OCCUPATIONAL PSYCHOLOGY

OCCUPATIONAL PSYCHOLOGY

An Applied Approach

Gail Steptoe-Warren

University of Coventry

PEARSON

Harlow, England • London • New York • Boston • San Francisco • Toronto • Sydney
Auckland • Singapore • Hong Kong • Tokyo • Seoul • Taipei • New Delhi
Cape Town • São Paulo • Mexico City • Madrid • Amsterdam • Munich • Paris • Milan

PEARSON EDUCATION LIMITED

Edinburgh Gate
Harlow CM20 2JE
Tel: +44 (0)1279 623623
Website: www.pearson.com/uk

First published 2013 (print and electronic)

© Pearson Education Limited 2013 (print and electronic)

ISBN: 978-0-273-73420-8 (print)
       978-0-273-73421-5 (ePub)
       978-0-273-78690-0 (eText)

British Library Cataloguing-in-Publication Data
A catalogue record for the print edition is available from the British Library

Library of Congress Cataloging-in-Publication Data
A catalog record for the print edition is available from the Library of Congress

Cover image: Alija/Getty Images

10 9 8 7 6 5 4 3 2 1
16 15 14 13 12

Print edition typeset in 9.5 pt StoneSerITCStd by 73
Print edition printed and bound by Ashford Colour Press Ltd, Gosport

Brief contents

Contents

Companion Website

For open-access **student resources** specifically written to complement this textbook and support your learning, please visit **www.pearsoned.co.uk/steptoe-warren**

ON THE WEBSITE

Lecturer Resources

For password-protected online resources tailored to support the use of this textbook in teaching, please visit **www.pearsoned.co.uk/steptoe-warren**

Preface

Throughout my career as an occupational psychologist, I have always maintained the importance of the link between theory, research and practice. Without theoretical underpinnings it is difficult to know what will work best. The major objective of this book, therefore, has been to produce a text that introduces the main concepts of occupational psychology in a clear and succinct manner with a focus on application. Within this textbook, chapters run in an orderly fashion with theories being described and examples provided to demonstrate their application. However, the real world of work never runs smoothly, with issues always arising. These issues may include a reduction in productivity due to reduced motivation and job satisfaction; conflict between an employee's work and home life leading to stress; and a change within the structure of the organisation resulting in redundancies. Attempting to incorporate some of the real world into the pages of a book is not an easy task as issues within organisations are never straightforward. However, we all have to start somewhere with our experience and it is safer to do it in a learning environment that does not have an impact on organisations, teams, management or individuals. To achieve this mock experience, a fictional organisational case study based on an organisation with the generic name of 'Sammie' is included from Chapter 4 onwards. The aim of using hypothetical case studies is to enable you to apply theory from the chapter into practice as well as understand some of the areas of practice within the field of occupational psychology. Also running throughout the book are real case examples, 'stop and reflect' questions, 'think about it' questions, as well as an explanation of the multi-level impact of the topic area from an organisational, management and individual perspective. The short-answer questions at the end of each chapter allow you to assess your learning as you progress and there are references for additional reading should you wish to delve deeper into the topic area.

The book was developed for a European audience of both students and practitioners as it takes the reader through individual, group and organisational perspectives while also considering historical developments and legal requirements. The text requires no previous knowledge or study of occupational psychology and can be used for degree-level study, continuing professional development and by practitioners. The chapters can be read independently to the whole book, which means that students and practitioners can dip in and out of topic areas.

Structure of the book

The book consists of 15 chapters. Chapter 1 provides an historical overview of occupational psychology from the pre-First World War era to the present day.

We consider the importance of scientific management, the use of psychometric tests to recruit soldiers and officers, and a diagrammatical explanation of how occupational psychology has an impact at individual, team, management and the organisational level. Without this historical knowledge we would not have developed our skills and knowledge within the discipline area to the level they are today.

Chapter 2 provides information about how to become an occupational psychologist. With the changes in responsibility for occupational psychologists moving from the British Psychological Society to the Health and Care Professions Council has come confusion. This chapter guides you through and demystifies the process. Also in this chapter is a section on consultancy, which has been included for two reasons. The first is that within the textbook are case studies where you will be asked to use the consultancy cycle. The second is that if you go through the British Psychological Society route to becoming an occupational psychologist, you will have to show evidence of two separate consultancy projects you have worked on. This is why the case studies are good to get you thinking about how you would tackle such a project in the real world.

Chapter 3 focuses on legislation applied to the workplace and takes both a UK and European perspective. As an occupational psychologist you will be suggesting interventions within organisations. If these interventions are not legal it leaves you and the organisation open to litigation. For example, you cannot go into an organisation and suggest that they sack the female part of the workforce as this would be discriminatory. Thus it is important that you understand the legislation and stay up to date with any developments.

Chapter 4 discusses theory, research and practice related to the topic of personnel selection and assessment. It includes job analysis techniques and methods, the importance of job descriptions and person specifications, and information on selection methods such as psychometric tests and interviews. The validity and reliability of these methods are also considered.

Chapter 5 considers performance appraisal, career development, counselling and coaching. Different approaches to performance appraisal are discussed and evaluated, identifying errors that may occur. With changes in the way people work, with some individuals having numerous jobs, a discussion of career types is presented. This helps us consider how individuals may develop their careers in the future.

Chapter 6 focuses on well-being, stress and work–life balance. With an estimated two million people suffering from an illness that has been caused or made worse by work, this topic area has become of interest to both government and organisations.

Chapter 7 evaluates the impact of individual differences such as personality, intelligence, individual values and beliefs at work. The chapter also discusses the importance of emotional intelligence in the workplace.

Chapter 8 explores the role of training. Models of training are discussed as well as the importance of following the training cycle, which involves identifying training needs, and designing, delivering and evaluating the training. Various methods of training are described and evaluated to help you choose the most appropriate one.

Chapter 9 focuses on a topic area that is classified as occupational psychology under the British Psychological Society knowledge areas, but falls more into the ergonomics camp. Design of work environments and work focuses on design aspects such as the design of tools to carry out a task; how the human body functions in relation to the task, and ill health as a result of poor work design.

Chapter 10 looks at issues of motivation, job satisfaction, employee engagement and behaviour modification. Motivation and job satisfaction are important aspects of employee engagement and when individuals do not engage in their work, productivity can decrease. There can be an increase in waste products as well as increased sickness absence. With the use of behaviour modification techniques some of these attitudes and behaviours can be changed.

Chapter 11 evaluates approaches of management and leadership and considers some contemporary theories such as servant leadership. Leadership development methods are also outlined.

Chapter 12 discusses groups and teams at work, outlining the benefits of working in groups as well as some of the catastrophic events that have occurred due to group work.

Chapter 13 takes an organisational perspective and considers how an organisation is made up, its structure, the values and beliefs of the organisation and its staff, its culture and how organisations change. Such change may be in response to a need to diversify the business in order to survive or a change in technological infrastructure.

Chapter 14 provides two examples of consultancy reports. These are based on the case studies in Chapter 4 – Personnel selection and assessment and Chapter 13 – Organisational structures, culture and change. Weblinks are provided to real-world business consultancy reports so that you can see their structure and content.

The final chapter, Chapter 15 considers the future of work. While we build on our past experiences, we also need to consider potential changes to the world of work. Issues such as flattening of organisational structures, organisational sustainability and the impact of globalisation are considered.

I hope you enjoy reading this book and wish you all the best in your future work.

Gail Steptoe-Warren

Guided tour

Learning outcomes set out what the chapter will cover and what you should be able to do after reading it.

Learning outcomes

After reading this chapter, you should be able to:

- understand the process to becoming a practitioner occupational psychologist
- use the stages of the consultancy cycle to complete the case studies in Chapters 4–12
- write a business/consultancy report for the case studies in Chapters 4–12
- understand ethical issues and apply principles of ethics in recommending interventions in Chapters 4–12.

Stop and reflect boxes suggest ways you can apply the topic to your life and think about your own relevant experiences.

Stop and reflect

Think of a critical incident that happened in your life. For example, the time you started school, college or university or went on a family holiday. Write down what you remember about the event such as the planning you did leading up to the event, and how you felt on the day. Ask someone else who is also familiar with the event to report on it. Are there any differences?

Exhibits show examples of techniques and theories being used in practice.

Exhibit 2.2 Example of title page

Personnel Selection and
Assessment Programme for
Senior Management

Prepared by Dr Gail Steptoe-Warren

Prepared on behalf of Sammie Services Limited.
14 September 2011

Exhibit 2.3 Example of contents page

Contents

	Page
1. Executive summary	1
2. Introduction/Terms of reference	2
3. Contextual theory	3–6
4. Supportive information	7–9
5. Case analysis	10–13
6. Proposed interventions	13–15
7. Recommendations	16
8. Conclusions	17
9. References	18

Practical examples describe situations in which you might need to use your knowledge of the topics being covered and ask you to think about how you would respond.

Practical example

An employee of an organisation has provided you with an interview as part of your information collection. After a week, the employee has decided that they want to withdraw their data from the project you are working on. Does the employee have a right to withdraw their data?

Yes. The employee has a right to withdraw their data.

Think about it questions pose essay-style problems for you to consider in relation to the topic of the chapter.

❓ Think about it

Think about problems of linking multi-organisational, individual career development theories to the performance appraisal process. Is it possible?

Real cases are mini case studies that illustrate a particular aspect of the topic.

Real case 6.1

Intel Corporation (UK) Ltd v. *Daw* (2007)

An employee, Daw, had suffered from postnatal depression after the birth of her two children, but had returned to work. She was promoted, which led to a substantial increase in her workload and number of hours required to complete the tasks. Daw complained about the increase and her health began to deteriorate. An email was sent to her employer informing them of her postnatal depression and that she felt 'stressed out'. Her workload was not reduced and she was signed off sick with depression and attempted suicide. The employee was offered a counselling service. However, the Court of Appeal held that the employer could not hide behind the counselling service and that the employer should have realised that the increase in workload and excessive hours impacted on the employee's health. Daw was awarded £134,000.

Short-answer questions test your knowledge and understanding of the topics that have been covered in the chapter.

Short-answer questions

1 What is one of the three differences between groups and teams?
2 What is one of the main benefits to an organisation for employing teams over individuals?
3 What is the final stage of Tuckman's stage model for group formation and development?
4 What is the problem associated with defining group development?
5 How would you apply Belbin's team roles to a group of six individuals?
6 What advice would you offer an organisation for avoiding groupthink?

Case studies at the end of each chapter provide fictional scenarios in which you can take the role of occupational psychologist and work through the steps you would take.

CASE STUDY
Groups and teams

The company
UK Serious Games is an organisation that designs and sells computer games for use in educational settings. The company was established in 2007 by a group of five postgraduates, who have combined expertise in research, education, computer games design and marketing. The company holds a number of contracts with schools and colleges around the country. The games are designed to be interactive and educational. For example, the company designed a computer game for schools to use for educating teenagers in road safety.

Further reading suggestions provide a good starting point if you want to explore the topics further.

Further reading

Crane A., & Matten D. (2010). *Business ethics. Managing corporate citizenship and sustainability in the age of globalization* (3rd ed.). Oxford: Oxford University Press.
EFPA (2005). *Meta-code of ethics*. Available: *http://www.efpa.eu/ethics/ethical-codes*
Grant, P. (2005). *Business psychology in practice*. London: Whurr Publishers.

Contributors

Gail Steptoe-Warren is an Occupational Psychologist, Senior Lecturer and Course Director in Occupational Psychology at Coventry University. She has an MSc in Occupational Psychology and an MSc in Forensic Psychology, and a PhD entitled 'The development of a situational judgment test to assess managers' strategic decision-making competencies'. Gail has worked on an extensive range of psychometric assessment projects and her experience spans the commercial, voluntary and academic sectors.

Emma Holdsworth decided to study at Coventry University as a mature student, having been in the motor industry for much of her working life. She graduated with a first class honours BSc in Psychology, and an MSc in Forensic Psychology with distinction. She has worked at Coventry University for the past three years as a researcher and part-time lecturer, both in occupational and forensic psychology. She is currently studying for her PhD. She is married with two young boys, and lives in Warwickshire.

Sophie Ward began studying psychology at A-level while working as a mentor developing stress management and counselling skills, and motivating students. She is currently a third-year undergraduate at Coventry University studying for a BPS-accredited BSc Hons in Psychology, furthering her knowledge and skills in order to pursue a career within the police sector.

Dela Lozanova was born in the Black Sea town of Varna, Bulgaria. She studied Bulgarian Language and Literature at The National High School for Arts and Humanities 'Konstantin Preslavski' – Varna. On her graduation, she was awarded a gold medal for being the best of the alumni. At the age of 18, Dela began her BSc Psychology course at Coventry University, and graduated in 2012 with a First Class degree. Dela is currently studying at Birmingham City University, and hopes to pursue a career in broadcast journalism.

Author's acknowledgements

I have a number of people to thank as without them this book would not have been possible.

My supportive and loving husband Dave who has encouraged me to write and develop my career. I love you.

My wonderful son Samuel who is the joy of my life and who is now, at age 13, taking an interest in psychology. I'm sure you're the future of psychology. You will notice, Samuel, that my case studies are named after you.

My dad Peter, who passed away in 2005 but was and still is my inspiration. Without his reverse psychology I would never have achieved what I have. I love and miss you, dad.

My mum Marlene, who is a wonderful and caring person. Her support is non-wavering and her belief in me is humbling. I am privileged to have you as my mum.

Dr Patricia Lindley who was my supervisor through my chartership process to becoming an occupational psychologist. Her encouragement and support of me has never stopped and I will be ever grateful. Thanks, Pat!

Dr Christine Grant who works alongside me. Her encouragement to get writing has always been there.

Emma Holdsworth who contributed a chapter to this book. Although Emma is now treading the path of forensic psychology, she would have made an excellent occupational psychologist.

My students who have inspired me throughout the years.

Lastly, and by no means least, thanks to Neha Sharma, Janey Webb and Jane Lawes at Pearson Education for their continued support and feedback. Without you, this process would not have been possible.

Publisher's acknowledgements

We are grateful to the following for permission to reproduce copyright material:

Figure
Figure 14.2 from Ipsos MORI

Table
Table 7.2 from 'The Bar-On model of emotional-social intelligence', *psicothema*, 18 suppl., 21 (2806).

Photographs
Alamy Images/Westend 61 GMBH: p. 219 (bottom);
Getty Images/NASA: p. 219 (top); Press Association Images/Denis Poroy: p. 220.

In some instances we have been unable to trace the owners of copyright material, and we would appreciate any information that would enable us to do so.

1

Introduction to occupational psychology

Learning outcomes

After reading this, you should be able to:

- understand the development of occupational psychology from before the First World War to the present day
- describe and critically evaluate historical theories
- critically evaluate the contribution of occupational psychology to present-day issues in the workplace
- explain how occupational psychology contributes to the individual, team, management and organisational level.

1.1 Introduction

Occupational psychology is the study of the way in which an individual's behaviour is influenced by an organisation, its rules, its culture, its communication networks and its structures. By applying theories and research in psychology to the workplace, it also considers the ways in which both individuals and groups contribute to the performance of the organisation of which they are part. Much of the research in this area has been conducted in real work settings rather than laboratories and has been undertaken to tackle problems in the workplace such as motivation issues, stress at work, leadership issues and organisational change.

As you will glean throughout this chapter, many of the major developments in occupational psychology history can be charted by recognising the work of key individuals. The development of occupational psychology did not occur under one umbrella of research and practice, but was a result of many factors such as the need for organisations to become more economic (worker efficiency) and in consideration of individual differences in the workplace (motivation and satisfaction). Other factors focused more on the organisational level rather than the individual, including mass production (in 1908 Henry Ford mass-produced the Model T car) and the increase in technological advancements (in 1901 Marconi transmitted the first trans-Atlantic radio message).

Stop and reflect

Think of your life so far . . . You have probably spent the majority of it as part of an organisation such as school, university and work. What factors have affected your behaviour in these organisations? What tasks have been challenging? Have you been satisfied and motivated? Did/do you have a good leader who empowers you? Have you got the right balance between work and home life?

Occupational psychology considers these factors and the impact they may have on individuals, teams, management and the organisation as a whole.

An overview of the historical developments within occupational psychology, which is fundamental to understanding how the discipline has developed, is presented as well as the importance of theories to our knowledge of both how organisations work and how individuals operate and behave within these organisations. This chapter will also outline how specific topic areas within occupational psychology influence individuals, teams, managers and organisations as a whole.

The chapter is presented in chronological order. However, due to the numerous contributors to the field, it in no way provides a full account of all developments. Instead, the aim is to provide a succinct overview of the significant contributions to our understanding of occupational psychology, starting with the pre-First World War era.

Terminology

Many terms are used to describe occupational psychology including industrial psychology–organisational psychology, work psychology and business psychology. For the purpose of this book, the term 'occupational psychology' will be used for consistency and will incorporate all the above terms. This terminology has been chosen because in the UK, the Health and Care Professions Council (the regulatory body for psychologists) has protected the title of Occupational Psychologist for those meeting the necessary criteria. Although there is a variation in terminology across countries (for example, Nordic countries use the term industrial–organisational psychology), the content of work carried out by occupational psychologists is comparable and therefore applicable across countries.

1.2 Occupational psychology in the pre-First World War era

Scientific management theory

It is Hugo Munsterberg (Munsterberg, 1913) who is considered the father of occupational psychology. He conducted experimentally-based research on monotony, attention and fatigue, and advertising, as well as physical and social influences in the workplace to assess whether they impacted on an individual's efficiency and productivity. One of Munsterberg's findings was that job efficiency decreased when workers talked to each other on the job. This led to a change in physical workplace design that made it difficult for workers to talk to each other. An increase in productivity was found, suggesting that the way in which the physical workplace environment is designed can influence productivity.

Munsterberg also argued that, to increase job efficiency, satisfaction and productivity, there should be a fit between the person and the job in terms of a person's mental and emotional abilities. To assess the person–job fit, Munsterberg developed tests and job simulations to assess an individual's knowledge, skills and abilities (KSAs) of applicants for the job. As Munsterberg (1913) stated, this new focus of psychology aims to 'sketch the outlines of a new psychology which is to intermediate between the modern laboratory psychology and the problems of economics: the psychological experiment is systematically placed at the service of commerce and industry' (Munsterberg, 1913: 3). It was at this time that research into the workplace started to flourish with empirical research being conducted at work.

Around the same time, Frederick Wilmslow Taylor (Taylor, 1911) put occupational psychology on the map in terms of scientific management. Scientific management theory argues that jobs can be studied systematically in order to determine the optimal performance, and employees can be selected according to specific characteristics required for the job. Taylor suggested that scientific principles could be applied to the study of work-related behaviour. He argued that jobs could be broken down into component measurable parts. The measurement could be conducted by timing each individual movement carried out on a specific job task, which would allow for the development of fast and more efficient ways to carry out a job. Taylor argued that this was scientific as it used empirical methods to measure changes. This represented the first real attempt at a job analysis (see Chapter 4 – Personnel selection and assessment). Existing employees were observed to ascertain what the important characteristics of good workers represented and training was provided so that employees knew the most efficient movements to carry out the job with rewards being offered to employees for effort.

Taylor based scientific management on five main job specialisation principles:

1 study the way the job is carried out scientifically
2 break down the job into its smallest component parts
3 determine the most efficient way of carrying out each component
4 provide training for workers to complete each component efficiently
5 provide financial incentives.

Job specialisation allowed workers to complete only one aspect of the job in which they had specialised. The advantages of this method were organisationally driven, such as less training of workers resulting in lower training costs, managers having greater control over their work and, as the employee is not specialised in a whole job, lower wages. However, disadvantages of this method include workers having a lack of variety in their work, a lack of opportunity to develop new skills due to working on specific components of a task, and a lack of development opportunities that may lead to a reduction in motivation and an increase in job dissatisfaction (this is discussed in detail in Chapter 10 – Motivation, job satisfaction, employee engagement and behaviour modification). Later studies, such as that by Walker and Guest (1952), investigated scientific principles at a car assembly plant to investigate the effect on job satisfaction. It was found that workers were satisfied with their working conditions, level of supervision and pay, but were dissatisfied with lack of autonomy over the methods used in their work, the time to undertake the work, repetitiveness and lack of diversity of the tasks and lack of interaction with other workers. Overall, the study found that scientific management had benefits in terms of efficiency, but could also have long-term negative effects in terms of staff satisfaction and motivation. Thus, Taylor's ideas were criticised for not considering human welfare and well-being. A further disadvantage of scientific management is that although it could be applied well to physical tasks, many jobs in today's workplace require problem solving and more cognitive-based tasks and therefore these principles would be less appropriate to the modern workforce.

1.3 Occupational psychology in the First World War

In the First World War, new areas of occupational psychology emerged with a focus on the use of psychological principles for the recruitment and selection of army personnel. A committee was set up for the psychological examination of army recruits. Robert Yerkes was chairman of this committee and pioneered the development of tests for selection and recruitment of army recruits. Yerkes (1921) developed the Army Alpha and Army Beta intelligence tests that were administered to over one million US soldiers to determine which roles the men were most suited to. Literate recruits were administered a written examination called the Army Alpha test and illiterate recruits were given a pictorial test called the Army Beta test. An example of an Army Alpha test question is 'A company advanced 6 miles and retreated 2 miles. How far was it then from its first position?' The answer is 4 miles, because 6 miles – 2 miles = 4 miles. The Alpha test was scored by adding together the total score on each of the eight tests and then converting it into a grade (e.g. A, B, C) according to the military's grading criteria. The eight tests included:

1 oral directions (drawing lines from circle one, passing through circle 2 and 3 to end in the middle of circle 4)
2 arithmetic problems
3 practical judgement

4 synonym–antonym

5 disarranged sentences

6 number series completion

7 analogies

8 information (such as, Germany is in Europe).

The Army Beta test consisted of seven subscales:

1 maze tasks

2 cube analysis

3 X–O series

4 digit–symbol substitution

5 number checking

6 picture completion

7 geometrical construction.

An example of the Army Beta test picture completion can be seen in Figure 1.1. Test takers were asked to identify what was missing from each picture. Scoring was similar to that of the Army Alpha test where total scores of the seven subscales were added together and converted into a grade. Yerkes argued that his tests assessed native intellectual ability that was not affected by education opportunities and/or culture. Three main facts appeared to emerge from the testing. Firstly, the average mental age of white American men was 13. Secondly, European migrants could be graded by their country of origin – for example, the Italians had an average mental age of 11.01. Thirdly, the average mental age for black men was 10.4. It can be seen that there was discrimination in mental age between country of origin and race.

Figure 1.1 Army Beta test example

These tests were paramount in the development of psychology as it represented the first group of intelligence tests and publicised the use of psychometric testing to other private and public sectors.

The answers for the example in Figure 1.1 are: 1) mouth, 2) eye, 3) nose, 4) hand, 5) chimney, 6) ear, 7) filament, 8) return address, 9) strings, 10) corkscrew, 11) trigger, 12) tail, 13) claw, 14) shadow, 15) ball, 16) net, 17) arm, 18) speaker, 19) arm in mirror, 20) diamond.

Walter Dill Scott also helped the army in the selection of its soldiers, forming the Committee for Classification of Personnel in the Army (CCPA). Whereas Yerke's test was developed to sift out those who were mentally unfit for the army, Scott's test assessed the familiarity of recruits with certain aspects of military work. Scott's test was applied to the selection of captains. He constructed proficiency tests for 83 military jobs. Proficiencies assessed are shown in Table 1.1.

Table 1.1 Scott's proficiency test characteristics

	Qualities assessed
Physical qualities	Physique, bearing, neatness, voice, energy, endurance
Intelligence	Accuracy, ease in learning, ability to grasp the point of view of the commanding officer easily, to issue clear and intelligent orders, to estimate a new situation, and to arrive at a sensible decision in a crisis
Leadership	Initiative, force, self-reliance, decisiveness, tact, ability to inspire men and to command their obedience, loyalty and co-operation
Personal qualities	Industry, dependability, loyalty, readiness to shoulder responsibility for his own acts, freedom from conceit and selfishness, readiness and ability to co-operate
General value to the service	Professional knowledge, skill and experience, success as administrator and instructor, ability to get results

Scott's test focused more on the character of the test taker. Such character tests appeared to feature heavily within the military. Carson (1993) found army regulations for recruits were based on the criteria of: 1) age (older than 18 and younger than 35); 2) being an American citizen or intending to become an American citizen; 3) being able to read, write and speak English; 4) not a convicted felon, not insane or a deserter. It is clear from these criteria that ability to operate at a high-ranking level (captain) was not part of the criteria. Scott argued that super mental ability did not guarantee competent leadership. It was not until Armistice Day in 1918 that intelligence became part of the selection criteria for new entrants and occupational placements within the military.

1.4 Post-First World War and pre-Second World War

Post-war, the focus of occupational psychology moved towards the welfare of employees at work. This is known as the human relations movement.

Human relations movement

The Hawthorne studies

A major contributor to this movement was Elton Mayo who was described by Smith (1998) as the founder of the human relations movement. Mayo's research (known as the Hawthorne studies after the Hawthorne works where the studies took place) investigated the effects of the physical work environment on worker productivity. The first experiment investigated the effects of lighting on productivity while varying the level of illumination workers received while working. From this, Mayo aimed to determine the optimum level of illumination for the best performance. It was found that productivity increased regardless of the level of illumination received. Further studies by Mayo varied the length and timing of individual workers' rest breaks. Again, regardless of whether rest breaks were increased or decreased, productivity increased. It was concluded that the reason for the productivity increase was better communication between managers and workers. The workers were consulted about the experiments and were given the opportunity to provide feedback so they felt involved in the process. Mayo also argued that the increase in productivity could be a result of an increase in attention from the management to the workers because of the experiments. Workers were also allowed to work in teams, which had not been allowed before the experiments.

The conclusions from these studies are that:

- work is a group-based activity
- the social factors concerning work are important to productivity
- there is a need for recognition, a sense of belonging to the team/organisation and job security
- workers are influenced by other workers in the organisation
- informal groups at work hold strong social controls over the behaviour and habits of fellow workers.

The Hawthorne studies have had a big impact on management in organisations. The studies have found that management involvement in staff work (through communication, praise, etc.) can increase motivation and productivity and that the design of the physical work environment also has an impact. However, there has also been some criticism. Parsons (1974) argued that individuals were given feedback on their job tasks and that the increase in productivity was due to the individual's skill acquisition. It was also argued by Parsons that, as the employees knew they were part of an experiment, their behaviour may have changed to please the experimenter and as a result had an impact on productivity.

Personnel selection

The emphasis during this time focused on production and efficiency, but leaders within organisations also wanted to know how to recruit the best workers for the job to ensure quantity and quality of goods and services. This led to an increase in research on personnel selection. For example, Weschler developed a battery of paper and pencil tests to measure intelligence and a simulator for taxi-cab drivers. The tests aimed to select men who:

1 would have fewer accidents
2 would earn more money for the company
3 would reduce labour turnover.

The written test assessed mental alertness and general intelligence. This involved a learning test, an arithmetical reasoning test and a picture completion test. The simulation test involved sitting a candidate in a dummy car and instructing him to look at a grey board, placed 10 feet in front of him. Intermittent lights of different colours were flashed at regular intervals. The driver had one foot on the clutch and the other on the accelerator and was told not to press the accelerator pedal as it was being fed at the proper rate. It was explained that on the flash of certain lights he was to react in certain ways by an appropriate movement of the hands or feet. For example, a yellow light represents slowing down and thus requires pressure from the foot on the clutch and brake. To validate the test, facts about the driver's previous performance were taken into account, such as the number of merits received, accidents, average daily revenue and revenue per cab mile. Comparisons were made with 'old' men for whom records were held. Results found the tests could pick out, to a certain degree, the safe from the unsafe, the efficient from the inefficient, and suggested that it would reduce labour turnover costs.

These developments in recruitment and selection processes and the rise in the Gross National Product in America had a positive effect on employment and companies started to create personnel departments for recruitment and selection of personnel. This involved carrying out job analyses and assessing individuals to see if there was a good fit between the candidate and the workplace (see Chapter 4 – Personnel selection and assessment).

As the Second World War began, there was a continued focus on personnel selection as well as a rising interest in group behaviour. This was due to a recruitment drive by the armed forces and will be discussed in the next section.

1.5 Occupational psychology in the Second World War

During the Second World War the Army Alpha and Beta tests were replaced with the Army General Classification Test (AGCT). This was a test of general learning ability and was used to place new recruits into military jobs. Over 12 million recruits were tested using the AGCT. The test consisted of subtests including the vocabulary test, which evaluated an individual's knowledge on the meaning of words; the arithmetic test, which tested knowledge of mathematics; and the block counting test, which required visualisation of missing information in graphical displays. High scoring recruits on the test were classified as 'rapid learners' and were assigned to Army Grade I jobs, medium scorers classified as 'average learners' who were assigned Army Grade II jobs, 'below average' were given Army Grade IV jobs and 'slow learners' were given Army Grade V jobs. This test used a mental standard to assign individuals to jobs.

In the same period there was a rising interest in group dynamics (discussed in more detail in Chapter 12 – Groups and teams); in particular, how individuals interact, how they influence each other, the development of norms within groups and the understanding of behaviour within groups. One of the main theorists within this area was Kurt Lewin. In 1945 Lewin established the Research Center on Group Dynamics, which investigated six areas related to groups (Research Center for Group Dynamics, 2010):

1 group productivity (why groups are ineffective in completing tasks)
2 group communication (social influence throughout the group)
3 social perception (how the group perceives social events)
4 intergroup relations (relations of members of the group)
5 group membership (how individuals adjust to the group membership)
6 training leaders (improve the functioning of groups).

The research focused on improving the efficiency of community leaders, conditions in which individuals from different groups have contact with each other, and increased belongingness and positive relationships within groups.

During the 1940s, 50s and 60s there was renewed focus on scientific management with the classic organisational theory as well as an upsurge of theories of motivation. This will be discussed in brief below and motivational theories can be read in more depth in Chapter 10 – Motivation, job satisfaction, employee engagement and behaviour modification.

1.6 Occupational psychology in the 1940s to 1960s

Classical organisational theory

Henri Fayol (Fayol, 1949) considered management functions and principles, as he believed that by focusing on these aspects he could increase efficiency in the workplace and minimise misunderstanding between management and employees. Fayol did not conduct any empirical research, but based his theory on his practical experience within organisations. He argued that management is a universal process that consists of functions and can be taught. He believed that managers have five principles, as can be seen in Figure 1.2 (overleaf)

There are many criticisms of the five primary functions (Argyris, 1957; Thompson & McHugh, 2002). These include the limited generalisability of Fayol's observations as the functions were based on his experience within organisations rather than through empirical research that could be replicated to test for validity and reliability. Fayol based his theory on management functions, but did not consider the influence this had on the workers, such as whether it decreased motivation or reduced productivity or that individuals would have minimal control over their working lives.

Planning: Developing plans of actions that combine unity, continuity, flexibility and precision. Must be coordinated on different level.

Organising: Providing resources including financial, staffing and raw materials. Building a structure relevant to the work.

Commanding: Managers with personal integrity, who communicate clearly and create initiative and loyalty.

Co-ordinating: Harmonising activities, to maintain the balance of the activities of the organisation. This involves weekly meetings with management.

Controlling: Controlling feedback, identifying weaknesses, developing plans, policies and instructions.

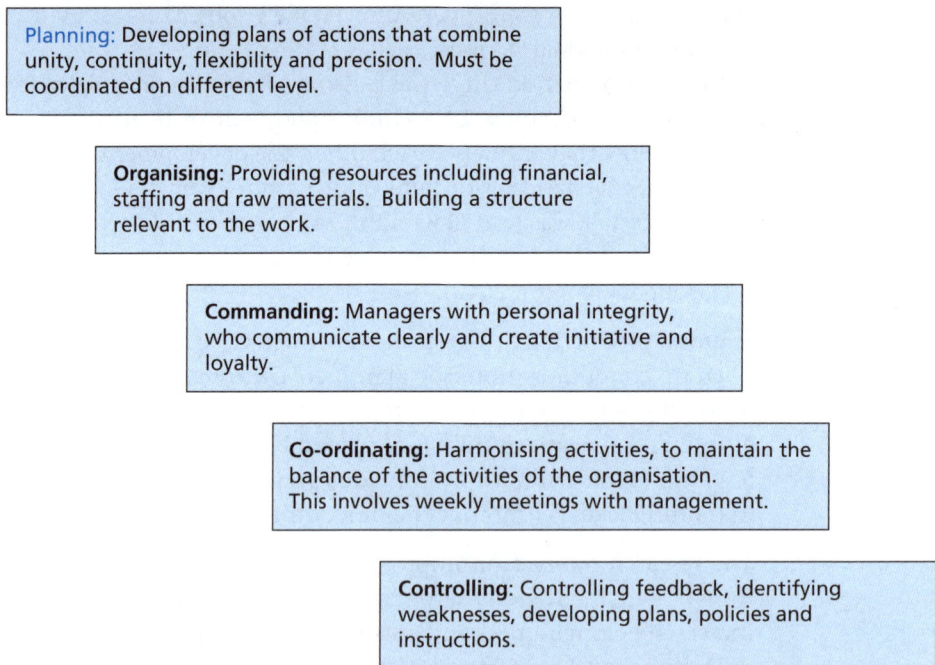

Figure 1.2 Fayol's five functions

Fayol (1949) also argued that successful management, where an organisation can be controlled, is based on 14 main principles. These principles provide guidelines for decisions and actions of managers.

1. Division of work: where repetition of a work task enhances speed and accuracy.
2. Authority and responsibility: give orders and exact obedience. Authority is linked to responsibility.
3. Discipline/obedience: seen as essential for the smooth running of the business.
4. Unity of command: employees receive orders from superiors.
5. Unity of direction: members of the group have the same objective.
6. Subordination of individual interests to the general interest: there should be no conflict between the individual interest and the organisational interest.
7. Remuneration of personnel: fair remuneration and rewarding deserving behaviour.
8. Centralisation: decisions are made from the top.
9. Line of authority: chains of command that do not hinder communication.
10. Order: everyone has their place, based on good organisation and good selection.
11. Equity: treatment of staff equally and fairly to encourage commitment.
12. Stability of tenure of personnel: stability in the job to ensure employees deliver to the best of their ability.
13. Initiative: being allowed to be creative.
14. *Esprit de corps*: to ensure the team does not become divided.

One of the main criticisms of these principles is that it assumes that all organisations are alike (Thompson & McHugh, 2002: 6).

? *Think about it*

Consider different industry sectors (public, charitable and commercial). Do you think they all operate in the same way? Consider the products or services they sell; the aim of the organisation (to increase profit, to provide care etc.); the size of the organisation; the stakeholders (customers, employees, trustees). Do the 14 principles apply?

Classical organisational theory was also adopted to examine the influence of power, structure and authority within organisations (Weber, 1947). Weber proposed a structure for a large number of employees called 'bureaucracy'. Bureaucracy represents an organisational form that is based on the ideal way to organise. It divides organisations into hierarchies where there is a clear line of authority and control. Weber based his theory on his observations of changes that were taking place during the Industrial Revolution. He believed that capitalism was the ideal way to organise activities based on a cost–benefit analysis: the amount of resource that was being put in and the amount of output (financial or products).

Bureaucracy is based on the following concepts.

- A hierarchical structure where there is a ranking of positions and each level of the hierarchy controls the levels below.
- Management by rules where decisions made at higher levels of the hierarchy can be implemented by those lower down the hierarchy.
- Organisation by functional speciality where activities are categorised by their function and performed by staff with the relevant skills.
- An 'up focused' or 'in focused' mission. The 'up focused' mission organisation's purpose is to serve its stakeholders, whereas the 'in focused' mission organisation's purpose is to serve itself and the people within it.
- Purposely impersonal where all employees and customers are treated equally regardless of individual differences.
- Officials where management are employed based on technical qualifications.

Weber's bureaucracy represents a system of power where leaders exercise control over subordinates. Weber defined **Power** in organisations as any relationship in which one person can impose his will on another person, regardless of any resistance. For example, this would be orders given by managers to subordinates. **Authority** was believed to exist when there is a belief in the legitimacy of that power. For example, if an individual believed that a manager could influence any rewards they may earn, then authority would be perceived by the workers. Weber classified organisations into three categories based on their legitimacy and uses of their power.

1 Charismatic authority: based on the outstanding characteristic of the individual
2 Traditional authority: where there is a respect for customs
3 Rational legal authority: based on a set of rules.

Weber argued that the rational legal authority is the most efficient because it provides a code that members of the organisation can follow; employees know the policies, procedures and rules to follow. Criticisms can be made of Weber's approach including the fact that it sets up a rigidity of procedures resulting in slow decision-making, which can lead to:

- delayed change in the organisation
- overspecialisation of tasks, which results in individuals not being aware of the consequences of their actions on other parts of the organisation
- employees having a lack of power over their jobs and working conditions.

Although Weber's approach can be criticised, the use of rules and procedures to deal with everyday tasks aims to anticipate all possible outcomes, making the working environment more certain. However, Crozier (2009) suggested that this may be a disadvantage as if almost every outcome is decided in advance, employees can gain control over their working lives only by exploiting zones of uncertainty. These result in employees playing strategic games either to meet their own needs or to stop others gaining a competitive advantage.

Motivational theories

Early theories of motivation focused on instincts where individuals were programmed to act and behave in certain ways. However, during the 1940s–1960s, the shift moved from the motivation 'instinct' driven theories to motivation 'content' and 'process' theories. Content theorists believed that factors internal to the individual such as food, drink and socialising direct behaviour to satisfy internal needs. These internal needs are individualised, depending on people's needs. The major content theories include:

- Maslow's Hierarchy of Needs (Maslow, 1943) suggests that individual needs exist in a hierarchy where lower needs such as physiological needs for drink, food, etc., have to be satisfied before those at the upper end of the hierarchy, such as self-actualisation, where individuals achieve their own potential, can be satisfied.
- Alderfer's ERG theory representing Existence needs, Relatedness needs and Growth needs (Alderfer, 1969) is a move forward from Maslow's theory, and suggests that the lower levels of the hierarchy do not need to be achieved before individuals achieve the upper levels.
- Herzberg's Two Factor theory (Herzberg, 1964), which is similar to Maslow's theory where lower levels representing hygiene factors would not motivate individuals to work, but those at the higher level (the motivator factors) would increase individuals' motivation.
- McLelland's Achievement–Motivation theory (McLelland, Atkinson, Clark, & Lowell, 1953) suggests that there are three primary needs including need for affiliation where an individual is motivated by social relationships, need for power where an individual wants to control their environment and have power over others, and a need for achievement where an individual takes responsibility for tasks and sets challenging goals.

The second set of motivational theories is known as process theories. The process theories take a cognitive stance to motivation and believe that an individual's decision to act in a particular way follows a rational decision-making process. The major theories in this area include:

- Vroom's expectancy theory (Vroom, 1964), where individuals choose their behaviour based on the outcomes they expect as a result of the behaviour. If the individual values the outcome they will continue the behaviour. For example, if an individual knows they will receive financial rewards for putting effort into the work task, they are more likely to work harder.
- Adams' Equity theory (Adams, 1965), which suggests that individuals compare their efforts and rewards with other workers similar to themselves. If you feel the effort you are putting in and the reward you are receiving is comparable with the effort/reward of others in a similar situation, then you are more likely to be motivated to put the effort into the work task.

Vroom's expectancy theory was further developed by Porter and Lawler (1968). They argued that rewards could be either intrinsic or extrinsic. Intrinsic rewards include satisfaction from undertaking a particular task and extrinsic rewards represent factors external to the individual such as pay, bonuses, etc.

Civil rights and occupational psychology

A major effect on the study of occupational psychology occurred in the USA in the 1950s with the Civil Rights Movement. For example, in 1954 the Supreme Court declared segregation in schools to be unconstitutional and at the same time the last all-blacks units in the armed forces were disbanded. In 1964, the Civil Rights Act was passed, which prohibited discrimination in employment due to race, colour, national origin, religion or sex. The Equal Employment Commission was created where any company wanting federal business had to have a pro-civil rights charter. The Civil Rights Movement for equality had an impact worldwide. In Belfast in 1964, the Campaign for Social Justice (CSJ) took over women's struggles to end discrimination in the workplace. Such legislation heavily influenced the development of employment practices such as recruitment and selection of individuals to jobs and the validation of psychometric tests used for this. This led to employees wanting more autonomy at work, feeling able to question authority and to be involved in decisions regarding their work.

1.7 Occupational psychology from the 1970s to the present

In the 1970s and 1980s there was a move away from motivational theories to participatory management (where employees are empowered to participate in organisational decision-making) including issues surrounding Total Quality Management (TQM). Employees are involved in discussions on issues such as customer service, within an organisation. This is based on management methods that enhance quality and productivity, which involves all employees as well as customers/

clients, having ownership of job roles and tasks, and being proactive. Jablonski (1992) identified six attributes of successful TQM programmes:

- customer focus (including customers within the organisation such as other departments as well as external customers)
- process focus
- prevention versus inspection (developing a process that incorporates quality within its production rather than rectifying after production)
- employee empowerment and compensation
- fact-based decision-making
- repetitiveness to feedback.

The aim of TQM is to manage business processes and people within organisations to ensure complete customer satisfaction. This requires clear reporting and decision structures, which in part resulted in the work of Weber being expanded and updated by Ritzer (2008). Whereas Weber argued the bureaucracy structure, Ritzer suggested a socially structured form of the fast food restaurant with McDonald's serving as the case model for this process, which is now known as McDonaldisation. McDonaldisation represents the process of rationalisation. This is achieved by taking a task and breaking it down into smaller tasks to its smallest level. The tasks are then rationalised to find the single most efficient way of completing each task. Any other method is classed as inefficient and discarded. According to Ritzer, McDonaldisation has four main dimensions.

1 *Efficiency*: this refers to choosing the optimum means to an end. For example, take Pizza Hut. It provides salad bowls to consumers and it is the consumer who fills up the salad bowl. It is, therefore, the consumer who is doing the work.
2 *Calculability*: an assessment of criteria based on quantifiable rather than subjective criteria, otherwise termed quantity over quality. For example, if we have a lot of something, then it must be good, such as a double cheese burger.
3 *Predictability*: there is uniformity in production and standardised outcomes. The food will taste the same, regardless of which restaurant of the same food chain you eat in.
4 *Control*: this is control over customers and staff and what they do as it is made routine. People don't have to think as much. This is occurring in all aspects of life including in car navigation systems that direct you to your destination (although at times the wrong direction!).

Stop and reflect

Consider a time that you visited a fast-food restaurant. Did you experience McDonaldisation? Evaluate whether McDonaldisation enhanced your experience of good customer service, for example the length of time you waited to be served.

As well as not always being the quickest way to produce goods, other negative effects of McDonaldisation include the de-skilling of staff. This is due to the use of consumers in roles such as cleaner, as the consumer is expected to tidy up their rubbish into bins after eating or drive-through customers take their rubbish with them.

The 1980s saw the beginning of a recession in the UK, with individuals being made redundant and those remaining in work taking on additional tasks. This led to an increased interest in work-related stress. Towards the end of the 1980s (in 1988 there was a 4.5% growth in the economy in the UK and a reduction in unemployment figures in the UK) there was a focus on research into work–life balance. Work–life balance is the balance between an individual's work life and personal life. Where work and personal life are not appropriately balanced, stress may occur. The majority of research at this time concentrated on women who had taken a break from work to have children and then returned to continue their career and thus was seen as a woman's problem. For a comprehensive overview of work-related stress, see Chapter 6 – Well-being, stress and work–life balance.

? Think about it

Consider the following scenario.

It is your son's first school play and you have promised that you will be there to see him. He is very excited and has been practising his lines with you for the last few weeks. His costume is ready. You drop him off at school, promising to go for a pizza after the play.

You arrive at the office and have a meeting at 10 am about the completion of the project you have been working on for the last six months. The customer is satisfied and is ready to pay for the work undertaken; however, they need a final report for 10 am the next morning.

How would you manage this work–life balance issue?

Here are three options, although there are many more.

1 Go to the play and for the pizza and work on the report through the night.
2 Go to the play and miss the pizza so at least you can finish the report and will get some sleep.
3 Do not attend the play or meal and stay behind at work to complete the report.

The concentration of research on employees continues into the 21st century, as does the increasing need to consider the impact of a global workplace and workforce. Some challenges for the 21st century are suggested below.

1.8 Challenges for occupational psychology in the 21st century

The 21st century has a number of challenges in terms of workers and the workplace. For example, there is an increasing move towards location-independent working where individuals can work from any location they wish. This reduces the overhead costs to an organisation in terms of providing space in offices, lighting and heating, etc. This, however, does have implications for managing and leading people who have little face-to-face contact with their superiors or work colleagues and rely on communicating through electronic media (Hertel Geister, & Konradt, 2005).

The ageing workforce is an area that will also require more attention, with individuals working until later in life. For example, physical changes may impede an individual's ability to undertake a job; thus an analysis of the physical abilities required for the job will need to be made clear. A further impact may be an increase in the number of younger people who are unemployed. If individuals work longer, there will be a reduction in the number of jobs available (Turner & Williams, 2005). An increased global awareness will also be required of employees as organisations operate across the world. This will involve communicating with people from different countries, different time zones and different cultures, which will have an effect on an organisation's working practices.

This is only a snapshot of potential changes. More detail about the changing nature of work and the impact it may have can be read in Chapter 15 – The future of work.

1.9 Conclusions

This chapter has provided an overview of historical developments from before the First World War to the present day. The world of work is ever-evolving with changes in legislation, economy and technological advancements. In becoming a practising occupational psychologist, it is, therefore, paramount to keep abreast of developments within the workplace. Occupational psychology is an ongoing process of change, learning and more change, and affects individuals, teams, managers and organisations. Figure 1.3 shows the influence of certain topic areas, discussed in this book, on different levels within the organisation.

All areas of occupational psychology, discussed in the following chapters, can have an influence on the individual, team, management and organisational levels, and Figure 1.3 indicates direct relationships between them. For example, not receiving the appropriate training can lead to poor performance appraisal, which may reduce job satisfaction and motivation. This may also affect the productivity of the organisation (which is not covered in individual topic areas, but needs to be considered at an organisational level).

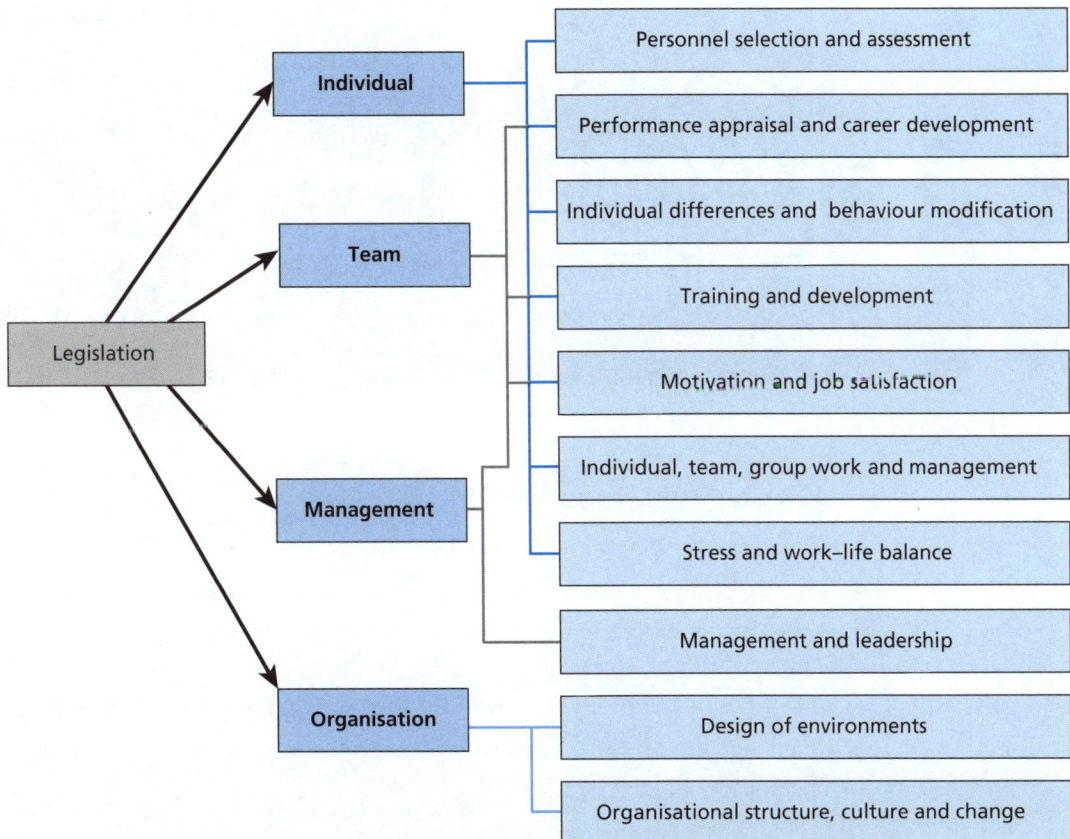

Figure 1.3 Use of occupational psychology at an individual, team, managerial and organisational level.

Short-answer questions

1 Describe the role of occupational psychologists in the workplace.
2 Critically evaluate the contribution of scientific management to occupational psychology.
3 Describe the importance of the use of selection tests for army recruitment.
4 Identify the differences between content and process theories of motivation.
5 Identify and evaluate future challenges for the discipline of occupational psychology.

Further reading

Koppes, L. L. (2007). *Historical perspectives in industrial and organizational psychology.* Hillsdale, NJ: Lawrence Erlbaum Inc. Publishers.

2

Becoming a practitioner occupational psychologist and the consultancy cycle

Learning outcomes

After reading this chapter, you should be able to:

- understand the process to becoming a practitioner occupational psychologist
- use the stages of the consultancy cycle to complete the case studies in Chapters 4–12
- write a business/consultancy report for the case studies in Chapters 4–12
- understand ethical issues and apply principles of ethics in recommending interventions in Chapters 4–12.

2.1 Becoming a practitioner occupational psychologist

The regulatory body for occupational psychologists is the Health Care and Professions Council (HCPC), which has been set up to protect the public. It regulates a number of professions including practitioner psychologists. The profession of psychology is divided into seven domains:

1 clinical psychologists
2 educational psychologists
3 health psychologists
4 forensic psychologists
5 counselling psychologists
6 sport and exercise psychologists
7 occupational psychologists.

Each of the seven domains represents protected titles. It is, therefore, a criminal offence for someone to claim that they are registered with the HCPC if they are not, or to use the protected titles. The HCPC provides a public register of appropriately qualified psychologists registered under one or more of the seven domains. This provides the general public with information about suitably qualified individuals who may be providing them with services. This is developed and maintained by the HCPC to ensure a high quality of education and training and continuing professional development within the profession. The HCPC also deals with complaints from the public regarding registered professionals and whether a professional is fit to practise. Two sets of standards are provided by the HCPC. These are the standards of proficiency, which are separate sets of standards for each profession regulated by the HCPC, and the standards of conduct, performance and ethics that apply to all professions regulated by the HCPC. Links to these documents are provided at the end of this chapter. The standards of proficiency are produced for the safe and effective practice of the profession. They are the minimum standards the HCPC set to protect the members of the public. The standards require individual practitioners to practise within the legal and ethical boundaries of their profession. For occupational psychologists, this involves acting ethically to balance the interests of the organisation with respect to individual rights. The practitioner should also be able to work in partnership with other professionals, and understand the contractual relationships with clients and promote psychological principles, practices, services and benefits. The standards also provide skills that practitioners are required to have, such as the ability to assess individuals, groups and organisations in detail, and to use the consultancy cycle.

The British Psychological Society provides a route to becoming a Chartered Member of the Division of Occupational Psychology and eligibility to apply for Occupational Psychologist status with the HCPC, although universities are now providing the route to chartership that meets the HCPC requirements to become a registered practitioner psychologist. The route to becoming a Chartered Member is a threefold process. Part one involves completing and being awarded with a first degree in psychology that is accredited by the British Psychological Society. This is known as having Graduate Basis for Chartership (GBC), previously known as Graduate Basis for Registration (GBR). Once GBC has been gained, the second part of the process requires the completion of an accredited MSc in Occupational Psychology. This is known as Stage 1 towards chartership as it is the first part of specific occupational psychology training. MSc training involves studying eight main areas of occupational psychology outlined by the British Psychological Society and agreed by the HCPC. These are:

1 human–machine interaction
2 design of work environments
3 personnel selection and assessment
4 performance appraisal and career development
5 counselling and personal development
6 training
7 employee relations and motivation
8 organisational development and change.

On successful completion of the MSc, the candidate can register for Stage 2 of the qualification through the BPS or with an HCPC-approved university that provides this training. Features of the qualification (BPS, 2012) include candidates being required to:

- take responsibility for their own learning and development
- develop and demonstrate competencies in relation to the knowledge base (MSc) and practice base (Stage 2)
- provide detailed information about the competencies that they are required to develop and the means by which their ability to demonstrate these competencies is assessed
- be supported in their development by supervisors with relevant expertise in the area of occupational psychology.

Stage 2 of the process to becoming an occupational psychologist involves providing evidence of breadth and depth of practice. Breadth of practice involves the demonstration of practical applications of skills that evidence the competencies required by the qualification in a total of five of the eight areas. Two examples of practice in each of these areas are required. Therefore, a minimum of ten assessments must be submitted and accepted in order to complete the breadth element. The second element is to assess depth. Depth involves the candidate showing evidence of practice using the consultancy cycle (discussed later) in at least one of four fields of practice. The four areas focus on:

1 work and the work environment
2 the individual
3 the organisation
4 training.

Two depth entries must be submitted and accepted for the depth section to be completed. Under the BPS qualification, on successful completion you will be awarded Stage 2 of the Qualification in Occupational Psychology. This then allows you to apply to the HCPC to become a Registered Occupational Psychologist.

2.2 Consultancy

To understand the process of consultancy, we refer to a number of terms relating to an occupational psychologist. These are defined as follows.

Consultant: a consultant represents a person who is an expert or professional who has a wide range of experience and knowledge within the occupational psychology field. She/he usually works for an organisation or is self-employed. The role of the consultant is to provide advice/recommendations on a particular area, e.g. restructuring of an organisation.

Client: a client is a person (or persons) who purchases services from a consultant. The client would seek advice on a specific issue concerning individuals, teams, management or the organisation itself.

Intervention: an intervention is a recommendation made to management about changes to current practices to improve performance or solve issues that have been identified.
Business/consultancy report: a business/consultancy report is a document that is presented to management to assist in the decision-making processes.

This section will introduce the reader to work undertaken by occupational psychologists in providing consultancy services. Organisations employ consultants for a number of reasons, including:

- to bring an external, new perspective to a project or organisational/business issue
- to access the expertise, knowledge and skills of the consultant.

The majority of consultancy work undertaken by occupational psychologists involves some type of organisational change. Typical areas where consultancy services are provided are covered by the eight main areas of practice identified by the BPS, discussed earlier. Whether working for an organisation or self-employed, occupational psychologists, as part of their practical training, have to show evidence of going through the whole consultancy cycle. It is important to note that, even when you have been registered as an occupational psychologist with the HCPC, it is imperative that you do not work outside your competency area. If you do not have relevant expertise in an area, you should not be providing independent services in that area. It is, therefore, required that you continue your professional development (HCPC, 2012). This involves maintaining a continuous and up-to-date record of your professional development; demonstrating that continuing professional development (CPD) involves learning activities relevant to future activities; and demonstrating that CPD has contributed to the quality of the practitioner's practice and service delivery, and benefits the service user. Also, you must provide, if requested, written evidence of how you have met the HCPC CPD standards.

The objective of employing consultancy services is to improve the effectiveness and efficiency of an organisation, or to aid in the identification of organisational issues and recommend necessary changes to overcome those issues (see the Sammie Services example below). This could involve advising an organisation on a restructure, creating effective work teams or changing the culture of an organisation. These are undertaken through a seven-stage consultancy process, which we will consider in the next section. The consultancy cycle used in this chapter is based on the BPS-defined consultancy cycle required for the Stage 2 Qualification in Occupational Psychology. Other types of consultancy processes, which you may want to read, include Block's (2011) flawless consulting.

2.3 The consultancy cycle

The consultancy cycle (see Figure 2.1) consists of seven stages (Cockman, Evans, & Reynolds, 1999) and provides a set of steps that consultants should progress through in the consultancy life-cycle. As you read through the consultancy steps, consider the Sammie Services example overleaf and think about how you would apply each step.

Stage 1 **Engaging**	Making initial contact and establishing a relationship
Stage 2 **Contracting**	Agreeing initial expectations, timescales and likely actions
Stage 3 **Collecting information**	Collecting key information
Stage 4 **Making sense of information**	Analysing information to identify strengths and areas for development
Stage 5 **Generating options, decisions and planning**	Deciding on actions to be taken
Stage 6 **Implementing the plan and taking action**	Carrying out the agreed actions
Stage 7 **Exiting**	Exiting from support

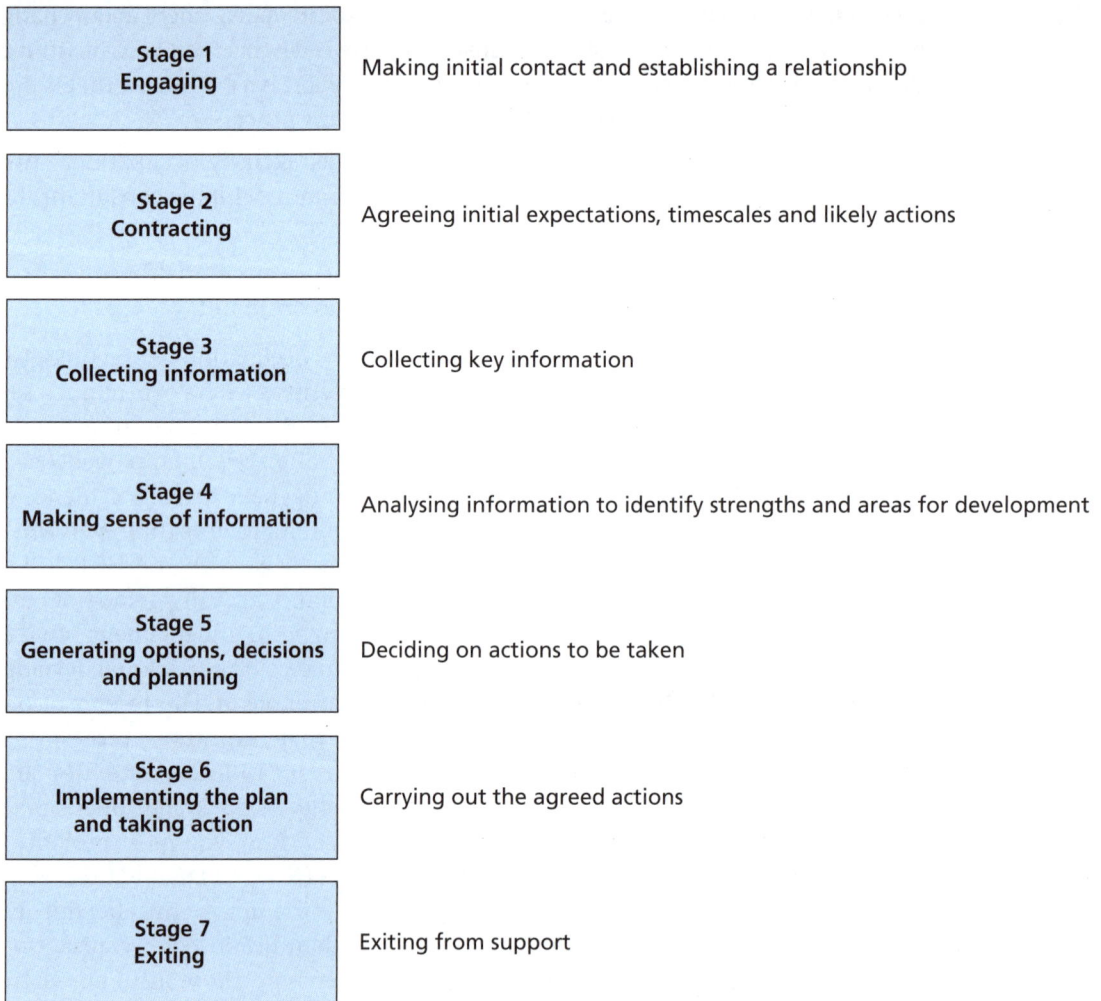

Figure 2.1 Seven-stage consultancy cycle

Reorganisation example: Sammie Services Plc

Following a strategic review by the trustee of Sammie Services Plc (a financial institution), decisions were made to focus on three customer segment areas (mortgages, savings and personal loans). This resulted in a decision to reorganise around the three segment areas. This would allow employees to focus their attention on developing skills in those areas. As a consultant, you are asked to work with the management team to ensure that the reorganisation is achieved in an effective and efficient way.

The first stage of the consultancy cycle, **engaging**, requires the consultant to make initial contact with the client. The main aim of this initial contact should be to concentrate on learning more about the organisation, who the key contacts are, who else will be working with you (if any from the organisation) and their roles within the work.

The second stage consists of **contracting**. This stage is where the consultant states explicitly what they will be doing. This may be quite a broad approach to start with, such as identifying communication problems within the organisation and suggesting interventions to remedy these issues. This stage is vital as it will establish the role of the consultant, what the consultant will do, the time-frame in which the consultancy will be undertaken as well as factors that may inhibit or promote the work undertaken. Questions should be asked of the client at this point. See Exhibit 2.1 for examples of questions.

Exhibit 2.1 Questions consultants should ask clients in the contracting stage

- What do you expect the outcome of the work to be?
- What is the level of commitment from management for this work?
- What is the timescale for the work?
- Which members of staff need to be involved and what are their roles/ responsibilities?
- Are there any risk factors that could inhibit the progress of the work?

The third stage of the cycle involves **collecting information**. Information can take a variety of forms including numerical information, work information, staff information, and organisational information. This information can be collected in a number of ways including discussions, interviews with staff and through company documentation. You do, however, need to consider the validity of the information provided.

The fourth stage requires **making sense of the information**. For example, an organisation may use a consultant to assess issues with their personnel selection and assessment process, as they have been employing individuals who require a lot of training on the job, which was not identified at the selection stage. This stage requires the consultant to ask some pertinent questions such as whether they have enough information, whether they need to collect more information, or whether any issues emerge from the information collected. For the issue of ensuring a good person–job fit, the whole process of selection and assessment would require scrutinising so that weaknesses in the process could be identified and interventions suggested.

The fifth stage of **generating options, decision-making and planning** involves synthesising the information obtained and restructuring the information so that options emerge. For example, it may be that a psychometric test is used to assess a certain ability where work-based samples would have been better to assess how the individual actually performs a specific task. The generation and selection of the ideas will need to be considered in line with the impact on staff, managers, teams and the organisation as a whole. When generating and making decisions on the options, a plan to take the decisions forward will need to be developed. The plan should include:

- the outcomes required
- the actions needed to achieve the outcomes

- the resources (including staff, physical resources and financial resources) required to implement the intervention(s)
- timescales for implementing the interventions
- evaluation strategies: Have the interventions solved the issues? Do additional issues require investigating?

The sixth stage involves **implementing the plan and taking action.** For the implementation to work, it is important to involve staff in the changes. This will ensure the staff feel a part of the process and are more likely to feel ownership. Clear time frames and implementation actions are required at this stage so that all involved are aware of what is to happen when and by whom.

The final stage is **exiting**. If the consultancy project has been successful, then exiting is relatively simple as outcomes have been achieved. However, if issues still exist at the evaluation stage, then it is more difficult. This may require a return to early stages of the consultancy process such as gathering and analysing more information.

The main tangible output of a consultancy project is a consultancy/business report. The report details the issues that have been identified as well as suggested interventions. A comprehensive discussion of what the report should include is detailed next and forms the format for the practice case studies in Chapters 4–13.

2.4 Writing a business/consultancy report

A business report represents the outcome of a consultancy project. These reports form part of everyday business life. The length of a report varies from one or two pages to much longer reports. We will be looking at the longer report as this report is generally what is expected from an organisation. Throughout Chapters 4–13, a relevant case study based on Sammie Services is provided. These case studies allow you to consider how you would apply the consultancy cycle to the case study and practise writing reports according to the guidelines detailed later in this chapter. Examples of two reports from case studies in Chapter 4 – Personnel selection and assessment and Chapter 13 – Organisational structures, culture and change can be found in Chapter 14 – Consultancy reports. Although the reports are academic in nature, they provide a good grounding for you to consider how you would show evidence of working through the stages of the consultancy cycle. However, a 'real' consultancy report may look very different, although it would consider similar issues; thus, links to a 'real' business consultancy report are also provided in Chapter 14.

The rest of this chapter details the layout of a business/consultancy report and the main headings that should be used.

Title page

The title of the report should be concise and clear, identifying the nature of the report (see Exhibit 2.2). The name of the author should be included as well as the person or organisation that requested the report. The completion date of the report should also be included.

Contents

The contents of the report should be laid out in a consistent format and you should include both page numbers and title numbers. A contents page should also be included to direct the reader to the relevant sections (Exhibit 2.3).

Executive summary

This section should be presented in prose and be similar in nature to an abstract for a journal article. Its purpose is to provide the reader with an easily digestible and lucid overview of the nature of the case and the issues inherent in the case: the key interventions proposed with the rationale for their proposal and a statement of the recommendations. These will have to be in summary form and, as this section is the most important part of the report, it should be written last.

This section should not contain the word 'I' but should be written in the passive voice. Instead of writing 'I would restructure the management team' you should write 'Due consideration may be given to restructuring the management team, to increase the reporting lines between staff'.

Exhibit 2.2 Example of title page

Personnel Selection and Assessment Programme for Senior Management

Prepared by Dr Gail Steptoe-Warren

Prepared on behalf of Sammie Services Limited.
14 September 2011

Exhibit 2.3 Example of contents page

Contents

Introduction/terms of reference

The introduction should outline the who, what and when of the report; who the report is written for, what the report is about, and when the report is being presented.

Contextual theory

It is necessary to examine the context in which any piece of investigation is undertaken, whether it is a piece of 'pure' research that is intended to be published in an academic journal, or a consultancy report that is produced as part of a consultancy exercise. Undertaking a piece of consultancy work without reviewing the appropriate literature and picking out the material most pertinent to the case under investigation is more like using 'gut instinct' than consultancy.

This section ought to cover those aspects of psychological theory that you believe are pertinent to the case that you are writing about. It should not be an attempt at a full literature review. You will need to be selective in your choice of material. The idea of the section is to explain to the reader of the report that there is considerable information and theorising already in existence that can shed light on the way forward for an analysis of the case and can provide support for any eventual recommendations.

It will not be possible to give a very full account of the theories that you focus on, but you should aim to enlighten the reader about what has been done in this field to bring ideas together, e.g. a theory. This section should also be presented in prose and should not contain the word 'I' but should be written in the passive voice. You will need to reference the theories in the same way that you would in an essay.

Supportive information

In a consultant's report it is usual to outline for the reader some 'facts' that the consultant's employer may need to be aware of in coming to a final decision about how to make progress. These 'facts' will vary according to the nature of the report, but will typically include topics such as the nature of the labour market (national, international and local), the costs incurred in advertising, in testing, in interviewing, in training, and the costs involved in losing staff. Figures are available on these topics from various sources, e.g. Social Trends, Mintel, or from the organisation itself.

This section should contain tables of data, graphs and commentary on them. All tables should be appropriately numbered and labelled (an example is provided in Figure 2.2).

The graph shows levels of hours worked and employment from 2008 to the end of 2011. It can be seen that both hours and employment have dropped from 2008 to 2011, but there is a small increase in both from Quarter 3 to Quarter 4 of 2011.

Case analysis

Although this may be thought of as the centrepiece of an investigation into a particular case, the analysis will only be as good as the overview of selected theory and

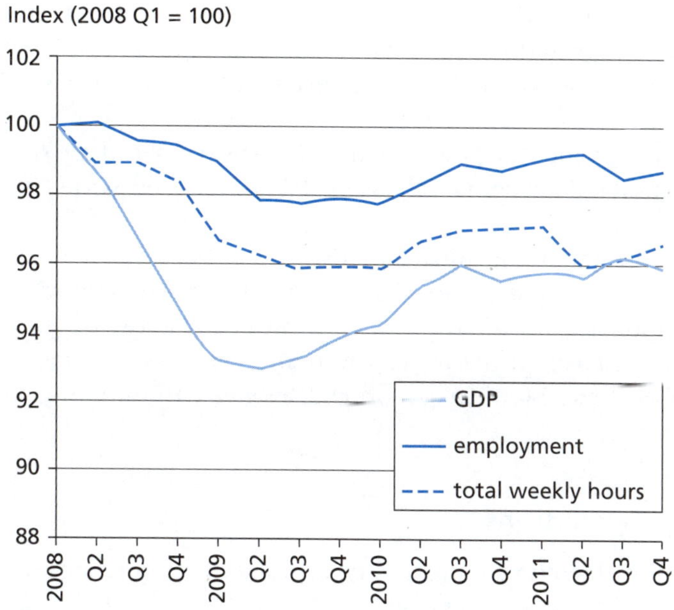

Index (2008 Q1 = 100)

Figure 2.2 Graph of UK employment and hours worked
Source: Office for National Statistics (2012a)

the choice of data on which to base the investigation. The outcomes of this section will inform the next section on the interventions that could be implemented and, from there, the recommendations to the employer.

Your task here is to pick out the points in the case that you have chosen that you believe need some form of remediation. You should note the *psychologically important* points that you have picked out from the case and comment on why they are deemed to be important and what effects they may be having within the organisation.

You may use sub-headings in this section, with each heading indicating to the reader the main issue. Once again your writing should not contain the word 'I' but should be written in the passive voice or in the third person, so instead of 'I consider that there are poor interviewers here' you may have 'It would appear necessary to examine the skill levels and effectiveness of the interviewing personnel'.

You would be advised to have a brief section that summarises the analysis at the end of this section.

Proposed interventions

This is the part where you become a consultant and make proposals to management about how they may change their current practice to improve their performance *in light of the case analysis.*

The highlighting above may have given away the idea that it is critical that any proposals for intervention and possible change are based on the actual analysis undertaken. It should also be evident that the analysis was based on an overview of theory pertinent to this study, so that any proposal for intervention should look at both the key issues that emerged from the analysis and the theoretical background to this analysis, as that area of work will be the basis on which sound proposals can be based.

This section could be prose-based, it could use sub-headings or it could use bullet points. It should not contain the word 'I' but should be written in the passive voice or third person.

The most important thing is that the **nature** of any interventions is clear and the **reasons** for these are explicit: important matters such as the **timing** of the intervention, e.g. 'within the next six months' and a cost–benefit analysis showing the possible **costs** to the organisation and the possible benefits should also be mentioned here. More weight should be given to outlining the nature of the interventions.

Recommendations

Here you spell out what ought to be introduced into the organisation to improve performance based on your analysis.

The purpose of this section is to give the client one page to refer to when they discuss the implementation of your consultative document. They will find it very helpful to have a snappy, transparent and well-presented set of recommendations that they can all refer to at the same time.

This is your chance to impress them with some clear-sighted view of what you think should be done. This section would almost certainly be most appropriately written as bullet points; it should not contain the word 'I' but should be written in a passive voice.

Conclusions

This should contain a summary of the main findings. Clearly state how you arrived at the conclusion.

References

These should include all the references to books, journals, websites, etc., that you cited in your report.

Within any research or consultancy, the importance of ethics is paramount. This means that you should act in a socially responsible and lawful way. When conducting any work with clients, you should **explain** the legal aspects related to your client's organisation; avoid any conflicts of interest such as personal relationships with clients or receiving personal benefits from the organisation. A number of ethical issues should be considered. The next section will provide an overview of some of the ethical guidelines that occupational psychologists should follow and are applicable to the work they undertake. However, this is not exhaustive and you may be faced with many more as you become a practitioner.

Each occupational psychologist will be confronted with an ethical dilemma at some point in their career. Ethics are the foundation of any consultancy and aid in the build-up of trust between consultant and client. Ethics represent behaviour and actions that a person and/or organisation adheres to. An occupational psychologist will have to consider the far-reaching consequences of their advice, such as the selection of individuals, restructuring an organisation or advising on issues such as work–life balance. Consequences of actions can be seen in Real case 2.1.

Real case 2.1

The phone-hacking scandal

The phone-hacking scandal involved the *News of the World* and other British tabloids. Employees of the newspaper were accused of phone hacking and police bribery that resulted in the closure of the *News of the World*, which produced its last edition on 10 July 2011.

The result of this case has had an impact on many individuals and organisations. These include the victims of the phone-hacking scandal such as the parents of murdered schoolgirl Milly Dowler; the resignation of a number of individuals spanning from Rebekah Brooks, the Chief of News Corporation, British Operations and John Yates, Police Assistant Commissioner in July 2011 as well as Britain's Press Complaints Commission (an industry-funded regulatory body) confirming (8 March 2012) it is to be abolished and replaced with a new agency.

Source: Associated Press, 2012.

? Think about it

When reading through the ethical guidelines, consider which ethical principles were breached by the case of the phone-hacking scandal.

For occupational psychologists, two main guidelines are followed. The first is the British Psychological Society's (BPS, 2009) *Code of Ethics and Conduct*, which is based on four main principles:

1 respect
2 competence
3 responsibility
4 integrity.

Respect is where psychologists value the dignity and worth of all persons. This includes age, disability, education, ethnicity, race, religion and sexual orientation. Psychologists should also respect confidentiality and obtain consent from clients/employees for the disclosure of information. Psychologists should also make clients/employees aware of their right to withdraw any of their data.

Practical example

An employee of an organisation has provided you with an interview as part of your information collection. After a week, the employee has decided that they want to withdraw their data from the project you are working on. Does the employee have a right to withdraw their data?

Yes. The employee has a right to withdraw their data.

Competence is where psychologists value the development of high standards of competence in their professional work. Occupational psychologists should recognise that ethical dilemmas will occur in their work and deal with these in the most appropriate way. They should also practise within their boundaries of competence.

Practical example

A client asks you to report results of a survey in a positive manner even though a lot of issues have been identified from the survey. What is your answer?

As an independent consultant you would report the results in the appropriate manner, regardless of what the client asks you. Your remit is to provide independent evaluation and independent advice to the client.

Responsibility is where psychologists respect their responsibility to the client. This involves the avoidance of harming clients, avoiding misconduct, debriefing all participants, and making clear conditions under which the contract may be terminated.

Practical example

A client raises concerns with you in an informal interview about stress they are feeling at work and the psychological and physical effects this is having on them. What do you do?

Your options could include, but are not limited to:

1 Discussing options with the employee such as speaking to their manager.
2 Referring them to stress management training.

As a consultant, you have a responsibility to take responsible action with any information you have while also maintaining confidentiality. For option 1, the action is placed on the individual; for option 2, you would need permission from the consultant to refer them to stress management training.

Integrity is where psychologists value honesty, accuracy, clarity and fairness with their interactions with people. Psychologists should be accurate in detailing their affiliations, qualifications, training and skills. Psychologists should also ensure clients are aware of the costs of the services provided. Multiple relationships may also occur such as providing consultancy services to a friend.

> **Practical example**
>
> A friend, who is a senior manager in a company, asks you to provide consultancy services regarding communication issues in their organisation. You have been friends for more than 20 years and are concerned that the consultancy project may be influenced by your friendship. What action do you take?
>
> *This project may result in a conflict of interest and therefore you may consider declining your services.*

A further set of guidelines is provided by the Health and Care Professions Council (HCPC, 2008), which is the regulatory body for psychologists in the UK. The HCPC's *Standards of conduct, performance and ethics* (2008) state that you should act in the best interests of clients; respect confidentiality; keep high standards of personal conduct; keep professional knowledge and skills up to date; act within the limits of your knowledge, skills and experience; keep accurate records as well as behave with honesty and integrity.

Remember: ethics is important in providing a valuable and fair service to your clients.

2.6 Conclusions

This chapter discussed the seven-stage consultancy cycle as well as ethical issues relating to business/organisational consultancy. This is imperative in providing an effective, efficient and fair service to clients. This book will consider case studies throughout and ask you to write a business report based on the case analysis. By following the business report style, a comprehensive report can be developed.

> ## Short-answer questions
>
> 1 Describe the process to becoming an occupational psychologist.
> 2 Describe the seven stages of the consultancy cycle.
> 3 Identify potential ethical issues relating to consultancy and explain how you may respond to them.
> 4 Identify the main sections of a business report.

Websites

Health Professions Council, which is the regulatory body for psychologists: *www.hcpc-org.uk*

Mintel, which provides market intelligence: *http://www.mintel.com*

Social Trends provides social and economic data from a wide range of government departments and other organisations: *http://www.statistics.gov.uk/statbase/Product.asp?vlnk=5748*

Further reading

Crane A., & Matten D. (2010). *Business ethics. Managing corporate citizenship and sustainability in the age of globalization* (3rd ed.). Oxford: Oxford University Press.

EFPA (2005). *Meta-code of ethics.* Available: *http://www.efpa.eu/ethics/ethical-codes*

Grant, P. (2005). *Business psychology in practice.* London: Whurr Publishers.

3

Legislation applied to the workplace

Learning outcomes

After reading this chapter, you should:

- have a clear understanding of UK and European legislation applied to the workplace
- understand the differences between indirect and direct discrimination
- have a clear knowledge of protected characteristics
- understand the concepts of positive action and occupational requirements
- understand how you can avoid discrimination in the workplace.

3.1 Introduction

As an occupational psychologist, it is imperative that you keep up to date with current legislation so that any work you undertake or interventions you suggest to clients withstands legal scrutiny. However, it is also important to remember that occupational psychologists are not legal experts and should not provide advice on legal issues (unless they have qualifications to do so). Occupational psychologists should seek advice from an appropriately qualified person on legal issues that may affect them in their practice.

Employment legislation is an important factor that protects the rights of both employees and employers. Employment legislation provides clear details regarding the rights and responsibilities of employees and employers so each knows what is required of them. Its aim is to allow all individuals equal and fair access to opportunities in the workplace. This represents non-discrimination where individuals who are in similar situations (such as applying for a job or promotion) should be treated similarly regardless of any protected characteristic(s) (such as disability, age, gender, sexual orientation or religion) they may possess.

Regardless of an organisation's size or industry sector, all organisations must abide by employment laws as the employer is legally responsible for any acts of discrimination, harassment and/or victimisation carried out by people in their employment and could face an employment tribunal, if found in breach.

This chapter provides information on legislation related to the workplace. Information will be presented on the Equality Act 2010 as well as European employment legislation. We will consider protected characteristics (such as age, gender and disability), providing examples of direct and indirect discrimination as well as real legal cases of discrimination so that you have a clear understanding of best practice in the workplace. This should help you in making lawful decisions regarding employment in the future. As the Equality Act (2010) has the same goals as the EU Employment Directive and the same discrimination laws, this chapter will discuss discrimination from a combined UK and European perspective. However, although legislation is discussed, it is important that you keep abreast of any changes in employment law and apply them to your practice. Links to appropriate websites are included at the end of the chapter and should be checked for any updates/additions to legislation before making any workplace recommendations.

The Equality and Human Rights Commission was set up under the Equality Act (2006) with the aim of eliminating unlawful discrimination and promoting equality and human rights. The Commission carries out enquiries and conducts investigations into organisations it suspects of having unlawfully discriminating policies. As part of an investigation, the Commission can require employers to provide information about its policies and practices such as its pay scales. Employers cannot refuse to provide this information. The Commission can also provide aid to individuals taking legal action enforcing their rights to, for example, equal pay.

On 1 April 2011, Her Majesty's Courts Service and the Tribunals Service integrated to form Her Majesty's Courts and the Tribunal Service. The Tribunal Service is responsible for the administration of criminal, civil and family courts as well as tribunals in England and Wales. The Employment Tribunal hears claims concerning unfair dismissal, redundancy payments as well as discrimination. The tribunal is an independent judicial body that determines disputes between employees and employers over employment rights. Thus, if you are working as an occupational psychologist within an organisation, employment legislation needs consideration. You can keep up to date on any changes in legislation by visiting the Direct Gov (2011) website.

3.2 United Kingdom law

The UK has a number of Acts concerning employment including the Equality Act (2010), the Human Rights Act (1998) and a Bill, the Dignity at Work Bill (2001). These will now be discussed further.

The Equality Act (2010) brought together all pre-existing discrimination laws into one place. Most of the Equality Act came into force in October 2010. Further additions to the law will be discussed later. This Act provides individual employees with greater protection from discrimination and makes it easier for organisations to understand their responsibilities. So that organisations can understand the main provisions under the Equality Act, Codes of Practice have been developed that provide explanations and examples of legal concepts to everyday situations. This Codes of Practice came into force on 6 April 2011.

Two main Codes of Practice are applicable to employers: the Code of Practice on Equal Pay and the Code of Practice on Employment.

Code of Practice on Equal Pay

The main aim of this law is to ensure that women and men receive the same pay (including pensions) and employment terms (such as holiday entitlement) for doing equal work. Equal work refers to work that is the same or very similar, provided that where there are some differences they are not of practical importance; where the job is different, but rated under the job evaluation scheme as being of equal value, or different, but has equal value in terms of skills, effort and decision-making. Although this code refers to equal pay between men and women, unequal pay systems are open to challenge on grounds of age, race, or any other protected characteristics under the Equality Act. The equal pay provision is applicable to all organisations regardless of size or sector (for example, public, private or charitable) and is set in both British law and European Union law. It is the responsibility of the employer to show that there are differences in the work being done, not the responsibility of the employee to show similarities. For example, a difference may be where two managers have different managerial and financial responsibility. However, a pay practice that treats part-time workers differently to their full-time equivalents is indirectly discriminatory. According to the Equality and Human Rights Commission (2011) there is a defence for difference in pay if the difference is due to a material factor. Material factors include differences in experience and qualifications, geographical differences such as paying more to those living in London, or individuals working different shift hours such as nights or weekends. However, a material factor is discriminatory if it is based on treating a woman or a man differently based on their sex. For example, if a woman employed as a cashier is paid less than a male cleaner, because the man is viewed as the main income earner for the family, this is discriminatory and not lawful.

Code of Practice on Employment

The main purpose of this code is to provide a detailed explanation of the Equality Act. The code helps employers understand their responsibilities and avoid unlawful practices and disputes. It also helps individuals understand the law and provides information about what they can do if they believe they are being discriminated against. Discrimination of protected characteristics (discussed later) is detailed. The Equality Act and Codes of Practice have been based on the European discrimination law, so that the two can be brought together more clearly.

Human Rights Act

The Human Rights Act provides further legal rights in the UK. The rights in the main represent everyday life including the right to an education, the right to marry and start a family. However, some parts of the Act are pertinent to the workplace.

Article 8 of the Human Right Act deals with the issue of privacy at work. The article states that 'everyone has the right to respect for their private and family life, his home and his correspondence'. This provides the person with the right to be left alone. If you monitor people at their place of work, the Data Protection Act (1998) applies. This includes videoing employees, checking telephone logs to check for private use and monitoring emails.

Although the Act does not prevent monitoring, it does provide guiding principles. The Act requires that the organisation be open in its monitoring, ensuring that employees are aware that they are being monitored, that alternatives to monitoring have been considered, that information is only used for the purpose for which the monitoring was initially carried out (such as detecting a crime), and that the information is kept in a secure manner. Covert monitoring is never recommended and can rarely be justified unless there is malpractice or criminal offences taking place and telling employees would make it difficult to source the information needed.

Issues that need consideration in terms of privacy are now described.

- The use of CCTV in the workplace involves the continuous monitoring of employees where results are recorded in a permanent format. This form of monitoring should only be used in areas where particular risks have been identified and where workers would not expect much privacy.
- Drug and alcohol testing is used to monitor employees operating dangerous machinery and transport workers. This can be undertaken if it relates to health and safety, and if workers have provided explicit consent.
- Internet and email use that is monitored by an organisation must first be agreed by the employee unless it is being monitored to:
  - detect criminal activity in the workplace
  - investigate the unauthorised use of telecommunication systems
  - ensure compliance with regulatory procedures.

Dignity at Work Bill (2001)

Dignity refers to the right to be treated in a respectful manner. A breach to the right to dignity occurs if an employer treats an employee less favourably than other people. This includes behaviour that is offensive, abusive, malicious, insulting or intimidating; unjustified criticism on more than one occasion; punishment without reasonable justification and/or changes in the duties or responsibilities of the employee to the employee's detriment without reasonable justification. An employer should have a Dignity at Work policy that complies with the Dignity at Work Bill. For example, such a policy would include an explanation of the statutory rights of all employees, examples of the types of behaviour that do not comply with dignity at work that may lead to disciplinary action, a clear statement of the procedure to bring complaints and details of how they will be dealt with, including details of a competent person to whom complaints are made, a clear statement of disciplinary procedures for infringement of dignity at work, providing appropriate training to management and annual monitoring of the operation.

Examples of breaches of dignity at work include bullying and harassment such as spreading malicious rumours, exclusion, making comments or threats about job security without foundation, deliberately undermining a competent worker and preventing individuals progressing in the organisation. The impacts of bullying are numerous and include mental health issues as well as physical responses. For example, Owoyemi (2011) in a qualitative study of 25 paramilitary personnel in a UK organisation found, through analysis of interviews, that the physical effects of bullying included hair loss, rashes and headaches. The psychological effects include anxiety, feeling scared, with two of the 25 personnel experiencing a nervous breakdown. The study also outlined the effects on work and the organisation. Effects included a loss of respect for management, reduced commitment and attitude to work as well as reduced productivity and performance. Thus, it is important to both the individuals within the organisation and the organisation as a whole that dignity at work is respected.

Another breach of dignity is through the use of harassment. Harassment represents behaviour that an individual recipient finds offensive even if it is not directed at them. Under the Equality Act (2010), four protected characteristics are not protected from harassment. Protected characteristics are discussed in more detail later. The four protected characteristics not covered by harassment law are pregnancy and maternity, marriage and civil partnership. Examples of workplace harassment can be categorised into three main areas: verbal, visual/non-verbal, and physical.

- *Verbal*: sexual innuendoes, jokes or teasing in reference to the protected characteristics; comments regarding the way a person dresses, their body or the use of insulting language or threats.
- *Visual or non-verbal*: looking at someone in a sexual manner; vulgar sounds or gestures including whistling; offensive pictures or obscene emails or other visual communication and other unwanted attention in the form of gifts or letters.
- *Physical*: inappropriate touching including patting, hugging and brushing against a person; physically blocking a person's movement; inappropriate display of body parts.

Harassment example

Peter, a librarian, had a knee operation. There were complications with the operation, which has resulted in Peter having a limp. Two male librarians have found Peter's limp to be amusing and have starting calling him names such as 'peg leg' and the 'limping librarian'. Peter is distressed by this ridiculing.

This is verbal harassment, as derogatory comments are made to Peter about his limp. This is known as victimisation, which occurs when an individual is treated unfairly, and is presented in a number of ways. The individual is treated unfairly because they have made a complaint about being discriminated against or harassed, they intend to make a complaint about discrimination or harassment, or they intend to act as a witness or give evidence to support another person's complaint regarding discrimination or harassment. For example, a manager shouts at Peter because he is making a claim of harassment with regard to a protected characteristic (disability) against his work colleagues. Such discrimination can be direct or indirect and discrimination occurs as a result of a particular protected characteristic, which will be discussed further in Section 3.4.

3.3 European law

The European non-discrimination law provides a set of rules that apply to the 27 European member states. The law against certain types of discrimination has been in existence since the 1950s, with the European Economic Community (1957) prohibiting sex discrimination in employment. Sex discrimination was the only legally recognised form of discrimination until 2000. However, public interest groups lobbied for prohibition of other types of discrimination such as religion, age, sexual orientation and disability. As a result of lobbying pressure, two Directives were implemented in 2000. The first was the Employment Equality Directive, which prohibited discrimination in employment on the grounds of religious belief, age, sexual orientation and disability. The second was the Racial Equality Directive, which prohibited discrimination on the grounds of race and ethnicity in the workplace and in the assessment of welfare such as social security.

3.4 Types of discrimination

Direct discrimination

Direct discrimination is when someone is treated less favourably than another because of protected characteristics. Protected characteristics include pregnancy and maternity, marriage and civil partnership, sexual orientation, sex, religion or belief, race, gender reassignment, disability and age. These will be discussed later.

Direct discrimination example

David, a senior manager of an engineering company, refuses Marlene's application for promotion to a middle management position. David did this as he believed that the team she applied to would not like a female having responsibility for an all-male engineer workforce. David believed that this would result in the team not following orders from Marlene and having a lack of respect for her, thus not allowing her to manage the team effectively.

This is an example of direct gender discrimination as Marlene is treated less favourably than others because she is female, rather than her ability to carry out the job.

Direct discrimination is lawful when the protected characteristic is age and it is to achieve a legitimate aim such as the requirement of a degree for holding a position as a teacher. Studying for a degree is usually post-A Level (age 18) and takes approximately three years, therefore an individual taking up a teaching post is likely to be at least 21.

Indirect discrimination

Indirect discrimination refers to a practice that disadvantages a protected characteristic. This can occur when there is a rule or a practice that affects all employees but disadvantages certain groups. Indirect discrimination is unlawful if it cannot be justified as a means of achieving a legitimate purpose.

> **Indirect discrimination example**
>
> Samuel, a senior security officer, advertises a vacant position for a security officer. The advert states that the person should have three years' experience and must be over six foot tall even though it would not affect the person's ability to carry out the job.

This would be indirect discrimination as, although it affects all applicants and it does not directly state that women should not apply, women tend to be shorter than men, thus it discriminates against them.

It is sometimes very difficult to assess whether a case of discrimination has occurred and whether it represents direct or indirect discrimination. The Real case 3.1 of *Homer* v. *West Yorkshire Police* provides an example of where even the professionals have a difference of opinion.

> ### *Real case 3.1*
>
> #### Age discrimination – *Homer* v. *West Yorkshire Police* (2010) (The Supreme Court, 2012)
>
> Mr Homer, a legal advisor with the police legal database, had over 30 years' experience as a police officer. At age 61, he applied for a promotion to a higher grade. He was rejected as his employers deemed a law degree as an essential requirement for the job. Mr Homer was offered funding to take the degree course, but he refused. Mr Homer filed a claim for indirect age discrimination. His claim was upheld by the employment tribunal based on employees between the ages of 60 and 65 not having sufficient time to study for a degree. West Yorkshire Police appealed the decision and were successful based on all employees without a law degree being treated equally. Thus, no age discrimination was found.
>
> Although Mr Homer did not have time to study for a degree, the degree was an essential requirement to be able to carry out the job efficiently, which could not be carried out without the degree. As there was evidence that a degree was needed, no discrimination could be found.

To help you understand the differences between direct and indirect discrimination, a discussion of the protected characteristics where discrimination can be found will now be outlined.

3.5 Protected characteristics

Direct and indirect discrimination occur in relation to protected characteristics including age, disability, gender reassignment, civil partnerships, race, religion or belief, sex discrimination and sexual orientation.

Age

Employment law protects people of all ages. Age discrimination has been unlawful in employment, education and training since 2006. This means that employers cannot treat you unfairly because of your age; cannot refuse to employ you because of your age (unless they can give a good business reason for discrimination); and are not allowed to bully or harass you because of your age.

> **Direct age discrimination example**
> An employer rejects Kate's application for promotion as she looks too young to hold a senior level within the organisation, even though she has the relevant experience and qualifications.

This is direct discrimination as Kate meets the requirements to carry out the job regardless of how old she is/looks.

> **Indirect age discrimination example**
> An employer insists that all candidates applying for an assistant administrator role undertake a fitness test. Fitness is not a key aspect of the job.

This is indirect discrimination as the fitness test would be something a younger candidate could perform better than an older candidate, thus resulting in indirect age discrimination.

However, individuals can be treated differently because of their age if the difference in treatment can be justified. Age is the only protected characteristic that allows for direct discrimination. For example, a young person playing the role of a teenager in a theatre production would be lawful, as would refusing a 20-year-old a position as a driving instructor, because by law they must be at least 21. These are clearly justified decisions and therefore not unlawful.

Disability

Under employment law a person is classified as disabled if they have a physical or mental impairment that has a substantial long-term effect on their ability to carry out day-to-day activities. Day-to-day activities include answering the telephone, reading a book, and using public transport. The terminology for discrimination of this protected characteristic is 'discrimination arising from a disability'. For discrimination to have occurred, an employer must know, or reasonably be expected to know, that the person has a disability. An example of this type of discrimination can be found in Real case 3.2.

Real case 3.2

Direct disability discrimination – *SCA Packaging Limited* v. *Boyle* (2009)

A woman, who had a propensity to develop vocal nodules and was controlled by a regime of avoiding raising her voice, was placed in a noisier work environment. It was argued that the noisier work environment would require her to speak louder and go against her voice management regime. After 33 years of working for the company she was made redundant. She started proceedings under the Disability Discrimination Act on the grounds that her employer did not make reasonable adjustments for her disability. A settlement of £125,000 was agreed.

It is the responsibility of the employer to make reasonable adjustments to help the employee to overcome a disadvantage resulting from their disability. In Real case 3.2, the employer placed the woman in a noisier environment, which would have meant that she had to talk louder to communicate and potentially cause further problems with her vocal nodules. If, however, a quieter working environment was provided to help the woman with her vocal nodules problem, this would have been deemed a reasonable adjustment made by the employer.

Before the introduction of the Equality Act (2010), indirect discrimination on the ground of disability did not exist. A change to the employment legislation has seen the addition of indirect discrimination for this protected characteristic in order to harmonise UK and European legislation.

Real case 3.3

Indirect disability discrimination – *Coleman* v. *Attridge Law*

Mrs Coleman claimed she was forced to quit her job due to requesting time off to look after her four-year-old disabled son and being refused. She accepted voluntary redundancy from the employer, but later filed a claim for constructive dismissal. The case was referred from a UK Employment Tribunal to the European Court of Justice (ECJ), which ruled in favour of Coleman who argued that able-bodied people can be unlawfully subjected to disability discrimination. An undisclosed sum was awarded.

Real case 3.3 is an example of indirect disability discrimination because, although the rule for taking time off work other than holidays and sickness applied to all employees, the fact that Mrs Coleman required time for another reason (her disabled son) resulted in her having to leave her job. Even before an individual is recruited, employers have to be aware of discriminating on the grounds of disability. As part of the employment legislation, employers are not allowed to ask questions about health or disability before they offer a candidate a job or send out a health questionnaire for them to complete before they have been offered the job position. Questions that relate to an individual's time taken off work due to sickness relating to a disability are not allowed. This is to ensure that individuals are considered on their ability to perform in the job well and not ruled out on health or disability. Questions can be asked once the person has been offered the job position or included in a group of successful applicants to ensure that a person's health or disability would not prevent them from carrying out the job. If a person has a disability or health issue that may affect their ability to carry out the job, an employer has to show that reasonable adjustments have been considered that would allow them to perform the job – for example, providing larger computer screens for those with visual impairments.

Gender reassignment

The protected characteristic of gender reassignment provides protection for transsexual people. The protected characteristic relates to people proposing to, having started or having completed the process of gender reassignment. Individuals do not have to be under medical supervision, which was a requirement of previous legislation; thus, a man deciding to live as a woman does not have to undergo any medical procedure to be protected against discrimination.

Direct gender reassignment discrimination example

Michael is a transsexual man who is about to undergo a medical procedure for gender reassignment. Michael is told at his performance appraisal that he is not being put forward for promotion to team leader as his team would not like the thought of a male becoming a female.

This is direct discrimination as Michael is treated less favourably than others, due to his gender reassignment and not his ability to perform in the job.

Indirect gender reassignment discrimination example

Michael is a transsexual man awaiting a medical procedure for gender reassignment. Michael works at a bank where the wearing of uniform is a requirement. The policy states that bank staff should wear 'gender-specific clothes' which places Michael at a disadvantage.

As part of Michael's gender reassignment he has to wear female clothing. Although Michael does not find this a problem, the policy of wearing 'gender-specific clothes' disadvantages Michael as he hasn't undergone gender reassignment and according to policy he must wear male clothes. This represents indirect discrimination.

Marriage and civil partnerships

Individuals who are married or who are in a civil partnership are protected under employment legislation. However, single people are not protected.

> **Direct discrimination example**
> Andy applies for a job that requires a lot of travelling. He is unsuccessful in securing the job as he is married and it is assumed that he will be a less reliable employee.

As the decision of whether to employ Andy was made on a perception of his reliability due to him being married, rather than his ability to carry out the job, direct discrimination has occurred.

> **Indirect discrimination example**
> A workplace-discounted gym membership has become available, within a large financial institution, for husbands and wives, but this offer does not extend to civil partnerships.

This would be indirect discrimination as although it affects all applicants and it does not directly state that women should not apply, women tend to be shorter than men thus it discriminates against them.

It is sometimes very difficult to assess whether a case of discrimination has occurred and whether it represents direct or direct discrimination. The Real case example of Homer v. West Yorkshire *police provides an example of where even professionals have a difference of opinion.*

Pregnancy and maternity

Women are protected against discrimination on the grounds of pregnancy and maternity from the start of the woman's pregnancy until the end of her statutory maternity leave. Indirect discrimination is not covered for this protected characteristic under employment legislation.

> **Direct discrimination example**
> Joanne, a receptionist, books an appointment with her direct line manager to inform him that she is pregnant. Phil, the manager, terminates Joanne's employment as she will not represent the sleek image of the company while she is pregnant.

This is a form of direct discrimination as Joanne's ability to carry out the job has not been the reason for termination of her contract – rather, it has been a result of her appearance due to a protected characteristic.

Race

The protected characteristic of race includes nationality, ethic or national origins and colour and can be discriminated against both directly and indirectly.

Real case 3.4

Direct race discrimination – *BBC* v. *Souster* (2001) (Equality and Human Rights Commission, 2002)

Mr Souster was a presenter for the BBC Scotland's *Rugby Special* who complained that his employment had been terminated because he was English and that the BBC wanted a Scottish person to present the *Rugby Special*. The BBC put forward the argument that the Scottish and English share a British passport and therefore there could be no grounds for discrimination. The Court ruled against this argument and found that discrimination had occurred.

Real case 3.4 is an example of where discrimination can occur within the same country and puts forward an important point to the necessity of employers to understand what represents discrimination. Other examples of discrimination based on this protected characteristic include not employing an individual because they are black or not using a picture of an Asian individual on the company's website as they want white individuals to be the representative faces of the company.

Real case 3.5

Indirect race discrimination – *Aina* v. *Employment Service* (2002) (Equality and Human Rights Commission, 2002)

A black African male applied for a job as Equality Opportunities Manager. The individual had the relevant skills and abilities to undertake the job. The individual did not secure the position as the job was only open to permanent employees of a higher grade, of which he was unaware. The organisation had no black African employees working at the level required. At an employment tribunal, it was found that there was no justification for the requirement to be at that grade; therefore it was found to be indirect discrimination on racial grounds.

In Real case 3.5, racial discrimination occurred because no black African employee was at the grade required to apply for the job. Although the grade was required for all people, regardless of race, applying for the job, it disadvantaged a certain group (black African employees) and therefore represented indirect discrimination.

Religion or belief

Under this section of employment legislation, religion or belief includes any religion and a lack of religion. The religion must have a structure and belief system and discrimination can still occur if the discriminator and the recipient of the discrimination are of the same religion or belief. Discrimination involves treating a person or group differently because of their religion.

> **Direct religious discrimination example**
> A Muslim employee is dismissed for misconduct; however another non-Muslim is not dismissed for the same misconduct.

This is a clear case of direct discrimination as, although two employees acted in the same way, two different outcomes were evidenced with the only defining factor being religion.

> **Indirect religious discrimination example**
> A male employee of a fast food chain who wore a turban to work was told to wear a baseball cap. This was not feasible while wearing a turban.

A policy enforced by the organisation on dress code clearly puts a group of individuals at a disadvantage even though the policy relates to all employees, making this a form of indirect discrimination.

Sex discrimination

It is unlawful to discriminate against people based on their sex.

> **Direct sex discrimination example**
> A female employee is turned down for a management position because she is a woman and not thought to be tough-minded enough to handle the job.

Here, the characteristic of being tough-minded was not assessed but, based on the protected characteristic (female), a judgement was made that because the employee was a woman she would not be tough-minded enough to carry out the job, therefore making it direct discrimination. If being tough-minded was assessed as part of a selection process and the woman did not perform well on the assessment, the organisation could have evidenced that the woman did not possess the characteristic, which would be non – discriminatory based on sex.

> **Indirect sex discrimination example**
> A large call centre has a policy that all employees have to work full time.

This requirement may be more difficult for women who have to look after children and is therefore, indirect discrimination. If the job can offer a job share, then the organisation must do this. Indirect discrimination cannot be found if the policy, practice or rule can be shown to be a business need – for example, requesting an

individual to work full time on a project with a high profile client of the organisation so that there is consistency in the service provided to the client and good
relationships built up with the client.

Sexual orientation

Discrimination based on sexual orientation is unlawful under employment legislation. This protected characteristic covers lesbian, gay, bisexual or heterosexual
individuals.

> **Direct sexual orientation discrimination example**
>
> A job applicant, at interview, states that he has a same-sex partner. The appli-
> cant has the correct competencies and skills required for the job vacancy. The
> organisation makes the decision not to offer the position because he is gay.

The individual is treated less favourably due to a protected characteristic rather
than his ability to carry out the job. This represents direct discrimination.

> **Indirect sexual orientation discrimination example**
>
> A medium-size manufacturing organisation restricts employee benefits for family
> members to opposite-sex partners only.

Although the policy affects all employees, it disadvantages same-sex couples, thus
making it indirect discrimination.

Positive action

Some discrimination is, however, allowed in favour of individuals who have a protected characteristic. This is known as 'positive action'.

Positive action is where an action is taken to help an individual who has
a protected characteristic. Such action may be taken if there is an under-
representation of individuals with protected characteristics in a particular type
of work or if someone is at a disadvantage due to the protected characteristic.
An example of positive action may involve training individuals with protected
characteristics so that they can apply for jobs. However, within organisations,
positive action is voluntary action with no requirement for employees to
undertake it.

One way to employ positive action is through the job advertisement. Through
this you can encourage people who have particular protected characteristics to
apply for the job being advertised. However, it is unlawful to state that you only
want someone with that particular characteristic. Even when employing positive
action the employer does need to evidence that they have chosen the person with

the most relevant skills and abilities to perform the job. If you are applying an occupational requirement (discussed below), you are able to state that you want someone with a protected characteristic.

Occupational requirement

Occupational requirement represents discrimination in favour of a particular protected characteristic for recruitment, training, promotion, transfers or dismissal in certain roles. For an occupational requirement to be allowed, an employer must show that the requirement of discrimination is a proportionate means of achieving a legitimate aim. For example, a Muslim care home may be able to evidence that its carers need to be Muslim in order to cater for its clients' religious/spiritual needs.

For discrimination to be classed as an occupational requirement, it must be crucial to the role and not just an important factor.

3.6 Avoiding discrimination

As discrimination can have negative effects on both the individual and the organisation, it is important that all efforts are made to avoid it. By undertaking the following actions you can put into place strategies to avoid discrimination taking place. This is not an exhaustive list, but an overview of actions that organisations can take.

- Amend company policies and procedures to reflect the harmonised Equality Act and European legislation.
- Review recruitment and selection procedures as well as application forms in response to the prohibition of making pre-health employment enquiries.
- Review any pay secrecy clauses within contracts, procedures and handbooks, and assess whether they should be removed.
- Review any occupational requirements in relation to specific roles and assess whether they fall within the occupational requirement defence.
- Train staff on the Equality Act and include as part of the new employees' induction programme.
- Seek legal advice if you are unsure about anything.

By following these guidelines unlawful acts can be avoided.

3.7 Summary

As an occupational psychologist or any other business professional making recommendations to change policies and procedures within organisations, legislation should be considered. Without due consideration interventions could be unlawful, leaving both the individual making the recommendations and the organisation at risk of litigation. As legislation changes over time, it is important that you keep abreast of any changes so that you are able to provide the best advice to your clients.

Short-answer questions

A person is dismissed from work due to long-term sickness absence. The person has cancer, which is automatically classified as a disability. The absence has been caused by the medical condition. The person has not been dismissed because of their medical condition, but due to the time taken off work to receive treatment. Thus, it is as a result of the disability the person is off work.

1 What protected characteristic is being discriminated against?

2 Define direct discrimination.

3 Define indirect discrimination.

4 What positive actions can you take to help an individual who has a protected characteristic?

5 Provide two legitimate occupational requirement examples.

Useful websites

The following websites provide further information on legislative changes and updates.

ACAS provides impartial advice, training and problem-resolution services: *www.acas.org.uk*

Business Link provides business advice and support services: *www.businesslink.gov.uk*

Direct Gov is a UK Government service for people in England, Scotland and Wales. It provides practical advice and information about public services: *www.direct.gov.uk*

Employment Appeals Tribunal Ireland: *http://www.eatribunal.ie*

Information Commissioner's Office: UK independent authority to uphold rights in the public interest: *http://www.ico.gov.uk*

Industrial Tribunal and the Fair Employment Tribunal Northern Ireland: *http://www. employmenttribunalsni.co.uk/index/useful_info/legislation.htm*

The Equalities and Human Rights Commission is an independent statutory body that helps to eliminate discrimination, and protect human rights: *www.equalityhumanrights.com*

Code of Practice on Equal Pay: *http://www.equalityhumanrights.com/uploaded_files/ EqualityAct/equalpaycode.pdf*

Code of Practice on Employment: *http://www.equalityhumanrights.com/uploaded_files/ EqualityAct/employercode.pdf*

Code of Practice on Services, Public Functions and Associations: *http://www. equalityhumanrights.com/uploaded_files/EqualityAct/servicescode.pdf*

The Government Equalities Office helps to create a fair and flexible labour market and ensure quality: *www.equalities.gov.uk*

Handbook on European non-discrimination law: *http://fra.europa.eu/fraWebsite/ attachments/182601_FRA_CASE_LAW_HANDBOOK_EN.pdf*

Further information

England

Equality and Human Rights Commission Helpline

FREEPOST RRLL-GHUX-CTRX

Arndale House, Arndale Centre, Manchester M4 3AQ

Main number 0845 604 6610 Textphone 0845 604 6620 Fax 0845 604 6630

Ireland Human Rights Commission

4th Floor, Jervis House, Jervis Street, Dublin 1

Main number +353 1 8589601 Fax +353 1 8589609 Email: info@ihrc.ie

Scotland

Equality and Human Rights Commission Helpline

FREEPOST RSAB-YJEJ-EXUJ

The Optima Building, 58 Robertson Street, Glasgow G2 8DU

Main number 0845 604 5510 Textphone 0845 604 5520 Fax 0845 604 5530

Wales

Equality and Human Rights Commission Helpline

FREEPOST RRLR-UEYB-UYZL

3rd Floor, 3 Callaghan Square, Cardiff CF10 5BT

Main number: 0845 604 8810 Textphone 0845 604 8820 Fax: 0845 604 8830

4

Personnel selection and assessment

Learning outcomes

After reading this chapter, you should be able to:

- understand the importance of undertaking a job analysis
- describe the link between job analysis and other personnel products (job description, person specification and the variety of recruitment and selection methods)
- evaluate various job analysis methods and techniques
- discuss the use of competency-based assessment
- choose appropriate selection methods including interviews, psychometric tests, situational judgement tests, work sample tests, biographical data, personal references and assessment centres.

4.1 Introduction

Samuel, a psychology graduate, applies for a job at a call centre. He is successful in being called in for assessment. Some questions that Samuel may consider before attending the assessment include:

- What does the job consist of?
- How will they identify the competencies required to perform the job?
- What assessment methods will they use to make their selection?

In this chapter we will explore the role of job analysis and its link to identifying the job role and the competencies required to undertake the job role. There will also be an evaluation of a variety of assessment methods that organisations employ in the selection process, which Samuel may want to consider when preparing for the assessment process.

Organisations spend a considerable amount of money on recruitment and selection of individuals to jobs. Such costs include job advertisements, sifting of applications, undertaking a selection process as well as training individuals into the job role. It is important, therefore, for organisations to ensure the right person is selected for the job.

The definition of recruitment used throughout this chapter represents the generation of an applicant pool for a job vacancy in order to provide a number of candidates for selection. The definition of selection represents a choice of candidates from the applicant pool through the employment of appropriate selection methods such as interviews, psychometrics, situational judgement tests, work-based samples, assessment centres, the use of biographical data and personal references.

The process of personnel recruitment and selection progresses through a number of stages. These stages can be seen in Figure 4.1 and will form the structure of this chapter.

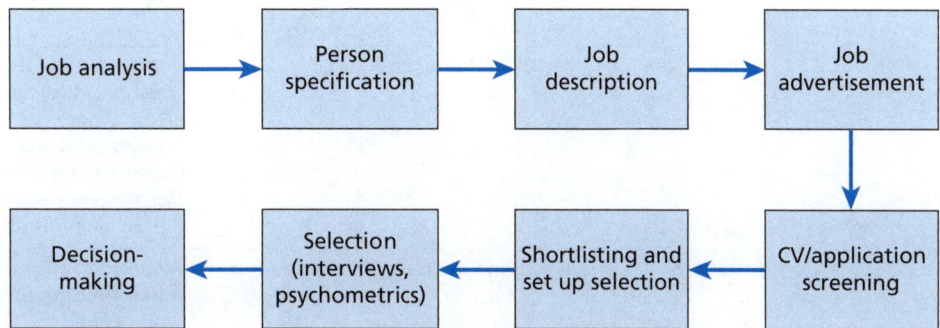

Figure 4.1 Recruitment and selection process

4.2 Job analysis

A job analysis is the first stage in the personnel selection and assessment process and can be described as the 'systematic procedure of collecting and analysing information about jobs' (Visser, Altink, & Algera, 1997). The job analysis can also be used in other areas of occupational psychology including training and development, performance appraisals, career development, to determine reward packages and to ensure that the job operates within the confines of the law. It involves the evaluation and understanding of the component parts that make up a particular job role within an organisation. The components consist of the tasks, responsibilities and duties to be undertaken; the knowledge, skills and abilities an individual must possess to perform well in the job; the technology/equipment to be used; the working conditions; and the position of the job within the structure of the organisation including reporting lines. Job analysis can be undertaken using a variety of methods which can be seen in Table 4.1.

Table 4.1 Methods of job analysis

Method	How performed	Advantages/disadvantages
Observation	Employee observed carrying out daily tasks by job analysts, camera or video equipment	*Advantages*: questions can be asked, inexpensive, gain first-hand knowledge of job *Disadvantages*: observer bias (overemphasises tasks), cannot observe cognitive tasks such as problem-solving.
Participation	Job analyst undertakes job	*Advantages*: hands-on experience of the job and how tasks relate to each other *Disadvantages*: not for jobs that require a high level of skill or technical expertise
Existing data	Taken from job descriptions, training manuals and previous job analyses (from own or similar organisation)	*Advantages*: time saving *Disadvantages*: out-of-date information, differences between jobs
Interviews	Structured or unstructured	*Advantages*: can ask follow-up questions, flexible, applicable to all job types *Disadvantages*: may miss information out, especially when a task becomes automatic; difficult to pull all information together
Surveys	Open-ended questions about a job	*Advantages*: allows for a large collection of data, cost-effective, time-saving *Disadvantages*: may miss key questions off the survey; cannot ask follow-up questions
Job diaries	Systematic documentation of tasks carried out	*Advantages*: good when jobs are difficult to observe *Disadvantages*: time to write diary, clarity of information provided, differing literacy levels of employees

As well as the methods, there are various standardised job analysis techniques. These include the Job Element Method, the Position Analysis Questionnaire, the Functional Job Analysis, Critical Incidents Technique and Cognitive Task Analysis. As these techniques are standardised the results from the test are more reliable. Each of these techniques will be discussed in more detail.

Job Element Method

The Job Element Method (Primoff & Eyde, 1988) focuses mainly on industrial or unskilled jobs. It adopts a person-focused approach, and takes into account the basic knowledge, skills and abilities that are required to perform the job. It aims to identify the characteristics (job elements) of satisfactory workers and, once identified, these are used to form the basis of the selection process. This technique has five main steps.

1 Select a group of experts: these include workers, supervisors, technical experts, etc.
2 Brainstorm a list of job elements.
3 Assign a weight to each of the elements considering the (T) trouble that would occur if the element was not considered; (P) practicality of including the element on the ability to fill the job; (B) barely acceptable, which considers the proportion of barely acceptable workers who have the job element; and (S) superior, which represents the effectiveness of the element in picking a superior worker.
4 Provide scale values based on the expert weightings.
5 Use results in the decision-making process, e.g. selection or promotion.

The advantages of this method include the identification of characteristics that are required for one to be good at a job and that it is based on past achievements rather than education or experience. However, this method blurs the boundaries of what is done by the worker and what gets done as it relies on identifying worker elements rather than on the targets set.

Position Analysis Questionnaire (PAQ)

The Position Analysis Questionnaire (McCormick, Jeanneret, & Mecham, 1972) is an employee-focused questionnaire that measures job characteristics and relates them to employee behaviours. The questionnaire contains 194 job elements. The items on the questionnaire are categorised into six key areas.

1 Information input, which considers how the employee obtains the relevant information to perform the job.
2 Mental processes, which involve the thinking and decision-making required in the job.
3 Physical activities, which the employee has to perform, and the equipment they will use as part of their role.
4 Relationships with other persons, including reporting lines as well as colleagues.
5 Job context such as physical or social contexts, including working in noisy environments.
6 Other characteristics such as other activities required as part of the job.

The advantages of this technique are that it can be used with a small number of job incumbents, but still generates reliable results; and it is inexpensive and simple to use as the questionnaire is structured, which allows for easy quantification. Disadvantages include people misinterpreting their job and the length of time to administer the questionnaire. Despite its weaknesses, in an analysis of 92 jobs, McCormick and Jeanneret (1988) found a reliability coefficient of 0.79 suggesting good reliability.

Functional Job Analysis (FJA)

Functional Job Analysis (Fine & Wiley, 1971) gathers information about tasks performed on the job and the way in which they are performed. This technique works on the assumption that whatever workers do, they do in relation to data, people or things (Brannick, Levine, & Morgeson, 2007). The job analyst collects data from a number of sources including job descriptions, technical documentation, organisational charts, books, as well as from observing and interviewing workers to learn about the job. This method provides a detailed overview of what the job entails (an example of the type of information gathered from this method can be seen in Table 4.2). The advantages of this technique are that it can be used with a large number of employees and it uses standardised statements to describe the nature of the job. However, it is extremely time-consuming and focuses on what the worker does rather than why they do it.

Table 4.2 Type of information collected from Functional Job Analysis

Data	People	Things
Synthesising	Mentoring	Setting up
Analysing	Instructing	Operating
Compiling	Supervising	Driving
Computing	Persuading	Manipulating
Copying	Serving	Tending
Comparing	Taking instructions	Handling

Critical Incident Techniques (CIT)

The Critical Incident Technique developed by Flanagan (1954) involves the recall and analysis of specific instances of employee behaviour on the job, both good and bad. The process involves the collection of factual stories about job behaviours that are crucial in performing the job effectively (Zemke & Kramlinger, 1982).

Flanagan put forward three pieces of information that are required from each critical incident:

1 the context of the behaviour and details of the lead-up to the behaviour exhibited
2 the employee behaviour
3 the consequences of the behaviour.

Types of critical incident represent behaviour that has actually occurred: behaviour that is of importance to the job, behaviour that is short-lasting, a behaviour that is not exhibited frequently, and a behaviour that has happened recently. This tool is powerful as it provides a multi-dimensional view of the tasks including actions that took place, interactions with other staff members as well as non-verbal behaviour. This technique also allows for rare events to be raised that more standardised questionnaire-based approaches may miss. However, problems with the critical incident technique do exist, such as employees not reporting events that may reflect badly on them; incorrect reporting of events due to gaps in memory; and the time required to collect a number of critical incidents.

Stop and reflect

Think of a critical incident that happened in your life. For example, the time you started school, college or university or went on a family holiday. Write down what you remember about the event such as the planning you did leading up to the event, and how you felt on the day. Ask someone else who is also familiar with the event to report on it. Are there any differences?

You may see that people report events differently. This makes it difficult to know which is the correct reporting of the event. With critical incidents in the workplace, such incorrect reporting can have an adverse effect such as jobs being incorrectly analysed, leading to problems with the development of a job descriptions as well as development of appropriate selection methods. Other issues can arise such as incorrect reporting of accidents in the workplace, meaning that any interventions may not solve future issues.

Cognitive Task Analysis

Cognitive Task Analysis adopts an employee-oriented approach. Unlike the other methods and techniques discussed, this approach aims to understand the mental activities employed by experts to complete the job task that is being analysed rather than focusing on the knowledge, skills and abilities required to perform the job. Five main methods of data collection and analysis have been identified by Seamster, Redding and Kaempf (1997) and include:

1 interviewing
2 team communication
3 diagramming
4 verbal report
5 psychological scaling methods.

The interview approach asks subject matter experts to outline the mental process used to complete each task. For example, a senior manager may be asked 'What do you need to know to make a strategic decision that other management levels will agree with?' The team communication approach analyses the mental processes of teams who communicate considerably to complete a job. For example, a combat engineer's assessment of mine location may be ascertained from questions asked of other team members. Diagramming can represent diagrams such as systems diagrams, dataflow diagrams or activity diagrams.

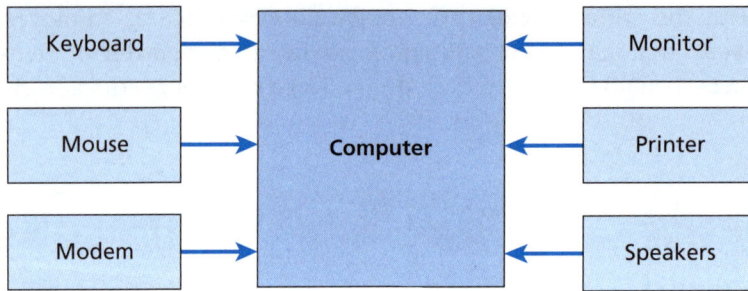

Figure 4.2 Systems diagram

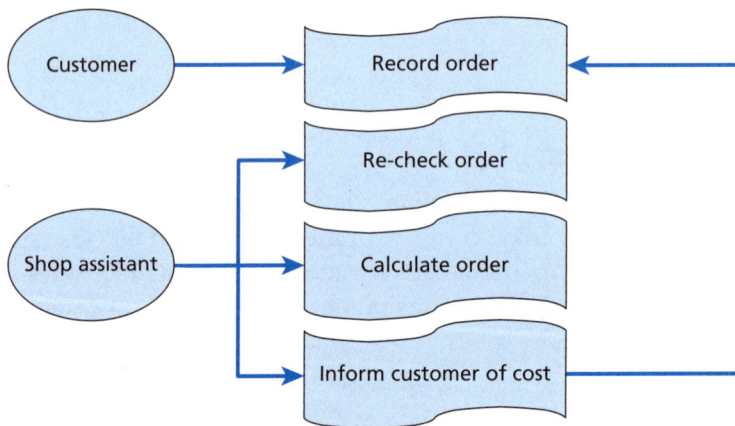

Figure 4.3 Dataflow diagram

The computer systems diagram in Figure 4.2 shows external features that could interact with the system. A dataflow diagram is a graphical image of the flow of data and interactions between the data. The dataflow diagram in Figure 4.3 shows a basic transaction in a fast-food restaurant.

An activity diagram is a graphical representation of stepwise activities/work flows. An activity diagram may be developed for completing a job application and would include stepwise activities such as requesting/downloading an application form, reading the job and person specification, completing the application form, etc.

The verbal report method involves asking job experts to 'think aloud' while completing a task. For example, a manager may have to make a decision on whether to invest in a new product or service. The 'think aloud' method allows for an understanding of how the manager reached that particular decision. The final method of psychological scaling involves subject experts ranking a variety of objects that are then clustered. For example, a police officer may be presented with a set of 30 cards that detail problems that may be encountered when carrying out an arrest (loss of radio control, injury, confronted with a weapon). The police officer would be asked to sort the cards into piles of similarity such as equipment issues or people issues. This would allow for an understanding of problems that are similar or different to each other. Once there is clarification of the component parts, a job description can be developed that outlines the tasks to be carried out as well as any responsibilities.

4.3 Job description

A job description provides information to candidates about the main duties, responsibilities and working conditions of a job. It also includes whom a person reports to. Although the job description outlines what an employee is required to do, it does not detail the expectations in terms of the skills that individuals should possess or the behaviour they should exhibit. An example job description is given in Exhibit 4.1.

Aside from the tasks to be carried out in the job, it is important to understand the competencies needed to be able to perform well in a job role. In its broadest sense, 'competency' refers to the sum of experiences and knowledge, skills, traits,

Exhibit 4.1 Example of a job description

Nursery Nurse

Organisation: Jelly Tots Nursery, Nuneaton, Warwickshire

Type: Permanent – 37 hours per week

£7.00 - £9.00 per hour depending on experience

Jelly Tots is a well established nursery providing care for babies and children from 12 weeks to 5 years of age.

Job purpose and duties

The Nursery Nurse will provide high-quality childcare and aid in the development of the children appropriate to their stage of development.

The duties include:

- To ensure daily routines are followed.
- To plan, organise and carry out activities appropriate to the child's stage of development.
- To maintain records.
- To communicate with parents and other visitors in a friendly and courteous manner.
- To ensure children are clean.
- To follow Health and Safety and Nursery Procedures.
- To respect confidentiality.
- To carry out projects as requested by the Nursery Manager.
- To be alarm key holder for the premises, including locking up and setting the alarm.

---

aspects of self-image or social role, values and attitudes a person has acquired during his/her lifetime (Mumford, Marks, Connelly, Zaccaro, & Reiter-Palmon, 2000). Competence is based on experience, in terms of what has been successful in the past and what has not, while also assessing whether the successful actions of the past would be successful if employed in the future. The competencies required for a job role are usually detailed in the person specification.

4.4 Person specification

A person specification is vital in the recruitment and selection of individuals who have the relevant knowledge, skills and abilities to perform well in the job. The development of the specification is undertaken by identifying whether the candidate needs to satisfy specific criteria and, whether they are essential, desirable or they disqualify a person from being eligible for the job. Examples of essential and desirable characteristics for the nursery nurse detailed in Exhibit 4.1 can be seen in Exhibit 4.2.

Exhibit 4.2 Example of a person specification

Criteria	Essential	Desirable
Qualifications		
Relevant childcare qualification	✓	
First-aid certificate	✓	
Experience/knowledge		
4+ years experience of working in a childcare setting	✓	
Understanding of health and safety procedures	✓	
Understanding of confidentiality issues		✓
Skills		
Good written and oral communication	✓	
Ability to work independently and as a team member	✓	
Good time-management skills	✓	
Attributes		
Reliable and responsible	✓	
Caring and friendly	✓	
Flexible approach	✓	

Many approaches to developing person specifications exist. One of these approaches is the Seven Point Plan. The Seven Point Plan developed by Rodger (1973) helps categorise job characteristics based on seven main groups:

1 physical attributes including appearance, health, physique and speech
2 attainments including education, qualifications and experience
3 general intelligence including intellectual capacity
4 special aptitudes including mechanical and numerical skills

5 interests including practical, constructional, social, artistic and intellectual

6 dispositions including dependability

7 background circumstances including domestic circumstances, family occupations.

However, organisations also adopt their own methods for detailing essential and desirable qualities, which may include talking to people already in the role, making assumptions of what the role involves or basing it on previous person specifications. Once a person specification has been developed, the job can be advertised.

4.5 Job advertisements

To attract potential employees to apply for a job, job advertisements (referred to as job adverts) are used. These are found in printed form (newspapers and trade magazines) as well as online (company websites and job searching websites), with research showing that job seekers are relying more and more on the World Wide Web to search for job vacancies (Van Rooy, Alonson, & Fairchild, 2003). It has been suggested (Cober, Brown, Levy, Cober, & Keeping, 2003) that job adverts play an important role in whether a person chooses to apply for a job. For example, it has been found that even the aesthetics of the job advert, including its font and colour (Cober et al., 2003) can have an effect, as well as its content.

? Think about it

Which of the two job adverts in Exhibit 4.3 do you think represents a good and bad advert?

Advert B is the better example as this contains information about the working hours, the type of responsibilities, and offers an opportunity to discuss the role further.

Perceptions of job adverts are believed to be a result of attitude formation, where positive or negative attitudes are based on how an individual perceives that cue (job advert) (Walker, Feild, Giles, & Bernerth, 2008). A second factor may be due to the job seeker's previous experience; those who have more experience are better able to discriminate between important organisational and job information. In a study by Walker et al. (2008), it was found that individuals with prior experience were more affected by the quality of the message content than less experienced individuals. It becomes increasingly important for job adverts to present the correct content to attract suitably qualified candidates. This also makes the sifting of applications easier as individuals would know what is required of them in the job and should write their application to show how they meet the competencies. The sifting process would involve working through the applications to assess who meets the competencies. If many candidates meet the essential competencies it may mean that you would need to assess for those that meet both essential and desirable characteristics and call those individuals to the selection process.

Exhibit 4.3 Examples of job adverts

Advert A

Nursery Nurses Wanted Now!

Warwickshire based Nursery

£7.00–£9.00 per hour

Interested? Call 07835 678987

Advert B

Help shape the future
of our children

Nursery Nurse - £7.00–£9.00 per hour.
Permanent post.

Due to an expansion in our well established
nursery, an opportunity has arisen for a
Nursery Nurse. The role involves providing
care as well as planning, organising and
delivering age and developmentally related
activities to children between 12 weeks and
5 years of age. Hours of work between 7 am
and 6 pm. To discuss the role further,
please call Erica on 07835 678987.

4.6 Selection process

The use of competency-based assessment in selection has grown in popularity. According to Golec and Kahya (2007), one of the most effective ways to facilitate selection is through competency-based employee selection. This approach is based on the assumption that each employee requires certain characteristics to be able to perform the job at the optimal level. These competencies can be identified through a job analysis (discussed in Section 4.2). The assessment of competencies is based on an objective approach where candidates are assessed against specific competencies required for the job role. One particular way to assess competencies is through the use of a competency-based structured interview.

? Think about it

Consider the example of Samuel at the start of the chapter. If a competency approach had been undertaken, would Samuel have a better understanding of what the job involved and the characteristics required for the job?

If this information was provided in the job description, Samuel may have been able to consider the types of assessments that could be involved in the selection process.

Competency-based interview

Interviews are one of the most common selection methods used by organisations (McCarthy, Van Iddekinge, & Campion, 2010). The aim of a selection interview is to predict future job success. The validity of these methods has been mixed and depends on the type of interview employed; however, a study based on a meta-analysis of selection interviews found a .38 validity coefficient for structured interviews based on a job analysis (Marchese & Muchinksy, 2007). This shows a moderate level of validity.

Competency-based interviews use a structured approach. The interviewer asks interviewees specific behaviour-based questions about events faced at work. For example, when was the last time you had conflicting demands at work? A candidate would provide an example of a conflict that they have handled and the interviewer can follow up with probing questions, such as asking what happened next, to elicit more detail. Candidates are encouraged to speak about specific events rather than generalise. The rationale for this type of interview is that judging how a person responded to an event in the past provides information about how they will respond in the future. An additional interview method can be used in competency-based assessment: the situational-based interview. The situational interview focuses on what a candidate would do, given a particular work situation. The question is based on a hypothetical situation that is relevant to the job role. For example, 'How would you deal with a staff member who refuses to provide you with a breakdown of work activities?' These types of questions allow less experienced candidates to demonstrate how they would act in situations that they have not experienced in their working life. Situational questions also allow candidates to answer the same hypothetical situation, making it easier to compare responses between candidates. It allows the candidate to talk about their input into a particular situation. However, whereas one study evaluating the design and implementation of a competency-based assessment centre to select doctors into postgraduate training in pediatrics found that candidates perceived the assessment method to be fair (Randall, Davies, Patterson, & Farrell, 2006), a study by Pulakos & Schmitt (1995) assessing 108 participants in either a behaviour-based (competency-based) interview or a situational-based interview found the behaviour-based interview to have a higher validity coefficient (0.32) than the situational-based interview (0.02).

? Think about it

Consider whether you would recommend the use of a competency-based or situational-based interview for the case of Samuel at the beginning of the chapter.

Factors that may influence the selection decision of interviewers include prior information, contrast effects, interviewer prejudices, physical attractiveness and over-weighting of negative information.

Prior information may be obtained from application forms, pre-interview references, work-sample or psychometric tests. This may predispose an interviewer to have a positive or negative view of the candidate before the interview and may affect the way in which the interviewer processes any further information about the candidate, as the interviewer will have an expectancy of how the candidate will perform in the interview. This was evidenced in a study by Macan and Dipboye (1990), who found that those candidates with higher qualifications were expected to give better answers in interview than those with lower qualifications. It was also found that interviewers had more favourable opinions of those possessing higher qualifications.

Interviewers may also compare job candidates with previous job incumbents who have performed well in the job or with previous candidates assessed for the vacant role. A study by Mills (2004) examined data collected from operational interviews with cabin crew from a major UK airline and found a contrast effect between the previous candidate's performance and the subsequent candidate's performance. Therefore, unless you are the first to be interviewed, you will always be compared with the interviewee before you.

Interviewer bias may also impact on selection decisions. Factors such as the candidate's race, gender and appearance may influence the interviewer's selection decision. A study by Graves and Powell (1995) found that female interviewers rated female interviewees more positively than their male counterparts, although males showed no differences in ratings.

The over-weighting of unfavourable information at interview can have a detrimental impact on how well the candidate is perceived to have performed at interview. Kanouse & Hanson (1972) attempted to explain this through cost–benefit analysis where individuals want to avoid potential costs and look for rewards and, in the case of personnel selection, this is the cost of hiring a poor performer. This is why more standardised measures of performance such as psychometric tests have grown in popularity.

Psychometric tests

Psychometric tests are now commonplace for use in selection of people into job roles. Psychometric tests fall under a number of categories including ability, attainment and aptitude.

Ability tests are also known as tests of maximum performance. These tests assess an individual's performance by how well they have done in the test. Ability tests can be split into tests of achievement, which assess an individual's present capability, and tests of aptitude, which assess an individual's likely performance in the future. Tests of achievement include tests that assess an individual's general mental abilities such as numerical reasoning and verbal reasoning, whereas aptitude tests assess job-specific skills such as spatial reasoning and technical aptitude. Such tests are underpinned by the 'psychometric objectivist' model (Anderson, 1992, Bertua, Anderson, & Salgado, 2005). This model uses selection techniques to measure an individual's abilities (competencies such as technical competence) and matches them to the abilities required for the job (identified in the person specification). The main assumptions of the model are as follows.

1 The purpose of psychometric assessment is the prediction of job performance.
2 In the main people do not change much. This suggests that certain capabilities could be fairly stable. This may be, for example, the leadership style that senior managers adopt.
3 Objective assessment of individual attributes is possible. By the use of psychometrics according to this model, it is possible to assess the core capabilities required for the job role.
4 Job performance is measurable. This assumes that there can be an assessment of an individual's performance on a job and whether individuals perform their prescribed tasks well.

This model suggests that by using various psychometric methods, a person's likely performance in the future can be predicted. This is known as predictive validity.

A further area of psychometric testing employed within organisations is the assessment of personality that assesses an individual's preferred or typical way of acting (Psychological Testing Centre, 2007). Personality refers to the differences between people, while focusing on the whole person as an integrated individual (Haslam, 2007). Personality is seen as a set of traits that are relatively consistent over time and situations. These individual traits represent a person's thinking, feeling and pattern of behaviour and provide an insight into how a person will act when placed in a certain situation. Researchers have identified a differing number of traits that describe an individual's personality. For example, Allport and Odbert (1936) identified approximately 18,000 different traits; Cattell (1943a) identified clusters of traits and reduced the number to 171 and, after factor analysis to assess whether traits loaded onto one another, developed 16 factors of personality for which a psychometric test was developed (Cattell, Eber, & Tatsouka, 1970). From this a second order of global factors emerged, namely the Big Five. The Big Five structure is now a widely accepted structure that looks at personality from the broadest level of abstraction, with each factor summarising a large number of distinct personality characteristics. Examples of these characteristics, according to the Big Five model, can be seen in Table 4.3 overleaf.

Many psychometric tools have been developed to measure the Big Five personality traits such as the Neo-Personality Inventory (Costa & McCrae, 1985). The importance of personality traits on performance has long been established with two meta-analyses, Barrick and Mount (1991) and Tett, Jackson and Rothstein (1991), finding that personality tests can be useful for predicting employee performance. These can be through either paper-and-pencil-based assessment tests or computer-based tests. Traditionally, assessment methods have focused on paper-and-pencil-based methods. More recently, computer-based testing has become popular. Much research has been undertaken on the mode effect (paper

Table 4.3 Characteristics of the Big Five model

Big Five Trait	Characteristics
Extraversion or surgency	Talkative, assertive, energetic
Agreeableness	Good-natured, cooperative, trustful
Conscientiousness	Orderly, responsible, dependable
Emotional stability v. neuroticism	Calm, not neurotic
Culture	Independent-minded, intellectual, polished

and pencil versus computer-based testing) of these. Bunderson, Inouye, and Olsen (1989) found that scores on a paper-and-pencil-based test were higher than those on a computer-based test, and Mead and Drasgow (1993) conducted a meta-analysis of cognitive ability tests and found that participants scored higher, although only slightly, on the paper-based method compared with the computer-based method, and Wallace and Clariana (2000) found that learners, who are less familiar with computers, will perform less well than those who are familiar with computers. These differences in scores could be the difference between a person 'passing' the test or 'failing' it. In terms of selection, it could be the difference between a person getting to the next stage of the selection process or not. Computer-based assessment does have its benefits such as improved test security, scoring efficiency and quicker feedback to candidates. The benefits of using the traditional paper-and-pencil mode of delivery, however, includes ease of administration, logistical freedom (do not need a room with a lot of computers) and cheaper set up costs (do not have to buy computers, licences or dongles).

Note: You can visit the British Psychological Society's Psychological Testing Centre at http://www.psychtesting.org.uk *to take practice psychometric tests and read more on psychometric testing.*

Situational judgement tests

A newer assessment method in personnel selection is Situational judgement tests (SJTs). SJTs are 'a measurement method that can be used to assess a variety of constructs' (McDaniel, Morgeson, Finnegan, Campion, & Braverman, 2001). Such constructs may include decision-making, leadership (Howard & Choi, 2002), delegation, integrity (Becker, 2005) as well as strategic decision-making (Steptoe-Warren, 2010). The test consists of a workplace scenario based on hypothetical situations, such as carrying out a risk assessment on a new business venture. Based on the scenario, the respondent is provided with a list of alternative actions that they may choose from in response to the scenario. The action they choose represents the action they are likely to take, should they be faced with the situation in the future. An example of a situational judgement test question can be seen in Exhibit 4.4.

Although used since the 1920s, SJTs have become increasingly popular (McDaniel *et al.*, 2001) due to their high face validity (McDaniel & Nguyen, 2001). Face validity refers to a test that looks appropriate (Parrot, 1991) in terms of measuring what it

Exhibit 4.4 Example of a situational judgement test question

You have been working for the same organisation for 10 years. There has recently been a recruitment drive due to an upturn in the business. Your new work colleague keeps criticising the way you carry out your tasks. What action do you take?

1 Ignore the comments and carry on with the tasks the way you always have.

2 Speak to your manager about the criticisms.

3 Speak to your work colleague and ask how they would carry out the task.

4 Tell your work colleague that you have done this job for 10 years and to keep their opinions to themself.

should be measuring. For example, if strategic decision-making was being assessed, then providing individuals with situational judgements where they have to make strategic decisions would be face valid, whereas providing them with situational judgements that asked them about a concept not related to strategic decision-making would not be face valid. This ensures that the test taker can relate to the test as being relevant. Robertson and Kandola (1982) argued that if an individual can see the test has job-relatedness, they will understand the reason for being asked to take the test and be motivated to try their best. This then aids in assessing the individual at their best performance. Much research has also shown that situational judgement tests are good at predicting job performance (Phillips, 1993; Weekly & Jones, 1997; Smith & McDaniel, 1998). Motowidlo, Borman, and Schmit (1997) argue that the reason that situational judgement tests have good predictive validity is that they measure actual job knowledge. It is argued that how an individual answers a question on an SJT is predictive of how they would act in a similar real work situation in the future.

One of the main reported advantages of the use of situational judgement tests, in selection, is that they tend to produce smaller sub-group differences than other methods of selection such as the selection interview. For example, Hanson (1994) assessed the differences found in mean scores for men and women and among racial groups compared with cognitive ability tests. It was found that there was a reduced difference in scores on the situational judgement tests. Therefore, men and women score similarly on situational judgement tests than other selection methods such as cognitive ability tests where greater differences have been found (Nguyen, McDaniel, & Whetzel, 2005).

Other forms of assessment are also used within selection procedures. Such methods tend to be less time-consuming and less expensive than setting up testing sessions or conducting in-depth interviews. These include work sample tests, the use of biographical information and obtaining references. We will now explore these in turn.

Work sample tests

Work sample tests are used as an assessment of an individual's ability to carry out specific work tasks. These tests have different formats such as hands-on tests where specific work tasks are completed and job knowledge tests that test the candidate's knowledge of the content of the job. These tests are best on tasks that are similar to those performed in the job. For example, an administrator demonstrates their typing skills or a first aider demonstrates CPR. Procedures for these tasks are standardised and scoring systems are developed by experts of the occupation being tested (Schneider & Schmitt, 1986). Work sample tests have also been found to have less adverse impact (Callinan & Robertson, 2000; Cascio, 2003), although more recent research from the public sector (Bobko, Rith, & Buster, 2005) has suggested that there may be more ethnic group adverse impact than initially thought. This may be due to the test not only measuring the work performance, but also assessing other constructs such as cognitive ability, which research has found to have adverse impact (Nguyen *et al.*, 2005). The benefit of using work sample tests is that they are based on an actual work tasks; it is difficult to fake ability to carry out a task and allows candidates to use and be tested on equipment that is required for the job role. Disadvantages of this method do exist, and include being costly as usually they can only be administered to one candidate at a time (especially where machinery is required); they cannot predict performance on jobs that take a long time (e.g. weeks) to complete; and they only measure the ability to perform the work sample and not the ability to perform well on the job as a whole.

Biographical data

Biographical data, also referred to as biodata, represents background information about a person and their previous life experience that may affect an individual's development or job performance. Information can be gathered through questionnaires and interviews with the candidate and correspondence with past employers. Information may include educational experiences, family and friend relationships, personal achievements and work experience. It also considers individual attitudes and values. Biodata works on the principle that past behaviour predicts future behaviour. For example, a study of 6,036 applicants for an automated systems controller for a government agency who responded to a 142-item biodata questionnaire, found that biodata predicted job performance on problem-solving (Dean, 2004). Biographical data is additional to the application form. The application form is usually based on factual data about the candidate including educational qualifications and work experience, whereas the biodata covers less easily provable information such as an individual's values, beliefs and personal interests. The use of biodata has been found to be predictive of training success, absenteeism, proficiency ratings, promotion and achievements (Stokes & Cooper, 1994), making it an important tool in selection decisions. However, problems do exist. For example, as the information is less verifiable, it is open to faking. Candidates may want to provide a favourable impression and thus over-exaggerate some aspects of information.

Personal reference

One of the most frequently used methods in selection is the personal reference. According to the CIPD (2010), 75% of organisations always take up references. The purpose of references is to obtain pre-existing information about a candidate's work history and the skills and abilities the candidate may have that are relevant to the current job vacancy. References are usually taken with existing employers and can be either verbal or written. Most organisations prefer written references as they provide the referee with the time to collect any relevant information about the candidate and to ensure that the information provided is factual rather than the referee providing subjective opinions. Verbal references tend to be used when information is required quickly. However, issues do exist such as not being able to contact the most relevant person, not having a signature on the reference and also the referee may not have the information to hand regarding the candidate. A telephone reference may also encourage bias as there is no written evidence of the conversation, only notes taken by the person taking up the reference. Before any reference is provided, the legal position must be clarified. Law covering references include the Unfair Contract Terms Act (1977), Data Protection Act (1998) and the Financial Services and Markets Act (2000), as detailed by the CIPD (2010).

A more comprehensive method of selection that employs a number of methods and aims to reduce bias is an assessment centre.

Assessment centres

The use of assessment centres in the selection of personnel is growing in popularity, with many organisations now adopting this approach to selection. An assessment centre involves a standardised process that assesses a number of dimensions using many methods. They typically last for a day and involve candidates completing a large range of tasks. The tasks set within an assessment centre test the roles set out in the job description as well as the essential knowledge, skills and abilities detailed in the person specification. Methods employed include interviews (both individual and group), psychometric tests, work-based samples, presentations, group exercises and role plays. This method of assessment has become popular in the UK where assessment centres have been used to select general practitioners and have been found to have good predictive validity; the way the person behaves in an assessment centre is predictive of how they will behave in the future (Robertson & Smith, 2001). Throughout the assessment centre candidates are observed by a number of observers who record and rate behaviour. To be a true assessment centre, LaRue (1989) argued that seven main elements must be present:

1 More than one assessment technique must be used with one representing a simulation (an exercise that is similar to a task that is performed on the job being assessed for).
2 More than one assessor is used who has had relevant assessor training before the commencement of the assessment centre.

3 The decision to offer the job is based on a pooling of information from assessors on the assessments carried out.

4 Evaluation of the candidate's behaviour happens after the candidate's performance on the exercises.

5 Simulation exercises are employed that are relevant to the job. Candidates should demonstrate their abilities rather than just verbalise them.

6 All the dimensions have been determined by a formal analysis (such as job analysis).

7 The assessment methods employed should measure the identified dimensions.

Advantages of assessment centres include the ability to collect a vast amount of information so that individuals can be assessed on multiple dimensions. Assessment centres can also assess multiple participants at the same time, unlike other methods such as the individual selection interview, and they can be custom- ised to suit any job type. The disadvantages of assessment centres include the need to train observers so that they do not bring their own opinions or biases to the selec- tion process, which is both time-consuming and costly. It is also difficult to provide one-to-one feedback on performance due to the number of people undertaking the assessment centre. However, assessment centres are successful as they target specific competencies required for the job, use standardised methods of assessment that ensure consistency and fairness in the assessment process and provide a better opportunity to ensure a good person–job fit.

One way of evaluating which methods to employ for the selection of individuals is their predictive validity. The predictive validity represents the ability of an assessment method to predict future job performance. The relationship between assessment methods and performance is assessed using correlations (r) where $r = 1$ is a perfect relationship and $r = 0$ where there is no relationship. According to Taylor (1990), 0.35 and below are considered low or weak correlations, 0.36 to 0.67 represent moderate correlations and .68 to 1 represent high correlations. The closer the correlation to a score of one the better the predictive validity of the assessment method to job performance. A comparison of selection methods was provided by Schmitt and Hunter (1998), which shows the predictive validity of a variety of selection methods with work-based samples and structured interviews as moderate (see Table 4.4). Whichever selection method is chosen, the main aim is to get the best person for the job while ensuring fairness in selection.

Table 4.4 Comparison of selection methods (Schmitt & Hunter, 1998)

Measure	Validity (r)
Work sample test	0.54
Structured interview	0.51
Unstructured interview	0.38
Reference checks	0.26
Biographical data	0.35
Assessment centre	0.37
Personality test	0.31

4.7 Fairness in selection

A candidate's perception of fairness in selection methods is important because it may influence the job attractiveness to the candidate and determine whether a candidate, if offered the job, decides to accept. Schmitt and Gilliland (1992) developed a model of the way in which situational factors may influence a candidate's perception of the fairness of the selection process. It was argued that a candidate's perception of fairness of the selection decision is influenced by perceptions of equity and equality. Candidates view the selection process on four characteristics: 1) job relatedness, 2) an opportunity to allow the candidate to demonstrate ability, 3) sympathetic interpersonal treatment, 4) questions that are not considered improper. Hausknecht, Day, & Thomas (2004), in a meta-analysis, found that applicants who have positive views of the selection process are more likely to have a favourable view of the organisation, are more likely to accept job offers and to recommend the organisation to others. According to Hausknecht *et al.* (2004), applicant reactions are important for five reasons.

1 Candidates who find the selection process invasive may view the company as a less attractive option when searching for jobs.
2 Candidates with negative views of the organisation may dissuade other potential applicants from applying.
3 Candidates may be less likely to accept an offer from the organisation.
4 Applicants may file legal complaints and court challenges.
5 Applicants may be less likely to reapply for a vacancy with the organisation.

Equity and equality can be ensured through the use of standardised selection procedures (as discussed above). A benefit of psychometric measurements, over other forms of assessment, within the recruitment and development arena is that they are standardised. Standardisation refers to the uniformity of the procedure of administering and scoring the test. This involves having a standard set of instructions, which the test administrator reads to the test takers. It is important that instructions remain clear and simple so that there is no confusion to the test taker as to what is required of them. Conformity in scoring is also required; therefore, scoring keys enable consistency in scoring. By ensuring conformity, no subjectivity is required, ensuring that the selection method is fair. This ensures that there is fairness in assessment.

4.8 Decision-making

To make a decision on the best candidate, all the information you have collected from the selection process (application form, interview, psychometrics, work-based sample) requires evaluation. To obtain the most valid results a weighting system should be applied. This should be based on the importance of competencies or characteristics required for the job to be carried out effectively. For example, if the key competency for an administrator is typing, then that competency may be given a 60% weighting whereas answering the telephone may be given a 10% weighting. Once you have these weightings and information about how well each candidate performed on assessments of each of those competencies, candidates can be ranked based on quantitative scoring. This will aid in making a decision and provides an objective decision-making process.

Multi-level impact of personnel selection and assessment

Using poor selection methods can have a number of negative effects on the individual, the team and the organisation.

From an individual perspective, inappropriate recruitment methods may mean a person securing a position that they are not skilled in undertaking, or a person losing a job opportunity for which they have the relevant skills. From a team perspective, an individual who is not right for the job will mean a reduction in productivity, which increases the workload of the team. This will result in reduced motivation as workloads will not appear equitable (see Chapter 10 – Motivation, job satisfaction, employee engagement and behaviour modification), which will also lead to a reduction in job satisfaction. The lack of motivation and job satisfaction from the team could impact on the organisation with a reduction in productivity as well as quality of products and services and an increase in absenteeism. The costs may also be seen in disciplinary procedures, termination of contracts and re-recruitment of an individual to the job role.

It can be seen that poor decision-making can affect all levels of an organisation. It is, therefore, important to employ the most appropriate selection methods. The importance of making the right decision is paramount, but the legal aspects of personnel selection and assessment also need to be adhered to and should be considered when making any recruitment and selection decisions (see Chapter 3 for a summary of legislation appropriate to work). Such legal aspects relate to discriminatory practices in recruitment and selection.

Legal context

Further details of the legislative requirements of personnel selection and assessment are discussed in Chapter 3 – Legislation applied to the workplace.

Short-answer questions

1 Identify the stages of personnel selection and recruitment.
2 Explain the affect of poor recruitment and selection on individuals, teams and organisations.
3 Explain the importance of job analysis in the recruitment and selection process.
4 Describe the job analysis methods and job analysis techniques from this chapter.
5 Describe the different selection methods and the advantages and disadvantages of each method.

CASE STUDY
Personnel selection and assessment

The company

Sammie Services is a national supplier of CCTV and security equipment located in Birmingham city centre. The company provides products and services to both the domestic and commercial markets. It holds contracts with electrical suppliers and national house builders.

The company was established in 1999 as a family business and is managed jointly by the chief executive officer and the managing director. Both still maintain active involvement in the company and have ensured that it has prospered in times of economic downturn. The chief executive officer is an entrepreneur who has developed creative ways to secure business contracts. The managing director is a more 'hard nose' businessman who likes to maintain control of activities within the organisation and be involved in the recruitment and selection of individuals into vacant roles. At an interview for a local newspaper, on the success of the organisation, the managing director stated: 'the success is due to hard work, long hours, a tightly controlled workforce and financial acumen'.

Growth of the business

The company has grown from two senior managers, two engineers and two sales executives in 1999 to two senior managers, five middle managers, ten sales executives and 30 engineers. However, the company has gone through a 24-month period of losing sales executives to competitor companies. This is problematic as the sales executives are taking their network of customers to competitors, which is having a negative impact on sales within Sammie Services.

Sales executive role

The sales executive is responsible for securing sales in CCTV, security products and maintenance throughout the UK. These staff are known within the organisation as 'baggers' as their aim is to bag business for the company. Of the ten staff, two cover the south of the UK, two the north of the UK, two the east of the UK, two the west of the UK and two in central UK. The baggers have a basic pay of £15,000 and a commission rate of 5% for the first £50,000 and 10% for sales over £50,000. For commission to be paid, a target of £20,000 sales per month has to be met.

Staff turnover has been excessive for sales executives within the last 24 months. Six of the ten sales executives have left for competitor companies. On an exit interview carried out by their direct line manager, reasons for leaving included unrealistic performance targets, a low basic salary, the job not being what they thought it would be, as well as confusion over their terms and conditions (such as the use of the company car for personal mileage).

Issues to be considered

The problems have prompted the chief executive officer to employ an occupational psychologist to evaluate the problems that exist in the recruitment and retention of staff and make recommendations to rectify those problems. Basic information provided by the chief executive officer includes the following.

- Six of the ten sales executives have left to work for competitor companies. Five out of the six have gone to Stronghold Security Systems, which pays a good basic salary, although the commission basis is similar to Sammie Services.

- The highest earning 'bagger' has been with the company since 1999 and earns approximately £85,000 per year. For new sales executives, undertaking the company's six months on-the-road training has averaged about 1,000 commissions per month.
- The managing director selects all staff members by the use of an interview and a verbal reference from the candidate's previous employer. The chief executive officer has suggested using a situational judgement test to assess sales competencies but the managing director has made it clear that he does not believe in such 'rubbish' as he can identify a good salesperson as soon as they walk through the door.
- The company advertisement states that the salary is £15,000 per annum with an opportunity to earn unlimited commission. The advertisement also states that the company has other benefits such as a company car. Employment contracts state the rates of pay, but do not state the benefits that employees receive.

The task from this case study is to apply the consultancy cycle and write a report providing an analysis of the issues facing this organisation on selection and retention of staff. For details of the consultancy cycle, refer to Chapter 2, which provides a comprehensive overview. Chapter 2 also provides details regarding the structure of a business report which you will find useful for this task.

An example consultancy report can be seen in Chapter 14.

Further reading

Brannick, M.T., Levine, E.L., & Morgeson, F.P. (2007) *Job and work analysis: Methods, research and applications for human resource management.* (2nd ed.) London: Sage.

5

Performance appraisal, career development, counselling and coaching

Learning outcomes

After reading this chapter, you should be able to:

- understand the performance appraisal process
- compare and contrast different approaches to performance appraisal
- critically evaluate the links between performance appraisal and career development models
- describe the use of career counselling within the performance appraisal process
- describe the benefits of using career coaching.

5.1 Introduction

Peter, a senior manager of a university library, has been asked to conduct performance appraisals for his team of 30 staff. At present, the university is looking into a new performance appraisal process and reviewing potential approaches. Peter has been told that, for this year, he can use whichever approach he wishes on the basis that he feeds back the strengths and weaknesses of the process. The information provided will then be fed into the review.

In this chapter we will discuss and evaluate different approaches to performance appraisals as well as its links to career development, counselling and coaching. When reading the performance appraisal methods and tools, please consider which you would advise Peter to use.

5.2 Performance appraisal

Performance appraisals have become a general heading for a variety of activities, through which organisations seek to assess employees and develop their competence, enhance performance and distribute rewards (Fletcher, 2001). Performance appraisals are conducted to assess an employee's skills and abilities to perform well on the job. These appraisals are typically carried out by the employee's direct line manager or supervisor. The performance appraisal provides an opportunity for an individual and their manager to meet to discuss the individual's work performance, their development and any training or support they may require. Performance appraisals review past behaviour based on objectives/targets set (usually within the previous 12 months) and set objectives/targets for the individual to achieve within the following 12-month period.

It is important to ensure that performance appraisals are fair and equitable to increase motivation of staff; aid in the acceptance of the outcome of the performance appraisal; increase commitment to the organisation; and increase trust in the supervisor/manager.

Uses of performance appraisal

There are two main uses of performance appraisal.

1 **Evaluation**, which involves comparing the performance of the employee with a set of standards, previous performance as well as other employees. This form of performance appraisal usually helps determine promotion and salary increases.
2 **Development**, which represents enriching attitudes, experience and skills that improve the effectiveness of employees (Boswell & Boudreau, 2002). This would be undertaken through the identification of employee strengths and weaknesses, setting individual goals and providing the necessary training to achieve those goals.

Performance appraisal points for consideration

It is important when developing performance appraisal systems to consider how an individual's performance will be assessed and what the outcome of the appraisal may be such as salary increments, identification of training needs or promotion. A further consideration is the type of assessment that is required. For example, will a generic tool be used that uses general ratings regardless of the employee's job or position within the organisation? This particular method may save time and money, but it may miss important aspects relevant to the individual's job and include criteria that are irrelevant to that particular job. For example, a course director may be given an objective to contribute to the recruitment of students onto a particular course, whereas a lecturer may be assessed on that objective even though their role is purely to teach on the course. However, if an individual format is adopted the assessment will be applicable to a specific job. The individual approach ensures that specific competencies relevant to the job will be assessed such as decision-making; leadership; communication etc., and allow for strengths and weaknesses to be identified. Whatever type of assessment is used, it needs to be fair and equitable.

Any tool that is chosen to carry out the assessment should adopt a structured and systematic approach to ensure accuracy, objective assessment and face validity of the assessment tool, which is where the tool looks as though it is measuring what it is supposed to measure. This can be achieved by measuring some of the work-related behaviours exhibited by individuals such as meeting deadlines, number of days late or absence from the workplace. However, where an objective assessment of behaviours cannot be made, subjective assessments are used. These assessments tend to be given by an individual's direct line supervisor or manager and are based on their perception of an individual's performance. To ensure these subjective appraisals are fair, a number of strategies can be adopted.

1 Establish and communicate standards of behaviour to which all individuals should adhere.
2 Provide clear explanations of the performance appraisal ratings and potential outcomes of the process.
3 Provide training to appraisers and appraisees.
4 Allow for a two-way dialogue to discuss performance.
5 Have multiple appraisers, e.g. adopt a 360 degree approach to performance appraisal (discussed later).
6 Have clear performance criteria so that the individual knows what is expected of them.

A number of appraisal methods can be used to ensure a fair and consistent process – for example, trait methods, behavioural methods, competency approach, results method and 360 degree feedback. These will now be discussed and evaluated.

Trait approach

This approach involves the appraiser assessing individuals on certain traits such as friendliness, efficiency, reliability, trustworthiness and conscientiousness. These traits are related to the performance of the individual. For example, a receptionist in a hotel needs to be friendly to customers, needs to deal with enquiries/complaints efficiently and needs to be trustworthy in handling money and credit card information. Methods using the trait approach to assess individuals are detailed in Figure 5.1 (overleaf).

Graphic rating scale

The graphic rating scale is a form where the manager ticks off the employee's level of performance. The appraiser considers areas such as quantity of work produced, quality of work produced, conscientiousness, judgement, initiative and attitude. These are assessed using a likert scale. For example, 1 = inadequate performance, 2 = fair performance, 3 = satisfactory performance, 4 = good performance, 5 = excellent performance. This type of system is advantageous when there are many employees to appraise as it is less time-consuming than other methods such as

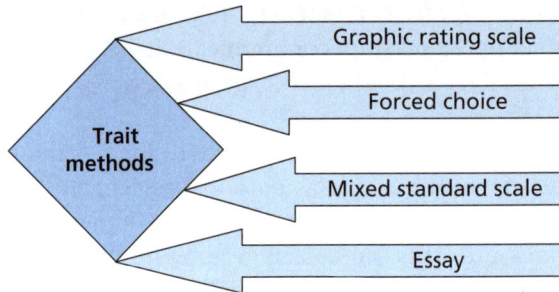

Figure 5.1 Trait methods of performance appraisal

the essay (discussed later). These methods also allow for a quantitative comparison to be made between and across employees. An employer will be able to assess how many individuals are performing at an excellent or an inadequate level. This method has high face validity as appraisees know that what they are being appraised on is relevant to the job. This also increases satisfaction of the performance appraisal process. Research by Roch, Sternburgh, & Caputo (2007) on the satisfaction of performance appraisal methods found that appraisees were satisfied with the graphic rating scale and reported it as being a fair method. However, different appraisers may use the scales in a slightly different way. One appraiser may rate individuals in comparison with others in their team whereas another appraiser may rate the individual on their development from the previous appraisal to the present. This means that there is an inconsistency in approach. Issues with the graphic rating scale have been overcome, to some extent, by the use of the forced choice method.

Forced choice method

The forced choice method involves the appraiser choosing from a list of statements the one that is most characteristic of the employee and the one that is least characteristic of the employee. Each statement is weighted or scored and individuals with the higher score are classified as the better employee. Examples of statements include 'Works hard', 'Performance is exemplary' and 'Is absent too often'. This method reduces appraiser bias due to the appraiser not knowing the weightings of each statement and thus not only being able to rate positive (higher ratings) aspects of the employee's behaviour. However, the appraiser can only rate the employee on the statements provided, which may not cover all characteristics required for the job, and may not allow for assessment of outstanding performance on certain job tasks. The result of this method is a bell-shaped normal distribution curve (Figure 5.2), which shows the distribution of performance across the organisation or department. The majority of individuals fall around the middle of the curve, with average performance, and very few employees are at either extreme of the curve, which represents poor or outstanding performance.

As can be seen in Figure 5.2, 40% of people will fall in the satisfactory range, 20% will fall in the fair and good range, and only 10% will fall at the extremes of

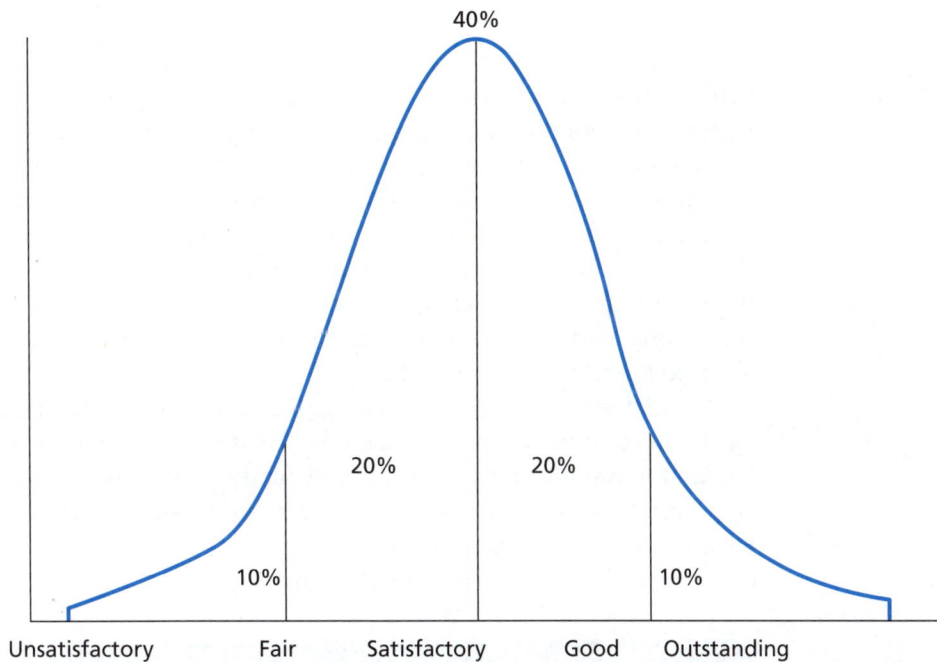

Figure 5.2 Normal distribution curve for the forced choice method

unsatisfactory and outstanding. The advantages of the forced choice method are that managers are forced to make tough decisions about the most and least talented members within an organisation. However, this method creates an increase in competitiveness between employees, which discourages teamwork and collaboration.

Mixed standards scale

The mixed standards scale provides the appraiser with a number of behaviours that are allocated a set of sentences. The sentences usually consist of three statements that describe higher, lower and average performance. For example, a team leader may have a higher statement: 'He/she is admired and respected by the team who trusts the judgement of the team leader'. The average performance statement may read: 'He/she has slowly become a leader of the team and the team is beginning to trust him/her'. The lower level statement could read: 'He/she is direct in their approach, which creates an air of distrust and conflict with the team members'. The sentences are random and the appraiser rates the individual on all three sentences using one of three rating options: 1) the employee fitting the statement; 2) the employee is better than the statement; 3) the employee is worse than the statement. The appraiser has to choose how to allocate each rating across the statements. The problem with this approach is that it only allows answers to the statements and does not allow for other aspects of an individual's job role to be included. Thus, important aspects of an individual's job may be missed. An approach that allows a subjective assessment is the essay approach.

Essay

The essay approach involves the appraiser writing a description of the employee's performance. This provides an opportunity for the appraiser to describe aspects of performance not normally covered by a questionnaire approach and concentrates on describing the strengths and weaknesses of an individual's job performance. This approach tends to be used in addition to questionnaire-type methods. The advantage of this approach is that it allows the appraiser to comment on any issue that is deemed relevant, which rating scales do not allow. However, this method is time-consuming, makes comparisons across appraisees difficult, and depends on the writing ability of the appraiser. The approach is also subjective and may not focus on the relevant job aspects.

Overall, there are many disadvantages of the trait approach, including appraisers feeling uncomfortable rating the employee as poor. Appraisers may also be open to bias; for example, if they have a particularly good working relationship with an employee they may provide inflated ratings over those with whom they do not have a good working relationship. This approach is also subjective compared with other methods such as behavioural methods.

> ### Stop and reflect
>
> Think about a job you have had or are currently doing. What traits are required for the job? How would you assess them?

Behavioural approaches

Behavioural approaches to performance appraisal involve recording employee actions. The aim of this approach is to describe actions/behaviours that should or should not be exhibited on the job. This may involve recording incidents and recording tasks that an employee does well or poorly on and providing feedback. Examples of behavioural approaches can be seen in Figure 5.3 and will be discussed in further detail later.

Critical incidents

The critical incident method involves the supervisor/direct line manager keeping a record of incidents that show both positive and negative aspects of the way an employee has acted. The record should include dates and times of the incidents as well as the people involved and actions taken by the employee. For example, an administrative assistant sees a filing cabinet left unlocked that holds confidential psychometric test information. The administrative assistant calls the occupational psychologist to report the problem. This would represent a critical incident where the employee had performed well. However, if the administrative assistant had not reported the problem and confidential information had gone missing, it would represent a critical incident where there was poor performance.

At appraisal time the employer reviews the documented incidents to provide an overall evaluation of the individual's performance. An appraisal interview is

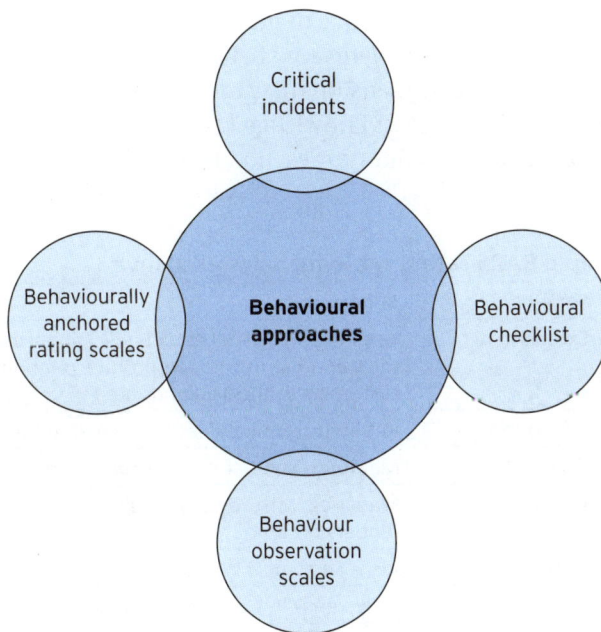

Figure 5.3 Behavioural approaches of performance appraisal

held and the appraisee is provided with the opportunity to respond to each of the incidents recorded and assessment is made based on those discussions. The benefit of this method of appraisal is that it records actual behaviours; however, there may be memory lapses due to time between the critical incident and appraisal, which does not allow the appraisee to respond fully to each incident presented to them.

Behavioural checklist

The behavioural checklist method involves the appraiser ticking statements on a list that they believe are characteristics of the individual's work performance. Such statements for an administrative assistant may include: 'Can meet office demands'; 'Keeps up-to-date with new policies and procedures'; 'Meets office deadlines'. This method requires a description rather than an evaluation of an individual's behaviour which the behaviourally anchored rating scales do consider.

Behaviourally anchored rating scales (BARS)

Behaviourally anchored rating scales (Smith & Kendall, 1963) are rating scales that are represented by points on a scale defined by effective and ineffective behaviours. These scales are defined by those individuals who use them. The development of the BARS follows four main stages.

1 List all the important dimensions for job performance (this can be achieved through the use of a job analysis that details all the component parts that make up a job role). See Chapter 4 – Personnel selection and assessment – for more detail.

2 Collect critical incidents of effective or ineffective behaviour.

3 Classification of effective or ineffective behaviour appropriate to performance dimensions. Performance dimensions may include relationships with customers, meeting deadlines and product knowledge.

4 Assignment of numerical values for each behaviour (see Table 5.1 for example ratings).

Table 5.1 Example BARS rating table for sales executive

Performance	Scale point	Behaviour
7	Excellent	Sales executive makes valuable suggestions for increased sales and has developed positive relationships with customers in the Midlands area
6	Very good	Initiated creative ideas for increased sales
5	Good	Maintains contact with customers throughout the year
4	Average	Manages, with some difficulty, to deliver quotes and tenders on time
3	Below average	Visits customers when asked by the sales manager
2	Poor	Only keeps in touch with a small number of customers
1	Extremely poor	Does not maintain customer contact or meet deadlines for quotes and tenders

The rating scale provides the employee with knowledge of what they need to do in order to be able to perform effectively. It is a clear and transparent method of performance appraisal. However, the rating scales take a long time to develop as they are job-specific rather than general ratings of performance.

Behaviour observation scale (BOS)

A behaviour observation scale contains a list of desirable behaviours that are required to perform a job successfully. Experts of the job concerned generate critical incidents based on the job role and categorise them into dimensions. Each of the behaviours is rated by the appraiser by indicating the frequency with which the individual engages in the behaviour. This is rated on a likert scale from 'almost never' to 'almost always'. An overall score is calculated by adding the appraisee's score on each behavioural dimension. However, the BOS is a relatively new tool and has less empirical evidence to support it, although it is favourable as it directs the employee's behaviour because it specifies what the employee needs to do to achieve a high rating.

Competency-based approach

The concept of competencies, developed by McLelland Atkinson, Clark and Lowell (1953), represents behaviours, knowledge, skills and abilities that are important for an individual to perform well in their job. Such competencies can also be referred to as attributes, factors or dimensions. Examples of competencies include teamwork, leadership, communication, initiative and understanding the business. Competency-based performance appraisal is a formalised way of establishing skills and behaviours that employees need in order to be successful

(Martone, 2003). The appraisal of these competencies includes measurement of actual performance against the competencies determined as required for good job performance (Chan, 2005). For example, Boyatzis (1982) used competencies to differentiate between successful managers and unsuccessful managers. The process involves an interview between appraiser and appraisee where the appraisee is asked to provide examples of when they have shown a particular competency within their job role. The appraisee describes the situation, the action taken and the outcome of the actions.

Using competency-based performance appraisals allows appraisers to determine how individuals carry out their work rather than just the outcomes of the work conducted. This approach enables behaviours to be identified that may require changing. However, Abraham, Karns, Shaw, & Mea (2001) conducted a pilot study investigating the competencies being used by organisations as part of their performance appraisal. The investigation considered whether management competencies, considered important to carry out the job effectively, were used as the assessment criteria at performance appraisal. It was found that, although competencies are used to describe successful managers, the same competencies were not used for performance appraisals. If such competencies are required to perform well in a job, it would seem sensible to use them as the criteria for assessing an individual's performance. It was suggested by Abraham *et al.* (2001) that future performance appraisals should use these competencies.

The benefits of using a competency-based approach to performance appraisal include:

- identifying areas of weakness where specific training can be provided (for example, providing leadership training)
- providing a clear set of criteria to employees on competencies required to be successful in the job
- providing a clear set of criteria to employees on competencies required to move to the next level in the organisation (career development)
- shifting the emphasis from organisational results to employee behaviours and competencies. This ensures that even if the organisation has performed poorly, it is the individual's performance that is assessed rather than the organisation's.

The main area of weakness with this approach is the risk of incorrect competencies being identified that are not relevant to the job, or important competencies being missed. This is where a comprehensive job analysis can help identify the competencies necessary (see Chapter 4 – Personnel selection and assessment).

The methods discussed so far have concentrated on the individual, focusing on an individual's traits and behaviours. The results method moves away from those approaches and focuses on the actual objectives to be achieved and the expected outcomes. This approach is known as management by objectives.

Management by objectives

This method of performance appraisal is based on the philosophy of rating performance by the achievement of goals that have been set by mutual agreement of the employee and their manager (Drucker, 1954). For this approach to work, both the manager and employee must be willing to work together on establishing goals. The objectives also need to be Specific, Measurable, Achievable, Realistic and Timely (SMART). Questions you may consider when assessing SMART objectives are detailed in Table 5.2.

Table 5.2 SMART objective questions

Specific	Is the objective precise, clear and well-defined?
Measurable	Is it clear as to what the outcome should be and the evidence needed to confirm it?
Achievable	Is the task within the employee's capabilities, and are the resources available to complete the task?
Realistic	Is it possible for the employee to perform the objective and does it fall within the business context?
Timely	Is there a deadline for the work to be completed and is it a feasible deadline? Are there any interim review dates?

This approach acts as a system of goal setting where objectives are set at an organisational level, departmental level, individual manager and employee level. Individuals are appraised on the achievement of the goals. Each goal statement must provide details of the actions the individual will take to achieve that goal. Periodic reviews of the goals are undertaken and any changes necessary are made to the goals. The individual then provides a self-appraisal of their performance that is discussed in more depth at the appraisal interview. The advantages of this method are that the employee is active in the goal setting and will therefore feel more in control of the goals and motivated to achieve them. This approach also has a good feedback mechanism as goals are reviewed periodically and can change as and when necessary. The disadvantages include the individual aiming to look good in the short term to meet goals, but not plan for long-term development. For example, if an individual has a goal to reduce the spend on machinery, they may make a decision not to repair broken items, which meets the goal set; however, productivity may suffer.

The methods discussed so far have taken a top-down approach where individuals are assessed by those higher in the organisational hierarchy. More recent approaches have focused on a multi-channel approach. This approach is known as the 360 degree feedback approach.

360 degree feedback approach

The 360 degree appraisal involves obtaining feedback on an individual's performance from managers, peers, subordinates and customers and in some cases a self-appraisal is also undertaken (see Figure 5.4). Feedback usually involves 8–10 people completing questionnaires regarding the individual's performance. The questionnaire needs to describe behaviours that relate to job performance.

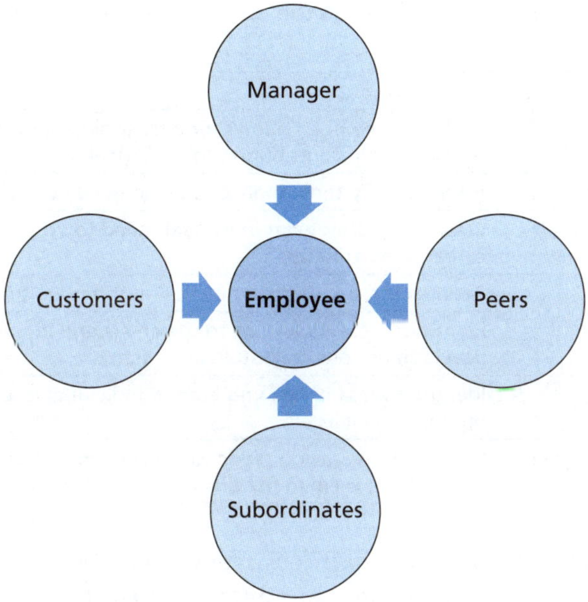

Figure 5.4 360 degree feedback

A manager's appraisal is central to the appraisal process as the manager judges an individual's performance in relation to objectives and targets set and aids in identifying areas where improvement is required. Peer appraisals bring a different aspect to the appraisal process as the peers may observe actual work behaviours carried out. Two areas of concern exist with this type of appraisal. First peers may provide a more positive view of their colleague's behaviour. Also, if peers are competing for rewards or promotions through the performance appraisal process, this may have a negative impact on the information reported by them. It is, therefore, important that a number of peers provide information on the individual's performance to ensure a fair and balanced appraisal. Subordinate appraisals also provide a valuable source of information as they work with the individuals on a daily basis. However, as with peer appraisals, there is the opportunity for bias, with individuals who are well liked receiving more positive reviews than those who are not. An important aspect of 360 degree feedback is customer appraisals. These provide an external view of the performance of an individual. The type of feedback received includes the quality of service provided, communication abilities, degree of professionalism and shows how an individual is viewed by external bodies. It has been argued in the literature that multiple rater feedback provides more accurate information as it cancels out individual bias (McDowall & Kurz, 2008) due to the number of people involved.

The 360 degree approach has many benefits over other methods of performance appraisal such as trait-based, behaviour-based, competency-based and results-based. According to Polman (2010), there are seven powerful features of the 360 degree feedback system, which are shown in Table 5.3.

Table 5.3 Seven powerful features of the 360 degree feedback system (Polman, 2010)

Feature	Description
Team development	Evaluation by peers allows for a truer picture of strengths and weaknesses in contributing to team goals
Personal development	Helps identify those individuals who need development
Career development	Clearly identifies what individuals need to do to enhance their career opportunities
Discrimination	Reduces the risk of discrimination as it has multiple raters
Customer service	Identifies areas important to customers and in need of development due to customer feedback
Training needs	Identifies areas of training both at individual level and organisational level
Sense of empowerment	Provides those giving feedback with a sense of empowerment by involving them in the process

Although the 360 degree approach has many strengths, its weaknesses need consideration. The method is time-consuming and costly, due to the number of people required to provide feedback and the collation of the information. It also assumes that those individuals providing people with feedback will provide accurate feedback. The method can also provide a culture of distrust as individuals are potentially reviewing each other.

Regardless of the approach or method adopted, it is useful for it to be followed by an appraisal interview so that the appraisee can provide their own view on their performance and development needs.

Appraisal interview

The appraisal interview involves an appraiser(s) and appraisee having a two-way discussion. There are two purposes to the interview process. The first is to reflect on the employee's past performance; identifying areas that require training, but also identifying major achievements. The second is to identify targets/objectives for the forthcoming period. A number of questions may be asked at the appraisal interview to evaluate an individual's performance (see Figure 5.5 for example questions).

The main aim of the interview is to have a two-way conversation about the individual's performance, provide constructive feedback and identify areas that can be developed in the future. However, research by Kikoski (1999) found that individual managers are not prepared to handle the performance appraisal interview and are reluctant to give negative feedback. This results in the individual being appraised receiving incomplete information about their performance.

Common errors in performance appraisal

A number of errors can influence the accuracy of the performance appraisal. These include distributional errors (central tendency, strictness and leniency), recency errors, contrast errors and rater bias.

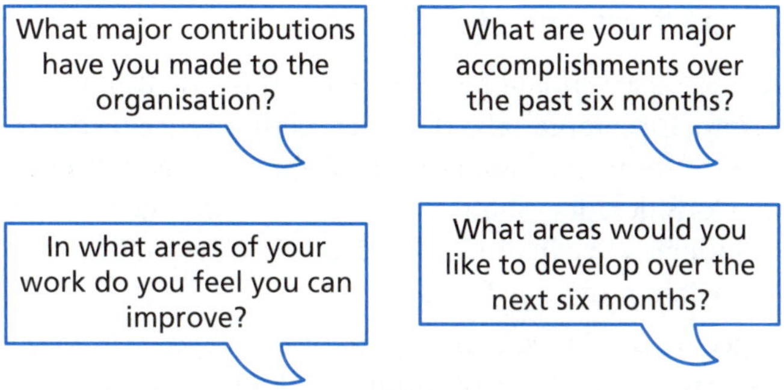

What major contributions have you made to the organisation?

What are your major accomplishments over the past six months?

In what areas of your work do you feel you can improve?

What areas would you like to develop over the next six months?

Figure 5.5 Examples of appraisal questions

Distributional errors Central tendency is where appraisers rate appraisees as average. For example, if you have a scale from one to five with one being poor, three being average and five being outstanding, the appraiser would opt for number three, the average. This can cause problems as poor employees may be rated higher than they actually are, which does not allow for key areas for development to be identified, whereas those who are good performers may be rated lower, which may cause problems with motivation and job satisfaction (see Chapter 10 — Motivation, job satisfaction, employee engagement and behaviour modification). Strictness is where the appraiser tends to use the lower end of the ranking system to rate individuals, whereas leniency is the opposite with the appraiser favouring the top end of the ranking system.

Recency errors are the tendency to allow recent events to carry more weight than events earlier in the review period. This could be negative or positive for the individual as, if an individual has just completed a project successfully, it would be likely to lead to a positive appraisal; however, if the project had been problematic, more negative ratings may be given.

Contrast errors occur when the rater compares the individual with other employees rather than the objective standard.

Rater bias results in either a halo or horns effect. The halo effect is when the rater's bias is in a favourable direction. This can be when an employee has areas for improvement, but these are not identified by the appraiser. The horns effect is when the rater's bias is in an unfavourable direction and the individual is given negative ratings, which can lead to frustration and dissatisfaction.

? Think about it

Identify the types of error in each of these statements.

1 Peter rates all his appraisees as average.

2 Peter rates Paul as favourable and identifies no areas for improvement even though Paul has had issues with meeting some deadlines.

3 Peter rates David's performance in comparison with Paul's performance rather than the performance criteria.

Providing performance feedback

Performance feedback should be provided to individuals regularly, not just at the time of performance appraisals. However, performance feedback is an important aspect of the performance appraisal process and the appraiser should prepare for the session. Consideration should be given as to the meeting place. The meeting should be conducted in a neutral place that is free from interruptions. According to Orvis (2008), when providing feedback:

- include specific task-based examples of the employee's strengths and deficiencies
- include specific suggestions of future development goals and self-development activities the employee could complete to address their performance weaknesses
- discuss both the employee's performance strengths and weaknesses, but limit the discussion of weaknesses to two or three priority areas.

The importance of narrative feedback was evidenced by Brutus (2010), who found that it involved the evaluator more in the process as well as providing a richer feedback message to the appraisee. The feedback message becomes much more personal than providing the appraisee with a number on which they have been rated. For example, a rating of 3 out of 10 may be provided on customer service (1 being poor and 10 being outstanding). Although 3 is at the lower end of the rating scale, it does not provide any information to the employee as to what the figure is based on and what they need to do to improve. If a narrative example is provided, then the employee has a clearer understanding of the problem and where they need to improve. For example, 'David needs to work harder on his customer service skills as he sometimes comes across as abrupt and rude' or on leadership vision 'David creates a clear vision and communicates this to subordinates, but lacks the confidence in communicating this to senior management'. This provides the employee with areas they need to develop such as customer service skills and expressing views to senior management.

Evaluating the performance appraisal

Regardless of the process or approach employed, an evaluation of the performance appraisal should be undertaken at the end of the process. This indicates how well the process worked and identifies problems that may have been encountered. This ensures that any future process can be enhanced by making changes where needed. To evaluate the effectiveness of a performance appraisal there needs to be some form of measurement. This could be assessing the changes in the employee's performance ratings (performance ratings should improve if appropriate support is provided by the organisation), or feedback from employees on the performance appraisal could be taken either through the use of anonymous questionnaires or through focus groups.

Performance appraisals can help in identifying areas that require development and reward areas of strength in individuals; they can also aid in the career development of individuals as specific talents of individuals can be identified. The career development discussion usually takes place at the end of the appraisal interview.

5.3 Career development, counselling and coaching

Career development

Careers according to Arnold (1997) are a sequence of employment-related positions, roles, activities and experiences encountered by a person. Career development is the life-long process of cultivating the shape of an individual's working life to make the best use of that person's skills, knowledge and interests (Peel, 1992). The focus of careers has moved away from a focus on organisational career development (developing an individual's career within a single organisation) to individual models where individuals are more fluid in their approach to attaining their career aspirations. This is due to the nature of the modern workplace where the job for life is rare and individuals tend to move from organisation to organisation. Examples of models that encompass these changes are the boundaryless career (Arthur & Rousseau, 1996), and the protean career (Hall, 2004). In terms of performance appraisal discussions, regarding career opportunities within these models would be difficult to achieve as they suggest career advancement through multiple organisations rather than through commitment to one organisation, which is the focus of the appraisal system. These models will now be discussed.

Boundaryless career

The boundaryless career (Arthur & Rousseau, 1996) suggests that the principles of careers include job mobility across multiple employers; the development of social networks to develop and maintain a career path; and that the individual has responsibility for their own career development. This is due to the changing nature of careers due to globalisation, technological advancements, industrial restructuring and downsizing (Baruch, 2003). For example, a study by Clements (1958) found that 38% of managers had worked for a single employer and only 13% had only worked for four or more employers. The movement to multiple employers witnessed an increase 26 years later when Alban-Metcalfe and Nicholson (1984) found in a comparable study that 9% of workers had worked for a single organisation and 43% had worked for four or more organisations. It can be seen from these two studies that individuals are more fluid in developing their careers across organisations. However, Sullivan and Arthur (2006) emphasised that mobility is not just physical, but also psychological. The psychological aspect represents creating and sustaining relationships across organisational boundaries. It is argued by Hall (2004) that the boundaryless career develops a mindset called protean career orientation.

Protean career orientation

Whereas the boundaryless career focuses on organisational mobility preferences, the protean career orientation (Hall, 2004) is where individuals rather than the organisation develop their own career path. These paths are not vertical or linear, but are flexible so that they adapt to changes in the world of work. Higgins (1998) argued that protean careerists are intrinsically motivated (they seek out new challenges) and hold a focus to achieve. Individuals have a particular mindset about the career path chosen based on their personal values. According to McGuire (1985), it is similar to an attitude that has a cognitive component (set of beliefs about the career); an evaluative component (what is a good or bad career for the individual); and a behavioural component (the tendency to act in a certain way). The careers are represented by four primary components (Briscoe & Hall, 2006).

1 *Dependent*: the person is neither values-driven or self-directed and is unable to define priorities or manage their own career development.
2 *Reactive*: the person is not values-driven, but can drive their own career development.
3 *Rigid*: the person is values-driven but not self-directed so cannot shape their own career.
4 *Protean*: the person is values-driven and self-directed and can define their career direction and identity.

It is the protean individual who is likely to achieve career aspirations due to their values and self-directed behaviour.

? Think about it

Think about problems of linking multi-organisational, individual career development theories to the performance appraisal process. Is it possible?

Individual-focused models and theories of career development help our understanding of the principal components, but an understanding of career development within organisations is also required. One model that considers both the individual and the organisation was developed by Bernardin and Russell (1993) (see Figure 5.6).

Career planning represents the steps an individual takes to achieve their goals, whereas career management is the process that organisations go through to select and develop employees in order to have individuals with the knowledge, skills and abilities to meet future needs. This approach views career development as advantageous to both the individual and the organisation, and as a dual approach involving both parties. However, problems may exist when an individual's career development advances too quickly or develops too slowly so that it does not meet the needs of the organisation. Career counselling and coaching can aid an individual's development.

Career counselling

Career counselling is a tool that can be used for career development. It can aid in the development of knowledge, skills and abilities required for improving job performance or developing an individual's career. Career counselling involves discussions with employees about their current job activities and performance as well as their career interests and skills (Bohlander, Snell, & Sherman, 2001) and can either

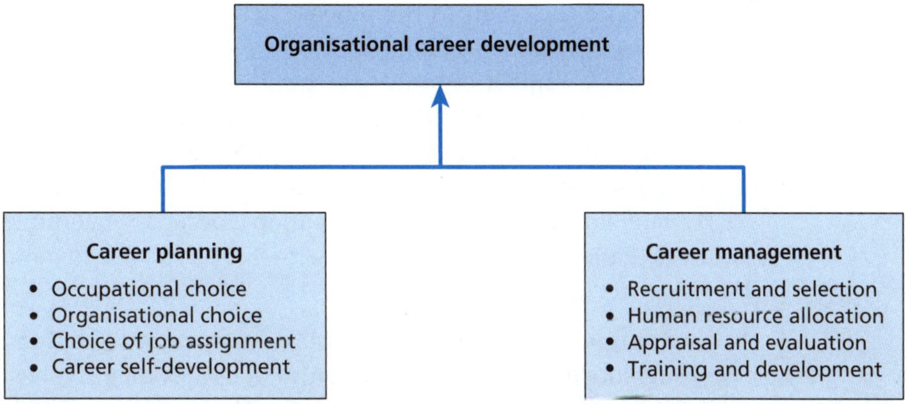

```
┌─────────────────────────────────────────┐
│     Organisational career development     │
└─────────────────────────────────────────┘
```

Career planning
- Occupational choice
- Organisational choice
- Choice of job assignment
- Career self-development

Career management
- Recruitment and selection
- Human resource allocation
- Appraisal and evaluation
- Training and development

Figure 5.6 Model of organisational career development (Bernardin and Russell (1993).

be undertaken by the individual's manager as part of the performance appraisal process or separately. One of the tasks within the career counselling session is to assess an individual's beliefs about themselves and the world of work, such as where they want to be, what they need to do to get there, and any actions required to get there. This session may also touch on areas that have been identified within the performance appraisal as being an area of strength or weakness. According to Egan (1990), it is at this point that individuals can be helped to set goals and progress can be made towards achieving them. Egan suggested three main steps in helping clients.

1 Identifying and clarifying the problem or goal (by listening, empathising and probing for more information).
2 Developing a preferred scenario (where does the client want to be/do).
3 Formulating strategies and plans (discussing options).

? Think about it

What are the benefits of including career development/counselling as part of the performance appraisal process?

Career coaching

Whereas career counselling focuses on an individual's progression in their job, career coaching focuses on aiding an individual's exploration of new careers, career change and other career-related issues. Career coaching is a collaborative process between the career coach and the client. The process usually involves the coach questioning and listening to the client to help discover individual interests as well as motivating the client and challenging them to achieve their ambitions. Coaching is individually tailored to meet the needs of the client. It usually involves sessions that introduce the client to the process, agree a plan of action for continuation of the process, conduct a number of assessments and provide feedback on those assessments. A number of tools have been developed that the coach may use to help the individual make the right career choice. For example, Holland's Strong Interest Inventory (reported by Palladin Associates, 2012) helps individuals identify their own personal career preferences. It is based on an individual's response to 317 familiar items describing occupations, occupational interests, hobbies and leisure activities, types of people and school subjects. The inventory is categorised into six general occupational themes.

1 **Conventional (the organisers):** individuals are interested in problem-solving through organising. High scorers enjoy activities that involve the organisation of information in an orderly manner. They are very detail focused, logical and like as much structure as possible. Occupations that fall under this theme include accountants, air traffic controllers and medical records technicians.

2 **Realistic (the doers):** individuals are interested in solving problems through hands-on activities. They enjoy working with machines and tools and work that involves physical activity and working outdoors. Occupations in this category include engineers, landscape managers and law enforcement officers.

3 **Investigative (the thinkers):** individuals enjoy abstract thinking problems. They are original and methodical, enjoy researching, collecting and analysing data. Occupations include psychologists, dentists and chemists.

4 **Artistic (the creators):** individuals enjoy solving problems through creativity and innovation. They enjoy being original, independent and self-expressive. They may be skilled in music, art, drama, writing and language. Occupations include librarians, artists and journalists.

5 **Social (the helpers):** individuals enjoy solving problems by helping. They enjoy working with people to inform, enlighten or cure. They are empathetic, patient and enjoy group activities. Occupations include social workers, occupational therapists and teachers.

6 **Enterprising (the persuaders):** individuals enjoy solving problems by persuading. They use words and feelings to motivate and persuade people. They are assertive, outgoing and persuasive, influential and goal-oriented. Occupations include chefs, travel consultants and human resources managers.

The benefits of this inventory is that it is updated constantly, thus the scores received on the inventory compare with individuals who have completed the inventory recently and are interested in occupations that did not exist when the questionnaire was first developed in 1927.

Although the Strong Interest Inventory was designed as a career choice test, the MBTI was not. However, a vast amount of research was carried out on the tool linking personality types with occupational categories. The information has been compiled into the CAPT (Centre for Applications of Psychological Type) atlas of type tables. This includes more than 300 type tables that encompass normative populations and career groups in occupations such as business and management, art, engineering, health, government and counselling (Reinhold, 2012). The tool is based on four preferences:

- introversion/extroversion – assesses where you direct your energy
- sensing/intuition – how you take in information
- thinking/feeling – how you make decisions
- judging/perceiving – how you live your life.

These preferences are then categorised into 16 types. Each type lists careers and preferences based on past research. For example, ISTJ is a type where individuals enjoy work that requires precision and high attention to detail. They are task-oriented and can concentrate for long periods of time, but do not like to be interrupted. Individuals with this type enjoy careers such as accountancy, engineering, legal secretary, teaching and airline mechanics. The benefits of career coaching include clarification of appropriate careers, developing actions plans for achievement of career preferences and providing information on how to develop knowledge, skills and abilities to achieve the chosen career. However, employing a career coach can be costly, which may dissuade individuals from using such a service.

Multi-level impact of performance appraisal and career development

Performance appraisals have an effect on all levels of the organisation from individuals to the manager and on the organisation as a whole. From an individual perspective, the performance appraisal provides an individual with feedback on their performance, allows them to gain a better understanding of their job role, identifying ways in which they can increase their performance, understanding and agreeing objectives for the following review period and provides an opportunity to discuss career prospects. From a management perspective, it provides an opportunity to discuss any strengths or weaknesses in performance, and an opportunity to understand any problems the individual may have, as well as an opportunity to understand an individual's career aspirations and training requirements. At an organisational level, performance appraisal provides information on which decisions regarding promotion can be made, information about training/development needs so that budgets can be set, provides organisational information that is linked to individual and departmental objectives, and provides an opportunity to update employee information such as achievements and new competency attainment.

Legal context

Further details of legislative requirements are discussed in Chapter 3 – Legislation applied to the workplace.

Government Equalities Office (2010). *Equality Act 2010.* Available: *http://equalities.gov.uk/equality_bill.aspx*

Short-answer questions

1 Evaluate the strengths and weaknesses of the trait, behavioural, competency, results and 360 degree feedback approaches to performance appraisal.

2 Describe the boundaryless and protean careers.

3 Describe difficulties in relating individual multi-organisation approaches of career development to the performance appraisal process.

4 Evaluate the importance of career counselling in relation to the performance appraisal process.

5 Describe the role of a career coach and methods/tools they may use.

CASE STUDY
Performance appraisal and career development/counselling

Sammie Carpentry is a family-run business that provides a variety of services including garden fencing, fitting of doors and window frames and household alterations such as partition walls, operating in the West Midlands and Warwickshire area. The company was formed in 2005 and currently employs six carpenters, one sales executive, one administrator and the owner Sammie. The majority of work the company obtains is through word of mouth and local newspaper advertisements.

The company is profitable and has received good customer feedback. At present, there is no performance appraisal process. The owner has just completed a management course and has realised the importance of the performance appraisal in developing his workforce.

The problem

At present the company does not have a performance appraisal system. Employees do not have any targets/goals set or have an opportunity for career development. The carpenters are paid the same regardless of the amount of work they complete or the quality of the work. The employees are raising concerns about their careers, potential promotions and fairness of pay and would like a clear process whereby they know how they can progress within the company.

Your task is to write a report to the owner advising him about the potential approaches that could be adopted for performance appraisal. You also need to discuss the importance of career development within organisations and how it can affect individuals, managers and the organisation as a whole. Ethical issues of implementing the interventions should also be considered.

Writing guidelines are provided in Chapter 2, Section 2.3 – The consultancy cycle, which provides you with a structure to follow.

Further reading

Butcher, D. (2002). It takes two to review. *Management Today,* 54–57.

Fletcher, C. (2008). *Appraisal, feedback and development: making performance review work* (4th ed.) Abingdon: Routledge.

Gillen, T. (2007). *Performance management and appraisal* (2nd ed.) CIPD toolkit. London: Chartered Institute of Personnel and Development.

6

Well-being, stress and work–life balance

6.1 Introduction

Emma, a long-serving member of an academic team within a university, has been told that her job is at risk due to the changes in government policy regarding funding of university places for students. Emma has to apply for roles within the university, but due to an increase in the need to employ overseas students, she will have to travel overseas, work unsociable hours to offer part-time evening courses as well as sourcing more research funding. Emma has two young children; one is in nursery and the other is at primary school. Emma's husband works away from home in the week and cannot help with childcare.

While reading through the chapter, consider sources of stress that Emma may be experiencing as well as sources of help for her.

The connection between health and work is an important one. According to the National Health Service's White Paper 'Choosing Health' (NHS, 2004), two million people suffer an illness that has been caused by or made worse by work. Such illnesses include stress, depression, anxiety and coronary heart disease.

The cost of such illnesses impacts both the employer and employee and includes loss of productivity, increased absence, increased turnover and an increase in the cost of training as well as potential litigation. It is the employer's duty to take reasonable care to ensure that its employees do not suffer an injury at work. Where an employer breaches this duty, an employer can be liable for negligence.

Real case 6.1

Intel Corporation (UK) Ltd v. Daw (2007)

An employee, Daw, had suffered from postnatal depression after the birth of her two children, but had returned to work. She was promoted, which led to a substantial increase in her workload and number of hours required to complete the tasks. Daw complained about the increase and her health began to deteriorate. An email was sent to her employer informing them of her postnatal depression and that she felt 'stressed out'. Her workload was not reduced and she was signed off sick with depression and attempted suicide. The employee was offered a counselling service. However, the Court of Appeal held that the employer could not hide behind the counselling service and that the employer should have realised that the increase in workload and excessive hours impacted on the employee's health. Daw was awarded £134,000.

Although the absence of ill staff can have an impact, present employees (known as presenteeism) who are ill also have an impact including a decrease in quality, increase in waste materials due to errors at work and a lower level of performance. Sainsbury Centre for Mental Health (2007) estimated that work inefficiency due to presenteeism costs £15.1 billion per year whereas absenteeism costs £8.4 billion. Due to these costs it is important to address issues that cause stress-related illness at work. To address some of the main issues, well-being, causes and consequences of stress, and coping mechanisms as well as possible changes that can create a healthy workplace will be discussed in detail.

6.2 Well-being

Well-being, according to Newell (2002), refers to a person's overall feeling – good or bad. Positive feelings include feeling happy, satisfied and pleased, whereas negative feelings include feeling depressed, unhappy and being generally unsatisfied. A person's well-being is sometimes confused with how satisfied an individual is at work; however, there is a difference between the two. For example, a doctor is performing at the appropriate level in their job and is satisfied at work; however, they are experiencing stress due to the number of patients they have to see and the budgetary constraints placed on them. Job satisfaction is, therefore, being experienced as one positive feeling, but the negative feeling of well-being is stress. Therefore, well-being is an umbrella term that covers a number of negative and positive feelings towards an individual's work.

One measure of well-being in the workplace is employee engagement. Work engagement represents an individual's commitment to the workplace and amount of energy they put into their work. If there is poor work engagement there is an increased likelihood that individuals will have more sickness absence, reduced productivity and reduced quality of work; and that they will leave the organisation and have more mental health symptoms. Having a positive well-being in the workplace has been found to be positively associated with an individual's psychological and physical health (Hallberg & Schaufeli, 2006). Thus, it can be seen that positive well-being is crucial to both individuals and organisations.

The National Institute for Clinical Excellence provides guidance on promoting mental well-being at work (NICE, 2009). The guidance is for those who have either a direct or indirect role in promoting mental well-being at work, including employers and their representatives. The actions include the following.

1 Have a strategic and coordinated approach to promoting employees' well-being. This will involve the development of policies and practices to promote well-being as well as promoting a culture of equality, fairness and open communication. Also, included in this action is the need for consideration of the process of job design, recruitment, training, and the promotion of well-being.

2 Assess opportunities for promoting employees' mental well-being and managing risks. This involves ensuring that systems are in place to assess and monitor well-being in the workplace so that risks can be identified and improvements can be made. This may take the form of employee surveys, monitoring absence and sickness, and staff turnover. Employees should be made aware of legal entitlements as well as taking responsibility for their own well-being at work. If issues are identified, employees should be supported with counselling or stress-management training.

3 Provide flexible working including part-time working, location-independent working, job-sharing and flexible working.

4 The role of line managers. Promote a supportive management style where managers motivate employees, provide training for them and deal sensitively with concerns or health problems.

5 Supporting micro-, small and medium-sized businesses. Provide support and advice on developing and implementing organisation-wide policies to promote well-being.

These guidelines are an important step forward in helping organisations promote well-being within their workforce. By implementing these practices, employers can meet legal obligations, reduce absenteeism and sickness, increase employee satisfaction and motivation, leading to an increase in performance and commitment to the organisation.

Real case 6.2

British Telecom

British Telecom (BT) has a mental health framework that focuses on promoting good mental health. BT provides an online risk assessment tool called STREAM, which involves the individual and their line manager completing 30 questions. A report is tailored to the individual and is colour-coded based on a traffic light system of red, amber and green. If the individual receives a red or amber report, a one-to-one meeting between the individual and their line manager must take place within 28 days so that an action plan can be drawn up.

The benefits of this system are that it provides a risk assessment for well-being and stress, allows for targeted interventions to be developed, and provides employees and employers with guidance on how to deal with stress.

6.3 Stress at work

Stress is a term that refers to the sum of physical, mental and emotional strains or tensions on a person. It also represents feelings of stress that result from interactions between people and their environment, which are perceived as straining or exceeding their adaptive capacities and threatening their well-being. In addition, stress has wide psychological and physical effects such as cardiovascular problems, musculoskeletal problems, headaches, gastrointestinal problems, sleep disturbance and depression (Ghaleb, 2008).

Stress was originally referred to as a biological reaction to a stressful stimulus. Selye (1946) found that when an individual is exposed to extreme heat or cold, they exhibit a set of bodily reactions. This he referred to as stress. However, today, when people are working longer hours, have more demands on their time from family and work as well as changes in the use of technology, individuals commonly use the word 'stress': 'I've had a very stressful day'. The concept of stress has almost become an accepted part of everyday working life. This type of stress generally refers to individuals also feeling under pressure. It is when the feelings of stress start to have negative effects on the individual and their working and family life that problems may ensue. The level of stress that can be coped with by each individual is very different. According to Lazarus (1993), stress represents a relationship between a person and their environment, which they perceive as significant to their well-being as the demands exceed the individual's coping resources. These differences in perception have been explained by the Cognitive Activation Theory of Stress (CATS), in which an individual's response to the stress stimuli is dependent on their expectation of responses they have in order for them to cope with the situation. If the coping mechanism is expected to provide positive results, the stress experienced by the individual will be reduced. If a lack of coping is expected to produce negative results, then ill health may manifest.

The way in which the body responds to stress is due to the person seeing a threat to their well-being. As a threat arises an individual's sympathetic nervous system is activated, which increases blood pressure and heart rate. Pupils are dilated and there is a reduction in pain sensitivity and an increase in our attention. These changes prepare an individual for fight or flight. The fight or flight response dates back to prehistoric times where individuals had to be aggressive to ward off predators and the flight response involved fleeing from predators. Although this does not occur in organisations, the notion still exists. The fight response can be seen when individuals become involved in confrontations and the flight response may be evidenced by an individual withdrawing from a situation. For example, an individual is involved in conflict with a peer at work. This has been a result of a misunderstanding regarding project deadlines. The issues have become very confrontational. If the individual is to 'fight', they would put forward their argument and stand their ground. If the individual decided to adopt the position of 'flight', they would withdraw from the situation to avoid a confrontation.

Work-related stress is a complex issue and is estimated to cost the UK in excess of £530 million and 14 million working days per year (Health and Safety Executive, 2007). A study by Smith, Johal, Wadsworth, Davey Smith and Peters (2000), which investigated the scale of occupational stress in a randomised sample of 17,000 people from Bristol, UK, found that over 20% of individuals (4,000) reported that they had high or extremely high levels of stress at work as a result of stressful working conditions that impaired their mental and physical health.

Stress at work, according to Melhuish (1978), can be described in four different ways, dependent on the level of pressure felt by the individual.

1 **Hypo-stress.** Stress can be caused by boredom or too little pressure being felt by the individual. This can manifest itself in depression, frustration and indifference.
2 **Eu-stress.** When an individual feels optimum pressure they can thrive in the work situation. Eu-stress is where stress is a motivating factor and encourages an individual to perform to their highest ability.
3 **Hyper-stress.** Stress becomes so extreme that stress reactions occur. Such reactions can vary from person to person. Symptoms when a person is in this state of stress can include feeling out of control, panic, and feeling that they are unable to cope with the situation.
4 **Distress.** Distress is a symptom of continuous stress. This can have a negative impact on both the individual and the organisation. The individual can experience physical and mental health problems and may voluntarily leave the organisation.

Theories of stress fall into two main camps: the interactional stress theory and the transactional stress theory.

Interactional stress theory

The interactional stress model has been directed by two main models. The first is the demand control model, also referred to as the job-strain model (Karasek, 1979), and the effort–reward imbalance model (Siegrist, 1996). The job-strain model's focal point is on the interaction between the work environment and the worker's autonomy in making decisions. The model allows for four job types.

1 **High strain jobs.** These are characterised by high demands and low levels of control. This type of job is the most risky to an individual's health.
2 **Active jobs.** These are characterised by high demands and high controls. This type of job is less risky to an individual's health.
3 **Low job strain.** These are characterised by low demands and high controls. This is characterised by below average levels of job strain.
4 **Passive jobs.** These are characterised by low level of demands and controls. Average levels of job strain may be shown as this type of job can be demotivating.

Later, the model also included social support as this was found to be a buffer to the experience of stress. However, there are disadvantages of this model. For example, it fails to consider external factors such as technological changes, legislative changes, globalisation and economic changes. However, there is evidence in support of this model. A meta-analysis by Stansfeld and Candy (2006) found that a combination of high demand levels and low decision autonomy was a risk factor for mental health problems.

The effort–reward imbalance model (ERIM) suggests that stress is caused by an imbalance between a person's effort and the reward they receive. Effort at work occurs due to a contract between the individual and the organisation; rewards can represent money, career opportunities, job security and praise. If the effort is perceived as outweighing the rewards, emotional distress ensues that can lead to stress being experienced. There are two main conditions where emotional distress can manifest. First, if a work contract is poorly defined and the individual has little choice of alternative work opportunities; secondly, if the individual accepts the imbalance for strategic reasons and/or over-commits due to occupational demands. Over-commitment includes attitudes, behaviours and emotions. This model allows stress to be predicted including coronary heart disease. Stansfeld and Candy (2006) found that high effort and low reward was a risk factor for common mental health problems such as anxiety and depression. The interactional stress theory and associated models have now been superseded by the transactional stress theory.

Transactional stress theory

The transactional stress theory (Lazarus & Folkman, 1984) takes into account the changing relationship between the person and the working environment. This involves three interlinked processes: 1) antecedent factors; 2) cognitive perceptual processes that result in the emotional experience of stress; 3) correlates of the experience such as impact on health. This theory is based on an individual's subjective experience and their coping resources. The manifestation of stress, according to this theory, can be psychological, physiological, social or behavioural. The theory also recognises individual differences in the perception of stress, thus explaining why one person may perceive an event or situation as stressful whereas another person may not. Much research has been carried out into causes of stress in the workplace and these are now discussed in more detail.

6.4 Causes of stress at work

The causes of stress at work have been the topic of research over many decades. As far back as 1967, the first Whitehall study of 18,000 men in the Civil Service was conducted, followed by a study in 1985 that included over 10,000 civil servants; one-third women and two-thirds men. Findings from these studies have been used to influence policy and help organisations with the development of appropriate policies and procedures to help improve well-being and the lives of employees. The main findings from the studies are reported by Cranwell-Ward and Abbey (2005) and are detailed below.

1 The social gradient. The studies showed that the organisation of work, the work climate, social influences and a lack of physical activity all play a part in the social gradient of health.
2 Demands and control at work. High demands and low control contribute to stress at work. As a person is promoted up the organisational hierarchy, the demands increase, whereas the lower down the hierarchy the less control a person has. People with lower control have higher sickness absence, mental health issues and heart disease.
3 Social support at work. Having supportive colleagues at work provides a buffer to stress and people who have strong social support have less sickness absence. Lack of social support is associated with stress at work.
4 Effort–reward balance at work. High effort without reward causes stress. The Whitehall study also found that this can relate to an increase in the risk of heart attack.
5 Job insecurity. Secure jobs have a very positive effect on health, well-being and satisfaction at work.
6 A healthy diet, exercise and quitting smoking reduce stress levels.
7 An active social life outside work can have a positive effect on an individual's health. This can include informal contact with friends and family and more formal involvement in groups and organisations.
8 Organisational change. Changes in management structure, management style and redundancy can all have a negative impact on an individual's health.

Organisational change in the last two decades has been dramatic. Globalisation has had a dramatic impact on the world of work. This is due to an increase in trade and competition across countries and the need for workers to be more mobile. This may also result in employees being more culturally diverse, as organisations may be located in different countries while still working together. Technological advances have also impacted on the workplace. The use of mobile technology such as smart phones that allow employers and employees 24/7 access to each other increases demands on individuals. Such variations in working practices may result in attitude changes towards work and job security. With an increase in redundancies and more outsourcing of work, individuals are not expecting a job for life, but have a constant sense of uncertainty that may lead to stress.

More recent research by the Health and Safety Executive (2000) identified types of stressors that can be split into two main categories: 'Content to work' and 'Context to work'. 'Content to work' includes the work environment, the work design, task design, workload/work pace and work schedule. 'Context to work' includes organisational culture and function, career development, roles in organisations, decision autonomy and control, home–work interface and interpersonal relationships at work. These will now be discussed in further detail.

❓ Think about it

Are there any other challenges that individuals and/or organisations face that can lead to stress?

Content to work

Work environment

An individual's work environment relates to physical barriers and distance. This can include the difference between working in an open-plan office, working in individual offices and remote working. Open-plan offices are made up of an open space that has barriers such as bookcases and privacy panels that provide an illusion of an individual working space. However, this does not detract from the noise that may be experienced in such an environment. An example of a large open-plan space where there may be a lot of noise is within a hospital setting. Ulrich, Zimring, Joseph, Quan, & Choudhary (2004) and Hweidi (2007) investigated the impact of such noise levels and found that noise within healthcare settings increases stress. This has an impact on the service provided to patients with research by Healey, Primus, & Koutantji (2007) showing that noise levels in work can increase medical errors committed by staff. The effects on staff include emotional exhaustion or burnout (Topf, 1989). Therefore, it is important that workspaces are designed to reduce the likelihood of stress occurring. (See Chapter 9 – Design of environments and work.)

Task design

Task design refers to tasks that involve short work cycles that become monotonous; work that appears meaningless to the individual; an underuse of an individual's skills or where a person's job has a high-level of uncertainty. Uncertainty can relate to job security, and also to the task at hand. For example, Beehr and Bhagat (1985) suggested that uncertainty related to two in-job role performances. The first is the uncertainty that an individual's effort will lead to a level of recognised job performance and the second is that performing well will lead to commensurate rewards.

To overcome issues with task design and reduce stress outcomes, the following actions can be taken:

- explain the task's aims and objectives and why it needs to be completed
- explain how, where and when those objectives will be achieved
- explain who is responsible for each task.

This will provide individual staff with a clear focus on the task. Further aspects of the task also need to be considered from a wider perspective such as whether the task fits with an individual's job role. This is where the importance of a clear job description can be seen (see Chapter 4 – Personnel selection and assessment for further information on job descriptions).

Workload/work pace and work schedule

Stress can be caused by a number of factors relating to the workplace including work overload and role conflict. Work overload occurs when a person perceives that they have too much work and too little resources to complete the tasks in the time allocated. Work overload can be split into two categories. The first is quantitative and the second is qualitative work overload. Quantitative overload is where, due to role expectations, there is too much work to do. Qualitative overload is where the employee does not have the experience or ability to carry out the role. For example, the pace of work may affect stress felt by individuals where there are demanding deadlines or the individual does not have control sover the pace of their work. An individual's work schedule can also impact on stress felt. This may include working unsociable hours, inflexible working practices as well as unpredictable or long hours. A study carried out in Belgium of more than 42,000 workers by Van Gyes (2006) examined stress factors according to nine factors, which included night work and shift workers. Shift workers reported very high workloads and night workers reported high levels of workloads. When the reported stress levels of shift workers and night workers were compared with those of regular workers, it was found that 43% of night workers reported experiencing stress-related symptoms and 41% of shift workers compared with 28% of regular workers, showing that working times do impact on stress experienced. Other factors contributing to work overload include role conflict. Role conflict occurs when there is a discrepancy between different expectations of the role. Two types of role conflict occur: intrapersonal and interpersonal. Intrapersonal role conflict occurs when an employee occupying a role believes they have many different expectations on them regarding that role. For example, a manager may feel that they have a role to protect their staff and lead them, whereas they are also responsible for representing the organisation and making tough decisions regarding their staff. Interpersonal role conflict occurs when there is conflict from more than one source. This may be a father who is a manager who is expected to work in the evening from home, whereas his wife and children expect him to spend time with them.

Context to work

Organisational culture and function

Stress factors in this category include poor communication and unclear organisational objectives. Poor organisational communication can lead to staff feeling left out or that senior managers are hiding something from them. This can lead to distrust between staff and managers which can result in reduced job satisfaction and stress symptoms. Unclear organisational objectives can also result in stress. When individuals are uncertain about how their work contributes to the organisational objectives overall, they may view their work as worthless. When individuals have clear goals that tie into the overall objectives of the organisation, they feel happier, more satisfied and less stressed. Thus, in order to reduce stress in workers, managers should link individuals' jobs to the overall objectives of the organisation and communicate these to individuals. An example of how this can be achieved is detailed below.

Example of how individual objectives can be linked to organisational objectives

A company trainer would complete the following as part of their job role:

- provide induction training for new staff
- identify staff training needs
- develop training materials
- deliver training to staff
- evaluate training programmes.

These tasks would link to the company's objective of providing quality goods and services. Without such training, individuals have no knowledge of what is required, the most efficient way to carry out a task or even the quality required by the organisation.

Career development

Poor opportunities for career development can also lead to stress within staff. Research has focused on the struggles of women in advancing their careers in the workplace. This has been evidenced by the glass ceiling and lack of career development opportunities. The glass ceiling refers to a barrier that stops women from progressing to high-level positions within an organisation. Clark (2010) reported that women make up 40% of employees in the UK, but are mainly employed at entry of middle-level positions and, of 600 companies surveyed across 20 countries, fewer than 5% of chief executives were women. This lack of parity also extends to women's earnings. Perrewe and Nelson (2004) found that women's earnings are still not at the same level as male peers, with women earning 76% that of their male counterparts. It was also reported that this lack of parity also extends to health care benefits and pensions.

? Think about it

Are there any barriers that affect a man's development within the workplace?

Roles in organisations

Role stress in organisations can have a negative impact on an individual's health. Role stressors have been categorised into three interrelated constructs: role overload, role ambiguity and role conflict (Peiro Gonzalez-Roma, Tordera, & Manas 2001). Role overload and role conflict were discussed in the 'content to work' section. Role ambiguity occurs when the individual does not have the necessary skills or knowledge to complete the job. This may occur when individuals do not receive feedback on how they have performed. For example, Bandura and Locke (2003) found an increased level of stress in academics who did not receive feedback, because they were more uncertain about their role performance. Role conflict occurs when a person's perception of what their role represents differs to what is expected by the organisation. In recent years this has been exacerbated by changes in working practices such as flexible and remote working, which has led to changing job specifications. This has resulted in job boundaries becoming blurred and individuals being uncertain about what is required of them. This uncertainty can lead to stress.

Decision autonomy and control

When an individual has a low decision-making autonomy, and a lack of control over their work they can feel frustrated, which may lead to stress. A worker who has autonomy and control over their work can make decisions as to when and how to do specific tasks, which leads to a feeling of power and provides a feeling that the organisation trusts them. This then leads to an increase in job satisfaction and commitment. For example, consider a practice nurse who has an appointment with a family that is travelling to Gambia on holiday. The family has booked an appointment with the nurse to seek advice on holiday vaccinations and medication. The nurse advises the family to take anti-malarial tablets and suggests relevant vaccinations. The family decides to go ahead with the vaccinations at the appointment. The nurse has gained the knowledge as part of their training about holiday vaccinations. The nurse does not have to consult the doctor to ask permission to provide the precautionary treatment.

Home–work interface

Having a good balance between work and home is becoming more important with dual-career families. This has led to research into work–life balance, which has become a major issue as we now live in a 24/7 culture where customers expect service regardless of the time of day or night. This has been enhanced by the use of technology such as mobile phones and the internet. These issues has been taken up by the European Commission (2010), which promotes issues such as childcare, parental leave and flexible working hours. Such issues in work–family life have been a result of dual-earner families. Such dual earning has occurred due to women's movements to return to the workplace after having children and the need for dual incomes due to wage reductions for males (Gornick & Meyers, 2003) and fathers spending more time parenting children. This has resulted in couples trying to juggle the demands of work, family and social life. As a result of the Work and Families Act (Legislation.Gov.UK, 2006), employees have the right to request flexible working if the individual has or is a carer for a child under six years old. Companies are now responding with the development of new policies such as the ability to undertake flexitime, job-sharing, on-site childcare services, shorter working hours as well as location-independent working (where individuals can work from any location such as home, office or even a coffee shop). The focus with this type of working practice is on outputs rather than time put into the job. However, although such work–life policies may help individual workers, it is the culture of the organisation that needs to be changed to adopt these working practices. (See Chapter 13 – Organisational structures, culture and change.) A work–family culture refers to an organisation's supportiveness to employees' family needs. Campbell Clark (2001) suggests a three-dimensional definition of this type of work culture:

- flexibility of working hours available
- flexibility of the job itself
- supportive supervision.

Another consideration in terms of work–life balance includes the demographics of the workforce such as the increasing number of older people wanting/needing to work later in life. This may be in part due to necessity as a result of the increase in pensionable age. However, the needs of these individuals may be different to those who have children. For example, research by Yeandle (2005) found that, between the ages of 50 and 75, a person's life may change with children leaving home, parents becoming grandparents, wanting new job opportunities, caring for elderly parents, managing chronic illness, unable to keep up with the fast pace of work and changes in the workplace. Therefore, work–life assistance may include providing access to training, reduced working hours, health promotion, extended leave options and career support services. Thus, a culture of diverse working conditions is required to ensure fairness across demographic groups.

Such a positive work-based culture has been found to reduce levels of distress, reduce work–family conflict and increase job satisfaction (Mauno, Kinnuen, & Pyykko, 2005). However, many myths exist about the implications for the organisation of implementing such policies. These include that work–life balance issues only exist for females and those with young children; that it will cost the organisation a lot of money to implement such policies; and that creating policies will put an end to work–life balance issues. However, other issues should be considered that may impact on work–life balance such as work effectiveness, management style and trust, role conflict and a culture where differences in working practices between individuals exist. This requires supportive managers and/or supervisors. This would require the manager to empathise with the worker concerning the need to provide a balance between work and family life as well as trust that the worker will be effective and efficient in their work. While a lot of research has focused on supporting females in the workplace (Mays, Graham, & Vinnicombe, 2005; Giscombe, 2005), there is a need to also consider the work–life balance of those who provide care for others within their family, including those who do not have children or carer responsibilities but also want a balance between their work and social lives. Therefore, organisations need to provide an equal system of parental leave for mothers and fathers and those with no care responsibilities.

? *Think about it*

Are there reasons other than childcare why individuals may want to have flexible working hours?

Interpersonal relationships at work

Interpersonal relationships at work relate to the day-to-day interactions between people including workers, co-workers and managers. Poor interpersonal relationships at work can include a lack of social support, feelings of isolation and interpersonal conflict. Social support at work refers to individuals being given the resources to carry out a task and the emotional support, which is a positive experience for the individual. A lack of social support can create stress. This may be due to an individual's expectations that their colleagues and manager would support them being dampened. A lack of social support can lead the individual to feel isolated and result in conflict. This conflict can lead to further negative behaviours, which can result in bullying.

Bullying at work refers to an employee being exposed to aggressive and negative acts over a prolonged period of time (Neuman & Baron, 1997). These acts can involve harassing, socially excluding, offending someone or interfering negatively with their work. Individuals who experience bullying feel powerless and unable to protect themselves. Zapf (2004) developed a model to explain the bullying process at work, which is signified by concentric circles, shown in Figure 6.1.

The outer circle represents social conflicts that occur within an organisation. This could be when an organisation is downsizing and individuals are competing against each other for available positions. The next circle symbolises social stressors that build up over time such as uncertainty when an organisation is being restructured or when an employee has high productivity demands. The third circle, interactional injustice, is represented by unfair working practices. The fourth circle represents negative social behaviours such as social isolation from work colleagues or attacks on a person's character. The upper circle is the feeling of being bullied. This represents the feelings of the bully victim.

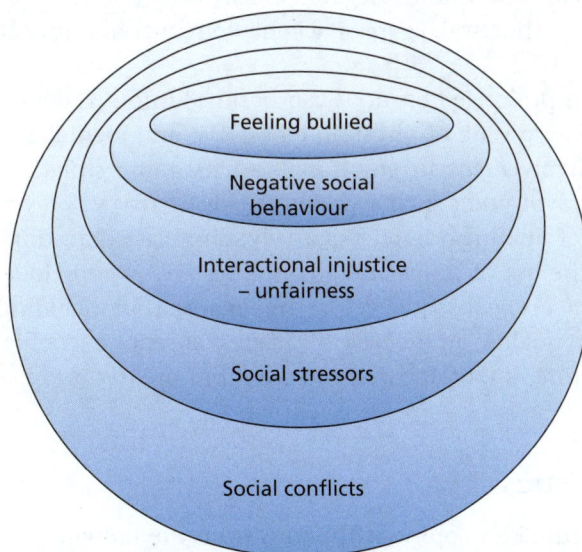

Figure 6.1 Bullying process (Zapf, 2004)

Bullying can be direct or indirect. Direct bullying can take the form of verbal or physical abuse whereas indirect bullying can be characterised by withholding information from a person. Research investigating the prevalence of bullying within organisations has varied from 17% in an Irish sample (O'Moore, Seigne, McGuire, & Smith, 1998) to 30% and above in British studies (Quine (1999) and Rayner and Keashley (2005). These acts can lead to negative health effects for individuals. According to a Finnish study, sickness absence was higher among bullied employees than non-bullied employees and an employee's chance of developing depressive symptoms was four times higher in those who reported bullying (Kivimaki, Elovainio, & Vahtera, 2000). Quine (2001) also found that nurses who had reported being bullied reported lower levels of job satisfaction, higher levels of anxiety and depression, and a great propensity to leave the organisation. The effects were also found to impact directly on the organisation's bottom line; Sheehan, McCarthy, Barker & Henderson (2001) estimated that bullying costs organisations £0.6 million to £3.6 million per year for an organisation with 1,000 employees. As can be seen, bullying impacts on the individual victim, causing stress, as well as the organisation. The consequences of stress are numerous.

6.5 Consequences of stress

The Health and Safety Executive (2011b) states that physical effects of stress include heart disease, back pain, headaches, gastrointestinal problems as well as psychological effects including anxiety, depression, loss of concentration and poor decision-making. Depression and anxiety are the most common stress-related complaints seen by general practitioners, with 20% of the UK working population affected. Stress can also lead to negative behaviours that may impact on health including social withdrawal, aggressive behaviour, alcohol/drug abuse and eating disorders.

When stress is prolonged burnout can occur. Burnout is defined by Pines and Aronson (1988) as 'a state of physical, emotional and mental exhaustion caused by long-term involvement in emotionally demanding situations'. This can be characterised by symptoms such as waking up as tired as when you went to sleep; lacking energy; evaluating oneself negatively; physical exhaustion; insomnia; and an increase in the use of drugs and alcohol. As well as individual consequences of stress there are also consequences to the organisation including a reduction in productivity and quality, an increase in sickness absence and a higher turnover of staff. It is, therefore, important that interventions are put into place to deal with stress at work.

Coping with stress

Research has focused on coping with stress from the individual employing their own coping methods to organisations implementing stress management programmes and, in severe cases, medical intervention. However, the way in which a person or organisation copes is dependent on the causes of stress. These coping methods are now discussed.

Individual coping strategies

From an individual coping perspective, Billings and Moos (1981) outlined three general coping methods that individuals may employ.

- Active Cognitive. The individual manages the appraisal of the stressful event. The individual changes the perception of their appraisal of the event by challenging irrational thoughts such as 'I can't do this on time' or 'I don't have the skills to carry out the task'. This allows the individual to cognitively restructure their perceptions of an event or situation to make it more positive.
- Active Behavioural. The individual deals with the stressful situation they are faced with. The issue is addressed and colleagues support the individual in working through the stressors faced. Social support represents a coping strategy employed by the individual.
- Avoidance. The individual avoids the stressful situation. Although the stressor is still present, it is avoided or ignored.

The option an individual may choose may depend on how confident they are in their ability to deal with the situation. This is known as self-efficacy. A person who has high self-efficacy is more confident and is better able to deal with stressful situations than those with low self-efficacy, as these individuals do not believe they can deal with the situation.

Other individual coping strategies also exist, such as:

- Reward substitution, where individuals stop seeing their work as a source of reward and see other activities or tasks they do as rewarding such as going to the gym, seeing family etc. Even those activities outside the workplace that may be boring or unpleasant should be viewed as rewarding. However, the realism of this can be questioned.
- Positive comparison is another way to make you feel better. This involves comparing the stressful situation with another situation that was even worse and which you coped with or, alternatively, making comparisons with people who are worse off than you.
- Optimistic action appears to be a more proactive approach and more realistic than the other two approaches as it involves bringing about change. The change is not made all at once, but in small stages. An individual would list all the issues they have with a current situation and then rate them on how serious they perceive each component. Individuals start with the least serious items and change them, which makes them feel more positive about the situation and allows them to deal with the more serious items on the list.

Organisational strategies

As can be seen, by the individual coping strategies, individuals are required to change either their behaviour or their cognitive thought processes. What this approach does not include is that organisations may be able to make changes to working practices or policies that may remove the stress altogether. For example, for work overload, time management training for staff may help reduce stress levels. This will enable the individual and the organisation to assess time spent on each task and reduce the time, change the way the work is carried out or reduce the amount of work to be carried out in order to reduce overload. Delegation is another way to manage workload. There is a limit to the amount of work any individual can do on their own. Delegation allows an individual to pass some of their work to another person who is qualified and skilled to carry out the task. Including checkpoints at certain stages of the job allows the delegator to maintain control of the work as well as ensuring the work is being completed to the standard required. Checkpoints enable the individual undertaking the task to ask any questions or raise any concerns they may have. Managers can also set realistic deadlines. This allows an individual to complete tasks that they are reasonably able to complete and reduces the stress felt by individuals when they are unable to meet unrealistic deadlines. Managers can also reduce role conflict by providing employees with clear definitions of their roles and responsibilities as well as providing them with the opportunity to participate in decisions that affect their jobs. Organisations can aid in the reduction of stress, but individuals also need to implement coping methods to deal with their feelings of stress.

Stop and reflect

Think about a time when you have felt stress symptoms. What coping mechanisms did you use?

Where individuals are not able to cope with stress at work and the organisation cannot make changes to relieve the stress, stress-reduction interventions (**Cox, Leather and Cox, 1990**) may be implemented. Interventions may be implemented at three main levels (see Figure 6.2).

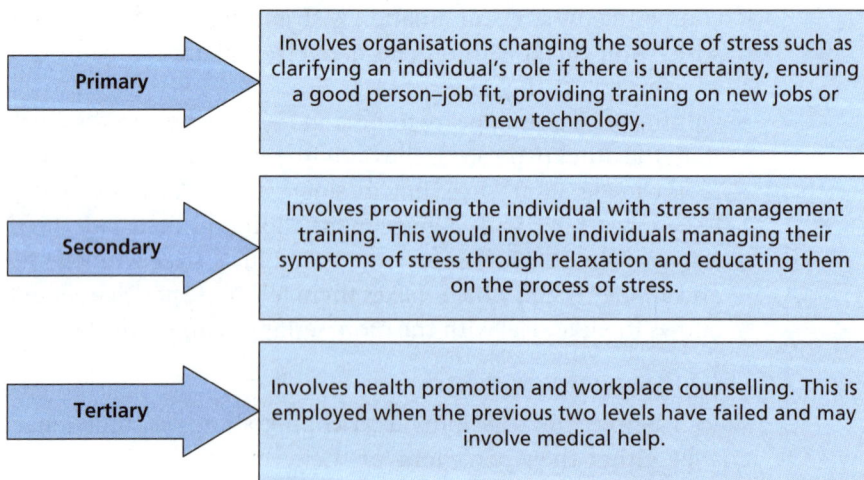

Primary → Involves organisations changing the source of stress such as clarifying an individual's role if there is uncertainty, ensuring a good person–job fit, providing training on new jobs or new technology.

Secondary → Involves providing the individual with stress management training. This would involve individuals managing their symptoms of stress through relaxation and educating them on the process of stress.

Tertiary → Involves health promotion and workplace counselling. This is employed when the previous two levels have failed and may involve medical help.

Figure 6.2 Stress reduction interventions.

6.6 Outcomes of stress reduction

The aim of stress intervention programmes is to avoid an unhealthy workplace culture. An unhealthy workplace culture is categorised by poor management, a bullying culture, poor customer service, high absence levels, reduced productivity and high work demands. The aim is to promote a healthy workplace. To understand the health and well-being needs of employees at work, a survey was developed and distributed jointly by the Health and Safety Executive (HSE) and the Health, Work and Well-Being Strategy Unit (HWWB) reported in a Research Report by Young and Bhaumik (2011). A total of 2,019 responses were obtained from people over the age of 16 in paid employment in an organisation that employed two or more people. Various health symptoms were reported. For example, 45% of respondents had experienced a health-related symptom; 10% experienced depression, bad nerves, anxiety; 9% experienced problems/disabilities associated with back or neck; and 8% experienced heart, blood pressure or circulation problems. The key findings from the survey cited the following health and safety initiatives that could reduce such ailments.

- More than 20 days' holiday per year (excluding bank holidays) and an employer pension scheme. Access to counselling and/or an employee assistance programme was reported by 40% of respondents and 38% reported having occupational health services.
- Flexible working practices including flexi-time, working from home, job sharing, working condensed hours and working reduced hours were reported by 57% of employees.
- Access to stress management help and advice was reported by 34%, as well as being able to talk to their line manager/supervisor about how to reduce stress at work.

Other initiatives included private medical insurance, access to the gym, subsidised canteen/restaurant as well as health screening and availability of healthy food choices, being supportive when individuals are receiving treatment for a stress- related illness. For example, Simon, Revicki, & Heiligenstein (2008) found that workers who received a year of treatment for depression and anxiety were more likely to return to full productivity than those who received no treatment.

Although the above are very personal to each individual, more generic initiatives were also reported such as managers responding to suggestions from staff, showing that they listen to staff and managers delivering on their promises. Findings also revealed more positive health outcomes with those who have good relationships with their work colleagues, whose values are consistent with the values of the organisation, where there are rewards for good work and development opportunities. However, the best method to adopt is trying to reduce the risk of stress occurring. This can be achieved through employers carrying out risk assessments. Unison (2012) states that every employer must conduct a risk assessment in the workplace, with risk assessments being key to preventing illness through stress. The process involves identifying the hazards by looking at sickness absence records, conducting focus group interviews on what employees deem to be risks, use of surveys, conducting return to work interviews after a period of absence related to stress, having informal talks with employees and conducting exit interviews when an employee leaves the organisation. The next stage is to decide who could be harmed. Although all staff can be affected by stress, some employees may be more susceptible due to the work they are undertaking or because they are just returning to work after a period of absence. The third stage is evaluating the risk. This involves considering actions that the organisation is already undertaking and assessing whether those actions are enough to reduce the risk. If not, the organisation must decide whether to avoid the risk by making the workplace safer, combating risks such as organising how work is conducted, adapting the work to the individual, developing a preventive policy and providing appropriate instructions to employees. The aim is to provide individuals with a healthy workplace by tackling potential risks before they become actual risks.

6.7 Healthy workplace

According to Bevan (2010), the benefits of a healthy workforce include an improved brand, improved retention, improved resilience, higher commitment, higher productivity, fewer accidents and reduced sickness. For example, there are at least one million workplace injuries caused by accidents each year (Bevan, 2010). The effects of these on the organisation include absence, sick pay, production delays and loss of contracts, which can be enhanced by poor health and well-being at work. Such factors can also impact on the retention of staff. Employees who find their work stressful become de-motivated and are more likely to leave their workplace. Recruiting and training of new staff can cost the organisation vast amounts of money. Retaining staff is, therefore, important to the organisation. Ways in which retention can be increased include supporting an individual to continue to work when they have become incapacitated; and providing support for employees returning to work after long periods of absence or after maternity leave or a career break. Providing support for staff encourages higher commitment and loyalty to the organisation. Committed employees work harder, are more productive and tend to have less sickness absence. It thus seems that the promotion of a healthy workplace may be important for attracting and retaining employees. It is now becoming commonplace for organisations to promote their flexible working and health support services when advertising jobs. Examples of such organisations include British Telecom, Procter & Gamble and Ernst & Young who believe that showing employees that the organisation cares helps in the attraction of a talented workforce. A healthy workforce, according to ACAS (2010), is typified by:

- line managers who are confident and trained in people skills
- employees who feel valued and involved in the organisation
- managers using appropriate health services to tackle absence and helping people return to work
- managers promoting an attendance culture by conducting return to work discussions
- jobs being flexible and well designed
- managers knowing how to manage common health problems.

To develop a healthy workplace, both individuals and organisations need to contribute to implementing practices such as those above, which reduce the likelihood that stress will be experienced or when stress is experienced that relevant interventions are in place to ensure the individual can cope with the symptoms of stress.

6.8 Summary

Stress is a complex issue that can have both positive and negative effects on individuals and the organisation including increased satisfaction, optimum performance as well as depression, decreased productivity and absence from the workplace. Organisations can enforce strategies that can reduce stress levels in individuals such as taking regular breaks, reviewing productivity targets to ensure they are realistic as well as ensuring appropriate help and guidance is available when stress is experienced. This will ensure that individuals are working in a healthy work environment and that organisations are employing happy and productive workers.

Multi-level impact of stress

Stress at work has an impact on individuals, teams, managers and the organisation as a whole. Individuals experiencing stress are more likely to have higher rates of accidents and/or injury. This may be a result of poor concentration or forgetfulness, which are common symptoms of stress. Stress can also lead to workplace conflict. This is due to individuals feeling anxious and isolated. If workplace conflict occurs this can lead to team problems and can take a lot of time for managers to deal with the issues arising from the conflict and negative effects on productivity.

At an organisational level the impact is vast. Sickness absence increases costs to the organisation in paying for an individual who is not performing, paying another person to undertake the role, and potential legal action if stress is found to be due to a failing within the organisation. Absence from work may seem the most obvious consequence of stress but another major issue may be the performance of individuals experiencing stress. There may be a reduction in productivity and quality, and an increase in waste materials due to error. A further impact on the organisation is the turnover of staff. If staff leave the organisation, there will be implications such as costs and time for recruiting other personnel as well as training costs.

Legal context

Please refer to the Equality Act (2010) and the Health and Safety at Work Regulations (1999).

Short-answer questions

1 Provide a definition of stress.
2 What is well-being at work?
3 What are the factors that lead to stress at work? Describe these factors.
4 Who is responsible for stress-related factors in the workplace?
5 What are the consequences of stress at both an individual and organisational level?
6 What characterises a healthy workplace?
7 What interventions can be put into place to reduce stress at work?

CASE STUDY
Well-being, stress and work-life balance

Sammie is the chief executive of a housing organisation that provides subsidised housing to individuals who have met a set of criteria set by the organisation such as overcrowding, health and safety issues such as damp. The organisation has 250 staff working for it. Staff have been asked to work extra hours including weekends because of a new project where there is to be an acquisition of a housing estate. This has led to an increase in applications for housing and individual staff members having to take on additional responsibilities. Additional work has not been discussed with staff, but delegated to them. There has also been a freeze on annual leave being taken over the next three months. Staff have also been informed that they will not receive a pay rise this year due to the economic climate.

The problem

Over recent months there has been an increase in staff absence due to stress-related illnesses such as anxiety and depression. This has resulted in a reduction in motivation. Managers have reported that they have had numerous reference requests for their staff members from other organisations where they have sought employment. There has also been reports of increased conflict between employees working on the new project and staff who have returned from sickness absence. More mistakes are also being made with applications being misfiled or incorrect criteria scores being allocated. The score affects where the applicant is on the housing list. These errors are leading to applicant complaints, which is taking up a large amount of time.

The chief executive has recruited you, as an occupational psychologist, to address the main issues within the organisation and suggest ways to make changes so that there is a reduction in staff absence, an increase in productivity and a reduction in mistakes and customer complaints.

For details of the consultancy cycle please refer to Chapter 2, which provides a comprehensive overview. Chapter 2 also provides details regarding the structure of a business report which you will find useful for this task.

Further information

Equality issues

The Equality and Human Rights Commission (EHRC): *www.equalityandhumanrights.com*

Health and safety

Health and Safety Executive (HSE): *www.hse.gov.uk*

Mental health issues

Rethink – voluntary sector provider of mental health services: *www.rethink.org*

Employer's Forum on Disability *www.employers-forum.co.uk*

Mind – Mental Health Charity: *www.mind.org.uk*

Other organisation

The International Stress Management Association: *www.isma.org.uk/*

7

Individual differences

Learning outcomes

After reading this chapter, you should be able to:

- critically evaluate the different theories of personality
- critically evaluate theories of intelligence
- explain the importance of emotional intelligence in the workplace
- describe the influence of an individual's values and beliefs to their behaviour at work.

7.1 Introduction

Rita, a sales consultant, has been in post for three months and is finding it difficult to attend meetings and to sell hair products. The role involves a lot of cold calling to hairdressers in the Midlands and Warwickshire area. Rita is finding it difficult to meet her sales targets. At the selection day for the job, Rita completed a personality questionnaire and was rated high on the introversion scale.

In this chapter we will discuss individual differences and the impact that they may have in the workplace. The individual differences approach assesses the differences that exist between people. Such differences occur in an individual's behaviour, emotion, cognition as well as their development. The main assumption of the individual differences approach is that in order to understand people we need to understand the differences between them as well as the commonalities. For example, people can be classified according to their personality and intelligence as well as their values and beliefs. The individual difference theory argues that no two individuals are born the same. There are many sources of individual differences. These factors can be seen in Figure 7.1.

Personality	Intelligence	Values and beliefs

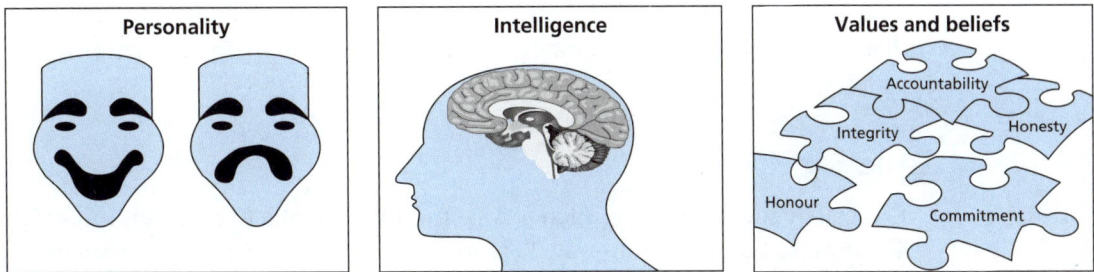

Figure 7.1 Individual differences

When reading the section on personality types, consider whether having an introvert personality would affect an individual's ability to carry out a sales role.

7.2 Personality

Personality refers to individual differences that are: 1) psychological in nature; 2) fall outside the intellectual domain (moods and feelings); 3) are enduring dispositions rather than transient states (habits and attitudes); 4) form generalised patterns (this represents the broad personality of a person) (Haslam, 2007).

There are many perspectives explaining personality: the trait perspective, the biological perspective, the psychoanalytic perspective and the cognitive perspective. These will now be discussed in further detail.

Trait perspective to personality

A trait represents a characteristic form of thinking, behaviour or feeling that is enduring over time (they don't change quickly), is consistent over time (behaves in a similar way in different situations), is a disposition (a tendency for a person to act in a particular way in certain situations) and are ways in which people differ from one another, for example hostility and shyness. The number of traits identified within the psychological literature is vast. Research by Allport and Odbert (1936) identified approximately 18,000 different traits that describe an individual's personality. It was argued that each individual has an individual trait (an overarching trait relevant to that person) and common traits (which are possessed by all people to some extent, e.g. outgoing), but the intensity of each trait in each individual may be different. For example, two people may be outgoing; however, one person may be more outgoing than the other, and the intensity is different. According to Allport and Odbert (1936), individuals possess three categories of traits: cardinal, secondary and central. A cardinal trait is a dominant trait that a person's whole life revolves around, such as being power hungry. Secondary traits are traits that are exhibited in specific situations, such as at work a person may prefer working in research or dislike working with financial information. Central traits characterise an individual's daily interactions such as the trait of sociability. It is these traits that make up a person's personality and that also makes them different from other people.

The Big Five

There are issues with using such a large number of traits to assess an individual's likeliness to act in a certain way. Research, therefore, concentrated on identifying a smaller number of fundamental personality traits. Cattell (1943b) used Allport and Odbert's (1936) list of traits in an attempt to identify a smaller number of traits, by identifying clusters, and then applying an umbrella term for each cluster. This reduced the list to 171. Asking 100 people to rate people they knew on the 171 traits and using a statistical technique known as factor analysis, Cattell (1943b) derived 12 factors to which he later added four more. From this, 16 Factors of Personality were developed, leading to the development of a psychometric tool to assess these factors now known as the 16 Factor Personality Questionnaire (Cattell, Eber, & Tatsouka, 1970). The primary traits were then factor-analysed to investigate personality structure at a higher level. From this a second order of global factors emerged, namely the 'Big Five' (discussed later in the chapter), which have been rediscovered by Goldberg (1990). Factor analysis combines similar variables into more meaningful factors. For example, if we look at the number of possible words we could assign to personality traits, there would be far too many to provide any meaningful description of a person's personality. Therefore, factor analysis helps reduce the vast amount of information into smaller sets of personality traits by assessing whether each factor correlates. For example, words associated with the trait extrovert may include outgoing, sociable, assertive, gregarious and lively. These words all relate to the same underlying trait of extroversion so would correlate with that and reduce the trait from five descriptors to one. Between the discovery and rediscovery of the Big Five, one of Catell's contemporaries (Eysenck, 1987) conducted a factor analysis of personality traits, but unlike Catell based it on a theory of personality. The theory focused on supertraits of **Introversion–Extroversion and Neuroticism–Stability.** Certain characteristics were associated with these supertraits and can be seen in Table 7.1.

Although Eysenck's theory was well established, there was a lack of consensus about the number of traits that make up a person's personality and the Big Five structure re-emerged (Goldberg, 1990). The Big Five structure is now a widely accepted structure that looks at personality from a broad perspective, with each

Table 7.1 Characteristics of Eysenck's supertraits

Extroversion	Sociable, outgoing
Introversion	Quiet and introspective
Neuroticism	Anxious, moody, vulnerable
Stability	Stable, calm, even-tempered

factor summarising a large number of distinct personality characteristics. The Big Five factors have been further researched by Costa and McCrae (1992) and have provided a robust measure of personality. The Big Five traits consist of:

1 *Openness to experience* (inventive/curious *v*. consistent/cautious)
2 *Conscientiousness* (efficient/organised *v*. easy-going/careless)
3 *Extroversion* (outgoing/energetic *v*. solitary/reserved)
4 *Agreeableness* (friendly/compassionate *v*. cold/unkind)
5 *Neuroticism* (sensitive/nervous *v*. secure/confident).

Peabody and Goldberg (1989) suggested that the five traits correspond to certain situational domains. For example, extroversion would relate to situations of power and energy; agreeableness in expression of love; conscientiousness is work-specific; emotional stability in terms of affect and control; and intellect is relevant to problem-solving and creativity situations. This has been evidenced by research, which has shown that conscientiousness is related to job performance (Barrick & Mount, 1991, Salgado, 1997) as well as predictive of leadership effectiveness (Judge, Bono, Ilies, & Gerhardt, 2002) and entrepreneurship.

However, there are criticisms (Block, 2010) of the Big Five approach to personality which include:

1 The approach does not explain all aspects of human personality.
2 The five factors are not independent of each other.
3 The identification of the five factors relies on interpretation by the analyst.
4 A large number of additional factors may underlie the main five factors.
5 Evidence of the five factors relies on self-report questionnaires.
6 The five factors are not based on any underlying theory (whereas Eysenck's factors were), so the underlying causes of them are not known.

A further area of debate has been whether an individual's personality determines the way they prefer to work within an organisation. Judge *et al*. (2002) demonstrated that people who have strong agreeableness traits also have a teamwork-oriented work culture. Thus, it appears that personality traits need to be considered when evaluating individual working styles. The importance of personality-profiling individuals has been shown in the workplace with organisations administering personality tests as part of their selection process.

Biological perspective to personality

Another way in which personality has been explained is by the biological perspective. This suggests that personality can be explained from three angles. The first is due to genetic influences, the second is through an individual's brain functioning, and the third is by way of evolution, which will now be discussed.

Genetics

The perspective that genetics has an influence on personality is based on research of family studies, twin studies and adoption studies. Family studies concern parents of children, as parents and children are 50% similar genetically. Thus, it is expected that children would share similar personality traits to their parents. However, problems do exist with this perspective as it is very difficult to distinguish what is related to genetic influence and what is related to their environment. In an attempt to overcome this problem, twin studies have been conducted.

Twin studies offer a different perspective as they try to rule out environmental influences as the twins would not differ significantly in their environmental experiences, and any differences can be argued to be based on genetics. Two types of twin studies have been conducted over many years. These studies are conducted with either monozygotic (MZ: identical twins) or dizygotic (DZ: fraternal) twins. For example, Rushton, Bons, & Hur (2008) collected data between 1983 and 1984 from twin registers at the University of London Institute of Psychiatry. Questionnaires were mailed to 1,400 twin pairs as well as their spouses and best friends asking questions on demographics, attitudes and personality. Questionnaires were returned from 322 pairs of twins (174 monozygotic twins – identical, and 148 dizygotic twins – non-identical) with a mean age of 32 years. The MZ twins were more similar on the self-rating scales than the DZ twins. As MZ twins share 100% of their genetic material and DZ twins share 50% of their genetic material, the result that MZ twins were more similar is not surprising. However, if genetics was the only contributor to personality, then the results should be that MZ twins are the same and not similar.

To understand the influence of genetics, adoption studies have been conducted. In these studies personality characteristics of individuals in relation to both biological and adoptive parents are examined. According to this perspective, the extent to which the adoptive children are similar to their biological parents, who gave them up at birth, evidences the genetic influence as they would have no environmental factors from their biological parents to be taken into account. In a similar vein, if a person is not similar to their adoptive parents, this suggests that environmental influences are few and that genes outweigh the environmental influences. A study by Cadoret, Troughton, O'Gorman, & Heywood (1995) of 242 males and 201 female adoptees who had been separated from their parents at birth, found that antisocial personality disorder was associated with biological factors but also with environmental factors, showing that genetics alone is not a predictor of personality.

There are limitations with the genetic approach. For example, it is difficult to separate the influence of genetics from environmental factors, and genes do not directly affect a person's behavioural disposition as this is influenced by brain functioning.

Personality and brain functioning

The majority of research into the link between personality and brain functioning has concentrated on traits. For example, Eysenck (1987) put forward that his dimensions of neuroticism and extroversion correspond to two discrete aspects of brain functioning. According to this theory, those individuals who are extrovert have low levels of brain arousal, which results in them seeking situations that are exciting and stimulating to raise their level of arousal. Introverts, on the other hand, have high levels of brain arousal and do not need the additional arousal, which results in them enjoying more solitary situations and activities. There has also been a link between cerebral blood flow and personality (Turner, Hudson, Butler, & Joyce, 2003) suggesting that differences in brain function may reflect differences in personality traits. However, research by Depue and Collins (1999) suggests that there are three main neurotransmitters associated with a system known as the 'neurobehavioural system' and it is the individual differences of chemicals within this system that are linked to traits of extroversion, neuroticism and constraint. These chemicals are dopamine, norepinephrine and serotonin. Dopamine is the basic modulator of physical endurance and drive; norepinephrine is the basic modulator of focused thinking and mental drive and serotonin is the basic modulator of psychological well-being.

Personality and evolution

Evolution refers to selected genes that contribute to the fitness and survival in species. This occurs over many generations. According to Macdonald (1998), different personality traits are suited to different ecological and social niches. Personality traits represent the dispositions to respond to certain environments and people move towards situations that suit their personality best. It is argued from the evolutionary perspective that organisms that do not adapt become extinct and those that do, survive. For example, someone with a highly aggressive personality can defend themselves and fight for available resources. However, these types of individuals may also become the target of aggression from others.

If we believe that personality has a genetic component, then we can start asking questions as to whether personality is adaptive over generations. If the answer to this question is yes, it would suggest that some personality traits enable fitness and survival more than others. For example, the trait of conscientiousness allows for planning and diligence aids survival.

Psychoanalytic perspective to personality

Whereas the evolutionary theory suggests that personality is adaptive over generations, the psychoanalytic perspective focuses on the early development years of an individual. The psychoanalytic theory of personality suggests that all early experiences influence human behaviour. A number of psychoanalytic theories are linked to personality; however, Freud's theory is the most prominent and criticised and will be the focus of this section. According to Freud, an individual's personality structure is made up of three stages. The first is the 'id', which infants are born with. The 'id' is not based on logic or reality, but is based on gratifying instinctual or biological needs such as drinking and eating, known as the 'pleasure principle'. The ego, on the other hand, is based on the 'reality principle'. The ego realises that satisfying certain needs may lead to guilt or even punishment. The role of the ego is, therefore, to repress such instincts, which begins the formation of the unconscious where the child begins to internalise socially acceptable norms, which develops the third structure known as the 'superego'. This structure makes feelings of guilt possible and provides an individual with boundaries on the types of gratification they may seek. Freud's theory of personality is based on a conflict model with the conflict occurring between the ego and the two structures of the id and superego. If the id allows for gratification, then the superego will generate feelings of guilt. If the ego does not allow the id to achieve gratification, tension develops. The ego develops defence mechanisms to ensure that conflicts are kept within the unconscious. Such mechanisms include denial, where an individual refuses to acknowledge an unpleasant event, and repression where there is motivated forgetting. It is the conflict that, according to Freud, is at the centre of an individual's personality structure.

The psychoanalytic theory is the most criticised theory of personality. Criticisms (McLeod, 2007) include the fact that it is based on case studies and represents an unscientific evaluation of personality; suggests that personality is deterministic, thus ruling out free will; it is difficult to prove wrong as it cannot measure and does not take into account mental processes such as thinking and memory. The importance of mental processes in personality was recognised in the cognitive approach.

Cognitive perspective to personality

Cognition refers to mental processes and activities such as thinking, remembering, planning and believing. According to this perspective, humans have a complex information process system and part of this system is the active processes of learning and memory. This system helps individuals relate to their environment and make meaning out of it. This suggests that we mentally engage with our environment in an active manner where we receive information, filter or pay attention to it and impose meaning on it. Kelly (1955) argued that each individual has personal constructs that determine the way in which they gather information from their environment, develop hypotheses and test them. This testing is based on our experience of past events. Kelly's theory is known as the fundamental postulate, which states that a 'person's processes are psychologically channellized by the ways in which he interprets events' (p. 46). For example, if you have approached a manager in the past about a problem and they have been friendly, you would be more likely to engage with them in the future. If the manager had been dismissive and patronising, you would be more likely to avoid interactions with them in the future. However, this perspective can be criticised as it does not take into account situational variables such as the manager being faced with a lot of problems on that day or that he had been in a difficult meeting before the work issue was raised with him. Thus, this seems a very simplistic view.

Ellis (1979) put forward an A-B-C model where individuals experience (A)ctivating events that result in our evaluation and interpretation of what is going on around us. Our interpretation of the event leads to development of Beliefs about the event and our role in that event. Once this belief is developed we experience emotional (C)onsequences based on our beliefs. Our beliefs, therefore, determine how we respond to events and the world with our behaviour and emotions.

Like all theories of personality, the cognitive theory is not without its criticisms. For example, nature and thoughts are abstract and it is difficult to define them; this theory of personality is weak as there is no solid explanation of its development.

? Think about it

Think about the case of Rita at the beginning of this chapter. What personality characteristics do you deem appropriate to be able to carry out that job? Do you think that Rita can develop those characteristics or are they stable?

Assessing personality

To assess a person's personality, a number of psychometric tests have been developed. One of the most commonly used tests is the Myers-Briggs Type Indicator (MBTI) (Devito, 1985). The MBTI measures types and is used to explain a person's personality characteristics. The measure is based on Jungian typing. Jung believed that individuals had two kinds of functions in their lives; how we take in information and how we perceive things. Within the two categories there are two opposite ways of functioning. We perceive information from our senses or based on our intuition, and we make decisions based on objective logic or subjective feelings. Jung suggested that we use all four functions in our lives. The theory has developed and this is the basis of the MBTI. Each individual, according to the theory, has a primary mode of operation within four categories:

1 our flow of energy
2 how we take in information
3 how we prefer to make decisions
4 the basic day-to-day lifestyle that we prefer.

Within each of these categories we prefer to be either introverted or extroverted, sensing or intuitive, thinking or feeling, judging or perceiving. A review of the measure was carried out by Carlson (1985) who reported that the measure has been used unsystematically in a variety of settings, but with favourable assessment of validity. Although there is satisfactory internal consistency, the samples are student samples so are not representative of the general population. One positive aspect of the MBTI is that it can predict workstyle preferences. Hirsch and Kummerow (1989) found that extroversion and introversion can influence the work that people choose. Extroverts like work environments that are actively oriented in which the individual has frequent interactions with others. Introverts prefer work settings that are quiet and allow for concentration. The benefit of understanding personality in the workplace is that it can help with career guidance to help understanding: what tasks individuals would be more happy with; interpersonal relationships, as by understanding personality we can have an understanding of how people will respond to certain situations; workplace counselling, by helping individuals to understand themselves and deal with their strengths and weaknesses.

Examples of questions on the MBTI include
- You enjoy having a wide range of acquaintances   YES/NO
- You are almost never late for appointments   YES/NO

A historical overview of testing can be found in Chapter 1 – Introduction to occupational psychology, and further details of psychometric testing for selection and assessment can be found in Chapter 4 – Personnel selection and assessment.

7.3 Intelligence

Intelligence has been a topic of debate for decades with parents wanting to know how intelligent their children are and employers wanting intelligent people working for them. Many theories of intelligence have been put forward. For example, Spearman (1904) suggested that intelligence is generated by a unitary quality within the human brain. This he termed 'g', which refers to general intelligence. This factor 'g' is a statistic that models the mental ability of results from various tests of cognitive ability. This theory was based on Spearman's observations of schoolchildren's grades that were positively correlated across differing and unrelated subjects. He argued that these correlations are due to 'g'. Spearman explained variations in intelligence scores being a result of two factors: first, the specific factor where variables associated with each individual mental task, such as an individual's abilities that would make them perform at a certain level on a cognitive ability test; and secondly, positive correlations caused by general intelligence. Many oppositions of 'g' have been put forward. For example, Thurstone (1935) conducted factor analyses which led him to develop a model of intelligence centred on primary mental abilities (PMAs). These PMAs represent different groups of independent factors that are different for everyone. Seven primary mental abilities were identified by Thurstone: verbal comprehension, word fluency, number facility, special visualisation, associative memory, perceptual speed and reasoning.

A further view of intelligence was that of Cattell (1943b), who argued that general intelligence consists of fluid and crystallised intelligence. Fluid intelligence represents abilities such as learning, problem-solving and pattern recognition. Crystallised intelligence is based on the acquisition of knowledge and each new thing an individual learns is added to their crystallised intelligence. When an individual learns, their knowledge can change, so when psychology students learn the different theories of personality or intelligence, it is added to their crystallised intelligence, but has not affected the way that they learn. Both types of intelligence increase through childhood and adolescence with fluid intelligence peaking at around the age of 30–40 and crystallised intelligence continuing into early and late adulthood. Whereas Cattell (1943b) suggested two forms of intelligence, Sternberg (1985) suggested a triarchic model consisting of three intelligences. These are: Analytical (A), Practical (P) and Creative (C). (A) responds to what is the general intelligence, (P) is an individual's ability to solve everyday problems and (C) refers to insight, synthesis and the ability to react to novel situations. To measure the three intelligences, Sternberg developed a battery of multiple choice questions that is known as the Sternberg Triarchic Ability Test (STAT).

Gardner (1993) suggested that individuals do not have an underlying general intelligence, but that they have multiple intelligences that form part of an independent system within the brain. The theory was based on empirical research from diverse populations. For example, research was conducted on brain-injured individuals who had lost one ability such as spatial thinking, but managed to retain other functions such as motor functioning. He argued that, as these abilities operated independently of each other, this was evidence of separate intelligences. According to Gardner individuals have seven intelligences:

1 Linguistic intelligence – speech and language
2 Logical-mathematical intelligence – abstract reasoning and solving logical and mathematical problems
3 Spatial intelligence – perceive visual and spatial information and perform tasks such as navigating
4 Musical intelligence – perform, read, write and decipher music
5 Bodily-kinesthetic intelligence – abilities used in sport and dancing
6 Interpersonal intelligence – understand others
7 Intrapersonal intelligence – understand oneself.

The main differences between Spearman and Gardner, apart from the number of intelligence(s), is that Spearman argued that intelligence could be measured by tests (IQ tests) whereas Gardner did not. Gardner's theory is more relevant to today as we live in a world where we see extreme talent such as individuals achieving at high levels in sports, or individuals who do not achieve expected levels in an English and Maths test, but excel in art or music. This suggests that there is no 'g' but rather multiple intelligences. The main criticism of this theory is that it suggests that intelligence is a cognitive style and not an independent construct (Morgan, 1996) as well as the theory not being empirical. The theory is incompatible with general intelligence and environmental influences and broadens the construct of intelligence so much that it becomes meaningless.

Stop and reflect

Think of a job you have carried out or a hobby you have participated in. Do you think they require different forms of intelligence? What intelligences are required?

Emotional intelligence

Emotional intelligence refers to an individual's ability to perceive, control and evaluate emotions. It has become prominent within the world of work as it provides a way in which people's behaviour can be understood and assessed. This may include areas such as management behaviour, conflict in the workplace and an individual's attitudes. According to Goleman (1998a) in order to be successful individuals need to:

- know their emotions
- manage their emotions
- motivate oneself
- recognise and understand other people's emotions
- manage relationships with others.

The importance of emotional intelligence has been recognised in the workplace. For example, Barsade (1998) conducted an experiment in which a group of participants played the role of managers who had to make decisions about which subordinates should have bonuses. A stooge (an actor who is planted by the researcher into the experiment) took part in group discussions and was sometimes cheerful, sometimes hostile and sometimes warm and friendly. The stooge always spoke first. The emotion the stooge showed affected the emotion shown by the participants. When the stooge showed good feelings, there was improved cooperation, fairness and performance within the group and money was distributed fairly. The opposite was true when the stooge showed negative emotions. However, although there was increased performance, it has been argued Goleman (1998a, 1998b) that emotional intelligence itself does not predict performance; rather it is competencies associated with being high in emotional intelligence that predict performance. For example, the ability to recognise and understand a person's emotion allows an individual to develop the competence of influence, because if you understand a person's emotion you can influence future emotions felt by individuals by acting in certain ways.

Different models of emotional intelligence have been put forward. For example, Salovey and Mayer (1990) developed an ability model of emotional intelligence. It is suggested that emotional intelligence is composed of two areas: the experiential area (ability to perceive, respond to and manipulate emotional information without necessarily understanding it); and the strategic area (ability to understand and manage emotions without necessarily perceiving or experiencing feelings). The two areas are then broken into two further areas (four in total) each known as branches. The first consists of emotional perception, which is the ability to have self-awareness of emotions and be able to express emotions and needs to other people. The second is emotional assimilation, which is the ability to distinguish between different emotions that you are feeling and be able to identify those with thoughts. The third branch is emotional understanding (understanding complex emotions such as feeling two emotions at once). The fourth is emotion management, where the individual can connect or disconnect from an emotion, depending on how useful it is to the situation. To test the validity of this model, a scale was developed called the Multi-branch Emotional Intelligence Scale (MEIS), which comprises 12 subscales that measure emotional intelligence. Evidence was found for discriminant validity of the scale (emotional intelligence was independent of general intelligence). This indicates the scale's ability to measure unique characteristics of an individual that is not measured by general intelligence tests. However, no evidence was found for the integration branch of the model and thus a new measure was developed. The new measure named the Mayer–Salovey–Caruso Emotional Intelligence (MSCEI) test involves specific abilities (of the four branches) being assessed by carrying out specific tasks. For example, a test taker is asked to rate the level and type of emotion that is expressed from pictures. Internal consistency of this measure has been rated at an alpha level of between 0.8 and 0.9 showing good internal consistency.

A mixed-model of emotional intelligence is the Bar-On (1997). Bar-On Emotional Intelligence referred to as EQ-I is a self-report questionnaire that measures a number of constructs related to emotional intelligence. Originally used from a clinical perspective, the measure assesses an individual's emotional well-being. The scales and subscales can be seen in Table 7.2. The questionnaire consists of 133 items and provides an overall score as well as scores related to the five composite scales and 15 subscales (Bar-On, 2006). The scale has been translated into 30 different languages and is a reliable measure of emotional intelligence having a Cronbach's alpha between 0.69 and 0.86, although it is not as reliable as the MSCEI.

Emotional intelligence is becoming more important in today's workplace. Individuals are not judged on how intelligent they are, but on how they perform in their job. For example, how they deal with clients, how they manage others,

Table 7.2 Bar-On composite scales and subscales

Intrapersonal (self-awareness and self-expression)	• **Self-regard** – accurately perceive, understand and accept oneself • **Emotional self-awareness** – aware of and understand one's emotions • **Assertiveness** – effectively and constructively express one's emotions and oneself • **Independence** – be self-reliant and free of emotional dependency on others • **Self-actualisation** – strive to achieve one's personal goals and actualise one's potential
Interpersonal (social awareness and interpersonal relationships)	• **Empathy** – to be aware and understand how others feel • **Social responsibility** – identify with one's social group and cooperate with others • **Interpersonal relationship** – establish mutually satisfying relationships and relate well with others
Stress management (emotional management and regulation)	• **Stress tolerance** – effectively and constructively manage others • **Impulse control** – effectively and constructively manage emotions
Adaptability (change management)	• **Reliability testing** – objectively validate one's feelings and thinking with external reality • **Flexibility** – adapt and adjust one's feelings and thinking to new situations • **Problem-solving** – effectively solve problems of a personal and interpersonal nature
General mood (self-motivation)	• **Optimism** – be positive and look at the brighter side of life • **Happiness** – be content with oneself, others and life in general

how they work as a team and how they deal with stressful situations. The ability to succeed at these include perseverance, motivation and interpersonal skills that form aspects of emotional intelligence. It can, therefore, be argued that an individual's emotional intelligence predicts performance. If our emotional intelligence is in line with our values and beliefs (also referred to as moral intelligence), it helps us make ethical decisions in the workplace and behave in an ethical manner.

7.4 Values, individual beliefs and behaviour

Values represent principles that guide an individual's attitudes, beliefs and behaviours and represent relatively stable characteristics. Values represent a person's cognitions, are connected to a person's motives and are desirable to the individual. Individual values can affect a person's beliefs about work, relationships and money. Virtually all aspects of an individual's life can be influenced by their values. For example, individuals who have a strong work ethic may have values that represent punctuality, commitment and working hard for a good day's pay. According to Schwartz (1992), values are 'desirable states, objects, goals or behaviours transcending specific situations and applied as normative standards to judge and to choose among alternative modes of behaviour'. This definition highlights two important functions of values. First, they are enduring and transcend situations; values can provide coherence and a sense of purpose to an individual's behaviour. Secondly, because they are normative standards, values can form the basis for generating behaviours, such as a strong work ethic.

Values can also be useful in making decisions, as they serve as strong informal guides that influence an individual's cognitive processes. For example, they specify modes of behaviour that are socially acceptable (Meglino & Ravlin, 1998). Values have a long tradition of shaping, directing, and guiding human behaviour, in and out of organisations (Box, Odom, & Dunn, 1991). Pech and Durden (2003) argue that decisions are often filtered through attitudes, beliefs and values, and that poor decision-making occurs when the filtering of the information conflicts with individual perceptions and results in poor assessment. For example, Gallen (2006) found from a study of 70 managers in 13 spas that their cognitive styles and their way of processing information had an effect on the strategies they preferred. In addition, their personal values directly affected their choice of strategies adopted.

Personal values and value systems result in characteristics or attitudes that in turn affect behaviour. For example, England and Lee (1974) identified seven ways in which values affect leaders. These included:

- the perceptions that leaders had of situations
- the solutions they generate regarding problems
- interpersonal relationships
- perceptions of individual and organisational success
- the ability to differentiate between ethical and unethical behaviour
- whether they accept or reject organisational pressures and goals
- whether they can affect managerial performance.

Depending on the type of leader and their own values and beliefs, perceptions of a particular scenario may vary considerably. This would translate into the business environment, as any decisions made by the manager would be based on their values and beliefs, which ultimately could restrict their choices. Essentially, values serve as blueprints or foundations for making decisions, solving problems and resolving conflicts. When these values become a hindrance to making the decision, solving problems and resolving the conflicts, problems arise. If the leader's values and beliefs are incongruent with the organisation's, problems may occur because the organisation and the individual want different things. This may affect the way the leader steers their followers to meet goals and objectives, which may not be in line with the overall objectives of the organisation.

Stop and reflect

Think of a time when your beliefs differed to those of your manager, work colleague or friend. What did you do and how did you feel?

Multi-level impact of individual differences

Individual differences can have a huge impact on individuals, managers and organisations. As each individual differs in personality, intelligence, values and beliefs, the impact of these may be reflected in how a person conducts a particular task in the workplace, how they interact with other people and their work style. For example, if a person is introvert they may prefer working alone, whereas a person who is extrovert may prefer to work with other people. At a management level, the values and beliefs held by a leader may influence the decisions they make at a local (departmental) level and at an organisational level, which may affect the strategic direction of the organisation.

Legal context

Further details of legislative requirements of individual differences are discussed in Chapter 3 – Legislation applied to the workplace.

Short-answer questions

1 What are individual differences and how can they impact on the workplace?
2 Critically evaluate theories of personality.
3 Discuss the differences between general intelligence and emotional intelligence.
4 What are values and beliefs, and how can they influence an individual's behaviour at work?

CASE STUDY
Individual differences

The company

Savings 'r' Us is an independent company that sells savings products to members of the public. Savings products include accounts, pensions and personal savings bonds. With the downturn in incomes, there has been a reduction in the number of savings accounts opened. As savings is the primary focus of the business, it is important that the company increases its account openings to remain competitive in its offerings.

Issues to be considered

Sammie, a branch manager of Savings 'r' Us, holds a meeting with all employees outlining the importance of opening new savings accounts. Sammie explains how the company benefits from an increase in savings accounts and outlines his vision of being number one in the savings market. In the week after the initial meeting, the opening of savings accounts increased, but towards the end of the month it went back down to the previous average number of openings. Sammie called a second meeting with staff to discuss the situation and any issues they had about the vision to increase the number of accounts being opened. Whereas in the previous meeting Sammie focused on the benefits to the company of opening new accounts he now developed a set of guidelines in securing new business. All staff were set a target increase of 10% on their normal monthly account openings (which averaged an increase in the team of an additional 100 accounts per month); set standard questions to ask customers such as 'Do you currently have a savings account with Savings 'r' Us?,' 'Do you have a few minutes where I can outline the benefits of opening a savings account?', and offering customers an additional £50 in their account once they had deposited £1,000 and left it in the account for six months.

Employees were told that if they did not meet their targets for three consecutive months they would be suspended without pay for one week and after a further three months their contract would be terminated. The threat of punishment did not increase the desired behaviour, but rather encouraged staff members to take sickness leave and look for employment elsewhere, which actually reduced the number of accounts opened.

The task from this case study is to apply the consultancy cycle and write a report providing an analysis of the issues facing this organisation.

For details of the consultancy cycle please refer to Chapter 2, which provides a comprehensive overview. Chapter 2 also provides details regarding the structure of a business report which you will find useful for this task.

For an example report based on the consultancy cycle, refer to Chapter 14.

Further reading

Haslam, N. (2007). *Introduction to personality and intelligence*. London: Sage.

8

Training

Learning outcomes

After reading this chapter, you should be able to:

- understand the costs and benefits of training
- engage with different training methods and types of training
- critically discuss the benefits and difficulties of assessing training needs
- understand the importance of practice and feedback
- understand the importance of training evaluation
- apply the training cycle to a case study.

8.1 Introduction

Marlene, a recent business graduate, applies for and is successful in securing a graduate training post with a large financial organisation. Although she has attained a good grade in her degree, she has no practical experience of business. To provide the best training for Marlene, the organisation should consider undertaking a training needs analysis to understand the skills that she needs to attain to perform well in the job, as well as consider the best training method for her.

In this chapter we will explore the role of training needs analysis and its importance in providing relevant training for individuals. An assessment of the methods used to train individuals will be undertaken as well as a discussion of the importance of practice and feedback and undertaking training evaluations.

According to Buckley and Caple (2007, p.8) 'training usually involves the acquisition of behaviours, facts, ideas, etc. that are more easily defined in a specific job context'. Buckley and Caple argue that 'training' is different from 'education', because training is more job-focused (such as learning new skills and abilities) and education is more person-focused (attaining knowledge). Education involves improving knowledge whereas training involves improving skills. However, there can be a debate as to whether education and training can be separated. For example, think of learning to drive a car. If you do not have the knowledge of how the car operates or the road signs that you have to abide by, the practical side (the training side) on its own will not allow you to pass your driving test. Another example is a nurse who needs to put a cannula into a patient. (A cannula is a small tube that is placed into a patient's arm or back of the hand so that intravenous fluids can be administered.) The nurse needs to have knowledge about cannulation before carrying it out. Education may include uses of cannulation, where to place the cannula, possible complications as well as procedures for inserting and removing cannulas. Without this knowledge the nurse will not be able to perform the task effectively and safely.

Training can also be categorised into formal, informal and on-the-job training. Formal training involves careful planning, has set outcomes or learning objectives and the person is conscious of their learning experience. A variety of methods (discussed later in this chapter) can be used for formal training transfer and the training programme can be evaluated. Informal training occurs spontaneously and in many different places such as at work, home and through interactions with other people. This takes place independently from trainer-led programmes, outside educational establishments and is not assessed. For example, informal learning may occur from discussions with colleagues on a particular topic area. On-the-job training involves the acquisition of skills while working on the job. It may involve following written and verbal instructions as well as observing others and then attempting the task. This form of training usually involves a supervisor or an experienced employee passing on their knowledge and skills to the trainee. However, a more informal on-the-job training can also take place which involves an employee being mentored by another member of staff. It is a relatively loose arrangement and employees will seek advice from their mentors as and when required. Although informal and on-the-job training is mentioned here, the main focus of this chapter will be on formal training because this is where, as occupational psychologists, we can ensure that effective training programmes are developed. The chapter will contain an overview of models of training as well as benefits and costs of training.

8.2 Models of training

To provide a comprehensive successful training programme, many models have been suggested. These models of training design include Instructional Design Systems (Branson *et al.*, 1975); Human Performance Technology (Jacobs, 1988); and Performance-Based Instructional Design (Pucel, 1989). We will now consider all three.

Instructional Design System

The Instructional Design System (IDS) aids in the design, development and delivery of training programmes. When we hear the word 'system' we may think of something that is extremely complex (such as a computer); however, this system is relatively simple. This model suggests five key phases of training programme development and is known as the ADDIE (Analys is, Design, Development, Implementation, Evaluation and control). Branson et al. (1975) suggest that by following these steps a comprehensive training programme can be developed. Figure 8.1 provides an overview of the five phases and tasks that should be conducted in each phase to ensure an effective training programme is developed.

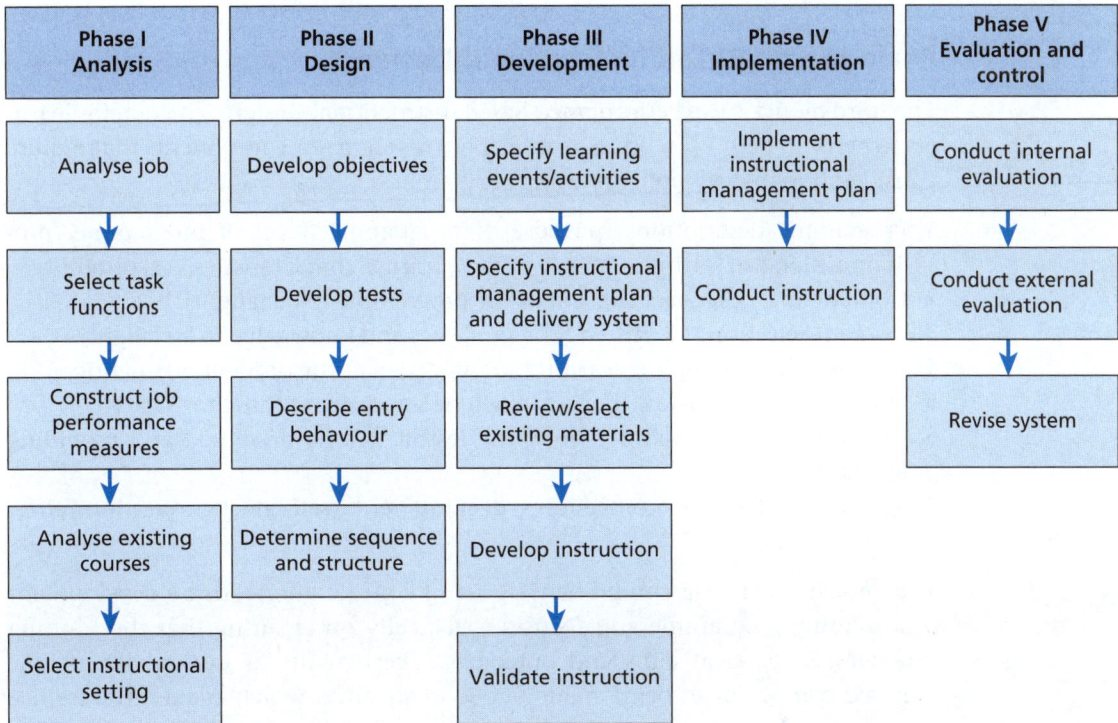

Phase I Analysis	Phase II Design	Phase III Development	Phase IV Implementation	Phase V Evaluation and control
Analyse job	Develop objectives	Specify learning events/activities	Implement instructional management plan	Conduct internal evaluation
Select task functions	Develop tests	Specify instructional management plan and delivery system	Conduct instruction	Conduct external evaluation
Construct job performance measures	Describe entry behaviour	Review/select existing materials		Revise system
Analyse existing courses	Determine sequence and structure	Develop instruction		
Select instructional setting		Validate instruction		

Figure 8.1 Instructional Design System example

The Florida State University five phases of ISD are ongoing as some issues may be identified in the evaluation stage that require the developer to return to an earlier stage. The benefits of an instructional design model include being quick and efficient in designing training programmes. All aspects are considered using the ADDIE model, thus nothing is left to chance and elements are observable and measurable.

Human Performance Technology

The second model, Human Performance Technology, also uses a system-based approach to ensure that individuals develop knowledge, skills and motivation to perform well in their job. The model is based on three main aspects: management functions that guide, control and facilitate employee development; development functions that examine problems and use resources to develop performance systems; and system functions that consider the materials, events and resources needed to achieve goals. The main aim of this model is to identify performance problems, assess needs and set goals. This model suggests that training is a result of specific issues with individual performance on the job. Once performance gaps are identified, relevant interventions can be implemented, which may include providing additional training. This method focuses on outcomes, which ensures that individuals have a consistent view on goals to be achieved. It identifies factors that inhibit performance, thus enabling a focus of any training to be on those issues.

Performance-Based Instructional Design

The third model is the Performance-Based Instructional Design, which helps learners to perform better at work. The model has seven major components that require consideration in developing training programmes.

1 Programme descriptions (purpose of programme, level of programme, programme length, setting, e.g. face-to-face, learner characteristics, e.g. disability)
2 Content analysis (exact content of the programme to be taught)
3 Content selection (identifying the processes and knowledge to be taught)
4 Content sequencing (the learning strategy such as the order of instruction)
5 Lesson structuring (how the lesson will be structured, timing for each slot)
6 Lesson delivery formatting (how the lesson will be presented and providing feedback)
7 Evaluation, feedback procedures development (self-checks, questionnaires, observations).

This model provides a comprehensive set of considerations in the development of a training programme and focuses specifically on ensuring that the training programme has clear aims and outcomes. The benefits of this model include required competencies being made public in advance, which enables the trainee to understand what is required of them, and performance standards are explicitly stated. Disadvantages include the model being based on certain assumptions such as: a trainee's learning is outlined in terms of performance; learners are active participants in the training; and they have responsibility for their own learning. If these assumptions are not met, training can fail.

8.3 Training

Training cycle

Although these three models describe the design of training programmes as phases, the training cycle recognises that training is cyclical. Figure 8.2 shows a diagram of the training cycle with each stage leading to the next with no fixed end point. For example, development of a training programme flows from the identification of training needs, design of the training, delivery of and evaluation of the training programme. However, when repeating the training, the evaluation from programme one would inform programme two, therefore changing the delivery.

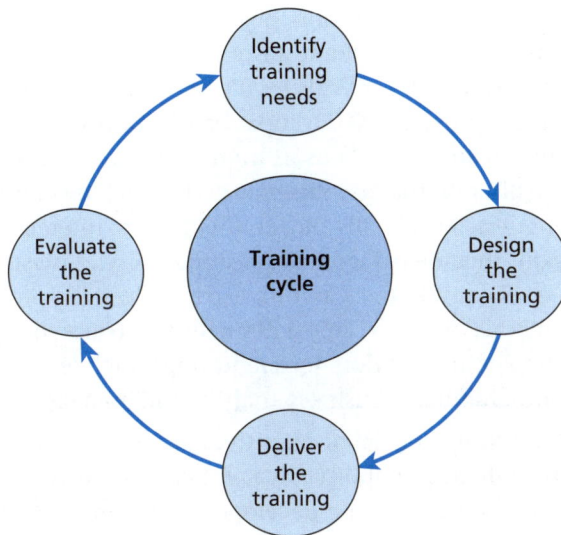

Figure 8.2 Training cycle

Identifying training needs: training needs analysis

A training needs analysis is the first stage in the training cycle and is a process that determines the training an individual needs to perform the job well. The trainee may already have developed some skills that are required for the job, thus re-training of those skills would be a waste of resource. For example, a secretary may know how to type documents, but may not know how to take notes using shorthand, therefore only training in shorthand would be required and not training in typing.

The training needs analysis is a process that can determine the gap between the knowledge, skills and abilities an individual already has and what they need to have in order to carry out the job. Knowledge, skills and abilities (KSAs) can be classified as follows:

- Knowledge is the content of technical information needed to perform the job at an acceptable level. Knowledge is usually obtained through formal education (school, college, university) and on-the-job experience. This knowledge is necessary for job performance, but is not sufficient on its own. For example, this may be knowledge of human resource procedures, but skills and abilities are also required.
- Skill is a special ability or technique that is acquired by training in either an intellectual or physical area. Skills can include listening, communicating, organisation, programming, health and safety, etc. These skills allow the individual to select the most appropriate behaviour or action to suit task requirements. This provides the individual with a certain level of autonomy in how best to carry out a particular task.

Depending on the occupation, different skills may be required. These include sensory skills, motor skills, sensori-motor skills, social skills and cognitive skills.

Sensory skills involve the senses of vision, hearing, touch, smell and taste. A cheese taster would use the senses of smell and taste whereas a translator would use the skills of hearing and vision. Motor skills involve movement such as walking, running, writing and hand movements. Occupations requiring motor skills include a plasterer, an athlete and an author. Sensori-motor skills involve both sensory experiences and motor skills. Jobs that use this type of skill include musicians, hairdressers and fashion designers. Social skills allow individuals to interact with others. Jobs requiring socials skills include bar workers, customer service personnel, call centre staff, nurses, and sales consultants. Cognitive skills allow the processing of information that an individual receives. This skill involves the receiving, interpretation, analysis and retaining of information. Jobs requiring a high level of cognitive skills include computer programmers, business analysts and managers.

- Abilities are natural competencies or cognitive factors possessed by the individual and represent the individual's abilities at a particular time. Although abilities are natural competencies, they can be developed over time. Examples of abilities include analysing data, working under pressure and the ability to communicate verbally.

To carry out a comprehensive training needs analysis to identify the gaps in knowledge, skills and abilities, six main categories need consideration. These categories consider both the business and individual needs.

1 *A context analysis of the business needs*. This takes into consideration how the training will help the individual/individuals to meet the objectives of the organisation. It evaluates whether training is actually required for an individual to perform on the job. As this category is related to business objectives, it can provide performance outputs that are required from the training such as an increase in sales by 10%. This provides a way in which to assess whether training has succeeded.

2 *A work analysis*. This type of analysis involves establishing what is required from the job such as the main tasks/duties to be carried out, the standards expected (e.g. quality), whether the standards are currently being achieved (if not, assessing whether specific aspects of the job are problematic) and the level of skill required to perform the job (e.g. a secretary typing at 60 words per minute rather than 20 words per minute) A method that can be used to undertake such an analysis is a Hierarchical Task Analysis (HTA). This is a structured approach that provides the training developer with knowledge of the tasks that individuals need to perform in order to achieve certain goals. For example, main tasks can be broken down into smaller tasks. An example of an HTA for ordering a printer cartridge is provided in Figure 8.3.

3 *A user analysis* focuses on both the trainees and the trainers. This analysis aims to establish: who will provide the training and their experience of training individuals; whether similar training has been conducted previously and the outcomes of that training (e.g. increased performance and quality); who the trainees are and their current level of knowledge, skill and abilities; and how the individuals prefer to

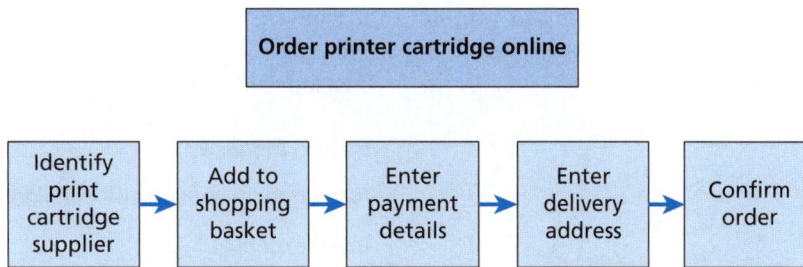

Figure 8.3 Hierarchical Task Analysis for ordering a printer cartridge

learn (seminars, lectures, workshops, role plays). This type of analysis ensures that the relevant training is provided and meets the needs of the trainees.

4 *A content analysis* involves looking at the foundations needed to carry out a particular task. This assesses whether individuals need to know certain information before they can perform a task. An example of this is when learning to operate a computer. An individual needs to know how to start up the computer, switch on the monitor, search for a file, etc. The individual can then build on that knowledge to perform specific tasks such as editing documents, saving documents and printing documents. Without the foundations a novice computer user would not be able to perform these tasks. However, certain tasks may require the foundations to be taught in a particular order. In terms of operating a computer, an individual would need to know how to switch on the computer before performing any tasks. A computer instructor would talk through the functions of the computer before the learner carried out any operations.

5 *A training suitability analysis* identifies whether an individual is suitable for training. Training does not change an individual, it can only change the way that they perform a specific task. For example, management training will not make an individual an expert in management if the individual does not have the capability to learn those skills. However, it is not just the capability of learning that is important, it is also the motivation of the trainee to learn. A study of 305 MBA students by Pham, Segers, & Gisselaers (2010) found that motivation significantly predicted the extent of training transfer.

6 *A cost–benefit analysis* considers whether the training is worth undertaking; specifically assessing the Return on Investment (ROI). The ROI is the cost of designing and delivering the training compared with the benefits such as increased productivity, quality, sales, reduction in waste from production, customer complaints, accidents and costs to carry out a task. If the benefits outweigh the costs, then the training would be beneficial. See Exhibit 8.1 for an example of a cost–benefit template.

? Think about it

Think of a task that you carry out on a daily basis. Develop a Hierarchical Task Analysis to describe the steps that should be taken to complete the task. Ask a colleague to undertake the task using your diagram to assess whether any steps in the process are missing.

Exhibit 8.1 Example of a cost–benefit template for training

A. Direct costs		
	Development of training	_____
	Training materials	_____
	Training room, equipment, catering	_____
	Travel expenses	_____
	Trainer fees	_____
	Trainee salaries	_____
Total cost of A		
B. Indirect costs		
	Administration	_____
	Marketing, telephone calls etc	_____
	Ongoing course development	_____
Total cost of B		

C. Pre- and-post-course on-the-job indicators

Error rate, waste materials, new business, return business _____

Time to completion (expected versus actual hours), delivery rate (early, on time, late) _____
Costs (expected versus actual costs) overtime, employee turnover

Calculate costs pre-training and costs post-training
(should be a saving if the training has been successful) _____

Calculate the costs of (A+B) – C. The benefits of C should outweigh

the costs of A and B. _____

Stop and reflect

Think of a time at school, college, university or at work when you have not been motivated to learn a new topic or task. Do you think this had an impact on your performance? If so, in what way?

Design the training

Stage 2 of the training cycle involves the actual design of the training programme. To provide a successful training programme, knowledge of how individuals learn is needed. This can be provided by laws of learning also known as principles of learning.

Principles of learning

The principles of learning provide insight into how people learn and what makes them learn most effectively. Thorndike (1932) argued for three basic laws: readiness, exercise and effect. 'Readiness' suggests that individuals have to be physically, emotionally and mentally ready to learn and the learner needs to be able to see a reason to learn (for example, to help them in their job). For individuals to be ready to learn, it is important for them to be shown the value of learning. This may be for promotion purposes or with personal development in mind. For example, training could be focused on developing skills such as being more assertive, being able to negotiate better or improving presentation skills. The second law, exercise, is concerned with practice. It was argued by Thorndike that if individuals repeat and practise skills, then they are more likely to retain that skill. The final principle, effect, is based on the emotional reaction of the trainee. If an individual is satisfied when they learn something new, it represents positive reinforcement that makes them more likely to repeat their learning experience.

Other factors can also affect whether a training programme will be successful. Pre-training activities can have an impact on how effective the training is. According to Salas and Cannon-Bowers (2001), pre-training activities fall into three main categories: 1) what trainees bring to the training setting; 2) variables that engage the trainee to learn and participate in development activities; 3) how the training can be prepared to maximise the learning experience. The types of characteristics that trainees can bring to the training setting include their cognitive ability (intelligence), their personal goals, and self-efficacy (the belief that one can perform tasks and behaviours). The variables that engage the trainee to learn is their motivation to use the knowledge, skills and abilities, gained from the training, on the job. Research suggests that pre-training motivation to learn predicts transfer onto the job (Tai, 2006; Bell & Ford, 2007; Chiaburu & Lindsay, 2008). Individual characteristics can have an influence on the success of the training, and so can the preparation of the training programme. The preparation of training to maximise the learning experience falls into four main sections (Salas & Cannon-Bowers, 2001).

1 The training presents information and concepts to be learned (this can be presented to trainees through learning objectives, details of which will be covered in the training programme).
2 Trainers demonstrate the knowledge, skills and abilities to be learnt (this can be through learning outcomes or competency outcomes).
3 Trainees' opportunities to practise the skills (for example, if a trainee is being trained in a computer application they should be given the opportunity to practise that application both during the training programme and post-training, on the job).
4 Feedback is provided to trainees during and after the practice session.

The use of feedback is important to help an individual learn new skills and rectify mistakes they have made. If an individual receives no feedback, they will assume that they are performing the task correctly.

Learning styles

A further consideration when planning training is the learning styles of the trainees. Learning styles provide trainers with categories that classify learners based on their approach to receiving and processing information (Buch & Bartley, 2002). Honey and Mumford (1982) identified four learning styles: Activitists, Pragmatists, Theorists and Reflectors.

1 **Activist** like to be involved in the experience of the task. They enjoy new experiences, but sometimes act without thinking through the potential consequences of their actions. These individuals are flexible and open-minded. Training techniques better suited to this learning style include brainstorming, problem-solving, group discussions and role plays.

2 **Pragmatists** enjoy trying out new techniques, theories and ideas to assess whether they work in practice. These individuals are practical in nature and enjoy solving problems, although they do not enjoy ruminating. Training techniques for this type of learning style include the use of case studies, problem-solving activities, discussions as well as time for reflection.

3 **Theorists** think through problems in a logical way. They collect all the facts and spend time analysing and challenging assumptions. Theorists like things to fit with their own mind-set and if they do not, they reject them. These types of learners prefer the use of stories in the learning experience as well as statistics and background information.

4 **Reflectors** like to ponder and observe from many different perspectives. They are cautious but thoughtful individuals who consider all possibilities and the consequences they may have. They listen to others before putting forward their own viewpoints. These learners are best suited to techniques that involve observation, receiving feedback and discussions.

? *Think about it*

Think of a cohort of 150 students that you need to teach. How would you encompass all learning styles so that each student will get the best possible learning experience?

Consider the types of methods that could be used such as lectures, hands-on experience, etc.

An alternative approach to Honey and Mumford's (1982) model is Kolb's (1984) model of learning, which is based on experiential learning. According to Kolb, there are two main processes of grasping information (concrete experience and abstract conceptualisation) and two processes for transferring experience into learning (active experimentation and reflective observation). These four processes can be converged into four learning styles.

1 **Convergers** perceive information abstractly and process the information through active participation. These learners enjoy discussions where there is

a two-way dialogue, but do not enjoy lectures where there is only impart of information.

2 **Accommodators** perceive information concretely and use active experimentation to process the information. These learners like hands-on experience and enjoy self-directed learning such as role plays.

3 **Divergers** perceive information concretely and process through reflective observation. These learners enjoy brainstorming, lectures and reflective activities.

4 **Assimilators** perceive information abstractly and process information through reflective observation. They enjoy reading, the use of case studies and private space to think.

To assess an individual's learning style, Kolb (1984) developed the Learning Style Inventory, which is a 12-item sentence completion exercise that asks individuals to rank learning strategies in order of preference. This inventory identifies four phases in the learning process: experiencing – learning from experience and being sensitive to people and their feelings; reflecting – taking alternative perspectives and reserving judgement; thinking – thinking logically and analysing ideas as well as planning; acting – taking risks, showing the ability to achieve and influencing. This allows trainers and trainees to understand the impact of their learning style and how best to develop material so that the individual learns well.

The learning style we adopt, according to Fleming (1995), is due to the way we receive and process information. Fleming argued that this is through modes: Visual, Auditory, Read/Write and Kinesthetic (VARK). There are various styles of presentation that trainers can use to ensure that individuals with various learning styles can understand the material being presented.

Table 8.1 shows techniques better suited to these types of learners.

The various teaching techniques in Table 8.1 can be combined so that the training session is based on all the different combinations of learning styles. For example, using a DVD as an introduction to a topic area, using workbooks to re-emphasise points, getting students to answer questions and asking students to apply their knowledge to performing an actual task. Using different methods of training also provides variety, which will help students keep focused on the training session.

Methods of training

The methods that can be used for training are varied. This section will discuss the most common training methods used within organisations such as lectures, case studies, role-playing, simulations, and computer-assisted training and job rotation.

While reading this section, think about the learning styles each method encompasses by referring to Table 8.1 (overleaf).

Lectures involve verbal presentation and are useful when information needs imparting to a large audience at the same time. This method of imparting information is cost-effective as it involves one presentation of the information and one lecture theatre and visual/audio equipment. Lectures are used widely within university settings, but do have drawbacks. Lectures tend to involve one-way

Table 8.1 VARK learning style techniques

Learning style	Teaching techniques
Visual	Pictures, graphs, diagrams, colourful posters and illustrations, DVDs, diagrams
Auditory	The use of voice to learn including lectures, discussion groups, podcasts, stories, role plays and verbal revision
Read/Write	Books, notes, lists, manuals, workbooks, write important words on whiteboard
Kinesthetic	Practical tasks, simulations, demonstrations

communication (from trainer to student); it is therefore difficult for the trainer to assess the level of student understanding. This type of training also makes it more difficult for students to ask questions because they are embarrassed or do not want to interrupt the trainer.

Case studies involve students analysing practice case reports. The case reports usually involve a real-life situation. The student is required to analyse the case report and, based on theoretical understanding, make recommendations for interventions (this is what you have been doing in your case study reports so far and continues throughout the remaining chapters). This method provides the student with practical experience rather than just theoretical knowledge. However, for case studies to be useful, the student needs to be clear about the link between the case study and the theory being taught.

Role play requires the student to adopt a specific role such as a customer. A scenario is presented to the student and they are asked to act out that scenario. This method of training is beneficial in providing the student with a safe environment to practise a particular task (such as dealing with a complaint) while also having real interactions with people. The participant receives immediate feedback from the trainer and provides the student with an opportunity to practise based on the feedback given. Disadvantages of this method include the trainee being too self-conscious to carry out the role play; and it is not appropriate for large groups due to the amount of time required to observe and assess the groups.

Simulations are usually computer-based and represent real-life situations. For example, flight pilots may use a simulator to practise flying an aeroplane. This method of training allows the individual to practise their skills in a safe environment (you wouldn't want a pilot to practise flying with 250 passengers!). A simulator also allows the trainee to study specific problems and make decisions and see the consequences of those decisions. Referring back to the pilot, it may be that a decision is made to increase the plane's altitude to avoid turbulence. The pilot would be able to understand the consequences of taking this action and associated risks by simulating the experience. However, the pilot will not get the same feelings with a simulator as when flying with passengers – such as increased levels of anxiety when an unusual situation occurs.

Computer-assisted training involves the use of computers as the main method of instruction. This type of training can involve the use of audio materials such as podcasts, visual material such as lecture notes, and practical tasks such as the use of a statistical package. This method is increasing in popularity as students want to work and learn. Computer-assisted training allows students to work at their own pace and their own convenience. Costs of training are also minimised due to a reduction in travel costs and face-to-face training time. There are some disadvantages to this method of training, including an individual's experience with computers, the student not being able to have immediate feedback on questions and a lack of interaction with other students, which can result in this type of training leaving the student feeling isolated.

Job rotation provides trainees with practical experience on the job. Trainees move through a variety of jobs in order to gain a broad understanding and experience of that job. For example, a management trainee may work in a variety of departments such as marketing, product design, quality assurance and accounts in order to gain a wide experience of how the organisation operates as well as its policies and procedures. However, the disadvantages of this method are that it is difficult to organise logistically as students would be required to be mentored by an experienced member of staff who may already be busy with day-to-day activities as well as the instability of moving people from job to job.

? Think about it

Refer back to the case study at the beginning of the chapter. What methods of training would be most beneficial to Marlene to gain practical experience?

Delivery of training

Once the method of training is decided, the content can be adapted. It is important to plan how the training will be delivered. For example, if there is a mixture of learning styles multiple methods may be required such as role plays and lectures. To ensure that the trainee has an understanding of the content to be delivered, the training should have clear learning objectives. Explanations of how the content of the training programmes meet the trainee objectives also need to be explained. The flow of the information needs consideration such as whether the information is sequenced appropriately. For example, training in hairdressing requires the theoretical knowledge before the practical application. Therefore, the flow of information would be the theory, which can then be applied to practice. A consideration of the time allocated to the training is also needed. Questions should be asked as to whether the time allocated is sufficient to cover all the training material in enough breadth and depth to meet the individual's learning needs. The trainer also needs to consider the diverse needs of the learner including race, ethnicity, religious beliefs, age and educational ability. Considering these factors at the outset ensures that the learner is provided with the best learning environment. However, other factors need to be understood as being critical to an individual's learning. These factors include the importance of practice.

The saying 'Practice makes perfect' has some evidence in research, which has shown that the more an individual practises a skill, the better they will perform. In a review of literature on practice, instruction and skill acquisition in soccer, Williams and Hodges (2005) found that practice plays an important role in the acquisition of skill. This was also evidenced in a longitudinal study by Ward, Hodges, Williams, & Starkes (2004), who evaluated practice history profiles in elite and sub-elite soccer players between the ages of eight and 18. It was found that the elite players spent twice as many hours a week practising than the sub-elite players in each age category, showing that practice increases performance. Although practice is important, the feedback on practice is also key to performing well. Feedback allows individuals to improve their performance or change their behaviour. A synthesis of over 500 meta-analyses by Hattie (1999), representing 20–30 million students, found feedback to be important in the student learning experience. In the absence of feedback, individuals may think they are doing well and continue with incorrect behaviour. Feedback is paramount as it identifies areas that need improvement and allows for adjustments to be made to improve performance. Feedback is also important as, when positive, it reinforces self-image and may motivate the individual to try harder. However, feedback should be rapid so that individuals can apply the feedback to the tasks just completed.

Evaluation of training

Evaluation is an important part of training. The use of evaluation tools and methodologies helps assess the effectiveness of the training and thus the value of the training programme to individuals and the organisation. Evaluation is usually the final aspect of a training programme. However, the training is a circular process where the evaluation allows for identification of what worked and what did not work in order that changes to the training programme can be made for future training events. Therefore, training is a developmental process. Evaluating training is difficult as it is hard to quantify and measure direct benefits that the course has had for individuals and organisations. Evaluation becomes easier when there are direct outputs to measure such as increasing the speed of typing or reducing waste from the production of a widget. One of the most common methods of assessing training is post-training surveys completed by the trainees. Trainees are asked to complete their views on a number of aspects of the course (usually using a likert scale from one to five stating how satisfied they are with certain aspects of the course) such as quality of materials, the use of examples and the quality of feedback provided. Other methods of training evaluation can be used and are detailed in Table 8.2.

More formal methods of training evaluation have been developed and are based on two main approaches (Phillips, 1991): goal-based and system-based approaches. Goal-based evaluations evaluate whether the training programme meets its objectives. A goal-based approach was proposed by Kirkpatrick (1959), who suggested that training evaluation can be carried out on four different levels. Level one involves the assessment of the trainee's initial reactions to the training process; Level two is an assessment of the learning process (the knowledge and

Table 8.2 Methods of training evaluation

Method	Function	Advantages	Disadvantages
Interviews	Understand trainees' perceptions of the training and their experiences	• Get depth of information • Flexible approach • Can probe for more detail	• Time-consuming • Interviewer bias • Difficult to analyse and compare responses
Observation	Gain first-hand experience of how a training programme is run	• View in real time • Can ask questions • Can observe people's behaviour	• Observer influence (can influence how a person behaves) • Difficult to interpret behaviours • Can be expensive
Focus groups	Use group discussions regarding the training experience	• Can obtain common perceptions • Obtain depth and breadth of information in short time period	• Hard to analyse responses • Difficult to get individuals together at the same time • Need a good facilitator
Questionnaires/ Surveys	Quickly obtain lots of information	• Can complete anonymously • Obtain lots of data • Inexpensive	• No chance for follow-up questions • May not get considered answer • Very impersonal

skills acquired by the trainees); Level three is based on a behavioural assessment that assesses whether the course has induced a behavioural change relevant to certain activities, and Level four assesses the impact the training has on the trainee's performance. Examples of questions you may ask using a goal-based approach can be seen in Figure 8.4 (overleaf).

Systems-based approaches focus on awareness, design choice and action that are inherent in decision-making and allow for individuals to work in a systematic way. For example, a model put forward by Stufflebeam *et al.* (1971) suggests the Context, Input, Process and Product (CIPP) model that incorporates both quantitative and qualitative analysis. The training evaluator focuses on Context evaluation, Input evaluation, Process evaluation and Product evaluation. The Context evaluation provides descriptive information about the training programme and the intended aims, objectives and outcomes of the training programme. The Input evaluation considers the infrastructure of the training, whereas the Process evaluation concerns the implementation of the programme, its procedures and strategies. The Product evaluation is concerned with the success of the training programme. An example of a CIPP model for the evaluation of a new MSc in Occupational Psychology is provided in Exhibit 8.2 on p. 145.

A more recent approach put forward by Bushnell (1990) argues that training evaluation should be based on Input, Process, Output, Outcome (IPO). Input

> How were the goals/objectives of the training programme met?

> Will the goals/objectives be met within the given training time-frame?

> Are there adequate resources to meet the goals/objectives (equipment, facilities, money)?

> Do goals/objectives require changing for the future?

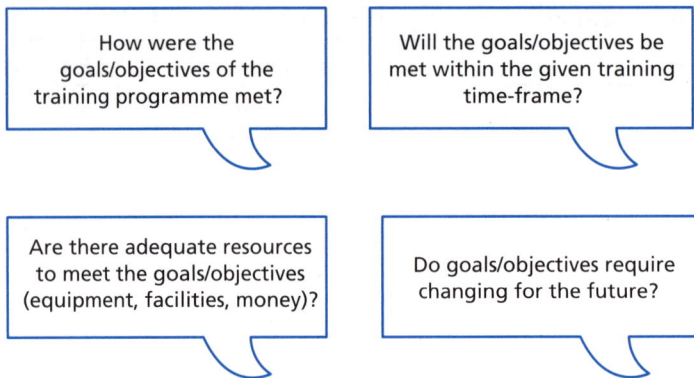

Figure 8.4 Questions for consideration when adopting a goal-based approach

evaluates the availability of materials, the individual's qualification and assessment as to whether training is appropriate for the individual. Process concerns the development and the delivery of the training programme; Output involves collection of data on the outcomes of the training intervention (for example, has error rate decreased? Has productivity increased?). Finally, Outcome measures the long-term results of the training such as return on investment due to increased productivity or reduced wastage. Both Stufflebeam *et al*'s. (1971) and Bushnell's (1990) approaches have an input level and a process level. Although labelled differently, both approaches consider the context or process and both consider the outcomes of the training. Thus, there is much agreement between these two approaches on what should be evaluated.

Stop and reflect

Think of Marlene at the beginning of the chapter. How would you apply the training cycle to identify the skills that she needs in order to be able to perform well in the job?

In summary, to ensure success of a training programme, it is important to be aware of a number of potential threats. Such threats include:

- inaccurate training needs analysis
- poorly motivated trainees
- training not linked to organisational objectives
- use of incorrect methods for trainees' learning style
- insufficient time for practice
- insufficient feedback.

Exhibit 8.2 CIPP Model for new MSc in Occupational Psychology

Context evaluation	• Assess objectives of MSc in Occupational Psychology
	• Assess background characteristics of learners (e.g. educational background, employment history, reasons for undertaking the course).
	• Are intended outcomes of the course satisfactory?
	• Outcomes include: Stage one towards the qualification in occupational psychology
	• Increase in percentage on post-graduate student satisfaction survey
Input evaluation	• Assessment of available resources (computers, library resources)
	• Evaluate quality of learning materials (handouts, lecture notes, contact hours, assignments)
	• Evaluate quality of teaching (lecturers)
	• The cost to study (to the student and the organisation)
	• Cost comparison of similar organisations and similar training programmes
Process evaluation	Examine the processes of:
	• lectures
	• workshops
	• guidance and counselling
	• assignments
	• examination processes
	• university regulations and guidelines
Product evaluation	• Examine outcomes of the training (progression rates, completion rates)
	• Assess student views on training provided (module evaluation and course evaluation)
	• Evaluation of content and assessment by external examiners and course accreditation bodies

8.4 Benefits of training

Many approaches and methods to training evaluation exist and it is important that you are not only evaluating the materials provided and the quality of teaching, but the benefits of the training, as it is the bottom line (monetary) value of training that organisations are concerned with.

The importance of getting training right is paramount as the cost to the organisation can be high. The cost of training includes the training course itself, travel expenses, and lost hours from work to attend training. For example, Campbell (2006) estimated that the amount spent in the UK alone by individuals and organisations on training programmes amounts to about £30 billion per year.

The benefits of training employees are numerous. These benefits include:

- reduction in poor quality/defective products and services
- reduced waste (e.g. materials in the process of production)
- reduction in absenteeism
- reduction in staff turnover (Pfeffer & Sutton, 2006)
- reduction in customer complaints and customer turnover
- increased staff loyalty/feelings of obligation (Shore, Tetrick, Lynch, & Barksdale, 2006) and motivation (Grant, 2008)
- a more flexible, empowered and adaptable workforce (Pfeffer, 1998)
- enhanced company image.

These benefits are only realised when a comprehensive training programme is implemented.

Multi-level impact of training

The impact of methods used and decisions made within the design, implementation and evaluation of a training programme can have an influence on individuals, teams and organisations. It is important, therefore, to follow the training cycle. If inappropriate training is implemented the effect can reduce an individual's motivation to learn, can lead to poor performance in the workplace as well as increase an individual's absenteeism. The effect can also be seen on team members and includes increasing pressure on the team to produce the work of the absent staff member. Also, the reputation of the team is at stake because if there is poor performance it reflects on the team as a whole. There may be a decrease in quality of work, work being completed late, and an increase in wastage. At an organisational level there could be an increase in costs due to wastage and return of poor-quality goods, complaints from customers, an effect on the reputation of the organisation and the organisation not meeting its goals or targets. It is therefore vital that training is appropriate and successful. Any programme that takes place must do so within the confines of legal guidelines.

Legal context

For further details of legislative requirements for training individuals in the workplace, please refer below. Additional details can also be found in Chapter 3 – Legislation applied to the workplace.

Government Equalities Office (2010). *Equality Act 2010.* Available: *http://equalities. gov.uk/equality_bill.aspx*

Short-answer questions

1 Identify the benefits of undertaking training.

2 Identify the stages of the training cycle.

3 Explain the six main categories in training needs analysis.

4 Describe the different methods of training outlined in this chapter, and the advantages and disadvantages of each of these methods.

5 Identify the threats to successful training and the effects of poor training on individuals, teams and organisations.

CASE STUDY
Training

The company

The store (Sammie Garden Centre) is a medium-sized garden centre that sells a large variety of products for the garden enthusiast. The products include plants, shrubs and trees, garden tools and electrical equipment, garden furniture and barbecues, outdoor heating and lighting, and hot tubs. The products range in price from £3 to over £6,000. The range has expanded over the last two years, as previously the centre sold only plants, trees, shrubs and garden tools.

The garden centre employs over 100 members of staff (reduced from 150 employed previously): 70 full-time and 30 part-time (working 16 hours per week). There are three store managers, which is a reduction from six store managers employed before the downturn in the economy. The store managers rotate their shifts from 8am until 4pm, 4pm until 10pm and weekends from 8am until 6pm Saturday and 8am until 4pm on Sundays. There is only one store manager in the store at any time. Their responsibility is to oversee the running of the store, as well as training employees.

There are a number of local competitors in the area, although they have smaller stores. However, recently, Sammie Garden Centre has become more expensive on a large range of products than other local stores. Customers are complaining that the store is expensive and that the level of customer service has reduced. Staff members are refusing to help customers to the car with their goods and seem less than helpful on the store floor when customers ask for information about products.

Training programme

The three store managers have worked their way up through the ranks from store assistant. Each store manager has responsibility for determining the exact training programme for each store assistant. The current training programme involves on-the-job training and mentoring of new staff by more experienced staff. The staff member providing the training and mentoring is paid an extra £10 per week for this. The responsibility of the staff member is to ensure that the new staff member meets the criteria set out by the senior management of the garden centre. The criteria include:

- having adequate knowledge of the products provided by the garden centre
- providing good, courteous customer service
- ensuring that the store meets health and safety requirements.

The trainer can use any method of training that they deem fit. At the end of the training period, the trainer has to sign a form stating that the employee has met the criteria. No additional training is provided for existing staff unless they are deemed to be underperforming. This has only occurred twice in the last two years. Store managers are expected to complete an online leadership training programme over six months that is undertaken in their own time.

Pay and conditions

Store assistants are paid a flat rate of £260 per week. Workers can work overtime at an increase of 15% on their normal hourly rate. Due to a reduction in sales, overtime has reduced and a rota has been set up for those wanting to work overtime. On average, individuals are able to work about 10 hours overtime a month.

The problem

There has been an increase in customer complaints over the last 12 months. The first set of complaints involve staff's lack of knowledge of the stock held, problems with using the tills, lack of awareness of special offers, lack of knowledge of credit agreements on hot tubs, expensive electrical equipment, and an inability to deal with returned goods without calling a store manager. The second set of problems involve staff reactions to customers including being discourteous and rude and refusing to help customers to the car with their goods. A questionnaire was sent to staff to assess their understanding of good customer service and of what was expected of them. The questionnaire results showed that staff had differing views.

Your task is to write a report to the senior management advising them about the issues related to the current training programme as well as issues concerning customer service. You should suggest interventions to overcome these problems. Ethical issues of implementing the interventions should also be considered.

Writing guidelines are provided in Chapter 2, Section 2.3 – The consultancy cycle, which provides you with a structure to follow.

Further reading

Kirkpatrick, J. D., & Kirkpatrick, D. (2007). *Implementing the four levels: A practical guide for effective evaluation of training.* San Francisco, CA: Berrett-Koehler Publishers.

Truelove, S. (2006). *Training in practice.* Oxford: Blackwell Publishers.

9

Design of environments and work

Learning outcomes

After reading this chapter, you should be able to:

- discuss categories of ergonomics
- understand the links between work design and health and safety
- develop preventive interventions to reduce health and safety risks
- understand types of human error
- know the key stages of a risk assessment.

9.1 Introduction

Christine, a copy typist, has been working in a legal firm for over 10 years. Her job involves repetitive typing for long periods of time. The workstations are old and were originally used for typewriters, but with computer technology the workstations are not appropriate and cause staff to crouch when typing. Christine has been diagnosed with musculoskeletal disorder.

This chapter focuses on how occupational psychology contributes to the design of work and work environments. It focuses on ergonomic principles as well as health and safety at work and human factors. Ergonomics can involve the assessment of factors such as design and use of tools, design and layout of the work environment, posture and movement required for the completion of a work task, the repetitiveness of a task and physical strength required to complete a task. To reduce the likelihood of accidents at work, the discipline of ergonomics aims to improve health and safety in the workplace. The importance of ergonomics in the workplace is to reduce occupational injuries and fatigue and to increase employee satisfaction. It involves the study of individuals and their environment.

Ergonomics came to the fore with the composition of the Ergonomics Society in 1959. However, the discipline of ergonomics research can be traced back nearly 50 years befor then. Taylor (1911) (as also outlined in Chapter 1 – Introduction to occupational psychology) worked at Bethlehem Steel Company where he observed workers shovelling coal. He provided each worker with a shovel that suited their weight and height and found that the worker's effectiveness tripled. This resulted in the company getting the same productivity from 140 workers as from 400 workers, therefore reducing costs. Also, in the 1900s, Frank and Lillian Gilbreth, a husband-and-wife team, developed the motion studies. From observations of workers, it was realised that no two individuals work in exactly the same way and each adopts their own individual working style. This led the Gilbreths to seek one ideal way to complete a job or task. Using a motion-picture camera, work tasks could be observed that allowed for breakdown of the work into fundamental elements as well as timing how long it takes to perform each fundamental element. Continuing research and development took place throughout the 1900s with the Hawthorne Studies in the 1920s (see Chapter 1 for further details) and in 1921 the Industrial Fatigue Research Board was formed, which researched topics such as the work environment and job design. Also established in 1921 was the National Institute of Industrial Psychology whose aim was to 'promote by systematic scientific methods a more effective application of human energy in occupational life and a correspondingly higher standard of welfare and comfort for workers'. The consideration of design of equipment continued throughout the war, with the Second World War seeing a concentration on design due to a number of aeroplane crashes by highly trained pilots, which were a result of poor control display configurations (Fitts & Jones, 1947). In 1957 in the United States, the Human Factors Society was formed and in 1992 the name was changed to the Human Factors and Ergonomics Society. The discipline has continued developing in areas such as computer technology, automation and health and safety at work.

9.2 Categories of ergonomics

Ergonomics can be categorised into four main areas:

1 physical ergonomics
2 cognitive ergonomics
3 the physical work environment
4 health and safety related to the workplace.

These areas will now be discussed in more detail.

Physical ergonomics

Physical ergonomics refers to how the human body functions and how physical aspects of the individual affect their work capabilities. An individual's body dimensions, also known as anthropometry, considers an individual's body shape and size. As people differ in their body shape and size, this information should be taken into account when designing workspaces. The simplest way that could be considered in designing workplaces is to design for the average person. Based on height, individuals will fit into the 5th, 50th or 95th percentile. The 50th percentile represents people of average height from the group surveyed, and the 5th percentile represents a small amount of individuals who are smaller than the majority. The 95th percentile represents a small number of people who are taller than the majority. Thus, 90% are considered average whereas 5% are smaller than the average and 5% are bigger than the average.

When designing work environments, consideration should be given to physical requirements as well as the mental aspects of the employees working in them. Physical requirements include posture, arm reach and clearance such as leg-room, elbow-room and head-room.

For example, consider the picture of the computer operator in Figure 9.1. The back of the chair supports the computer operator's lower back with the seat fixed at a comfortable height, which can be adjusted for different computer operators. The height of the table is level with the bent arms of the operator, ensuring that the keyboard is within comfortable reach. The computer screen is at a comfortable height for the user and at an angle that will cause minimum strain to the eyes.

When the basis of design is based on anthropometric data, there are four main areas that need consideration.

1 The user group. Who are you designing for? Consider age, gender and nationality. For example, the design of a desk for schoolchildren between the ages of 5 and 11 would be different to the design of a desk for working adults between the ages of 18 and 65.

Figure 9.1 Computer operator

2 Posture such as sitting, standing, reaching or moving. Maintaining the sitting or standing lumbar shape of the spine is important for posture and comfort.

3 Clearance for when people have to access work or get through restricted spaces. Clearance represents the minimum space to let a person into or out of an area – for example, emergency exits.

4 Reach represents the workspace envelope. It recognises that, although individuals may be sitting or standing, they will have to reach at some point in a task.

The workspace envelope represents the three-dimensional space in which a person works. In an office, your workspace includes your desk and chair and the immediate space around you. The limits of your workspace are influenced by your functional arm reach, which is impacted by the direction of reach and the task to be carried out. The design of the workspace includes where furniture is placed, the tools and equipment needed to carry out the job, and the amount of space the employee needs to carry out their work. Poorly designed workplaces can cause a number of health problems such as eye strain, back pain, repetitive strain injury and musculoskeletal disorders. These are discussed in more detail later.

? Think about it

Think about Christine at the start of the chapter. What considerations should be given to her working environment? The design of the workstation shown in Figure 9.1 may have helped her in being comfortable at work and reduce the likelihood of physical health issues.

Cognitive ergonomics

Cognitive ergonomics considers the human brain and sensory system in the processing of information. Human cognition includes touch, smell, taste, hearing and vision. It focuses on the fit between a person's cognitive ability, the work task and the work environment. This may involve designing a warning sign or designing a software package. The aim is that the majority of people will understand its meaning and act in the appropriate manner. Consider driving a car that has a speedometer that beeps when you have exceeded the speed limit. It is expected that the majority of people will recognise the beep as referring to the need to reduce the speed and the majority of people will ease the pressure on the accelerator pedal and reduce the speed at which the car is travelling.

Cognitive ergonomics is important in the use of highly complex technology. Consider the use of mobile phone technology and the reliance on this technology for social and business communication. Humans have an over-reliance on such technology and may keep all their contact information within the technology and may rely on conducting business with the technology. However, this can be dangerous. See Real case 9.1.

When technology goes wrong

Blackberry phones in 2011 had days of disruption in Europe, the Middle East, Africa, India, Brazil and Argentina. The blackout on the Blackberry service left millions of users without email, web browsing and Blackberry messaging. Blackberry's owner blamed the outage on a backlog of emails to Europe, the Middle East and Africa (BBC, 2011). According to the *Telegraph* (2011), nearly half of Blackberry users say they will get a different device when they change handsets.

Physical work environment

Environmental factors may also require consideration in the design of a workspace. There are three primary methods of assessing how humans respond to their work environments:

1 Subjective methods. There involve rating scales such as those from 1 (completely dissatisfied) to 5 (completely satisfied). These assessments are easy to carry out. Questions that may be asked include issues such as a person's comfort or problems with their working environment.
2 Objective methods. These provide direct measures of a person's response such as their body temperature, and levels of vibration experienced by the individual when carrying out a task.
3 Behavioural methods/models of human response. These involve assessing a person's change in posture when conducting a job as well as making adjustments to the environment so that they can work more quickly and more efficiently. This model relies on providing a reason for the change in behaviour and requires the observation of the behaviour by a trained observer. The difficulty with this method is that it is difficult to understand cause and effect.

Such factors that may be considered within workplace assessments include noise, lighting, air quality, radiation and vibration from work equipment. These will now be discussed in further detail.

Noise. Repeated and excessive exposure to loud noise can damage the ear leading to hearing problems including full hearing loss (see Real case example 9.2 of work

Work-induced hearing issues

GMB member David Carr, 65, has received £6,000 compensation from Barnsley Metropolitan Borough Council after suffering from **noise-induced hearing loss and tinnitus**. He was exposed to excessive noise while working as a road-worker, JCB driver, HGV driver and mower for the council (Hazards, 2011).

induced hearing loss). It can also lead to organisational issues such as the inability to communicate effectively in the workplace. When investigating levels of noise, annoyance level is the most often used criterion although there is also consideration of loudness and nuisance (Parsons, 2000). Noise levels are assessed by measuring the noise throughout a factory, office or other workplace. The average noise level is then taken.

Lighting. Lighting levels should be appropriate for the task to be undertaken. Working in dim, low-level lighting can cause eye strain as well as headaches. Excessive exposure to ultraviolent and infrared light can also cause problems including headaches. If bright lights shine on to a computer screen, it may make it difficult to see the work being carried out.

Air quality. Working in dusty or environments with fumes without appropriate ventilation can cause breathing problems, asthma attacks and lung disorders. Even basic issues such as the re-circulation of air in air-conditioning units can increase the risk of infection and air pollution.

Radiation. Radiation exposure, such as that from the sun, can lead to skin cancers. Work including gardening, building, sports coaching, such as golf, and those who deliver post would be exposed to more ultraviolet radiation than individuals who work indoors such as office workers and factory workers.

Vibration. Vibration of the hand or arm, or whole body vibration, can cause damage to an employee's spine, hands and stomach.

To ensure that organisations protect their employees and others in the workplace, health and safety legislation is enforced. It is the responsibility of both employers and employees to abide by this legislation.

Health and safety at work

Until the 1970s, health and safety law in the UK consisted of more than 500 pieces of legislation, and was administered by nine government departments. The legislation was reviewed by the Robens Committee, which found that there had been no reduction in the number of people injured or killed in the workplace. A new Act was, therefore, developed to put a duty of care on employers to ensure the health and safety of their employees.

The Health and Safety at Work etc. Act (1974) (reported by the Health and Safety Executive, 2006) provides a framework for organisations to ensure the health and safety of all its employees or anyone affected by work such as clients and contractors. A number of duties are set out in the legislation, which include:

- Placing a duty on employers to ensure health, safety and welfare of employees as far as is reasonably practicable.
- Requiring employers to consult with trade union safety representatives on issues affecting health and safety of employees.
- Writing a health and safety policy if staff numbers exceed five.
- Ensuring that non-employees who may be affected by work tasks are not exposed to risks to their health and safety.
- Placing a duty on anyone responsible for the workplace to ensure premises, plant and machinery do not endanger people using them.

- Placing a duty on every employee while in the workplace to take care of themselves and any other person who may be affected by their actions.
- Employees not misusing or interfering with anything that affects health and safety.

The Management of Health and Safety at Work Regulations (1999) (reported by the Health and Safety Executive, 1999) requires employers to conduct risk assessments, discussed later in the chapter, in order to eliminate or reduce risks. As well as carrying out risk assessments. Employers need to:

- implement health and safety measures identified from risk assessments
- monitor and evaluate the interventions
- set up and provide information to employees about emergency procedures
- provide information, supervision and training for employees to carry out work tasks.

The importance of such legislation is to reduce injuries and death at work. See Real case 9.3.

Real Case 9.3

Health and safety at work (2012)

A door manufacturer has been ordered to pay more than £48,000 in penalties after a machine operator lost part of three fingers when he trapped his hand between heated platens on a press.

Yesterday (12 January) at Derby Crown Court, the judge fined the company £25,000 and ordered it to pay £23,154 in costs.

After the hearing, HSE inspector Noelle Walker said the case showed the 'importance of providing physical safety measures where they are practicable, instead of relying on informal systems of work where a mistake or misunderstanding can lead to such a serious injury'.

The European Union also has a set of Directives relating to health and safety. The European Agency for Safety and Health at Work (EU–OSHA) provides information and guidance in Europe. Although regulations for health and safety are the same throughout Europe, directives are tailored to the national laws of member states. Within the EU, the key directive is the Health and Safety Framework Directive (89/391/EEC). This provides protection for employees by the use of preventive measures that protect against occupational diseases and accidents. Employers are required to:

- ensure free health and safety for workers in all their work
- provide risk assessments and ensure protective measures are implemented
- keep accident records
- provide measures for first aid, firefighting and evacuation of workers

- provide information and consultation for health and safety at work
- provide health and safety training for all employees.

9.3 Health issues

Health issues affect the individual in their ability to conduct their day-to-day work activities and can also affect the organisation in terms of reduced productivity and health-related litigation claims. Examples of cases of litigation are considered when outlining health-related issues in order to explain the impact of poor work or environmental design on both the individual in terms of health and the organisation in terms of financial payouts and a reduced reputation for providing a healthy workplace. Strategies to mediate some of the issues are also described and may be considered by organisations when evaluating risk reduction.

Eye strain occurs when an individual stares at a computer for a prolonged period of time. This is made worse if there is insufficient light or a computer screen that flickers. Symptoms can include headaches, tiredness, itching/watery eyes, blurring and/or double vision.

Strategies to reduce risk of eye strain are:

- use screens that don't flicker
- have evenly distributed lighting
- take regular breaks from the computer
- have regular eye checks
- look away from the screen at regular intervals and focus on something in the distance.

Back pain is suffered by many office workers especially those who use computers for a long period of time. This may be due to poor posture and/or poorly designed chairs.

Real Case 9.4

Back issues

A specialist nurse who needs risky surgery on her spine after she slipped on a wet floor as she arrived at work has received £17,500 compensation. The Unite member, who is employed by an NHS Trust in London, suffered injuries to her ankle and has **a displaced disc pressing on a nerve in her back** (Hazards, 2011).

Strategies to reduce risk of back issues are:

- use fully adjustable chairs
- use a computer screen with an adjustable monitor

- take regular breaks
- use the correct posture (sit with back straight).

Repetitive strain injury causes damage to wrists and fingers as well as other body parts. The cause of injury is the repetitive movement of the joint – for example, a typist whose wrist is constantly bent with repetitive movement of the fingers. The symptoms include aching, burning sensations, weakness, numbness, pins and needles and stiffness.

Strategies to reduce repetitive strain injury are:

- use wrist rests to support wrists
- place elbows by your side when typing
- ensure your chair and workstation are at the correct height
- have regular breaks.

Musculoskeletal disorders include inflammation of tendons in the shoulders, wrists, hands and shoulders (known as tendonitis); irritation of the median nerve, which runs through the bony channel of the wrist (known as carpal tunnel syndrome); inflammation of tendons in the fingers, which causes loss of dexterity (known as trigger finger syndrome). Other signs of musculoskeletal disorder include deformity, cramping, loss of balance, burning, numbness, stiffness and tingling.

Real Case 9.5

Carpal tunnel syndrome

GMB member Andrew Bowler, 51, has received £60,000 in compensation from Nottinghamshire County Council after the landscape gardener developed **carpal tunnel syndrome** as a result of using vibrating tools at work (Hazards, 2011).

? Think about it

Think about Christine at the start of the chapter. Are there any strategies the organisation could implement to reduce the likelihood of musculoskeletal disorder occurring?

To reduce the likelihood of these health problems occurring, certain factors should be considered when designing the workspace, including:

- the tasks the employee is required to conduct and the actions they need to undertake to complete the task
- the position of the employee when undertaking the task, e.g. sitting or standing
- the postures the employee will adopt, e.g. bending, stooping
- how far users can reach both horizontally and vertically
- the individual's body dimensions.

When designing a workspace for employees, the sitting position should be considered as well as the standing position. For a job that is seated, the maximum work area would represent the maximum reach of the person's extended arm. The normal work area represents the bent elbow (90 degrees) sweeping movement. A standing workspace represents the space at which an object can be reached for and grabbed comfortably. There also needs to be consideration of the visual workspace. Frequently viewed items such as computer screens should be positioned directly in front of the user.

For organisations to comply with legislation and ensure safe work environments, risk assessments need to be carried out.

9.4 Risk assessment

All UK workplaces are required by law to carry out a risk assessment under the Management of Health and Safety at Work Regulations (1999). A risk assessment involves the identification of what could cause harm to people within the workplace as well as ensuring legal compliance. It allows for the identification of risks that may lead to injury or ill health or death. According to the Health and Safety Executive (2011a), a risk assessment involves five stages.

- *Stage 1*. Look for hazards. This may involve basic steps such as walking around the organisation and looking for items that could cause harm. Ask employees whether they have noticed any hazards. Look at accident and sickness records to ascertain if common problems are occurring.
- *Stage 2*. Decide who might be harmed and how. Groups of people should be identified, such as members of the public visiting the organisation, contractors and employees.
- *Stage 3*. Evaluate risks and decide if existing precautions are adequate or whether more precautions are needed. Can a hazard be removed altogether? If not, assess whether the likelihood of a risk occurring can be reduced – for example, providing safety equipment when using machinery.
- *Stage 4*. Record findings and tell employees about them.
- *Stage 5*. Review assessment and revise if work changes or if there is an accident.

Although all risks cannot be eliminated, there is a need to protect people as much as is reasonably possible. Once risks are identified, it is then possible to consider possible strategies to reduce or mitigate the risks.

❓ Think about it

Think of a hairdressing salon. Consider some of the hazards that you may find in a hairdressers. What risks do they pose? Consider ways in which you could reduce these risks.

An example risk assessment for a hairdressers can be found at the Health and Safety Executive: http://www.hse.gov.uk/risk/casestudies/pdf/hairdressers.pdf.

Although organisations can conduct risk assessments and mitigate some of those risks, accidents that are a result of human error can also happen. This will now be considered in more detail.

9.5 Human error

Human error represents a failure of planned actions to meet their desired outcomes due to a deviation of what should have been done and what was done. On average, between 60% and 80% of general accidents are due to human error (Reason, 1990). The error itself is not intentional and it is assumed that the factors leading to the error are outside the control of the individual. Errors can also be subdivided into slips and lapses, and mistakes.

Slips and lapses mainly occur during the completion of routine tasks and are usually a result of attention being distracted away from the task. Reasons for such errors may include a number of factors, which will now be discussed.

Misidentification

This is the result of objects required for the task being similar which leads to confusion. For example, an off button and on button that are similar in shape and size. The employee may press the incorrect button due to its similarity especially if the buttons are located close together.

Non-detection error

Non-detection occurs when an employee is interrupted while working or is fatigued.

Stop and think

Think of a time when you have been tired and forgotten to do something such as lock your door at night, switch off lights or forget to put on your alarm clock. Although this may not have had a massive effect on you, forgetting to complete an action at work may have more significant consequences.

Attentional failures

Errors due to attentional failures usually occur because an individual's attention is focused elsewhere.

A further error is mistakes. Mistakes occur when formulating and constructing plans. Reason (1990) suggested two categories of errors due to mistakes.

1 Rule-based errors involve rules and procedures that decisions are based on, in terms of which course of action to take. For example, if a fire alarm sounds there are rules and procedures for people to evacuate the building safely. Errors occur when people are involved in problem-solving activities that are familiar, but previous solutions are not applicable to the current situation.

2 Knowledge-based errors are based on reasoning such as when a person, faced with a new situation to which there are no existing solutions, has to find an on-the-spot solution. Existing ideas may be used that are not relevant to the situation, or evidence is sought to confirm or disconfirm the problem-solver's belief of what actions should be taken.

Errors can also occur due to a number of reasons including, but not limited to, incorrect performance of task, performing tasks out of sequence, failing to perform a task, omitting an action from a task and performing an action not required. Research has focused on why such errors occur. According to Reason (2000) there are two main approaches to human error. The first is the person approach and the second is the systems approach. The person approach attributes blame to an individual person for causing an accident. The assumption is that the accident occurred due to negligence, lack of skill or knowledge, carelessness or a lack of motivation. This approach uses fear and punishment to improve safety. The systems approach recognises systemic inputs to the occurrence of accidents. It recognises problems with human–system designs (the way the person interacts with a piece of machinery, for example) as well as environmental factors such as noise and heat. This approach recognises that humans are fallible and systems need to be developed to take this into account.

Due to the importance of identifying the aetiology of errors/accidents, research has focused on identifying issues that may lead to system failures. Wiegmann, Zhang, & Van Thadden (2001) suggest three stages with a fourth stage being added later.

● *Stage 1*. This is the technical period where developments of new mechanical systems are rapid and most accidents are caused by mechanical malfunctions, especially in the design, construction and reliability of the equipment.

● *Stage 2*. This is the period of human error, where human faults rather than mechanical malfunctions cause the breakdown of the system.

● *Stage 3*. This is the socio-technical period. This stage considers the interaction of human and technical factors.

● *Stage 4*. This is the organisational culture period. This recognises that operators are not performing their duties or interacting with technology in isolation. They are working in a coordinated team that has a particular culture.

A further consideration may be organisational failure. Reason (1992) identified ten organisational failures, and three latent workplace factors that produce situations which can be used as early warning signs of an accident occurring. The organisational factors are:

1 organisational deficiencies
2 incompatible goals

   3 inadequate communications
   4 poor planning and scheduling
   5 inadequate control and monitoring
   6 design failures
   7 unsuitable materials
   8 poor operating procedures
   9 inadequate maintenance
  10 poor training.

The latent workplace factors are **violation-producing conditions,** where there is a lack of familiarity with the task, poor interface between human and the system, and irreversibility of errors. **Error-producing conditions** include a lack of organisational safety culture, management and staff conflict and poor supervision. **Inadequate defences** are where both human and technical elements fail to deal with an accident in terms of protection, warning, recovery and containment or escape. A model to explain why there may be inadequate defences was proposed by Reason (2000) and is known as the Swiss cheese model. The model explains errors occurring due to a series of events taking place in a particular order, which are lined up (such as holes in Swiss cheese). The model differentiates between two types of hole: latent failures and active failures. Latent failures represent existing failures, and active failures represent acute failures. Active failures are a result of unsafe acts committed by individuals and normally have a short-lived influence on the system.

Real Case 9.6

Active failure

The Chernobyl power plant disaster occurred on 26 April 1986 and was a result of human error. Facility operators switched off control systems of one of the plant's reactors. The reactor reached unstable, low power conditions, which triggered a power surge that led to a number of blasts that blew off the reactor's steel lid and led to leakage of radiation into the air.

Figure 9.2 (overleaf) shows an example of the trajectory of events that cause errors if the holes are lined up. This occurred in the Chernobyl disaster, as both human error and poor system designs such as poor alarm systems and poor safety procedures led to the trajectory of events being level, resulting in disaster.

However, if holes are in different places the continuation of events is not allowed and stops the error. Figure 9.3 (overleaf) shows an example of events that have been stopped.

For any major accident to occur, each error needs to penetrate defences. Therefore, developing systems that do not allow the continuation of errors is paramount. This has resulted in a focus on error management.

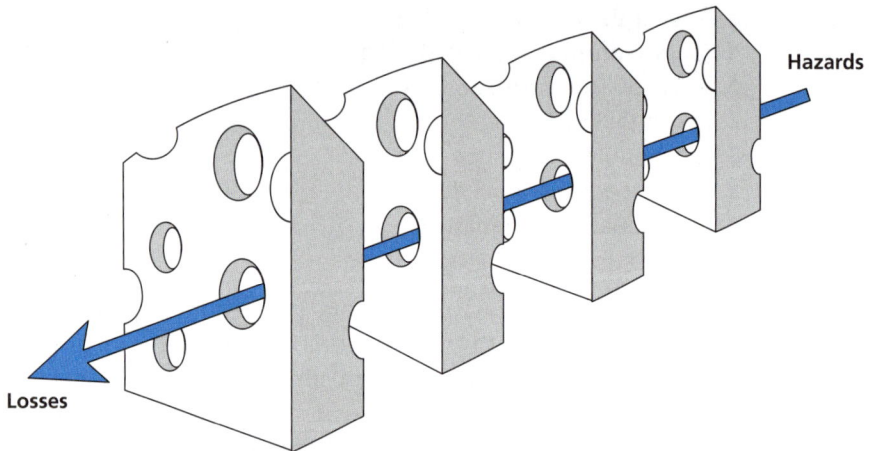

Figure 9.2 Swiss cheese trajectory of errors

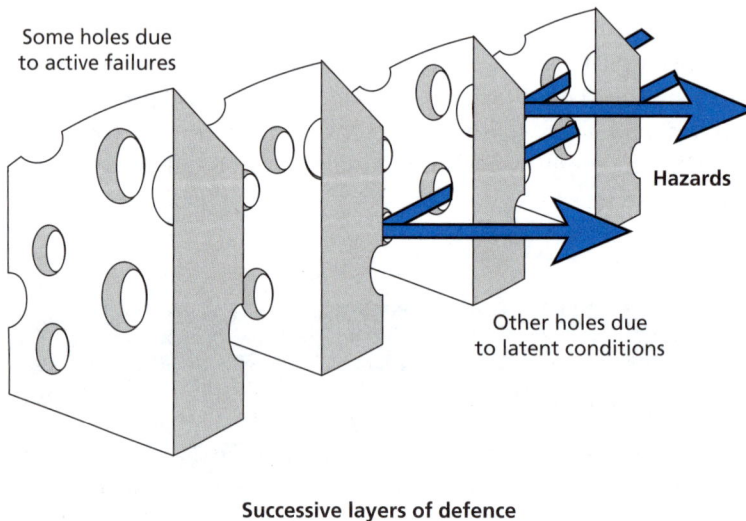

Figure 9.3 Swiss cheese stoppage of errors

9.6 Error management

Error management involves the use of all available data to enable us to understand the cause of errors including what actions we can take to reduce the likelihood of recurrence.

Error management, according to Reason (2000), is concerned with two main aspects. The first is to limit the incidence of errors occurring, and the second is to develop systems that can tolerate the occurrence of errors. For organisations to engage in error management, a safety culture is needed. Definitions of safety cultures have been diverse, with Pidgeon (1991) defining them as 'a set of beliefs, norms, attitudes, roles, social and technical practices that are concerned with minimising the exposure of employees, managers, customers and members of the public to conditions considered dangerous or injurious'. Carbrera, Isla, & Vilela (1997) suggested that a safety culture represents the shared perceptions of organisational members about their work environment and, more precisely, about their organisational safety policies.

The main impetus of the recognition of a safety culture as being important to error management was the statement from Judge Fennell after the fire at King's Cross. Fennel stated that 'a cultural change in management is required throughout the organisation' (Fennell, 1998: 127). In 2001, as a result of the investigation into the Ladbroke Grove rail accident (which occurred in 1999), there has been a focus of attention on the role of safety management and culture within the rail industry. Such a positive safety culture, according to Pidgeon and O'Leary (2000), is based on four factors:

1 senior management commitment to safety
2 realistic and flexible practices for handling well-defined and ill-defined hazards
3 continuous organisational learning through practices such as feedback systems, monitoring and analysing
4 a care and concern for hazards within the workplace.

According to Cooper (2000), there are three main components to a culture of safety. The first is based on the situational aspects, which is characterised by the organisational structure, its policies and procedures. The second is behavioural components that can be measured through observations and self-report question-naires. The third is the psychological component that measures a person's values, beliefs, norms and attitudes towards safety. Research has found that individuals' perceptions of a safety culture are associated with fewer work-related injuries and greater safety-related behaviours (Zohar, 1980, 2000). Zohar (1980) identified seven components for safety to be important within organisations: the organisation classifying safety training as important; management attitudes towards safety being positive; effects of safe employee conduct on promotion; identification of levels of risk at the workplace; the status of the safety office within the organisation; effects of safe conduct on social status; and the status of the safety committee. Zohar (2002) also found that the type of leadership style had an influence on the safety culture where safety-specific transformational leadership (see Chapter 11 – Management and leadership approaches) predicted occupational injuries through the effects of perceived safety climate, safety consciousness and safety-related events.

As can be seen there is an interaction of many factors – culture, leadership, individual and organisational – that contribute to how we respond to safety at work. However, a positive safety culture should be fostered to reduce injuries and increase an individual's well-being at work as well as to reduce error rates within organisations.

Multi-level impact of ergonomics

On an individual level, poor ergonomics can cause health-related illnesses such as musculoskeletal disorder, a reduction in worker productivity and job satisfaction. It can also result in increased work-related accidents. At an organisational level there may be an increase in work error rates, an increase in occupational accidents and increased financial costs due to sickness and litigation.

Legal context

The design of safe working environments is covered by a number of legislation directives. For further information, it is worth reading:

The Health and Safety at Work etc. Act (1974)
The Management of Health and Safety at Work Regulations (1999)
The Workplace (Health, Safety and Welfare) Regulations (1992) (Health and safety executive, 1992a)
The Manual Handling Operations Regulations (1992) (Health and safety executive, 1992b)
The Health and Safety (Display Screen Equipment) Regulations (1992) (Health and safety executive, 1992c)

Equality Act (2010). Further details of the Equality Act (2010) are discussed in Chapter 3 – Legislation applied to the workplace.

Short-answer questions

1 Discuss the four main categories of ergonomics.
2 Identify three health risks that can result due to a poorly designed work environment and suggest interventions.
3 Describe the stages of risk assessment and why it is important for risk assessments to be conducted.
4 Define the main sources of error within organisations.
5 Outline the Swiss Cheese Model and explain how to reduce the likelihood that errors will occur.

CASE STUDY
Design of environments and work

Sammie's telesales team employs more than 50 telesales staff. Much of the work involves using the telephone and using a computer to log bookings and contact details of follow-up calls. After working for the company for 18 months, Stephanie complained of aching shoulders, a painful neck, eye strain and headaches.

After an initial assessment, the following issues were identified.

- Stephanie holds the telephone between her ear and her shoulder when talking to potential customers.
- The computer display screen was difficult to read due to glare and reflections coming through the window next to Stephanie's desk.
- The chair Stephanie uses is not adjustable and she appears to be too low to reach the keyboard comfortably.

The task from this case study is to apply the consultancy cycle and write a report providing an analysis of the issues facing this organisation on selection and retention of staff.

For details of the consultancy cycle please refer to Chapter 2, which provides a comprehensive overview. Chapter 2 also provides details regarding the structure of a business report which you will find useful for this task.

For an example of a consultancy report please refer to Chapter 14 – Example consultancy reports.

10

Motivation, job satisfaction, employee engagement and behaviour modification

Learning outcomes

After reading this chapter, you should be able to:

- critically evaluate the major theories of motivation and job satisfaction
- describe the impact of motivation and job satisfaction on employees and the organisation
- suggest interventions to increase motivation and job satisfaction in organisations
- describe the concept of employee engagement
- be able to recommend interventions to increase employee engagement.

10.1 Introduction

Marc, an operations manager for a petrol tanker company, has noticed a downturn in performance, an increase in absenteeism and has heard staff complain about how they are not enjoying their work driving heavy goods vehicles. It has also become noticeable that staff are comparing their bonuses, which are based on performance, which has caused a lot of conflict regarding inequity in payments. Marc will need to look into this issue in more depth and make changes in the organisation to increase motivation and satisfaction. What theory could you apply to this and what changes would you make?

10.2 Motivation

Motivation at work refers to 'psychological forces that direct a person's behaviour in an organisation, a person's level of effort, and a person's level of persistence in the face of obstacles' (Jones & George, 2004). Effort and persistence differ from person to person and from situation to situation. For example, a sales executive may be motivated to sell products in order to meet their sales target and achieve their bonus, but once their target has been met they may no longer be motivated to sell. Sources of motivation may come from within a person (intrinsic) or from external sources (extrinsic) where a person tries to gain a reward or avoid a punishment. From a management perspective, intrinsic motivation is more difficult to encourage. A manager can attempt to provide work that stimulates an individual's intrinsic motivation, but cannot create the motivation for them. In terms of extrinsic motivation, a manager can develop rewards that will increase an individual's motivation to perform.

Although the idea of motivation seems relatively simple, in terms of internal drives and external factors, managers need to understand how motivation can be developed in order to increase performance and commitment to an organisation. Many theories of motivation have been put forward to understand an individual's behaviour at work and these can be categorised into content and process theories. Content theories explain the specific factors that motivate individuals and assume that all individuals possess the same set of needs, which suggests that certain characteristics should be present in all work. Process theories, however, focus on differences in the needs of individuals and take a cognitive approach to explain those differences.

Theories categorised within the individual need (content) camp include:

- Maslow's (1943) Hierarchy of Needs theory
- Alderfer's (1969) ERG theory
- McClelland's (1978) Three Needs theory.

Theories categorised within the cognitive (process) camp include:

- Vroom's (1964) Expectancy theory
- Adams' (1965) Equity theory
- Locke's (1976) Goal Setting theory
- Skinner's (1953) Reinforcement theory.

These will now be discussed in more detail.

Content theories

Maslow

One of the main theories of motivation is Maslow's (1943) Hierarchy of Needs (see Figure 10.1, overleaf) (overleaf). Maslow argued that all individuals are driven by needs and a need is something that an individual requires. On fulfilment of the need, satisfaction ensues. Maslow's hierarchy consists of five levels of need that represent a pyramid.

At first glance, the hierarchy does not appear to be related to the workplace; however, each need can be represented by different work factors. For example, the physiological needs include providing lunch breaks and payment for work; security needs include providing a safe working environment and job security; love and belonging needs represent a feeling of belonging within the organisation and team spirit; esteem needs represent recognition of achievements and status within an organisation; and self-

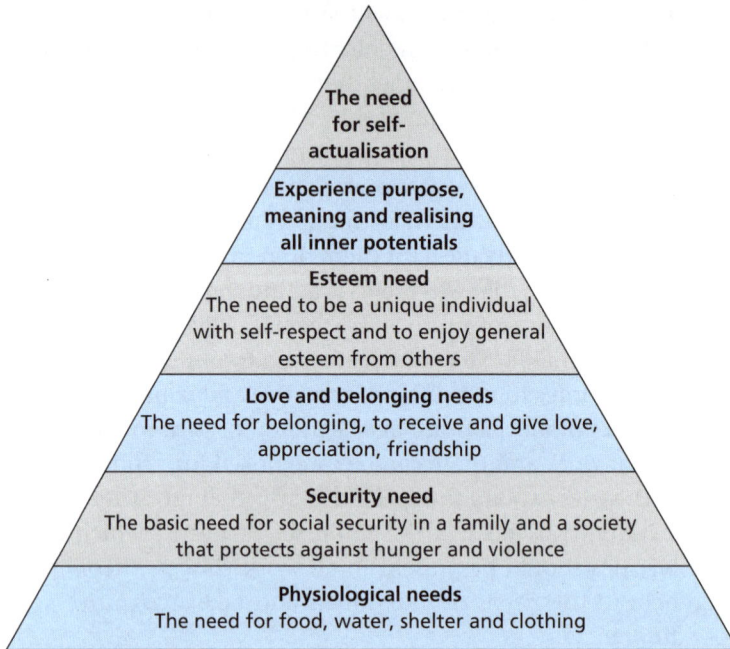

Figure 10.1 Maslow's (1943) hierarchy of needs

actualisation provides individuals with challenging and innovative work. According to Maslow's theory, once a need has been satisfied it stops becoming a motivating force and the next need will be activated. Thus, for managers to motivate employees, the manager needs to determine the rewards related to the level at which each individual is. This may be a different level of the hierarchy for each employee.

Many criticisms of Maslow's approach have been put forward and developments of the theory have been made by Alderfer (1969), discussed later in this section.

Criticisms of Maslow's approach

Criticisms of Maslow's theory focus on both the needs as well as the scientific evidence. Criticisms include:

- Only one need can be motivated at a time, thus a person may require a safe working environment, but does not need to have the feeling of belongingness at work.
- The concept is difficult to test and thus questions its scientific value to understanding motivation.
- The needs are argued to be innate, thus individuals have little control over them or in what order they achieve them.
- Although it appears plausible that we would first take care of our lower needs, such as physiological needs, there are examples where this is not the case – such as an artist who feels fulfilled by the art that they do (self-actualisation), but lives in poverty (physiological).
- This approach does not account for individuals who regress down the hierarchy due to situations such as redundancy or retirement.

Alderfer

Alderfer's (1969) ERG theory was a revision of Maslow's theory. Alderfer classified individual's needs into three categories: existence, relatedness and growth (ERG). Existence refers to our concerns of material existence motivators; relatedness is our motivation for maintaining interpersonal relationships; and the growth need represents our desire for personal development. As can be seen in Figure 10.2, the needs identified by Maslow are basically reduced down to three tiers.

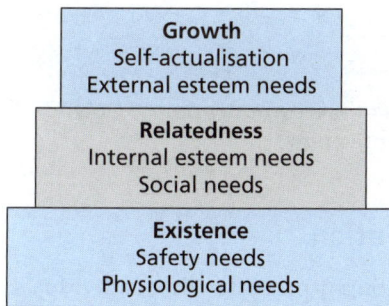

Growth
Self-actualisation
External esteem needs

Relatedness
Internal esteem needs
Social needs

Existence
Safety needs
Physiological needs

Figure 10.2 Alderfer's ERG theory diagram

Alderfer suggested that, as you start to satisfy needs higher in the hierarchy, they become more powerful rather than the motivating force decreasing as suggested by Maslow (for example, if you have control, you want more control). This theory also allows individuals to pursue different level of needs and acknowledges that people will differ in the order of needs, thus the self-actualised artist situation can be encompassed into this theory. There is also acknowledgement that if an individual fails to achieve a higher need or if a situation of redundancy arises, they could regress to lower needs that are easier to satisfy. The practicalities for managers are that they must recognise that individuals have different needs that are fluid.

McClelland

McClelland also disagreed with Maslow's theory, stating that needs are not necessarily innate, but can be learned and socially acquired. This theory is known as the Achievement Motivation Theory (also called Manifest Need Theory). These needs are classified into three categories: need for achievement (n-Ach), need for power (n-Pow), and need for affiliation (n-Aff). Individuals with a high need for achievement (n-Ach) seek to excel and succeed at work. They set themselves challenging, but achievable goals; they like to work independently or with others who are high achievers and feel rewarded when they achieve their goal. Individuals with a high need for power (n-Pow) like to lead others and have power. Power for these individuals falls into two categories. The first is personal power, which they achieve by having power over other people. The second is organisational power, where they want to direct teams of people in order to achieve the objectives of the organisation. Individuals with a need for affiliation (n-Aff) prefer working with and having friendly interactions with other people. These individuals are team players, sociable and want to be liked. Individuals with a need for achievement are suited to jobs such as sales where they are given challenging but achievable goals. Those with a need for power operate well as managers or team leaders, and those with a need for affiliation are suited to roles such as customer services.

This theory has made an important contribution to the need theories of motivation as it suggests that individuals have control over their needs, rather than Maslow's innate assumption that individuals lack control. Control over one's motivation has also been the view of the process theories of motivation.

Stop and reflect

Think about a job you have had or are currently doing. Do you think the needs approach contributes to your motivation?

Process theories of motivation

Process theories focus on the thought processes that individuals use when going through a set of alternative choices, suggesting that motivation is under the control of the individual, but can be affected by external factors.

Adams

In Adams' (1965) Equity theory, it was argued that individuals have beliefs relating to the fairness of treatment they receive at work. A balance in fairness motivates an individual. An imbalance reduces an individual's motivation. The main factors within this theory are input and output, where people calculate the amount of effort they put into their work compared with how much they are getting out. Effort can relate to time, performance, education whereas outputs include compensation, recognitions and perks (see Figure 10.3). Employees go through a process of evaluating their input–output ratio with similar employees. If one employee is perceived as receiving equal output for equal input, fairness is achieved and the scales are balanced, whereas if there is inequality between employees motivation reduces.

When an employee is under-rewarded for their contribution, anger and frustration occur. For example, you have been in your job for ten years when a new employee begins work. The employee is the same age and gender, and has

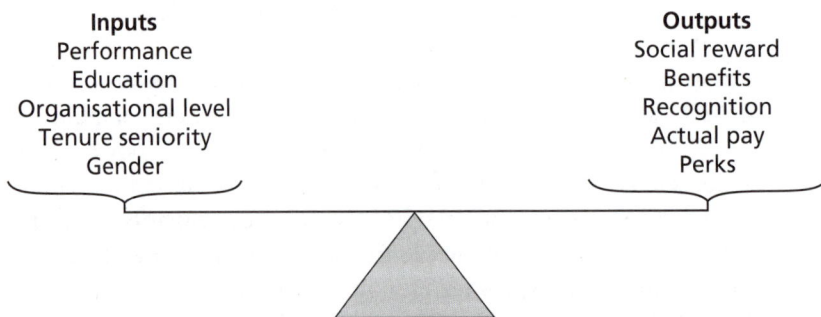

Inputs	Outputs
Performance	Social reward
Education	Benefits
Organisational level	Recognition
Tenure seniority	Actual pay
Gender	Perks

Figure 10.3 Balance of inputs–outputs: Adams' Equity theory

the same educational background, but has less work experience than you and is paid £5k more than you per annum. This would result in a feeling of inequity and a reduction in motivation. Such a reduction in motivation can also reduce an individual's feelings of commitment and loyalty to the organisation, which means they are more likely to seek employment elsewhere and are less likely to go above and beyond their duties to achieve at work. If an employee is over-rewarded for their input a sense of guilt can be felt, which also creates an imbalance. This may result in the individual working harder to even out the input–output ratio. Therefore, organisations need to develop reward systems that are both equitable and fair and whereby employees value the outcomes. This may be more important now than ever because under the Equality Act 2010 (Government Equalities Office, 2010) individuals can freely discuss their salary without any negative impact on them from the organisation.

Locke

An alternative view known as the Goal Setting theory was put forward by Locke (1976), and suggests that an individual's behaviour is motivated by their goals. A goal represents something that an individual wants to achieve. For example, this could be to meet a sales target of £20k each month, or to finish a report by 4pm on Friday. However, there are differing goals. For example, goals can be specific or general (specific = the report to be finished by 4pm on Friday; general = the report requires completion). Goals can also vary in difficulty from easy to achieve to difficult. Goals that are challenging but achievable increase motivation and lead to better performance. A major factor affecting performance in the achievement of goals is the role of feedback in motivating individuals. If feedback is given, performance is increased more than when feedback is not received by the worker, because feedback enables the individual to understand how close they are to achieving their goal or what changes they need to make to achieve their goals. The reason that goal setting theory may increase motivation in employees is that it allows the individual to direct their attention and focus their effort on achieving that goal. A good example of goal setting theory is the company WeightWatchers, where an individual has an overall goal of losing a certain amount of weight (say 14lb). The goal is then split down into smaller sub-goals of weight loss of 2lb per week over a seven-week period. This target is challenging, but achievable. Locke and Latham (2006) identified eight categories of study that have moved this theory forward.

1 *Goal choice*: suggests that self-efficacy, past performances and social influence affect the level of goals that are set.
2 *Learning goals*: suggests that difficult goals do not always lead to increased performance, but simply urging people to do their best may do so.
3 *Framing*: suggests providing people with difficult goals may be effective when individuals view them as threatening.
4 *Affect*: suggests that individuals who perceive a goal as difficult to attain view a change in affect.
5 *Group goals*: suggest that goal setting is also effective with groups.

6 *Goals and traits*: suggest that people with a learning orientation choose tasks that require the acquisition of knowledge and skill. Individuals with a performance orientation avoid tasks where people may judge them unfavourably because of errors they may make.

7 *Macro-level goals*: suggest that an organisation's vision and low levels of dysfunctional optimism is partially mediated by the setting of co-operative goals.

8 *Goals and subconscious priming*: suggests that a goal does not have to be in a person's conscious awareness every second.

Vroom

A further model of motivation was developed by Vroom (1964). This represented a mathematical model of motivation at work known as the Expectancy theory. According to this theory, expected rewards lead to behaviours by focusing on cognitive states that lead to motivation. In short, individuals are motivated when they believe that they will be rewarded or have desirable outcomes. If there is a lack of belief, then they will not be motivated to behave in a certain way. The mathematical equation developed for this theory is:

$$\text{motivation} = \text{expectancy} \times \Sigma \, (\text{valence} \times \text{instrumentality})$$

Expectancy is the belief about the outcome of the behaviour (I will get an additional £100); valence is the value the individual assigns to the outcome of the behaviour (I value an additional £100); instrumentality is the belief that the outcome received for performing the behaviour will occur again if the behaviour is exhibited (if I do the same again I will get £100). Thus, if an individual performs well at a task they will be rewarded for their performance and the rewards will continue when they perform at that level again. Vroom argued that if a reward is not valued by the individual, this reduces the motivation to perform.

A more recent development of Vroom's theory and one that removes the mathematical model is that of Green (2000). Green suggested that instead of individuals having expectations they have beliefs. The first belief is confidence – that is, the confidence that the effort put into a task will lead to better performance. The second concerns the relationship between performance and outcomes where managers give employees rewards for good performance. By providing relevant rewards, trust is also maintained between the employee and manager. Finally, the satisfaction belief is the belief that outcome (reward) provided by the manager should satisfy the employee. It is therefore important for managers to realise that employees will be satisfied by different outcomes. However, there are situations where this does not occur, which can lead to a reduction in motivation. For example, a student has put a lot of effort into an assignment (researching the topic area and time spent) and is confident that they have done well (the reward would be a good grade). On receipt of the feedback, the student receives a lower grade than expected, which leads to dissatisfaction. Feedback is important here as the student may have put a lot of effort into the assessment, but lacked understanding of the topic area. In this scenario, effort does not always link to reward.

Skinner

The above theories are based on the early theory of reinforcement by Skinner (1953), known as the law of effect, where individual behaviour that is followed by positive consequences is likely to be repeated, whereas individual behaviour followed by negative consequences is not likely to be repeated. For example, an individual works late on a Friday to ensure that a project deadline is met. The individual receives praise from their manager for putting in the extra time and completing the project. The positive consequence of praise would encourage the individual to repeat this behaviour in the future. The flip side to this would be the manager nagging the individual to be more productive and, once they are, the nagging stops. This negative consequence of nagging would likely result in the behaviour not being exhibited in the future. The positive consequence represents positive reinforcement and the negative consequence negative reinforcement. Two other methods within the reinforcement theory that can be used to control behaviour are punishment and extinction. Punishment represents the removal of positive consequences and applying undesirable consequences. In the example of the individual staying late on Friday to complete the task, punishment would represent reducing the payment of the individual's salary due to not meeting the project deadlines within the normal working hours between 9am and 5pm. The final method is that of extinction. Extinction represents the absence of reinforcements. For example, the individual does not receive any praise for staying late to complete the project; he may feel that the behaviour is not being rewarded so is unlikely to exhibit that behaviour again in the future. The benefit of this theory is that it allows us to understand how people learn behaviour. An alternative set of theories to the content and process theories, and ones that are based on more up-to-date research, are the job design theories.

10.3 Job design theories

The job design theory addresses four main questions.

1 What motivates people to work?
2 What job characteristics are significant (e.g. autonomy, task significance, career progression)?
3 How can alternatives of job design be identified (e.g. analysis of procedures and work processes, technical analysis, scanning of organisational culture and structure)?
4 What job design changes can be implemented (e.g. increased communication channels, increased opportunity for promotion)?

The job characteristics model (Hackman & Oldham, 1976) is based on the notion that the work task is important for employee motivation. Research has suggested that jobs that are monotonous and boring reduce the motivation of employees, whereas making the job more interesting and meaningful increases

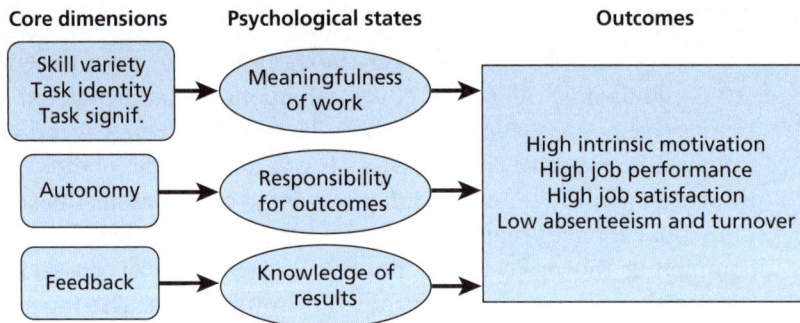

Figure 10.4 Job characteristics model (Hackman and Oldham)

motivation. According to Hackman and Oldham (1976), there are five main core dimensions that impact on three critical psychological states, as can be seen in Figure 10.4.

High levels of motivation occur when experiencing the three psychological states when working. Meaningfulness of work applies to work that you can relate to and understand how it contributes to the organisation as a whole; responsibility for outcomes refer to an individual's autonomy to make choices about how to carry out the work; knowledge of results refers to providing feedback on how well an individual has performed as well as providing an emotional connection with the customer or client. These three psychological states are derived from the core dimensions identified in Figure 10.4. Skill variety refers to using a variety of your skills so that you do not become bored, but not so many that you become overwhelmed; task identity involves identifying with the work so that you take pride in the task; task significance is the understanding of how your individual task is contributing to something bigger such as the goals of the company. Autonomy refers to your level of freedom in making decisions and scheduling your own work, whereas feedback refers to knowledge of how effective your performance has been. Having the right individual level of core dimensions, as well as the three psychological states, results in the positive outcomes identified in Figure 10.4. These relate to both individual (motivation and performance) as well as organisational (outcomes and low absenteeism). If there are any negative issues with any of these components, then changes need to be made so that outcomes remain positive. Some of these changes may involve:

- varying the type of work that individuals undertake so that they can use a variety of their skills
- providing individuals with autonomy over how they conduct their work
- linking an individual's work to the overall goals of the department/organisation.

Although some strategies that increase motivation of individuals have been suggested, research has also been carried out into managing individuals' motivation within organisations.

10.4 Managing motivation within organisations

Linder (1998) conducted a survey to assess motivational factors and their level of importance. The participants were asked to rank motivating factors from most motivating to least motivating. Ten factors were rated from most to least motivating, which allows for strategies to be developed by managers to increase motivation in the workplace.

- Having interesting work
  Strategy: develop specific goals for individuals and teams.
- Having a good level of pay
  Strategy: provide incentive pay where pay is linked to performance.
- Being appreciated for work done well
  Strategy: provide feedback, recognition, reward and promotion.
- Having job security
  Strategy: provide levels of job security relevant to the current economic climate
- Having good working conditions
  Strategy: provide appropriate resources to carry out work and a safe working environment.
- Having loyalty between employers and employees
  Strategy: share information between employees and employers.
- Having fair discipline
  Strategy: be clear and consistent on appropriate behaviour and relevant disciplinary action.
- Being sympathetic with employees' personal problems
  Strategy: show interest in employees and develop positive relationships.
- Opportunities for promotion and growth within the organisation
  Strategy: provide training and development opportunities for staff.
- Feelings of inclusivity
  Strategy: involve employees in decision-making.

By adopting these strategies, positive outcomes, as identified by Hackman and Oldham (1976), can be attained for both employers and their employees.

More recently, Glanz (2002) developed the CARE (**C**reative Communication, **A**tmosphere and appreciation, **R**espect and reason for being, **E**mpathy and enthusiasm) model, which helps managers to motivate their employees and reduce turnover of staff. The model involves managers being open and honest in their communication strategies; showing appreciation to staff and recognising their hard work; learning about individual employees' strengths and weaknesses; valuing employees; providing the relevant resources for them to undertake their work; and fulfilling individual needs. The CARE model, in particular, is easy to implement and is a cost-effective way to increase motivation and job satisfaction at work. When considering work motivation, the link with job satisfaction needs thought as it is difficult to separate the two. For example, if an employee is satisfied, they are more likely to be motivated. However, much of the literature has considered the two independently. Thus, for the purpose of clarity, job satisfaction will be considered separately to work motivation in this chapter, but both should be considered as affecting the other.

10.5 Job satisfaction

Many definitions of job satisfaction have been put forward, but the most inclusive definition by Locke (1976) is 'a pleasurable or positive emotional state resulting from the appraisal of one's job or job experiences'. Put simply, job satisfaction refers to how happy a person is with their job. The more happy a person is, the more satisfied they are.

Job satisfaction has also been related to positive outcomes in the workplace. For example, it has been linked to an increase in productivity (Judge & Bono, 2001), increased life satisfaction (Judge & Church, 2000), and a reduction in absenteeism (Hardy, Woods, & Walls, 2003). Job performance is a major concern for organisations because, in order to remain viable and competitive, organisations need high levels of efficiency and quality in their production. This relationship between job satisfaction and job performance has been a focus of numerous researchers. Judge and Bono (2001) found a correlation of .30, which suggests there is a relationship between satisfaction and performance. However, according to Bowling (2007), after controlling for factors such as personality, work, locus of control and organisation-based self-esteem, the job satisfaction– performance relationship is eliminated. This suggests that other factors need to be considered when measuring associations that theories of job satisfaction have tried to achieve. One of the early theories of job satisfaction is Herzberg's (1974) who suggested that people's level of motivation and job satisfaction is a result of two main factors. The first is Motivation where six main factors were identified and Hygiene is the second factor where six main factors were identified and can be seen in Figure 10.5.

According to the two factor theory, individual employees are satisfied by motivation factors such as recognition, responsibility and achievement, which represent intrinsic factors. Feelings of dissatisfaction are associated with hygiene

Factors leading to dissatisfaction (hygiene)	Factors leading to satisfaction (motivation)
• Company policy • Supervision • Relationship with boss • Work conditions • Salary • Relationship with peers	• Achievement • Recognition • Work itself • Responsibility • Advancement • Growth

Figure 10.5 Two factor theory (Herzberg)

factors such as working conditions, salary and company policies, which represent extrinsic factors. Herzberg suggested that the factors leading to job satisfaction are independent of those leading to job dissatisfaction. Therefore, if managers remove factors that dissatisfy individuals it may not result in motivation or satisfaction as they are independent of each other. Therefore, if we want to motivate and satisfy people we need to concentrate on the intrinsic factors such as allowing people opportunities for advancement and recognising their achievements. This particular theory interlinks motivation and job satisfaction.

Job satisfaction theories are categorised into three main approaches. The first is the dispositional approach that purports that job satisfaction is innate. The second approach is the social information processing approach that suggests that job satisfaction is due to a person's job and factors in their environment. The third approach is the interactive approach where there is interplay of innate factors and situational factors. These will now be discussed in detail.

Dispositional model

The dispositional model assumes that by measuring an individual's characteristics, job satisfaction can be predicted. One reason for such a prediction comes from an individual's genetic makeup. For example, Avery, Abraham, Bouchard, & Segal (1989) in a study of monozygotic twins reared apart, found that even when the twins were not raised together they had job satisfaction scores that correlated positively. This suggests that job satisfaction is consistent over time as well as situations. Evidence was found by Straw and Ross (1985) that job satisfaction was reported over both situation and time over periods of three and five years.

However, it is not clear in the literature how dispositions affect job performance.

Social information processing model

The social information processing model suggests that individuals socially construct the world around them. Individuals look to their co-workers to make sense of their work environment, which leads to the development of attitudes about their work. If an individual's co-workers are positive about their work and their work environment, then the individual is more likely to be satisfied, whereas if an individual's co-workers are negative, they are more likely to be dissatisfied (Jex, 2002).

Integrated approach

The integrated approach represents a combination of the dispositional model and the social information processing model.

As job satisfaction has been linked to performance, development of measures to assess job satisfaction has been extensive.

10.6 Measurement of job satisfaction

The measurement of job satisfaction is important within organisations so that positive/negative attitudes of individuals towards their work and working environment can be assessed. Measurements can either be qualitative or quantitative. Quantitative approaches include rating scales where individuals are asked to rate their attitude to certain aspects of their job. For example, 'I am happy with the level of autonomy I have to carry out my work'. This would be scored on a rating scale from 'completely disagree' to 'completely agree'. Qualitative approaches include interviews with staff members on their attitude to their work and concentrates on what makes an individual happy or unhappy in their work. The second approach is a more subjective approach and relies on individuals feeling comfortable in disclosing how they feel about their work.

Measurement of job satisfaction can adopt two approaches. The first is the global approach that assesses an individual's overall satisfaction with their job, whereas the facet approach assesses an individual's satisfaction with certain aspects of their job such as their level of autonomy, their salary and benefits and their relationships with their colleagues. Although the global approach tells us whether a person is satisfied or dissatisfied, it will not provide information relating to changes that could be made to increase satisfaction, whereas the facet approach can identify areas of satisfaction and dissatisfaction so that actions can be taken.

Many questionnaires have been developed to assess satisfaction at work including the Job Descriptive Index (JDI) developed by Smith, Kendall, & Hulin (1969), which adopts a facet approach to measurement. Five facets are measured: promotion, pay, supervision, the work itself and co-workers. Individuals are asked to answer 'Yes', 'No' or 'Can't decide' to a series of statements that describe an individual's job. Using a facet approach in the measurement of job satisfaction, organisations can assess individual aspects of an individual's job that contribute to satisfaction/dissatisfaction and can implement interventions to manage or change aspects of a person's work and work environment.

10.7 Managing job satisfaction within organisations

As job satisfaction is an important aspect of an employee's well-being and performance in the workplace, it is important that it is managed within organisations. This can be achieved through many factors such as:

- *The company's policy:* policies that show equity and fairness.
- *Working conditions:* ensuring safe working conditions and having appropriate equipment to carry out tasks.
- *Achievement:* recognising individual achievements and ensuring employees are in the correct positions that allow individuals to use their skills.

- *Autonomy:* allowing individuals to be responsible for their work and choose how to carry out their work tasks.
- *Employee benefits:* competitive salary, pension and work–life policies.

The importance of both employee motivation and job satisfaction is also related to the emerging area of employee engagement.

10.8 Employee engagement

Employee engagement refers to an approach that ensures employees are committed to their work and organisation and are motivated to succeed. This increases an individual's self-worth and well-being. In other words, it is a positive attitude held by employees towards their organisation and their work. Kahn (1990) defines employee engagement as 'the harnessing of organisation members' selves to their work roles; in engagement people employ and express themselves physically, cognitively and emotionally during role performance'. The physical aspect refers to the energy an individual puts into their work; the cognitive aspect refers to the beliefs the individual has about the organisation such as the vision of the organisation, its working conditions, and the way of doing things (policies and procedures) within the organisation; the emotional aspect refers to the attitudes individuals have towards an organisation. This may influence the individual's behaviour where they may put in extra work, feel more motivated and satisfied with their job.

One of the most comprehensive research studies of employee engagement is the Gallup Organisation (2004) survey, which uses the Q12 instrument. The Q12 survey assesses how satisfied individuals are with their jobs, which consider whether employee needs are being met as well as their emotional commitment to the organisation. Results of the research show that when employees score in the top half on employee engagement they have 56% higher success rate with customer loyalty, 50% higher success rate on productivity outcomes, 44% higher success rate with employee turnover and a 33% higher success rate on productivity outcomes (Coffman & Gonzalez-Malina, 2002). Harter, Schmidt, & Hayes (2002) conducted a meta-analysis on the Gallup studies and also found that high levels of employee engagement resulted in customer satisfaction, productivity, profitability and good safety outcomes. Thus, it is important that organisations create and encourage employee engagement.

Salkey (2005) suggested four dimensions for creating employee engagement:

- *Line of sight:* 'I know what I do to contribute to business goals and outcomes'.
- *Involvement:* 'I know I can make decisions to influence business results'.
- *Share information:* 'I have the information I need to guide my decisions'.
- *Reward and recognition:* 'I know I will be rewarded for my contribution'.

? Think about it

Do you think there are any other dimensions that may contribute to employee engagement? Why are these important?

The main focus of the four dimensions is to make the employee feel that they, as individual employees, are contributing to the overall business objectives and that they feel empowered to make decisions on how to carry out their work based on sound business information. It is also important for individuals to feel recognised for their work. This is where employee engagement is influenced by theories of motivation and job satisfaction – for example, Adams (1965) Equity theory (discussed earlier in this chapter), where individuals are motivated if they believe their input into the job is rewarded equitably. If the outputs are equitable (compared with similar workers), then the individual will feel satisfied with their job and be engaged within their organisation. If they are inequitable (to others in a similar role) negative behaviours may be exhibited such as withdrawal from the organisation.

According to Robinson, Perryman, & Hayday (2004), behaviours associated with employee engagement include being helpful to work colleagues, willing to put in extra work and time for the organisation, a desire to work to make things better and keeping up to date with advancements in the field. Robinson's research also found that an employee's feeling of being valued is a key driver of engagement. The benefits of employee engagement include increased efficiency, higher productivity, higher customer satisfaction and lower turnover rates (Buhler, 2006). A study by Towers Perrin (2007) of 50 international organisations in different industries found over a one-year period that those organisations with higher employee engagement had a 19% increase in operating profits whereas companies with lower levels of employee engagement had decreased operating profits by 32%. Therefore, employee engagement is key to the survival and operations of an organisation.

In order to increase/maintain employee engagement, Seijts and Crim (2006) put forward the 10 C's of engagement.

1 *Connect.* Leaders must show that they value their employees.
2 *Career.* Leaders provide meaningful and challenging work and opportunities for career development.
3 *Clarity.* Leaders should communicate a clear vision so that employees know what they need to achieve.
4 *Convey.* Leaders clarify their expectations about employees and provide them with feedback so that they can improve on tasks or their skills.
5 *Congratulate.* Leaders should provide praise and recognition for good performance.
6 *Contribute.* Leaders should make clear how the individual is contributing to the overall business objectives so their contribution feels valued.
7 *Control.* Employees have control over the pace of their work.
8 *Collaborate.* Leaders to encourage team work.
9 *Credibility.* Leaders strive to maintain the company's reputation and ethical standards.
10 *Confidence.* Leaders create confidence in the organisation by promoting good ethical standards.

Employee engagement (Baker & Warga, 2010)

Harrah's International is the largest provider of branded casino equipment, and employs over 65,000 employees worldwide. The challenge for the company was to double the size of its existing casino in Chester, Pennsylvania. With new legislation in table games it had the opportunity to increase staff by 700. The objectives were to hire 600 staff in 120 days who were upbeat and positive and create a fun environment. Providing an online platform to engage people during their new employment training, and creating a model for employee feedback, resulted in an increase in scores on the employee feedback survey and established employee loyalty.

As employee engagement is important to organisational commitment and the business as a whole, it is key that managers adopt the ten approaches to ensure employees feel engaged within their organisation.

10.9 Behaviour modification

Behaviour modification is based on the principle of learning. Behaviour modification involves the use of behaviour change techniques that either increase or decrease behaviours. Within an organisational setting, behaviour modification is important in increasing motivation, morale and productivity. This can be achieved by minimising negative behaviours and maximising positive behaviours. A number of methods to achieve these outcomes have been put forward.

Nearly 100 years ago, Pavlov (1927) conditioned dogs to salivate at the sound of a bell. To do so, Pavlov presented food with the presentation of the bell and eventually the dog salivated (in anticipation of food) on the sound of the bell whether food was presented or not. Thorndike (1911) focused on the law of effect which argued that when behaviour leads to desirable consequences it is more likely to be repeated. For example, if an employee performs a job well and is praised for their efforts, the positive consequence of praise will increase the likelihood that the behaviour will be exhibited again. This is known as reinforcement, which can be either positive or negative. Positive reinforcement is where a behaviour is followed by a reinforcer, which results in the behaviour being strengthened. Negative reinforcement is followed by a removal or reduction in aversive stimulus (such as intense heat within a manufacturing plant) which reinforces a person's behaviour (carry on working). Thus, negative reinforcement strengthens a behaviour because a negative condition is stopped or avoided as a consequence of the behaviour. However, certain factors impact on the effectiveness of the reinforcement – for example, the time between the behaviour and the reinforcer. For a reinforcer to be effective it should be immediate. The longer the delay, the less effective the reinforcer is.

The use of reinforcement was further developed by Watson and Rayner (1920) who tested the role of conditioning on humans. This was known as the 'little Albert' study. Watson conditioned Albert to fear white rats by exhibiting unpleasant noises on the presentation of white rats. The unpleasant noises represent a negative consequence that Albert associated with the white rats. Albert became afraid of the rats, showing that both positive and negative conditioning is possible. In the 1930s, Skinner, based on the work of his predecessor, made a significant contribution to psychology with the theory of behaviour modification. Using animals (rats) and birds (pigeons), Skinner found that the consequences of behaviour predicted behaviour. This was shown when Skinner placed a rat inside a box that is now termed the 'Skinner box'. The box had a lever at the side. While the rat moved around the box it would accidentally move the lever and a food pellet would drop into the container next to the lever. The rats soon learned to go straight to the lever after a couple of times in the box. Thus, the positive consequence of receiving food meant that the rats would perform the behaviour repeatedly. In a work situation, if an employer gave you £1,000 bonus each time that you completed a project on time, you would more likely work harder to complete the project. A further reinforcement is the removal of a negative consequence. Negative reinforcement strengthens the behaviour because it stops an aversive consequence. For example, if you do not complete the project on time, you give your employer £1,000. Whereas positive and negative reinforcement strengthens behaviour, punishment weakens behaviour or eliminates it entirely. For example, an employee is told that they will have to forfeit their holiday if they do not complete the project on time. However, Bandura (1971) argued that behaviour modification is a result of learning by copying or imitating what others do – for example, observing a role model in the workplace exhibiting a desirable behaviour.

More modern views of operant conditioning that relate to workplace behaviour modification were posited by Luthans and Kreitner (1985). The basic premise involves five main steps: 1) the identification of critical performance-related behaviours; 2) measuring the frequency of those behaviours; 3) the analysis of antecedents and consequences associated with the behaviour; 4) the application of positive consequences when the desired behaviour is exhibited (positive consequences include money, performance, feedback and recognition); 5) the evaluation of changes to the behaviour in relation to its impact on the individual's performance. However, for behaviour to change, it needs to be understood in relation to a specific context – for example, dealing with conduct problems in employees. One such assessment of behaviour is the ABC method. A-B-C represents Antecedent, Behaviour, and Consequence. Antecedent refers to what happens before the behaviour occurs. Behaviour refers to what actions a person does or what they say. Consequences refers to what happens after the behaviour.

Workplace example of the A-B-C method of behaviour modification

Antecedent	A new performance-related bonus is announced to staff
Behaviour	Employee performs to the required standards
Consequence	The performance-related bonus is awarded to the staff member.

Although the five-step approach by Luthans and Kreitner (1985) appears reasonable, Martin and Pear (2007) suggested seven characteristics that need consideration in behaviour modification:

1 A strong emphasis on defining problems related to behaviour that can be measured in some way.
2 Treatment techniques provide ways of changing an individual's environment to help them to function more efficiently.
3 The methods and rationale can be described.
4 The techniques are applied to everyday life.
5 The techniques are based on the principles of learning.
6 There is a strong emphasis on scientific techniques and demonstration that these have caused the behaviour change.
7 Strong emphasis on individual accountability for everyone in the behaviour change programme.

A key aspect of behaviour modification is measuring the behaviour before strategies for change are implemented. This measurement is needed to ensure that what you have implemented has had a direct impact and is not due to other factors.

Workplace example of a behaviour change assessment

Samuel, a manager of a food processing company, notices that some of his staff members were turning up to work late on a Monday morning. Before taking any action, Samuel records the arrival times of all staff members over a period of four weeks. Samuel found that certain members were consistently late on a Monday morning. Therefore, a behaviour change plan could be developed. To assess whether change has been successful, the arrival times of members of staff would be recorded during implementation of the plan and after implementation, to ascertain whether the behaviour change has occurred.

There are, however, limitations to behaviour modification at work. These include being able to reinforce only observable behaviours. Thus, individuals who perform more cognitive-focused tasks will not be able to change using this method. If the reinforcement is used regularly, the novelty wears off and individuals come to expect that reinforcement. Therefore, it is essential for reinforcements to change. Employees do not have to learn self-discipline as they do not have to identify ways in which to correct their own behaviour.

There are also ethical considerations such as a manager's ability to manipulate individuals using reward and punishment.

Multi-level impact of motivation, job satisfaction and employee engagement

Motivation, job satisfaction and employee engagement can affect individuals, management and the organisation. From an individual perspective, a lack of motivation can lead to a decline in job satisfaction and employee engagement. Individuals may withdraw from the organisation, have a reduction in quantity and quality of goods which may lead to an increase in waste products, show increased absenteeism and lack commitment to the organisation. This may also affect management, as it will need to ensure the operations of the organisation are still running smoothly as well as ensuring employees are satisfied and motivated to ensure commitment to the organisation. This means that the manager will need to understand the needs of employees as well as those of the organisation and try to harmonise the two so that they work in parallel. From an organisational perspective, dissatisfied and de-motivated employees who disengage from work can impact on the profit of the organisation as poor productivity and quality may result in the loss of business. Negative attitudes towards the organisation may influence the brand image of the organisation as the company may be deemed to be a poor employer, which may affect the quality of staff employed by the organisation.

Legal context

Details of legislative requirements are discussed in Chapter 3 – Legislation applied to the workplace.

Short-answer questions

1 What motivates you? Which of the motivation theories best suits your motivation?
2 What do you believe is the importance of motivation/job satisfaction theories to managers/leaders?
3 What is employee engagement and why is it important?
4 What can managers do to increase employee engagement?
5 What do you believe are the negative effects of a lack of motivation, job dissatisfaction and employee disengagement?

CASE STUDY
Motivation, job satisfaction and employee engagement

Sammie's Fashion Supplies provides jewellery, make-up and hair accessories to fashion accessory stores within the UK. The company was formed in 1980 and its headquarters are based in Liverpool. There are 90 employees working for the company in varying roles such as product manufacturing, packing, sales and accounts.

Seventy-five per cent of employees have worked for the company since its inception in 1980. The company prides itself on its four core values.

1 quality of products
2 timeliness of delivery

3 safety of staff and customers

4 impact on the environment.

The company also prides itself on respecting staff as individuals and providing development opportunities (career development and education). As there has been success with the current operations, the company has decided to expand its business into Europe and America using the internet. This will require a vast financial investment from the organisation as well as changes being made to individuals' jobs. Some staff are concerned about this expansion as a similar company has attempted such an endeavour, which proved unsuccessful and resulted in a loss of jobs.

The problem

Over the past 12 months, staff motivation and satisfaction seem to have declined. Staff sickness has also been on the increase and there has been a high turnover of staff (12 compared with an average of two per year a year ago).

Your task is to write a report to the owner, advising him about the potential reasons for the individuals' change in attitudes. Interventions to increase positive attitudes should be put forward. You also need to discuss the importance of motivation, job satisfaction and employee engagement within organisations and how it can affect individuals, managers and the organisation as a whole. Ethical issues of implementing the interventions should also be considered.

Writing guidelines are provided in Chapter 2, Section 2.3 – the consultancy cycle, which provides you with a structure to follow.

Further reading

Albrecht, S. L. (2012). *Handbook of employee engagement: Perspectives, issues, research and practice*. Cheltenham, UK: Edward Elgar Publishing.

11

Management and leadership approaches

Learning outcomes

After reading this chapter, you should be able to:

- describe the concept of management and the concept of leadership
- critically evaluate the various theories/approaches to leadership
- understand leadership development options that can be implemented in organisations
- suggest leadership development interventions.

11.1 Introduction

Anna-Marie is a senior manager in a large financial organisation. Her approach is very directive: she tells staff what tasks to undertake and manages them on a daily basis. The staff feel as though Anna-Marie does not trust them to work on their own initiative and have started to feel de-motivated. This has had an impact on the productivity and quality of work the staff have produced.

In this chapter we will discuss and evaluate different approaches to management and leadership. As you are reading through the chapter, please consider the type of management style Anna-Marie adopts and whether this is the most appropriate style.

The terms 'leadership' and 'management' are used interchangeably within the literature; however, the words describe two separate concepts. Managers direct subordinates and seek to control and order individuals and the workplace. Leaders set a vision or direction for their people and inspire individuals to work towards that vision. Put simply, managers have subordinates and leaders have followers. The topic of leadership and management is one of the oldest areas of research within occupational psychology. Research has focused on characteristics that make a good leader

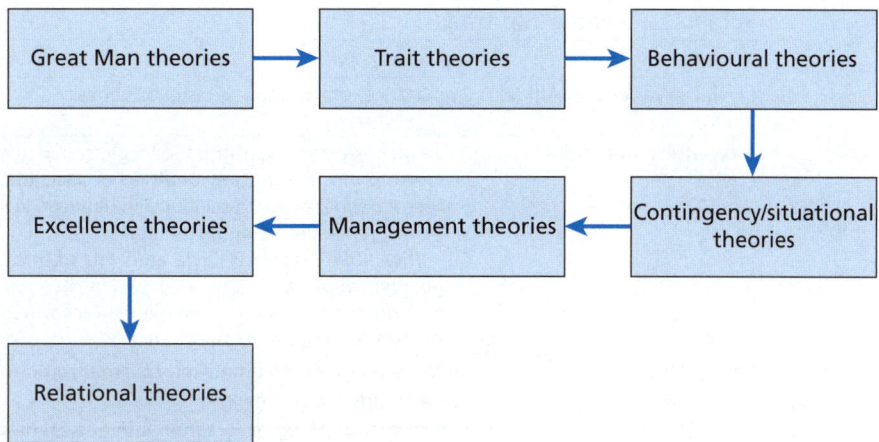

Figure 11.1 Leadership theories

and how they influence others. This chapter will discuss theories of leadership and management as well as empirical research that assess characteristics of good managers.

Figure 11.1 provides an overview of the theories, which will now be discussed in more detail.

11.2 Theories of leadership

Great Man theory of leadership

In the early 1900s, it was believed that the ability to lead was innate. This was known as the Great Man theory, which put forward that some individuals are born to be leaders (Stogdill & Coons, 1948). This name came from the notion that great politicians and religious leaders possess certain characteristics or traits. This approach leans towards the nature debate that leaders are born and not made. At this particular time, gender issues were not considered as most leaders were male. Towards the 1940s, this view began to wane with the emergence of the trait theory of leadership.

Trait theory of leadership

The trait theory is based on the assumption that individuals are born with certain personality or behavioural traits that are common in all leaders. The approach suggests that if you can identify people with specific traits, then you can identify good leaders. Many traits have been suggested although no agreement of key traits has been made. Examples of traits representing good leaders can be seen in Table 11.1 (overleaf).

It is interesting to see that the earlier review by Lord, De-Vader and Alliger (1986) identified masculinity as a trait related to leadership, suggesting that leaders are male. This is due to the relatively recent involvement of women in these roles (Collinson & Hearn, 2003) and the promotion of leadership styles in women

Table 11.1 Leadership traits

Authors	Leadership traits
Lord, De-Vader and Alliger (1986)	Dominance, masculinity, conservativeness
Kirkpatrick and Locke (1991)	*Drive* (achievement, ambition, energy, tenacity and initiative) *Leadership motivation* (personalised or socialised) *Honesty/Integrity* (trusting relationship between leaders and followers) *Self-confidence* (emotional stability) *Cognitive ability* (process large amounts of information and develop strategies) *Knowledge of business* (to enable well-informed decisions to be made and understand consequences)
Bennis (1998)	*Building teamwork* (committed to organisational goals) *Understands the business* *Conceptual thinking* (select innovative strategies) *Customer driven* (create value for the customer) *Focused drive* (goal-focused) *Drives profitability* (cost-effective and efficient operations) *Systems thinking* (connects processes, events and structures) *Global perspective* (addresses cultural and geographic differences) Emotional intelligence (understands own emotions)
Daft (1999)	Alertness, originality, creativity, personal integrity and self-confidence

that tend to promote more interactions with employees, information-sharing and employee participation in decision-making (Meyerson & Fletcher, 2000). However, research by Welle (2004) found that women hold 51% of managerial and professional positions and therefore traditional stereotypes should be challenged.

There are other limitations to this approach. To identify traits of a good leader, a subjective assessment has to be made which leaves it open to bias. There is also disagreement within the literature over which traits are the most important ones for effective leadership and whether the same traits apply to leaders in different organisation types such as a military leader and a charitable leader. Northouse (2007) also identified the weaknesses of the trait approach including the list of traits for leaders being never-ending and ever-growing and that it fails to take situations into account. The approach also views traits as fixed, stable structures. For example, Zaccaro, Kemp, & Bader (2004) defined leader traits as 'stable and coherent integrations of personal characteristics that foster a consistent pattern of leadership performance across a variety of group and organisational situations'. If traits are stable, an argument could be put forward that experience, teaching and leadership training are pointless.

The strengths of the trait approach according to Northouse (2007) are that it focuses on the leader; it has a long history of research to support the theory; and it suggests that people need to perceive leaders as special people with certain traits. Other benefits of this approach are that by identifying traits, a benchmark of what is required in leaders can be determined. Leaders are also able to identify their strengths and weaknesses against each of the traits required.

The trait approach, however, does pose questions about whether leaders are born or made.

? Think about it

Identify, from the media, a person whom you believe is a good leader. Identify traits that you believe make this individual a good leader. Think about whether these traits could be developed through training.

Behavioural approach to leadership

Behavioural theories emerged in the 1950s and 1960s in response to the criticisms of the trait approach. As traits are difficult to measure, the focus of leadership turned to the behaviour of leaders and how this was related to its followers. The view was that leaders are made, not born. This approach views the behaviour of leaders (what they do) as more important than their physical, emotional or mental traits and argues that leaders can be trained through teaching of relevant skills and observation of others.

The two most famous studies from the behavioural approach were conducted in Ohio State University and Michigan University. The Ohio State studies involved administering the Leader Behaviour Description Questionnaire to individuals in the military, manufacturing organisations, student leaders and administrators from a college. Two distinct aspects of leadership were identified: consideration and initiating structure. Consideration involved concern for subordinates, being supporting as well as recognising achievements. Initiating structure, referred to as task-oriented behaviour, involves planning, organising and coordination of work.

At the same time, studies were undertaken in Michigan with the aims of determining the methods and principles of leadership that led to satisfaction and increased productivity in staff. Two general leadership behaviours were identified: an employee-orientation and a product-orientation. The employee-orientation represents leaders showing concern for members of the organisation, whereas product-orientation leaders focus on the task to be completed. It was found that an employee-orientation increases productivity.

Based on the behavioural approach to leadership, Blake and Mouton (1964) developed the Managerial Grid (Figure 11.2, overleaf) which considers the concern for people and concern for production. Five alternative behavioural styles of leadership are presented.

The x axis of the grid represents concern for people and the y axis represents concern for production.

- The *impoverished style* (co-ordinate 1, 1) represents managers who have low concern for production and people. The main concern for this management type is to avoid being responsible for any mistakes that occur.
- *Country club management* (co-ordinate 1, 9) represents managers who have a high concern for people and a low concern for production. These managers try

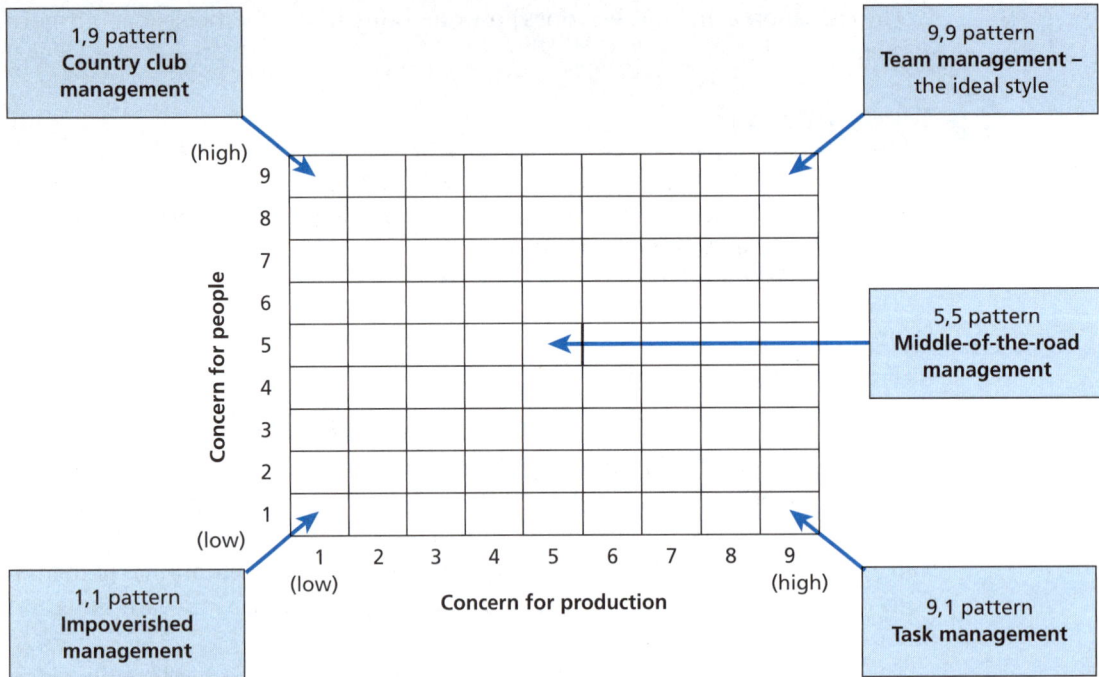

Figure 11.2 Managerial grid

to ensure that their subordinates feel secure and comfortable in their roles. A friendly environment is promoted, which these types of managers believe will increase productivity.

- The *task management style* of leadership (coordinate 9, 1) has a high concern for production and a low concern for people. This type of manager believes that payment for work equals production. Managers use rules and procedures to pressurise employees to achieve goals.
- The *middle-of-the-road style* (coordinate 5, 5) aims to provide a balance between the goals of the company and the needs of its employees.
- The *team style* (coordinate 9, 9) has a high concern for people and production. Teamwork is encouraged and individuals feel part of the company, which increases commitment to meeting goals.

Blake and Mouton concluded that the team management style is the best as it lowers employee turnover, increases performance and job satisfaction. Other team roles have been discussed by Belbin (1993) and are discussed in Chapter 12 – Groups and teams.

The behavioural approach to leadership does help managers in determining the most appropriate behaviour to be a good leader. However, it does not provide any advice regarding which behavioural styles match certain situations, making it difficult for individual leaders to adapt their behaviour to the situation. This was the main impetus of the contingency/situational approach to leadership.

Contingency/situational leadership

The limitations of the behavioural approach are made redundant by the contingency/situational approach to leadership. This approach suggests that leadership styles differ across situational contexts and explains leadership in terms of situational variables, also known as contingency theories. The contingency theories put forward that leadership styles and their effectiveness depend on situational factors and that leaders need to adapt their leadership style according to the situation faced. Therefore, this approach does not suggest that there is one optimal approach to leadership, but that leaders should be flexible (French, 2007). The first contingency model of leadership is Fiedler's (1967) Least Preferred Co-Worker Model. According to this theory, it is the quality of the leader–member relation, the structure of the task and the amount of power the leader has that influence the effectiveness of leadership. The leader–member relation represents the amount of loyalty, dependability and support the leader receives from their employees. The measure of this is based on the manager's perception of how well they are getting on with their employees. If the manager and the employee have a good relationship, there is a high task structure and managers are able to reward or punish their employees accordingly. If there is a negative relationship, the task is not structured and the manager shows little authority over their employees. The amount of authority and power the manager perceives they have been given by the organisation is known as position power. Within this theory there is no good or bad leader as each leader has their own preference on the leadership style they adopt. Task leaders perform better in groups where there is competition – for example, a leader of a sales team where targets are difficult and challenging, but are achievable. Relationship-oriented leaders are better in customer service type roles, such as a leader of a retail shop. Problems with this theory do exist. For example, the theory does not explain what the leader needs to do to become more effective, so it is difficult to recommend training interventions to improve leadership.

A further theory is that of Path–Goal theory developed by House (1997). This theory focuses on types of leader behaviour including directive, supportive, participative and achievement-oriented. Directive leaders provide exact instructions to their employees and expect employees to follow those instructions. This makes it clear to employees what is required of them and what they should be achieving. Supportive leadership is where the leader shows the employee that they are concerned for them and provides their employees with a supportive working environment. Participative leadership involves leaders consulting with employees and taking on board employees' views before making any decisions. Finally, achievement-oriented leadership involves the leader setting the individual challenging goals and believing in employees achieving to a high level. According to this theory, any leader could adapt one of these approaches based on the situation they are faced with and by adapting the behaviour, according to the situation, they will ensure a more successful outcome. This theory fails to consider any emotional bonds that may occur between leader and employee and the influence of emotions on behaviour. For example, if you have a good, trusting relationship with your leader, you are likely to go above and beyond what is required of you to achieve organisational goals. This is not considered by this approach.

Although consideration was given to adapting behaviour according to the situation, very little consideration was given to adapting leadership behaviours dependent on the employee. As the interaction between the leader and employee can affect factors such as trust, motivation and satisfaction, it is clearly important that such interactions and relationships be considered. A theory that takes into account relationships between leaders and employers is the Situational Leadership Theory developed by Hersey and Blanchard (1977). This theory specifies different leadership behaviours based on an employee's level of maturity in relation to their work. For example, a high-maturity employee is confident in the task they are undertaking, whereas a low-maturity employee lacks such self-confidence. If a person is less confident the leader would need to be more directive in tasks the employee is to carry out, clarify what is required, monitor the task being undertaken and provide sufficient feedback. This would allow the employee to know what is expected and when they are completing the task to a satisfactory standard. Once the employee moves into a high-maturity state, less interaction and feedback would be required. It thus appears that the leader must first assess the maturity level of their employee in relation to the task they are asked to carry out and adapt their leadership style accordingly.

A criticism of the theories presented in the contingency/situational approach is that they look at styles in black and white. You are either adopting one type of leadership style or another. However, Tannenbaum & Schmidt (1958) suggested that this view was too simplistic and that leadership does not represent one extreme or another (employee- or task-focused), but can be understood along a continuum and leaders can fall somewhere between the two.

Tannenbaum & Schmidt (1958) suggested two extreme leadership styles of autocratic and democratic that fell at each end of the continuum, and persuasive and consultative that fell in between. An overview of these styles can be found in Table 11.2.

Table 11.2 Leadership styles (Tannenbaum & Schmidt, 1958)

Autocratic	Makes decisions without input from employees and tells the employees what actions to take. The autocratic leader does not expect to be questioned by subordinates.
Persuasive	Makes decisions without input from the group, but uses persuasion to make people buy into the decisions made. The leader thus sells the decision as a good one to subordinates.
Consultative	Subordinates are asked to contribute to the discussion of decisions to be made. Although the decision is the responsibility of the leader, the thoughts and feelings of subordinates are taken into account.
Democratic	The leader presents the problem to employees and asks for a discussion of the problem and potential solutions. The leader chairs the discussion and the decision is made by the group as a result of the discussion.

Stop and reflect

Think of a group that you have been involved in. This may be in work, school, college, university or in a sporting activity. Think of the leader of that group (this may be a formal leader or an informal leader). What leadership style do you think they have? What are the positives and negatives of them adopting that style?

The democratic approach to leadership where individuals are empowered to be involved in decision-making was furthered by Adair (1973). Adair developed the action-centred leadership model where there is a focus on teamwork and developing trusting relationships between leaders and subordinates. The model is based on three factors, as can be seen in Figure 11.3.

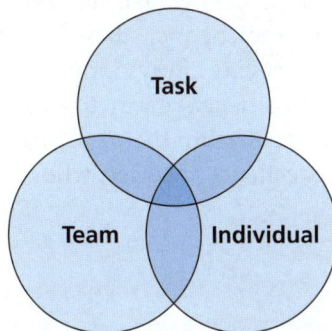

Figure 11.3 Action-centred leadership model

Based on this model, the action leader must direct the task to be completed. This is achieved by outlining the task, planning actions, allocating relevant resources, ensuring the plan is on time and of relevant quality and making adjustments to the plan as and when required. The leader should also support individuals by listening to their problems, recognising and praising their achievements as well as providing opportunities for the individual to develop. Finally, the leader must provide direction and co-ordination to the team by ensuring clear communication, motivating team members and providing clear goals to ensure the group feels a sense of purpose in the work they are carrying out. As well as the various leadership theories, various management theories have considered what makes good leaders. These will now be discussed.

11.3 Management theories

Management theories were initially developed from Taylor's (1911) scientific management studies and those of Fayol (1949) (see Chapter 1 – Introduction to occupational psychology). However, management research tended to focus on trans-actional leadership where individuals are motivated by systems of punishments.

Transactional leadership

Transactional leadership is based on two key factors: rewards (such as money or recognition) and punishment (negative feedback or disciplinary action). When a task is accomplished by an employee, that employee is rewarded. If the employee fails to accomplish the task or does not meet the expectations of the leader, the employee is punished. The transactional leader provides clear structures to ensure subordinates know what is expected of them as well as an understanding of rewards for employees when they achieve and punishments when they underachieve. The employee is solely responsible for his/her success or failure. Excuses such as the employee did not have enough time or resources are not acceptable under this type of leadership.

There are advantages and disadvantages to this theory. On the plus side it is a relatively simplistic theory and is based on research evidence of human responses (read research by Pavlov and Skinner for further details). However, there are many downsides to this theory. For example, the theory is based on the assumption that everyone is rational and that employees are always motivated by rewards and punishments. The theory may be used in a negative way to exploit workers, thus providing one of the most controversial leadership theories. There was, therefore, a move from this theory towards the excellence theories, whose name suggests a more positive approach to leading.

Excellence theories

The excellence theories came into being in the 1980s and 1990s. These theories considered interactions of traits, behaviours, situations and group facilitation in providing effective leadership and provided an attempt at integrating all previous theories. However, these theories did not focus on followers, but on the achievement of goals.

To ensure achievement of goals, Covey (1991) put forward eight characteristics that leaders should possess.

1 They are continually learning (educated by their experiences – they read, undertake training, listen to others, are curious and expand their competence).
2 They are service-related (see life as a mission not as a career).
3 They radiate positive energy (cheerful, pleasant, happy, optimistic and have positive energy).
4 They believe in other people (believe in unseen potential of others, are compassionate, forgive and forget).
5 They lead balanced lives (keep up with current affairs, have lots of friends, but few confidants and have a good sense of humour).
6 They see life as an adventure (resourceful, creative, have willpower and stamina).
7 They are synergistic (they are change catalysts, work hard and work smart and are productive).
8 They exercise for self-renewal (exercise minds through reading, creative problem-solving, writing and visualising).

However, little empirical evidence exists for excellence theories and at the end of the 1980s and into the 1990s and beyond, leaders started to recognise the importance of employees and, as the name of the theory suggests 'relational' connections between leaders and employees were made.

Relational theories

Relational theories of leadership (also known as transformational leadership) concentrate on the connections between leaders and their followers.

Transformational leadership

The concept of transformational leadership is where leaders aim to inspire their followers, empower them to achieve, have a clear vision and instill confidence. This particular view of leadership combines the trait approach with the behavioural approach. Although individuals have certain traits, they also behave in a particular way that 'excites, arouses and inspires followers' (Robbins, Millett, & Waters-Marsh, 2004). These individuals tend to be charismatic. The charismatic leader creates common goals, provides opportunities for individuals to develop, inspires and influences others. Examples of transformational leaders provided by Burns (1978) included Rousseau, Castro and Moses, who it was argued possessed values of liberty, justice, equality and collective well-being. It was argued by Bass (1985) that transformational leaders were at the opposite end of the spectrum to transactional leaders and the three main characteristics of a transformational leader are: 1) charismatic and inspirational leadership (the leader envisions a future, communicates how to achieve it, sets standards and uses him/herself as an example by which followers copy; 2) intellectual stimulation (the leader encourages followers to continually question assumptions and come up with innovative ideas to solve problems; 3) individualised consideration (the leader treats people individually).

Bass and Avolio (1994) suggested that leaders exhibit behaviours that can be categorised into five transformational styles.

1 **Idealised influence.** Individuals express their beliefs and values. Realise the importance of building trusting relationships, take responsibility for new opportunities and have a strong sense of purpose.
2 **Inspirational motivation.** Individuals communicate their optimism regarding the future, have a compelling vision of the future and talk enthusiastically about what needs to be achieved and expresses confidence in ability to achieve.
3 **Intellectual stimulation.** Individuals seek different perspectives to problem-solving, encourage creative thinking, question ideas that have not been questioned before.
4 **Individualised consideration.** Individuals spend time teaching and coaching individuals. They consider individuals' needs, abilities and strengths, and listen to people.
5 **Idealised attributes.** Individuals build respect, have power and competence, make sacrifices for others and instill pride in others.

The importance of behaviours that individuals exhibit was furthered by Hooper and Potter (1997, 2000) who identified seven key competencies of leaders: setting direction, emotional alignment, acting as an example, developing people at all levels, effective communication, acting as a proactive change agent and showing effective behaviour in crisis situations. An example of a transformation leader can be seen in Real case 11.1.

Real case 11.1

Richard Branson, Chief Executive Officer of Virgin Group

Richard Branson is a famous entrepreneur. He is the driving force for between 150 and 200 companies employing over 8,000 people in more than 26 countries. From a small student magazine business and mail order record company in the 1970s, Branson expanded his business empire to include travel, drinks and investment funds to name a few.

When looking at the success of Virgin, Scully (2008) stated that Richard Branson has leadership behaviours that verge on the eccentric. He empowers his teams, sets high expectations, and hosts ostentatious celebrations with teams across the world making the brand successful within the organisation as well as outside. It is clear from the success of Richard Branson's brand that he also has a strong focus on strategic leadership in terms of directing his organisations in a direction that meets the needs of customers and allows the brand to continue to be successful. However, although the decisions to direct the organisation towards a particular future tend to come from a strategic leader, it is the followers who tend to implement the decisions, thus it is important that they have faith in the decisions being made and believe that they have the relevant capabilities to implement the changes. This is where the human assets approach proves advantageous.

Human assets approach

The focus of the human assets approach is based on policies and principles relating to people. There is knowledge of employees' capabilities that are used to achieve goals. People are rewarded for initiatives at all levels of the organisation, which increases commitment. Leaders who adopt this approach become involved in recruitment of staff higher up in the organisational hierarchy. For example, at Pepsi Co, Wayne Calloway interviewed for the top 600 jobs in the company, regardless of its world-wide location (Farkas & Wetlaufer, 1998). These individuals also become involved in career development plans, performance reviews and developing incentives for their staff. This ensures that employees who are motivated and do well are appropriately rewarded. This, in turn, increases commitment and loyalty to the company.

Whereas the human assets approach focuses on policies and principles relating to people, the Leader–Member Exchange theory also considers relationships between individuals. The LMX theory focuses on the quality of the relationship between the leader and follower. It is argued that if the relationship between the leader and follower is good, there will be a positive effect on the follower's satisfaction. If the relationship is bad, there will be a negative effect on satisfaction that could lead to poor performance and a lack of commitment. These relationships result in an in-group where there are good relations with the leader and an out-group where there are bad relations with the leader. Another approach that considers people is the servant leadership theory.

Servant leadership

Servant leadership is based on a belief system that focuses on individuals. It provides core values that encourage innovation from and development in leaders with a focus on serving their stakeholders. Greenleaf (1977) developed a value-driven and person-oriented theory of leadership that has many similarities to transformational leadership in that the leader has a vision, exerts influence, is seen as highly credible, but differs from the transformational leader in that the servant leader puts the needs of others as the highest priority. The leader's main aim is to serve others. Success occurs when the followers achieve their goals.

Real case 11.2

Servant leadership – First Fruits

First Fruits is one of the largest apple producers in the world, based in Washington with 2,000 employees.

'Sure we have to make money . . . but profit isn't our main motive. It becomes the byproduct of treating people with dignity, respect and mutuality, and as equals in every sense of the word. We believe if we ever stopped doing that we would implode.'

Real case 11.3

Servant leadership – Medtronic

Medtronic was founded in 1949 and is now the biggest medical technology company. Its mission is to alleviate pain, restore health and extend life. All this is built on the approach of servant leadership.

Other companies that have adopted the servant leadership approach include Starbucks and Federal Express. Reasons for adopting this approach may include the organisation having a double bottom line which means that they focus on people and profit. This creates a high level of trust and loyalty to the organisation, which attracts good employees and customers.

Spears (2004) identified ten main characteristics of servant leaders from Greenleaf's work:

1 *Listening* – they should listen to others.
2 *Empathy* – they should accept and recognise fellow workers.
3 *Healing* – they should recognise the emotions of others.
4 *Awareness* – they should be aware of issues including ethics and values.

5 *Persuasion* – they should convince rather than coerce others.
6 *Conceptualisation* – they should be able to have a vision of the future while maintaining day-to-day activities.
7 *Foresight* – they should know the consequences of their future decisions.
8 *Stewardship* – they should motivate people to maintain trust for the betterment of society.
9 *Commitment to the growth of people* – they should be committed to individuals within an organisation as well as to the organisation as a whole.
10 *Building community* – they should lead the way by demonstrating their unlimited liability for a community-related association.

The basis of these types of companies is that they are close to their customers and they focus on all stakeholders including employees, customers and the community in general. These companies strive to develop management talent from lower down the ranks of the organisation, making career development within the organisation possible, thus encouraging people to stay with the organisation.

11.4 Modern concept of leadership

There has been an increasing awareness of problems with leadership that has come about from both the *News of the World* scandal, in which phones were hacked and allegations of police bribery made, as well as the expenses scandal in 2009 where certain MPs were jailed for claiming too much on their expenses. This has led to an interest in the theory of authentic leadership that, if adopted, may restore confidence in our leaders.

Authentic leadership

Authentic leadership theory is still in its infancy with some of the first applications to leadership being in the sociological and educational domain (Hannah & Chan, 2004). The theory of authentic leadership is described by Avolio, Luthans, & Walumbwa (2004: 4) as 'those who are deeply aware of how they think and behave and are perceived by others as being aware of their own and others' values/moral perspectives, knowledge and strengths: aware of the context in which they operate; and who are confident, hopeful, optimistic, resilient and of high moral character'. However, Shamir and Eilam (2005) expressed concerns about the breadth of this definition and suggest a narrower focus based on four characteristics that an authentic leader exhibits.

1 Authentic leaders are true to themselves (do not conform to the expectations of others).
2 Authentic leaders are motivated by their own convictions rather than by attaining status or personal benefits.
3 Authentic leaders are originals, leading from their own viewpoint.
4 Authentic leaders' actions are based on personal values and convictions.

In this definition the leadership style is not described, allowing for an individual style to be adopted such as transformational, servant or any other type of positive leadership. These types of leaders work hard, lead with purpose and have a vision. The authentic leader has a deep sense of self and knows where they stand on important issues (Avolio and Gardner, 2005). Research has shown that adopting an authentic style of leadership increases subordinate trust in their leader, contributes to worker-engagement (Hassan & Ahmed, 2011) and increases organisational commitment (Shamir & Eliam, 2005). It appears that this leadership style may be of benefit to individuals as well as the organisation as a whole. However, more empirical research is required to provide evidence of the worth of this leadership type.

When leaders are new to organisations or when a particular leadership style is not working in an organisation, leaders and managers may undertake leadership development.

11.5 Leadership development

Leadership development enhances the quality and effectiveness of leadership in an organisation. Commonly adopted approaches include training seminars, executive coaching, action learning and 360 degree feedback.

Training seminars are a popular method of leadership development as they can address a large audience. These seminars consist of generic information such as strengthening external networking skills or casting your vision, and tend to be seminars about one hour long. Disadvantages of training seminars include them being delivered over a short time-frame, not meeting individual needs, not providing the individual an opportunity to master the skills through practice and feedback, and providing no implementation strategies. According to Falk (2003), such problems result in the learning not being transferable to the job, thus questioning the worth of these seminars to changing behaviour and practice.

Executive coaching addresses these issues as it is based on a relationship between a leader and a coach and is tailored to the individual. The coach identifies development needs of the individual leader and puts actions in place to address those needs. This form of leadership development adopts a long-term approach. As individuals apply knowledge to the workplace, they can learn from the application of knowledge to practice in terms of what works for them as individuals and their organisation. Executive coaching thus represents an effective approach to changing behaviour and it is estimated that 70–88% of large companies use coaching (CIPD, 2005). An approach that shares some characteristics of the executive coaching approach is action learning.

Action learning is an approach where individuals learn by completing real tasks on the job (Revans, 1998). Individuals learn by taking part in group discussions, solutions are discussed and may be changed so that they are tailored to the organisation. Liedtka (1998) assessed the effectiveness of action learning used by 542 managers of a large financial organisation. It was found that the action learning approach was a useful and practical way of developing new skills and knowledge and allows for the retention of knowledge and skills attained. However, there are some criticisms to this approach. First, some tasks experienced by leaders may not be experienced on a regular basis so may not be practised and the skills lost. For example, Conger and Toegel (2002) found that, to develop true skills, leaders need repeated exposure to tasks. Secondly, as this approach to development is very task-focused, it does not provide an opportunity for reflective learning. Reflective learning allows individuals to step back from the task and analyse it from different perspectives. Undertaking an analysis allows individuals to assess what has worked and what has not and thus can enhance future performance.

Another technique used in leadership development is the **360 degree approach**. This involves leaders being given feedback that has been gathered from a variety of people and can include subordinates, peers, customers and suppliers. It has been found by Shipper and Dillard (2000) that this approach is one of the best approaches to leadership development. 360 degree feedback allows leaders to see themselves from other people's points of view. However, receiving feedback does not necessarily lead to a change in behaviour. For example, Cacioppe and Albrecht (2002) examined 360 degree feedback provided to 304 managers from more than 1,000 subordinates. It was found that although the feedback provided the leader with a vast amount of information, it does not provide information about how to change or help with the implementation of those changes. To achieve this, a mentor based in the organisation may be able to assist.

Mentoring involves a relationship between the leader and a senior member of the organisation. The senior member provides knowledge, advice and support to the leader. As the senior member knows the organisation, its values and beliefs as well as its goals and mission, it allows for development that fits the aim of the organisation. This has been shown to be effective in developing leaders within organisations (Day, 2000). Although mentoring has been shown to be effective, there are disadvantages such as the time taken to be a mentor; differences between mentor and mentee; and power dynamics between leader and senior member of staff. However, when a strong successful relationship is formed, evidence of increased career satisfaction as well as higher organisational income has been found (Chao, Walz, & Gardner 1992).

All the individual approaches to leadership development have their own benefits, but it does seem more appropriate to use a combination of approaches. Providing feedback using the 360 degree approach, using an executive coach to identify and work through areas of improvement, and providing training seminars for information and action learning to apply theory to practice using a mentor, will provide a rounded approach to becoming a good leader. A meta-analysis conducted by Burke and Day (1986) that reviewed four studies that combined three or more development techniques found that multi-dimensional approaches had a greater impact on both learning and performance.

According to McDonald (2002), a three-track approach to leadership development that integrates the following principles is more effective.

1 Structured learning track that provides a forum for learning about leadership models, provides frameworks and tools, and provides interaction with current leaders.

2 An individualised development track that enlists participants in tailoring their learning. It features assessments including 360° feedback, goal setting, action planning, and selection by participants of current work-related opportunities that match their goals. This track is most effective when a coach works with a participant throughout the programme.

3 An applied learning track gives participants a chance to expand beyond their functional areas. It consists of assembling teams from the leadership programme to tackle specific strategic projects and/or questions defined by current leaders.

This approach allows for theory and practice and takes an individualised approach so that key areas of individual weakness can be targeted. However, other factors do need to be considered when developing leaders. This is the development of leaders to operate globally. To be successful, leaders need to be aware of cultural, economic, technological and political differences between countries in which they operate. In a 62-nation, 11-year study with 170 researchers worldwide, a project was undertaken entitled GLOBE (Global Leadership and Organisational Behaviour Effectiveness). The research was reported by Grove (2005). Data from 17,300 managers in 951 organisations was collected. Some of the research considered whether practices and values associated with leadership are universal. The research found that there were 21 primary leadership dimensions that span across cultures as being a contributing factor to leadership effectiveness. Each of these primary leadership dimensions has between two and four attributes. For example, one of the 21 dimensions represent a Team Integrator, which has attributes of communicative, team builder, informed and integrator. Based on this research six culturally endorsed leadership dimensions (containing the 21 original dimensions) were found (see Figure 11.4).

Charismatic/value-based	Team-oriented
• Charismatic/visionary	• Team collaborative
• Charismatic/inspirational	• Team integrative
• Charismatic/self-sacrificing	• Diplomatic
• Integrity	• *Malevolent (reversed)*
• Decisive	• Admin competent
• Performance-oriented	
Self-protective	**Participative**
• Self-centred	• *Autocratic (reversed)*
• Status conscious	• *Non-participative (reversed)*
• Conflict inducer	
• Face saver	
• Procedural	
Humane-oriented	**Autonomous**
• Modesty	• Autonomous
• Humane-oriented	

Figure 11.4 Culturally endorsed leadership dimensions

Those characteristics that are italicised in Figure 11.4 are reversed. This means that if asking questions based on those 21 characteristics, individuals do not automatically agree with all questions (as they are considered positively), but have to consider them separately as some may be negatively worded. This research has provided a huge step forward in the identification of culturally similar characteristics required of leaders who operate globally. This will help leaders become successful when working with clients from different parts of the world of managing individuals in different countries, although more research is needed in this area.

Multi-level impact of leadership

Leadership impacts all levels of the organisation, from individuals, management and the organisation as a whole. At an individual level, poor leadership can lead to a reduction in motivation and job satisfaction, leading to a decrease in productivity and an increase in absenteeism and turnover of staff. At a managerial level, if employees are not performing to the required standard, the leader or manager is not achieving their targets or meeting organisational goals. If organisational goals are not met, the organisation cannot develop/maintain business, thus leaving it vulnerable to competitors.

? Think about it

If you were asked to make a suggestion about the best approach to leadership development, what would it be and why?

Legal context

Further details of legislative requirements are discussed in Chapter 3 – Legislation applied to the workplace. Additional details can be sourced at the Government Equalities Office (2010).

Equality Act 2010. Available: *http://equalities.gov.uk/equality_bill.aspx*

Short-answer questions

1 Evaluate the strengths and weaknesses of the leadership styles discussed in this chapter.
2 Describe the concept of the managerial grid.
3 Discuss the most appropriate leadership style for global leaders.
4 Name three methods of leadership development as well as their strengths and weaknesses.

CASE STUDY
Management and leadership

Sammie Waste Management Services has been in existence since 1972 and employs 60 staff. The company provides domestic waste services and recycling to residents and companies in central England. The previous chief executive officer (CEO) has retired and a new manager who has a financial services background has taken over the role. The previous CEO was a very approachable leader who empowered staff to make decisions and suggest improvements to services. Staff were rewarded for innovations that saved the company time, money and other resources. Each Christmas, the CEO organised a Christmas party for all staff members and their partners, paid for by Sammie Waste Management Services. One staff member stated 'Sammie, the previous CEO was a kind and thoughtful man who cared about the company and staff. I must say we are concerned about the new man who is very in your face and cares more about the money than staff'.

The new CEO, having a financial background, is very money-focused and likes to cut costs where possible. Staff are told what to do and are timed for the task undertaken. The CEO makes all decisions without consulting staff and staff feel uncertain about their future. The incentive scheme has been scrapped as well as the Christmas party. Staff are increasingly having time off sick as well as leaving/looking for alternative employment.

The problem

The current leader is not motivating staff with the leadership style he has adopted. Staff feel disempowered and are looking for employment elsewhere. The CEO has recruited you, as a consultant, to write a business report outlining any issues with his management style and making suggestions about leadership development. The CEO is open to ideas at this stage as he has realised that the waste disposal industry is very different to the financial services sector.

For details of the consultancy cycle, please refer to Chapter 2 which provides a comprehensive overview. Chapter 2 also provides details regarding the structure of a business report, which you will find useful for this task.

Further reading

Falk, I. (2003). Designing effective leadership interventions: A case study of vocational education and training. *Leadership & Organisation Development Journal, 24*(4), 193–203.

Northouse, P. G. (2007). *Leadership: Theory and practice* (4th ed). Thousand Oaks, CA: Sage Publications.

12

Groups and teams

Emma Holdsworth

Learning outcomes

After reading this chapter, you should have developed an understanding of:

- how human groups have evolved throughout history
- definitions of groups and teams and their subtle distinctions
- the benefits to organisations of employing work groups and teams
- the theories that help us understand how groups form, and the problems associated with defining 'group development'
- different group roles and their interdependence for group effectiveness
- the factors and characteristics of groups that affect group performance and ultimately the organisation's performance.

12.1 Introduction

Elizabeth works for a global charity organisation that fights poverty. She has been tasked with setting up a new office in Europe, where she needs to put a new team in place. Elizabeth will need to consider these questions. How should the group be recruited? Who will run the new group? What roles should there be within the group? Do all the group members need to be based in Europe all the time?

The aim of this chapter is for us to understand the nature of work groups and teams within organisations. This particular area of organisational psychology represents a significant overlap with social psychology, the primary focus of which is the relations between people and groups. Sociologists are also interested in individuals within groups but in the context of larger social structures and processes such as gender, race, class and social roles. Social psychology focuses more specifically on how an individual's thoughts, feelings and behaviours are influenced by other people. How individuals behave as a member of a group or team is directly influenced by their membership of that group or team. In other words, people tend to behave in certain ways that are associated with other members of the group, and the purpose or function of the group.

The human social development of groups has historically been based on the dimension of work. Many thousands of years ago, hunters and gatherers worked in groups as a means of survival. Somewhat later the agricultural era generated an economy that was able to sustain larger communities, resulting in a surplus that allowed specialised trades such as craftsmen and merchants to develop. These trades added to the surplus, encouraging growth in communities. Large communities needed organisation and protection in order to develop into empires. There was a hierarchical structure to empires based on power and wealth, which were regarded as only heritable commodities.

The same pattern of evolution can be seen in the industrial era, although at a much faster rate. The development of industry called for the development of literacy that, in turn, created a need for education. The impact of the industrial era greatly impacted on human groups, increasing the population. People migrated to cities in search of jobs, and the middle class that had stemmed from the trades developed in the agricultural era grew at an ever-increasing rate. The consequence was that empires, ruled by an elitist minority, were forced out by the industrial revolution. This created a fundamental change in the power relationships and organisation of groups. Empires were replaced by nations, which fostered the principle of elected leadership, rather than inherited leadership.

The evolvement of agriculture and industry has essentially determined the course of history and human social development. History has shown that groups are a natural function of economic change and demonstrates the importance of the impact of work on human socialisation. The progression of industry has served to divide humans into groups. White-collar workers during the 1930s formed the minority of individuals in industrialist societies, where most jobs that involved manual labour in factories were occupied by blue-collar workers. However, white-collar workers became the majority as the number of desk jobs increased during the 20th century. This level of categorisation of workers is clearly very broad; however, it is important to see how work represents a fundamental grouping factor of individuals. The grouping of individuals in work extends beyond the broad industrial level to the individual organisational level. Organisations within different industries are continually moving towards the employment of teams. As industries grow, so does competition among businesses. This engenders a natural trend for achieving higher standards and greater diversity in the products and services that organisations offer. This must be matched by greater diversity in the skills among the employees of the organisation. These different skills need to be harnessed and amalgamated to maximise the organisation's ability to achieve to its best potential.

There are different types of social phenomena (e.g. group polarisation, social loafing) that arise from the simple effects of grouping individuals together at work, which can adversely affect group performance. There is also a number of group factors (e.g. cohesion) that can improve group performance. The group's performance is intrinsically linked to the organisation to which it belongs. It is therefore not surprising that organisations have a vested interest in developing means of reducing the adverse affects and enhancing the positive influences associated with group performance. An understanding of the psychological factors and processes that underpin these group phenomena will help to generate practical means of reducing the adverse effects, enhancing the positive factors, and ultimately maximising organisational group performance.

12.2 Definitions of groups and teams

'Groups' and 'teams' are terms used interchangeably without a clear distinction between the two, although there are subtle differences in their definitions. A work group can be defined as a 'collection of individuals who have regular contact and frequent interaction, mutual influence, common feeling of camaraderie, and who work together to achieve a common set of goals' (Luthra, 2007). The definition of a team is very similar, but teams have three specific properties over and above groups:

1 the actions of individuals must be interdependent and coordinated
2 each member must have specified roles and responsibilities
3 there must be common task goals and objectives.

This latter point is the same for groups, but the distinction is that group members can fulfil their jobs alone whereas team members cannot. The specified roles of each team member in the completion of their common task means their jobs are to a large degree interdependent. The terms 'groups' and 'teams' are often used without necessarily reflecting this distinction. For example, a work group might be a group of sales people at a motor dealership, although they are frequently referred to as a 'sales team'. Their common task is to achieve monthly sales targets prescribed by the motor company and/or the motor manufacturer. Although they all need to contribute to the achievement of these targets, they can fulfil their jobs independently of one another. By contrast a work team involves a number of people who have been brought together because of their skills, to work on a time-specified project. The diversity in these skills is what makes the team; it is the fundamental requirement for achieving the end product. For example, Disaster Management Teams (DMTs) consist of local bodies employed by the government for the effective management and handling of any disaster, both natural (earthquakes, floods) and human-made (road, rail, air accidents, community disturbances, riots). The main objectives of the team are risk reduction, preparing resources to respond to the disaster, responding to the actual damage caused by the disaster, and limiting further damage. The team may generically consist of medical professionals, experts in the field of crowd control, relief workers and administrators. There would also be experts in a particular area depending on the nature of the disaster, such as seismologists in the event of an earthquake. The members of the team have discrete skills, but they must work cooperatively and collaboratively to complete their objectives. The coordination of their individual activities is also vital in ensuring that the disaster is managed effectively.

12.3 Function of work groups and teams in organisations

It is easy to think of many instances when work teams are evident, and when vital functions could simply not be performed by individuals working alone. For example, we rely on medical teams to coordinate their skills for a variety of purposes, from assisting the birth of a new baby to performing heart bypass operations. We rely on the coordination of members of airport ground crew and flight crew to make sure we arrive safely at our destination. On a more down-to-earth level, we might switch our radio or television on each morning to listen to current events, brought to us by journalistic news teams.

There are clearly activities that require the employment of teams rather than individual workers, but there is a variety of particular reasons why many organisations prefer to employ teams over individuals. This may be due to downsizing the organisation through the collapsing of ranks, or expanding the organisation by increasing the output or diversity of the organisation's product or service. The employment of work groups provides a means of both actively involving employees in collective efforts and solving organisational problems. The main benefits for an organisation in the employment of teams include the reduction of departmental barriers (teams frequently include members from different departments), the enhancement of production or service levels, the identification of organisational issues, the division of duties and responsibilities, and a reduction in absenteeism. Although it might seem that employing teams must be the way forward for many organisations, it is important to recognise that the structuring of the workforce into teams is not in itself sufficient. There is a variety of factors that are specific to the psychology of groups and teams, which can either increase the team's performance, or reduce it. The performance of a team is intrinsically linked to the performance of the organisation. Consequently, teams can either lead to the success of an organisation, or its failure. It is perhaps not surprising then that many organisations are keen to enhance factors relating to improved performance and eliminate those that contribute to poor performance. We will explore the specific factors that underpin both the advantages and disadvantages of teams to organisations later in this chapter, but now we will look briefly at the main benefits of teams to the organisation.

Benefits of employing groups to the organisation

Over the last two decades a number of different worldwide pressures have driven organisations towards developing infrastructures based on workflow teams rather than individual jobs in functionalised structures. This is in response to increasing levels of competition within industries that have undergone radical change because of the rapid developments in worldwide communication and technology. Work teams offer skill diversity, flexibility in working, and are able to respond quickly and adaptively to the demands of dynamic industries. In this sense, teams have modified the organisational design of many businesses.

The performance of organisations has been directly linked to the function of work teams. Delarue, Van Hootegem, Procter, & Burridge (2008) identified four major dimensions of organisational performance:

1 attitudinal outcomes (commitment, trust and involvement)
2 behavioural outcomes (turnover, absenteeism and extracurricular activity)
3 operational outcomes (productivity, quality of the product or service, innovation and flexibility)
4 financial outcomes (added value and profitability).

From a review of 31 studies, Delarue *et al.* found that nine of the studies discovered a positive relationship between team work and improved attitudes and behaviours, including reduced absenteeism and staff turnover, and increased levels of motivation and employee satisfaction. Well over half the studies (18) demonstrated significant improvements in operational outcomes, and a quarter of the studies found significant improvements in financial outcomes. It is probably the latter two dimensions in which organisations would be most interested, as they are more directly related to organisational performance than the former two dimensions. Teams offer increased productivity and flexibility over individual workers, therefore it is not surprising that Delarue *et al.* found the dimension of productivity to be most positively influenced was operational outcomes. Work teams clearly have a positive influence on financial outcomes, but to a lesser degree; probably because for many organisations there are likely to be a variety of other contingent factors in relation to profitability (Delarue *et al.*, 2008), such as external market forces and the fiscal basis on which the organisation operates.

12.4 Formation and development of groups

How groups naturally form and develop has been explained by various different theories. We will look at two well-known but distinct theories to demonstrate the diversity of theories, before concluding with a discussion of the common underlying problem observed by Chang, Bordia, & Duck (2006) which is how to operationally define 'group development'. The first theory is Tuckman's stage model, which accounts for the four basic sequential stages representing group formation and development (see Figure 12.1). Tuckman (1965) observed these stages in a review of the literature on clinical groups, although the model is relatively simple and therefore can be applied to most work groups. The second theory is Gersick's punctuated equilibrium model (PEM) (Gersick, 1988), which by contrast

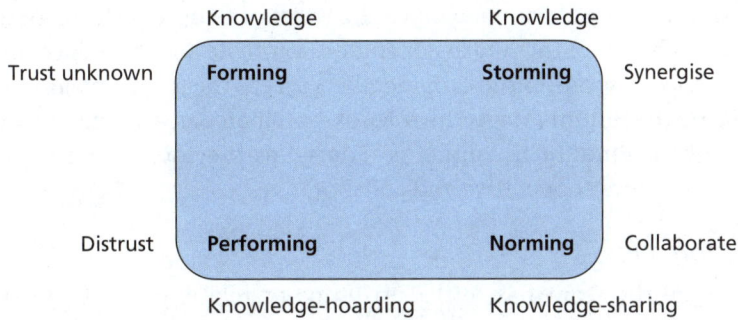

Figure 12.1 Tuckman's Four-stage model

views group formation and development as a stable and continuous process. Gersick's model was based on observations of eight project teams and eight student project groups with a fixed project time-line. The two models may appear to be contrasting but Chang, Bordia, & Duck (2003) argue that the models are complementary in their explanation of the formation and development of groups.

Stage model

Forming

At the forming stage, the group is not yet a group, just a collection of individuals. It is at this stage that team members are introduced, declaring their purpose and objective within the team. Members cautiously explore the boundaries of acceptable group behaviour. This is a stage of transition from individual to member status, and of testing the leader's level of control and type of formal and informal guidance.

Storming

The storming phase involves the transition from formation to intense group activity. All the members will have their own ideas as to how the process and outcome should look. Personal agendas are likely to come to the fore, which may create unexpected challenges. Storming is probably the most difficult stage for the team because it is at this point that they begin to realise the measure of the tasks ahead, which may be different and more difficult than what they had previously imagined. Impatient about the lack of progress, members argue about what actions the team should take to complete the task. A feeling of distrust may emerge and so members will try to rely solely on their personal and professional experience, and resist collaborating with other team members.

Norming

The norming phase is when the team reaches a consensus about the process required to achieve the team's objective. This collaborative agreement leads to everyone developing an enthusiasm for the achievement of their task objective. At this stage, this enthusiasm may have the effect of tempting the team to go beyond the original scope of the process. Members reconcile any differences or competing loyalties and responsibilities. All members accept the team, any ground rules set down during the forming stage, the roles of each member, and the individuality of fellow members. Emotional conflict is reduced as previously competitive relationships become more cooperative and collaborative.

Performing

By now the team has settled in terms of relationships between members and members' expectations. They can begin the process of task completion by diagnosing, problem-solving, implementing changes, and continually revising their accomplishments. At last, team members have discovered and accepted other's strengths and weaknesses. In addition, they have learned about their own role and some valuable information about the roles of others. The team finally meets to discuss their achieved objective and the dissemination of their objective during this phase. When the team finally completes this last meeting, there is frequently a bittersweet sense of accomplishment coupled with the reluctance of members to say goodbye. Many relationships formed within these teams continue long after the team disbands.

Punctuated equilibrium model

In contrast to the sequential progression that underpins Tuckman's stage approach, the punctuated equilibrium model (PEM) (Gersick, 1988) conceptualises group development as a stable process punctuated by a discontinuous shift that occurs at the midpoint of a group's lifecycle. In Gersick's study, groups quickly developed a structure, established members' roles, and followed a pattern of interaction that was maintained up until the midpoint of the group's lifecycle. At the midpoint there was a dramatic shift as tasks were organised, role responsibilities were reallocated, and efforts to meet project deadlines were significantly increased. Gersick proposed that groups adopt a framework of behaviours and assumptions in relation to their project emerging in the first half of their time together. Progress during this stage is not made explicit as members may not know how any new information generated can be used until the original framework is revised. At the midpoint there is a transition in groups as they shift in their approach as they draw on the implicit progression they have made in order to make significant advances towards their objective. The group adjust their pace to ensure the task is completed within the time-frame set. Gersick argued that the transition places the team on a new course by formulating new plans that are set in motion, which must be effective as the team are unlikely to change their plans again. However, this may be specific to project teams that have a very specific time period, and therefore a relatively short period of time working together. The emphasis of Gersick's model is on the adjustment of pace at the midpoint, and the members' awareness of time pressures that motivate group members to change their pace and course in order to ensure they meet the project deadlines. The stage model is linear, i.e. each stage is progressive and determined by the previous stage, but the PEM is non-linear, i.e. the course of the group's development is subject to contextual factors rather than previous activity. However, Chang, Bordia and Duck (2006) argued that both linear and non-linear models are relevant to the development of groups.

12.5 Defining group development

One of the key problems in the group development literature is the lack of any universal agreement as to what 'development' constitutes, which creates some confusion as to how we should conceptualise this phenomenon. Chang *et al.* (2006) conducted a review of group development literature and discovered multiple definitions, with nearly as many accompanying theories. The 'development' of a group could potentially refer to growth in cohesiveness, the development of interpersonal relations among group members, the development of loyalty to the group leader, changes in group values and priorities, and changes in the interpretation of the group task and output (Chang, Bordia & Duck, 2006). The researchers tackled the literature by organising their definitions of development along three principal dimensions.

1 *Content.* This dimension refers to the content of the developments that exist on a continuum, ranging from changes of a specific aspect of the group over time at one end, to general or comprehensive changes in the overall picture of the group at the other end.
2 *Population.* This dimension refers to the populations of groups that exist on a continuum, ranging from specific populations such as project teams at one end, to general developmental patterns across all groups at the other end.
3 *Path-dependency.* This dimension refers to the path-dependency of groups that exist on a continuum, ranging from path-dependent groups at one end, to non-path-dependent groups on the other. Path-dependency refers to continual changes within the group that are determined by what has gone before, i.e. they are historically dependent. Non-path-dependency refers to any changes that happen as a matter of time, rather than the previous activities of the group.

The three dimensions identified by Chang, Bordia & Duck (2006) are useful for demonstrating the contrasting positions of the PEM and the stage model in relation to one another. The PEM focuses specifically on the group's awareness of time pressures, defining its development in terms of changes in relation to course and pace. The PEM would therefore sit on the specific end of the content dimension continuum. The development of the PEM was also based on project teams, which places it on the specific population end of the population dimension continuum. Changes in the group's course according to the PEM were determined by time awareness (which occur at the midpoint) rather than their previous activities; therefore the model would sit at the non-path-dependent end of the third dimension. In contrast, the stage model is more comprehensive as it considers generic sequential processes in the development of groups, placing it on the general end of the content dimension continuum. The model also applies to all work groups and therefore sits at the general end of the population continuum dimension. Finally, the stage model is based on the group's progression; each stage of the model is dependent on the previous stage, placing it on the path-dependent end of the third dimension.

12.6 Group roles

Not everyone within a group or team has the same function. Different individuals have different skills, jobs and responsibilities. For many teams, individuals will have been recruited as a member of the team because of their particular skills and abilities; hence their role within the team will be prescribed before their recruitment. For example, an accountant might be recruited to oversee the financial activity of the team; hence their role is already predetermined. However, for some work groups, there are less prescriptive roles which may be established after the group has formed. There are abstract, generic group roles that are associated with either the group's task, or the characteristics of the members of the group.

Stop and reflect

Think of a time when you were involved in a group or team – this does not have to be a work team, it might have been a group or team related to sports or music. How were you recruited? Was it for a particular skill or ability, or was your role in the group established after it was formed? If so, how was it established?

Formal and informal roles

Roles can be broken down into two types: formal and informal. Formal roles are those that are specified by an organisation usually within a job description. These roles are well defined in order to avoid any ambiguity about what is expected of the employee. The formal roles of members within a group need specific parameters to avoid any overlaps with other group member's roles. An overlap in members' jurisdiction or responsibilities can lead to role conflict. Conflict within teams can be damaging to the team's performance, but we will go into this in more detail later in this chapter. Informal roles are the product of group interaction. Groups tend to invent these roles but they do not exist in a formal sense. An example of this is when someone in a group takes on the role of organising social gatherings, or arranging participation in charity events. The member may take on the role of arranging events, inviting people, collecting money and paying for the venue. Another example might be of a member who is elected as a mediator to resolve conflict between group members. They will have been recognised by other team members for their qualities in diplomacy and reconciliation. Although organisations may be concerned that employees spend too much time in their informal roles, the fulfilment of these roles have beneficial purposes for both the team and the organisation (e.g. resolving intra-group conflict), which may not be as well defined as their formal roles, but are still important to the team's success. Time and effort spent in informal roles equates to what is known as 'process loss', which is when employees spend time at work on matters not directly related to their work. Process loss can clearly be detrimental to production levels and subsequently the profits of the organisation. However, process loss is not always counter productive. A certain amount is to a large extent inevitable and it is therefore better for the organisation to control the amount rather than to avoid the causes of process loss altogether. Low levels of process loss as a function of social cohesion among group members may eventually lead to better group performance.

Belbin team-role inventory

The Belbin team-role inventory is an established measure for the identification of individual team roles. Belbin differentiated between clusters of behaviour and tendencies to interrelate with others in a particular way. Belbin researched personalities in management game settings with the use of the self-perception inventory; an instrument for quantifying individual team-role preferences. The test aims to determine what kind of team role a person has. The scores on the scale range between 0 and 100, where the highest score shows the participant's primary role, their second highest score shows their secondary role, and the third highest score shows their tertiary role. Belbin found that certain combinations of team roles result in poor team performance and other combinations lead to success. Belbin's focus is on the establishment of roles within a team, where measures of self-discovery in combination with the perceived needs of the team determine the assumptions of members' duties and responsibilities.

Belbin (1993) argued that, within a team, particular individuals take on specific roles. The blend of these individual roles has a crucial influence on the team's performance. A poor blend is likely to lead to poor performance, and the right blend will enhance the likelihood of the team's success. The composition of the team therefore is of crucial importance. Belbin constructed a list of nine potential 'roles' required for effective teams.

1 **Plant**: creative, imaginative, unorthodox. Plants are capable of solving difficult problems, but they might neglect details and fail to communicate effectively.
2 **Resource investigator**: extrovert, enthusiastic, communicative. Resource investigators explore opportunities and develop external contacts, but they tend to be over-optimistic and lose interest once their initial enthusiasm has passed.
3 **Coordinator**: mature, confident. Coordinators clarify goals, promote decision-making, and delegate duties among other team members, but other members may regard them as manipulative.
4 **Shaper**: challenging, dynamic, thrive on pressure. Shapers have the courage to overcome obstacles, but they tend to provoke others, which might lead to team conflict.

5 **Monitor evaluator**: sober, strategic and discerning. Monitors are able to see all available options and judge them appropriately, but they can be overly critical and lack the ability to inspire others.

6 **Team worker**: cooperative, mild, diplomatic. Team workers listen, build, and calm team conflict, but they tend to be indecisive in challenging situations and can be easily influenced.

7 **Implementer**: disciplined, reliable, conservative. Implementers turn ideas into practical actions, but might be inflexible and slow to adapt to new changes.

8 **Completer finisher**: painstaking, conscientious, anxious. Completers search out errors and omissions, finalise details and deliver on time, but they are inclined to worry unduly, and may be reluctant to delegate.

9 **Specialist**: single-minded, self-starting, dedicated. Specialists provide knowledge and skills that are uncommon and provide a narrow but necessary proportion of the output, but because their focus is on technicalities, they are unable to see the big picture.

Belbin's approach to team building has been commonly used among team managers within organisations (Lessem & Baruch, 2000). The literature on groups and teams has found support for Belbin's team roles (e.g. Senior, 1997), but what happens when the team consists of fewer than nine members? Belbin referred to the importance of 'team balance' in team success, where each of the roles can be identified in at least one member's profile, by observing a score for that particular role in excess of 70. To overcome the clear limitation of a team of fewer than nine members in applying this theory, Belbin proposed that for the absent primary roles, secondary roles with scores between 30 and 60 would be adequate (Senior, 1997). Van der Water, & Bukman (2009) formulated a mathematical model, that demonstrates the balance of Belbin's team can be maintained when there are fewer than nine members, by assigning the most suitable roles as either primary or secondary. However, ensuring the right balance of primary and secondary roles is a complex process. There is also likely to be a risk of role conflict if members of a group occupy more than one role. Belbin's nine roles may be overly defined and too many in number, and can in fact easily be reduced to personality types. Fisher, Hunter, & Macrosson (2001) conducted a study investigating the convergent and discriminant validity for Belbin's team roles. Convergent validity is the extent to which constructs are similar to other theoretically similar constructs, whereas discriminant validity is the extent to which constructs are distinct from other theoretically different constructs. The researchers found convergent validity for the nine roles using personality assessments, but were unable to find support for distinct roles and argue in support of Broucek and Randell (1996), who suggest that Costa and McCrae's (1992) NEO-PI/NEO-PI-R Five Factor Inventory may be just as effective. Fisher *et al.* (2001) used Costa and McCrae's Big Five as a team model to fit with seven previously identified project tasks: planning, defining resources needed, scheduling, implementing, measuring progress, reporting, and maintaining human relations (see Table 12.1). Each of the five personality traits possess certain characteristics that lend themselves to certain tasks; hence, rather than define the individual's role by features of the task as Belbin did (e.g. 'completer

Table 12.1 The fit between Costa and McCrae's Big Five and project tasks (Fisher, Hunger, & Macrosson, 2001).

Project task	Personality trait
Planning & defining resources	Openness (inventive, insightful)
Implementing	Extroversion (outgoing, energetic)
Scheduling	Conscientiousness (efficient, methodical)
Measuring progress & reporting	Neuroticism (anxious, fearful)
Maintaining human relations	Agreeableness (trusting, stable)

finisher'), Fisher et al. provide a dyadic alignment of personality traits with specific project tasks. This presents with less specificity than Belbin's team model but arguably greater practical utility.

The trait of openness lends itself to the planning stage of a task, which requires imagination, insight and enthusiasm. Extroverted characters will be useful at the implementation stage of a task, which requires energy for fine ideas to be synergised into action. Conscientious team members who tend to be efficient will be useful for ensuring the project is running in accordance with planned targets and time periods. Team members high on neuroticism will find their mildly obsessive tendencies towards perfection useful in measuring a team's progress and producing reports. Finally, agreeableness will be a vital team member component to guard against the negative influence of team conflict.

The focus on matching certain personality traits with roles that require such traits makes good sense. However, this may be a little idealistic because it neglects the social dynamics created by a mix of differing personality traits. Halfhill, Sundstrom, Lahner, Calderhone, & Nielsen (2005) found that groups tend to be homogeneous in terms of personality variables. The more heterogeneous the group, the more likely their performance was to decrease. As we will see later in this chapter, disparities in member demographic variables can create the conditions required for team conflict, which in turn reduces team performance. It therefore makes sense that disparities in members' personality types are also likely to negatively impact on team performance; potentially with team conflict acting as a mediating variable (Halfhill et al. 2005). The opposite of this is that similar personality types are likely to have a similar work ethic, generating high levels of group cohesion, working collaboratively to maximise group performance. There is likely to be potential for using Costa and McCrae's Big Five as a team model for project work, but it might be prudent in doing so to attend to the domains (lines of communication, work environment) that foster interpersonal relations among group members, in order to reduce the potential for interpersonal conflict among very different personality types.

12.7 Group factors and group performance

There is a belief that group performance is better than an individual's performance: 'two heads are better than one'. Some work projects or tasks clearly need not only more than one person, but diversity in skills in order to complete the set objective. However, when individuals work in groups, the mere element of working with other people generates a number of group phenomena that can either have an adverse effect or a positive influence on the group's performance. Naturally, organisations will be interested in reducing the former and enhancing the latter. We will now look at group phenomena that directly affect the group's performance (group polarisation, groupthink, social loafing, team conflict, group cohesion, brainstorming, group fit). First we will look at a specific group concept that explains how groups develop specific criteria within a number of domains, which ultimately determines their performance.

Group norms

Group norms refer to unwritten rules of group behaviour. These norms can vary from the style of dress, the manner of speech, to how hard everyone works. These norms can have a powerful influence on an individual's behaviour because the group enforces these norms through formal work activity and informal social activity. A more formal type of norm is a production norm, which dictates how many articles the members should produce within the course of their work. This can be seen in piece-rate factories where individuals get paid per item produced. With this type of system, all members of the group are given financial rewards that are directly linked to their level of production. From the organisation's point of view this does not always motivate groups to perform well because individuals will be reluctant to increase their level of production if it does not conform with the group norm for production. However, it has been found that goal setting can be an effective means of encouraging groups to adopt norms that are consistent with the organisation's production requirements (Lichtman & Lane, 1983). This differs from individual goals as the whole group is signed up to achieving the goal rather than one person. The level of production the group needs to engage to achieve their goal becomes the group production norm.

Stop and reflect

Group norms don't just apply to work groups; they can also apply to activity groups, sports teams or social groups. For instance, groups of friends can have norms or unwritten rules about how to behave in certain situations. Can you think of a norm in one of your friendship groups? How did the norm develop? Was it a norm that was clearly spoken about or was it something that the group simply 'knew'? Was it a positive norm or a negative norm? Did it help the group achieve anything, or did it cause problems? What happened if someone broke the norm?

Groups tend to establish norms only with respect to factors that are significant to the group. Norms might apply only to particular group members, and in such cases tend to specify the role of these members. Group norms vary in terms of how they are enforced, but in most cases sanctions are applied to members of the group who break the norms.

Group norms function as key determinants of the group's performance. For example, if a work group has a norm that is pro-management, they are likely to be more productive than a group with an anti-management norm. Managers can influence the setting and changing of norms by evaluating current norms in relation to the group's performance, and replacing any counterproductive or dysfunctional norms with pro-organisation, facilitative norms.

Most norms develop slowly over time in one or more of the following three ways:

1 explicit statements made by supervisors or colleagues
2 critical events in the history of the group or the organisation
3 distinct behaviours carried over from previous situations.

Compliance with group norms is essential to the group's survival, which is why norms are enforced. The group norms represent a regulatory body for all group activity to prevent disorderly conduct that may place the group's status within the organisation at risk. They are also useful to the organisation as knowledge of the group's norms allows for the prediction of the group members' behaviour. Predictability subsequently empowers the organisation with the ability to design strategies for improved group performance.

Group polarisation

Groups are frequently tasked with making decisions, the outcomes of which carry a risk for both the group and the organisation. For instance, there will often be a number of courses of action the group must decide on, each with different potential outcomes. There will be outcomes that represent advantages to the organisation, and outcomes that will represent disadvantages. In deciding which course of action to take, the group will assess the level of risk of a disadvantageous outcome, and estimate the value of potential benefits against the value of potential losses. The decisions taken by groups tend to differ from those taken by individuals, but not necessarily in the way one might expect. Early theories of group decision-making offered by psychologists such as Allport during the 1920s indicated that individuals would make more extreme decisions than groups. The argument was that groups would ultimately reach a decision that conformed to the average level of risk perceived by each of the group members. However, this has been shown not to be the case. Groups are more likely to make more extreme decisions than individuals, the phenomenon of which has been defined as group polarisation. It was formally defined as 'risky shift' on the basis that individuals prone to risk-taking exaggerate their position within groups. However, it was later discovered that this can also occur in the opposite direction, i.e. individuals prone to conservative decision-making exaggerate their position of safety within groups. Thus the group phenomenon that exists is one of polarisation; whether the majority consensus is risky or safe, the final group decision will be an exaggeration of the consensus. Group decisions can subsequently be extreme compared with the average levels of risk in the decisions taken by an equivalent number of individuals.

The decision is likely to generate an outcome in the predicted direction, but the measure of the outcome is likely to surpass original estimates.

The two most common theories drawn on to explain the effects of group polarisation are social comparison theory (Isenberg, 1986) and the persuasive argument theory (Turner, Wetherell, & Hogg, 1989). Social comparison theory incorporates the individual's perception of the self and their motivation to be socially desirable. When a group initially forms, members are not aware of one another or each other's opinions. Therefore they tend to moderate their own opinion towards what they perceive is the central tendency for the group. However, as discussions commence and members become more aware of each other's opinions, in order to achieve social desirability members polarise their opinions in favour of the common consensus. This allows them to distinguish themselves in the group's valued direction.

In contrast to focusing on the social perceptions and motivations of group members, the persuasive arguments theory (PAT) concentrates on the content of group discussion. The PAT posits that during their discussions, groups become exposed to persuasive arguments from its members, which encourage others to alter their initial opinion. The strength of persuasion that an argument holds depends on its originality and validity. For an argument to be able to persuade group members to change their initial position, they must perceive the argument to be one that carries weight and is unlike any arguments already presented. As the more persuasive arguments are likely to be possessed by those representing the majority position, shifts in opinions will favour the majority position.

Both the social comparison theory and the PAT are compelling in their explanation of group polarisation. However, not all members of a group will be intent on achieving social desirability, and therefore their opinion is less likely to be motivated by social factors. Depending on the nature of the decision, some group members may place priority with the appropriateness of their decision outcome rather than their social status within the group. The persuasive argument theory certainly explains why initially diverse opinions among group members can become concordant in the presence of convincing arguments favouring a decision outcome. However, it does not necessarily explain why opinions surpass simple agreement and become polarised towards achieving extreme outcomes. Isenberg (1986) conducted a meta-analysis to explore the underlying mechanisms for group polarisation and found that both the social comparison theory and the PAT provide causal explanations. However, Isenberg concluded that the causal factors described by both theories operate in combination; i.e. PAT operates in the absence of social comparison theory and vice versa. However, persuasive argument processes have been found to have a significantly stronger effect than social comparison processes (Isenberg, 1986).

Groupthink

Groupthink was a concept developed by Janis (1972) to describe a tendency for groups to engage in concurrence-seeking. In a hurry to reach an agreement, groups fall foul of making inappropriate decisions. This is frequently because members instinctively favour a particular course of action to the extent that minority opinions are ignored, relevant information is not sufficiently reviewed, and the group tend to believe they cannot be wrong. Groupthink therefore interferes with effective decision-making within groups. Consequently, poor decisions inevitably lead to unsuccessful and sometimes disastrous outcomes. Groupthink is a phenomenon best explained by providing classical examples of its occurrence. Consider the following three cases in point:

Real case 12.1

Space shuttle disaster

On 1 February 2003 the Space Shuttle Columbia disintegrated over Texas during re-entry into the Earth's atmosphere, killing all seven crew members. The loss of Columbia was due to damage sustained during its launch when a small piece of foam insulation broke off the main propellant tank. The debris then struck the leading edge of the left wing, damaging the shuttle's thermal protection system, which is designed to protect the shuttle from heat during re-entry into the Earth's atmosphere. However, even while Columbia was still in orbit, engineers suspected damage, but NASA managers limited the investigation because they had concluded that little could be done to prevent the incident. The consensus that nothing could be done had prevented NASA managers from engaging in necessary urgent investigations and the development of contingency plans. Their position was one of calculating potential risks rather than making an assessment of the actual damage and seeking preventive solutions.

Real Case 12.2

US banking crisis

The worst financial crisis since the Great Depression in the 1930s hit the world's economy in 2007. Foreign money pouring into the US from rapidly developing economies in Asia created a credit bubble; property prices rose, and credit was easy to come by. As property prices fell in 2007, interest rates rose, the result of which was a liquidity shortfall in the US banking system. Throughout the world,

financial institutions collapsed and governments were forced to bail out banks. The outcome of the crisis resulted in depressed housing markets, a downturn in stock markets, a decline in consumer wealth, and many people being evicted from their homes. Following the major banking crisis the Independent Evaluation Office (IEO) uncovered serious lapses in judgement made by the International Monetary Fund (IMF). A report conducted by the IEO in February 2011 stated that 'the IMF's ability to correctly identify the mounting risks was hindered by a high degree of groupthink, intellectual capture, a general mindset that a major financial crisis in large advanced economies was unlikely, and inadequate analytical approaches . . .' The IEO report claims that the IMF failed to observe key elements underpinning the developing financial crisis. The IMF favoured the US/UK approach to achieving rapid financial growth through 'light-touch regulation and supervision', to the point of making recommendations that other advanced countries follow suit. The IEO concluded its report by making suggestions that the IMF should in future actively seek alternative or dissenting views.

Real case 12.3

Weapons of mass destruction

In 2003, President Bush's State of the Union address made very specific claims about Iraq's weapons of mass destruction: '500 tons of sarin, mustard and VX nerve agent; mobile biological weapons labs', and 'a design for a nuclear weapon'. Just one year later, President Bush was calling for an investigation of failures in intelligence about such weapons preceding the invasion of Iraq. There had been a wave of surprise around the world at the clear, substantial failure of intelligence that subsequently led the United States into war. But the United States went to war largely because the president and most of his top advisors believed that Iraq possessed stockpiles of weapons of mass destruction. The Bush administration had undertaken a brave attempt at overthrowing a foreign government in order to stop the spread of these weapons of mass destruction. Fighting terrorism and replacing a destructive dictatorship with a democracy were laudable, unquestionable leadership objectives of the US presidency. It is now clear that such weapons did not in fact exist. The communication and interpretation of intelligence of Vice President Dick Cheney and his allies encircled the president, blocking out views that went against their own. This filtering of dissent meant the course of action the government took was not only ill-informed, but reflected the thinking of only a select few of the US presidential team.

From these three cases we can see that groupthink can generate exceptionally damaging outcomes. Janis's model of groupthink (see Figure 12.2) identifies the antecedents (B – 1) that lead to concurrence seeking (Janis, 1972). These antecedents

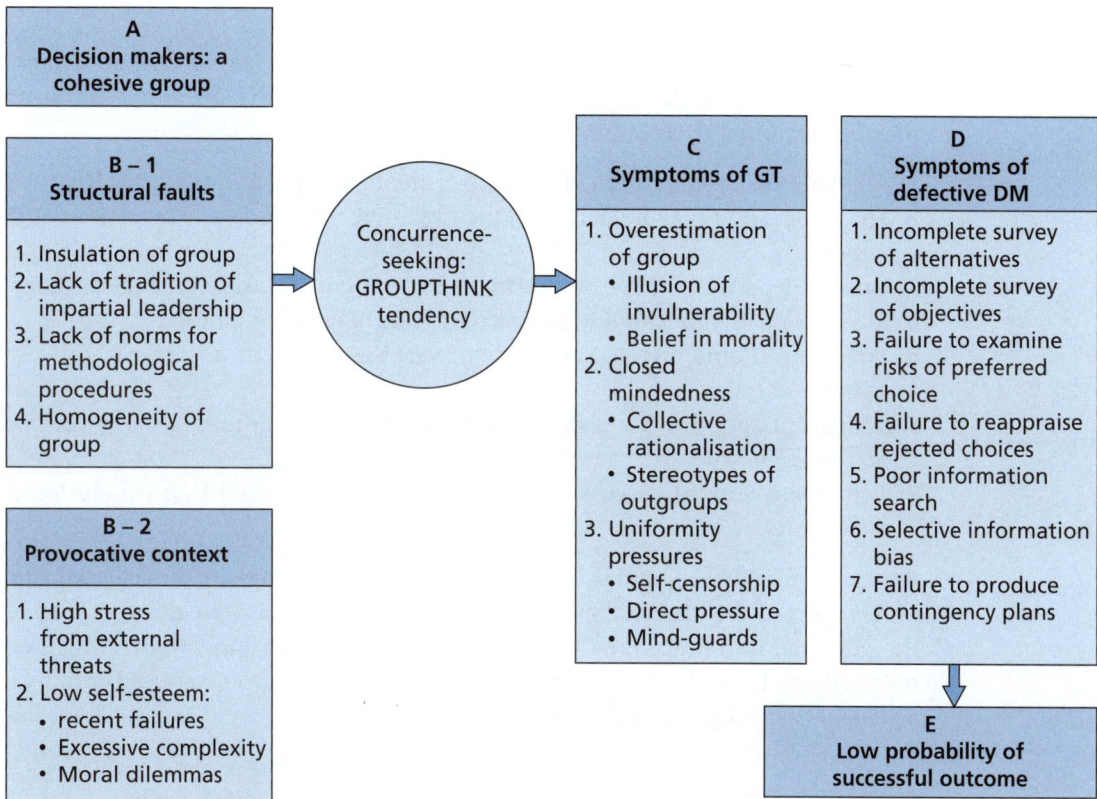

Figure 12.2 Groupthink

include the absence of group norms and homogeneity of group members. This presents an interesting problem as we have already observed that homogeneous groups tend to be more productive than heterogeneous groups (Halfhill et al. 2005). However, it is easy to see why group members who are similar in their views might miss pertinent information in their decision-making processes. Early symptoms identified in Janis's model such as closed-mindedness evidence early signs of groupthink that are observable in the three cases presented. For example, we can clearly see that the Bush administration's brave attempt to overthrow a foreign government in the interests of fighting terrorism is indicative of their belief in morality. This alone of course was not necessarily the problem, but their pursuit of the moral good prevented thorough and accurate interpretations of intelligence. Groups, just as the Bush administration, may reach a cognitive state where they are unable to see that their decision is so right that it must be wrong. The most well-thought-out and supportable decisions are those that tend to invite conflict in opinions during their making, which in turn demand the appraisal and reappraisal of all available intelligence. As we can see from the symptoms of defective decision-making in Janis' model, there is a general failure of the group to explore other possibilities and closely examine the risks their choices carry.

Avoiding groupthink

Many groups are at risk of groupthink; however, the good news is that understanding groupthink and the antecedents allows organisations to avoid it. Groupthink may be prevented by adopting some of the following measures.

1 All members should be encouraged to evaluate group decisions critically.
2 The leader should avoid declaring their own preferences and expectations at the outset.
3 Outside experts should be invited to offer their opinions and challenge any views.
4 At least one member should be given the role of devil's advocate.
5 The group should discuss and evaluate warning signals from external sources or critiques.
6 If large enough, the group should be split into smaller groups to make decisions on the same issue.
7 The group should discuss and evaluate minority dissenting or alternative viewpoints.

It is interesting to note that this last measure was advice given by the IEO to the IMF in its report of the financial banking crisis. These measures were designed to avert the potential for groupthink to arise, but they would also apply to averting group polarisation. They are arguably reasonable measures that groups should employ on a general basis to ensure effective group decision-making.

Social loafing

Social loafing describes the tendency of individuals to exert less effort when they are part of a group. Because all members of the group are pooling their effort to achieve a common goal, each member of the group contributes less than they would if they were individually responsible. The contribution of efforts can mask the source, which allows social loafers in the group to hide behind the efforts of others. Social loafing occurs when individuals feel that they are not personally accountable or that their efforts are not needed by the group. This obviously means that not all members of the group are contributing to the same level, therefore social loafing is a problem for the performance of many groups.

Stark, Shaw, & Duffy (2007) developed a multi-level, interactive framework for predicting social loafing in teams that incorporates team-member attitudes (preference for group work), individual differences in competitiveness (winning orientation), and task interdependence (the degree to which members rely on one another). The findings demonstrated that preference for group work was negatively correlated with social loafing, i.e. the greater the preference for group work, the lower the scores on social loafing, and vice versa. This relationship was predicted by low scores on winning orientation (i.e. were not highly competitive), and low scores on task interdependence (i.e. participants rely little on each other).

It would appear that social loafing is a complex psychological phenomenon that results from a combination of attitudes and preferences. In terms of preventing social loafing, from the findings of Stark et al. (2007) organisations would need to consider the individual's preferences to working in groups and their ability to work as part of a team. However, organisations are becoming increasingly focused on monitoring and documenting the performance of employees within a number of different domains, including contributions to group-related processes. 'Brainwriting' for example, as an alternative to brainstorming (which we will discuss towards the end of this chapter) reduces the opportunity for social loafing because members' contributions to the session are recorded on a computer.

Team conflict

It is a natural phenomenon that when individuals are grouped together on a work task, conflict is likely to arise at some point. Rifts between members of a team can be undermining both to team-member satisfaction and the performance of the team. Lau and Murnighan (2005) conceptualised rifts within teams as 'faultlines' that exist when there is considerable disparity between member demographics, such as age, gender and ethnic origin. This can be the cause of divisiveness within the group, which creates the conditions for intra-group conflict. These conditions are tensions among group members that may be managed up to a point, but invariably create weak spots or underlying fractures that are susceptible to conflict. This group state is the opposite of group cohesion, which is the bonding force that keeps groups together and committed to accomplishing their task. Although the conflict may exist initially between two members of a group, the divisive nature of conflict may pervade the rest of the group as other members are implicitly required to take sides. This creates subgroups that sustain and build on the original conflict rather than resolving it. Conflict is likely to deflect the group's energy and attention away from their task and create stress among its members. This is likely to lead to poor team member satisfaction and ultimately degrade their work performance.

However, conflict in work groups is not always bad news. Conflict can be functional as long as it originates from within the work task rather than interpersonal member relations. Examples of relationship conflict might be differences in political opinions, interpersonal style, morals, views and work ethic. On this last point, diversity in work ethics should not be confused with task conflict. Work ethic relates to members' attitudes and approaches to work in general, rather than their specific view of the group's task. Task conflict, however, arises from differences in members' views on organisational policies, processes, distribution of resources, allocation of work, and interpretations of task-specific information. Although relationship conflict is clearly likely only to negatively influence the group's performance, a low level of task conflict may in fact stimulate ideas and progression. Task conflict is likely to arise when one member or more of the group resists conforming to the views of other group members. Therefore conflict is useful for combating the negative effects associated with groupthink (group pressure and conformity; Janis, 1972), where the group ignores minority thinking at its own peril. There can be advantages to diversity; different points of view in constructive discussions can synergise and generate new ideas, methods, solutions to problems (Amason, 1996) and decision quality (Mannix & Neale, 2005). However, when conflict stems from interpersonal relations, it interferes with group information processing and undermines team satisfaction and performance. From this, we can conclude that reducing the conditions and factors associated with interpersonal conflict, and enhancing those associated with task conflict, would be beneficial to group performance.

However a meta-analysis conducted by De Dreu and Weingart (2003) found that both interrelationship conflict *and* task conflict were negatively associated with team-member satisfaction and performance. From an information-processing perspective any anticipated conflict, even if it is task conflict, still detracts cognitive processes that need to remain focused on the task. Carnevale & Probst (1998) found that participants were cognitively more flexible and creative in their thinking when they anticipated a cooperative negotiation (low conflict) with another individual. Conversely, when participants anticipated hostile negotiation (high conflict), this substantially reduced cognitive flexibility and creativity. This effect was described by Carnevale and Probst as 'cognitive load', where the type of cognitive processes rooted in creative thinking that need to be free of interference are disturbed by negative cognitive arousal and anxiety.

It would seem that other factors might be responsible for determining whether task conflict can have a positive influence on team performance, such as the nature of the task and members' attitudes to resolving the conflict. Jehn (1997) differentiates non-routine tasks and routine tasks in how they can affect group performance. Non-routine tasks can be beneficial to team performance because there tends to be a lack of standard solutions associated with routine tasks. Non-routine tasks therefore may require group discussions where contrasting views are more acceptable and functional in developing greater levels of scrutiny and effective problem-solving. However, routine tasks ordinarily have well practised and standardised operating procedures. Group discussions regarding routine tasks may be perceived as time-consuming and unnecessary by group members. Therefore any conflict in relation to routine tasks may be more likely to hinder performance rather than improve it. In terms of members' attitudes towards dealing with task conflict, in order for diversity to be functional and synergise new, dynamic thinking, those involved in the conflict may need to compromise and adapt their earlier views. Members of the group are more likely to make compromises when interpersonal relations among group members are positive. In turn, positive interpersonal relations means interpersonal conflict is unlikely. Thus, we may conclude that for teams to handle task conflict and use it to their collective advantage, maintaining positive member relations is of considerable importance.

Group cohesion

Group cohesiveness is a great source of interest in the literature looking at groups and teams, because it is frequently associated with enhanced group performance (e.g. Mullen & Copper, 1994). Group cohesiveness is also the best summary representation of the psycho-social variables present in the study of groups. Before we look at how cohesiveness determines group performance we shall consider what constitutes group cohesion.

Group cohesiveness is a force that attracts group members and keeps them together. Cohesion is a type of bonding that occurs because of shared and intense motivations towards the group's objectives, and the esteem associated with being a member of the group. Historically there has been a mixture of definitions for group cohesiveness with some authors favouring a unitary construct (e.g. Carron, 1982) whereas others have favoured a multi-faceted construct (Festinger, 1950). Festinger (1950) identified three facets that comprise group cohesion: member attraction, group activities requiring task commitment, and prestige or 'group pride'. Group pride has largely been ignored in the literature, with the focus tending to be on group cohesion as dyadic; a combination of the relations between members and the nature of the work task. Gross, & Martin (1952) identified two underlying dimensions accounting for member attraction and group activities: interpersonal cohesiveness and task cohesiveness. Interpersonal cohesiveness relates to interpersonal relations among group members, which if positive is likely to lead to open communication and effective coordination of each member's contribution to the task. Task cohesiveness refers to the shared commitment from the group members in achieving the group task (Hackman, 1976), which if positive is likely to lead to an increase in the members' individual efforts in the group's task.

Group cohesiveness has been studied in a wide variety of settings where the concept of 'togetherness' is particularly relevant, including military units, sports teams and therapy groups. A cohesive group is one that sticks together; one whose members are bonded to one another, and to the group as a whole. Cohesiveness often engenders feelings of solidarity, harmony, loyalty and commitment among its members to the achievement of group goals.

There is a general consensus that group cohesion is a positive force oriented in strong member relations and motivation towards achieving task-related objectives. A highly cohesive group as we have observed is the opposite of a group that is susceptible to conflict. Group norms are strongly enforced in highly cohesive groups and subsequently function as a means of sustaining group cohesion. Communication levels between members of a cohesive group are high. This facilitates the clarification of the group's aims and objectives. As a result members of cohesive groups are generally more satisfied with their jobs, and the team are more likely to perform better in relation to their task. Beal, Cohen, Burke, & McLendon (2003) conducted a meta-analysis and found that the three components of group cohesion identified by Festinger (1950) – interpersonal attraction, task commitment and group pride all related to group performance. The belief that highly cohesive groups will improve their work performance has led many organisations to enhance this group factor, by encouraging the participation of members in bonding experiences, such as those offered by Outward Bound. Organisations believe these extra-curricular activities will bond members together through their unique, shared experience and ultimately increase their level of effort in the group's work task.

Although the concept that high group cohesion leads to better group performance, the findings are not always consistent in the literature on this topic.

One of the key problems is that there are a number of operational definitions and measures to match (Casey-Campbell & Martens, 2009). Mullen and Copper (1994) identified a divergence in cohesion literature, where some researchers assess group cohesion experimentally by comparing the performance in high and low cohesive groups, whereas others assess correlations between group members' perceptions of cohesion and performance. The method used in the research is important in relation to the findings, as Mullen and Copper (1994) found a stronger link between group cohesion and performance among correlational studies than experimental studies.

Chiocchio and Essiembre (2009) identified a further divergence in cohesion literature in terms of how performance is measured, which is either by behaviour or outcome. Interestingly, the strength of the influence of cohesion on either of these two measures is dependent on the type of team. The researchers assessed the effects of cohesion in project teams, production teams and service teams in both organisational and academic settings. The researchers found that the link between cohesion and performance was stronger in project teams than the other two types. Furthermore, in project teams the link was stronger for behavioural measures than outcome measures, but stronger for outcome measures among the other two work teams. This might be because production and service teams are continually generating output in relation to their work, which may be less distinguishable from behaviour than in a project team. Project teams may have a number of deliverables in relation to their task, but these are less continuous than they would be in the other two work teams. The time-limited nature of project teams may mean members place greater importance on behaviour than do more settled work groups. Chiocchio and Essiembre (2009) also found that task cohesiveness was more important than social cohesiveness, but only in project teams in academic settings. This might well be because although academics work on projects collaboratively, they tend to work in isolation, hence social cohesion is not necessarily a requirement for performance.

Brainstorming

Brainstorming involves generating ideas without any concern for criticism about the appropriateness of the ideas. All ideas, no matter how impractical they may appear, are called for in a brainstorming session in order to generate a pool of ideas that can be later evaluated and modified. Groups can be superior to individuals in generating ideas and solutions to problems. The theory behind brainstorming is that group members will inspire one another to generate ideas that they would not have thought of alone. Participating in a brainstorming session provokes cognitive facilitation, which is where other group members' ideas trigger new cognitive associations and ideas that would not come to mind in a solitary idea-generation session (Paulus, Larey, & Dzindolet, 2000).

Brainstorming is one of the most widely accepted processes for generating creative ideas within organisations (Nijstad & Stroebe, 2006). However, research by Gallupe, Bastianutti, & Cooper (1991) failed to find superior performance among groups. It was found that, rather than inspiring one another, group members inhibited one another. Individuals may be reluctant to volunteer ideas because of a lack of confidence both in their ideas and their ability to communicate them. Members of the group might decide while waiting for their turn that their ideas are not good enough to share. A later study by Gallupe, Bastianutti, & Cooper (1994) found that if individuals were asked to enter their ideas into a computer there was an increase in performance. However if there was a delay in individuals being able to submit their ideas there was a decrease in performance. Clearly there are benefits from removing some of the environmental pressures, but ideas need to be promptly communicated and subsequently recorded or there is a risk they may not be recaptured. Researchers have referred to this alternative method of brainstorming as 'brainwriting', which has been found to produce superior generation of ideas compared with brainstorming (Paulus & Yang, 2000). Brainwriting allows group members to share written ideas silently. This reduces negative factors associated with brainstorming such as interpersonal conflicts, domination by group members, conformity pressure, and digressions from the topic under discussion (Van Gundy, 1983). Brainwriting also has the potential to reduce social loafing (Paulus & Yang, 2000) as the mode of communication clearly evidences the level of input from each member of the group. Brainwriting also offers clear convenience and cost advantages over brainstorming for international groups who do not work in the same country. The increasing globalisation of many organisations means that many work groups will be working in different locations throughout the world. An online forum will allow members to brainstorm ideas in a cost-effective way, and in a less socially pressured way.

Group fit

The fit perspective refers to the interactive processes between two entities. The concept of fit within organisational psychology typically refers to the person–environment fit, the person–organisation fit, and the person–job fit. It has become relevant to work teams because of the increasing diversity in team members' knowledge, skills and experience (DeRue & Morgeson, 2007). Work teams therefore need high levels of inter-communication and co-ordination, which are dependent on a good level of 'fit'. Group fit was classified by DeRue & Hollenbeck (2007) as either internal or external. Internal group fit refers to the way member factors such as demographics, personality traits and values relate or correspond with one another. External group fit refers to the alignment of the group's characteristics with the organisational culture and task environment. A high level of internal group fit is likely to generate group cohesion, whereas a low level of fit is likely to indicate poor cohesion, and subsequently poor group performance. External fit such as group organisation fit (G–O) and group task fit (G–T) are either actual fit, or perceived fit. Actual fit can be determined by a comparison of one of the attributes of the group with a comparable attribute of the organisational environment (Kristof, 1996) or by the group's ability to be challenged by and complete the group task. Perceived fit is the group's perception of their compatibility with the organisational environment and their given task.

Shin and Choi (2010) found that perceived G–O predicts cohesion, and perceived G–T predicts group efficacy. As both group cohesion (Mullen & Copper, 1994) and group efficacy (Stajkovic, Lee, & Nyberg, 2009) directly relate to performance, the group's perception of fit may have a greater indirect impact on the group's performance than the actual group fit.

Legal context

For further details about employment legislation see Chapter 3 – Legislation applied to the workplace.

Short-answer questions

1 What is one of the three differences between groups and teams?
2 What is one of the main benefits to an organisation for employing teams over individuals?
3 What is the final stage of Tuckman's stage model for group formation and development?
4 What is the problem associated with defining group development?
5 How would you apply Belbin's team roles to a group of six individuals?
6 What advice would you offer an organisation for avoiding groupthink?

CASE STUDY
Groups and teams

The company

UK Serious Games is an organisation that designs and sells computer games for use in educational settings. The company was established in 2007 by a group of five postgraduates, who have combined expertise in research, education, computer games design and marketing. The company holds a number of contracts with schools and colleges around the country. The games are designed to be interactive and educational. For example, the company designed a computer game for schools to use for educating teenagers in road safety.

Company growth

The company has grown steadily over the past few years due to a growing positive reputation among UK educational institutions. The company now have three offices situated around the UK (London, Birmingham and Manchester) and a total of 62 employees. Each office comprises a small team of researchers headed by a team leader, a team of programme designers headed by a team leader, administration and reception staff, accounts staff, and an office manager. Their success has been due to the three following principles that the company has adhered to:

1 being aware of, and sensitive to current, educational topics
2 designing games that combine fun (to motivate students and pupils) with learning (to target the identified topic)
3 professional and efficient manner in handing their contracts.

The first principle has involved extensive research in the area of topicality, educational issues and pedagogy, which is the study of the best methods of teaching. The second principle has involved the recruitment of highly skilled individuals in the design of computer games who rely on research to generate the design, and understand the aims of each product. The third principle has been developed through the culture of the organisation, which from the start has fostered the belief that their success and future growth is dependent on delivering effective products and high standards of service. Their staff turnover has been exceptionally low; the company provides a strong remuneration package and staff satisfaction levels are high. Although initially during their set up they engaged in a substantial amount of marketing activity, the need for this has dwindled as their reputation among educational institutions has generated more than enough business.

New project

The company has recently developed a new game that educates teenagers in the damage caused by drug and alcohol abuse, which so far has been highly successful in the UK. The success of this game indicates that it would work in Europe. However, after a preliminary survey, only a few current employees are willing to work in Europe on the new project, which would be for approximately 18 months.

Your job

You are tasked with generating a report for the company, advising them how to develop a project team to adapt and launch their game in Europe. They are seeking your services because they are keen to ensure the right team is put together, which may involve recruiting some new staff. It is important to the continued success of the company that the team complete their objectives within the time-frame because of set budgets for the project.

Points to consider

- Who would manage the new team?
- What specific roles would the team need? (This should reflect general stages of the project requirements, including research, design, marketing, dissemination.)
- What skills would team members need to possess for this project?
- How many of the team (from none to all) could be based in Europe?
- What communication processes and systems could be put in place to ensure the team complete their objective within budget and on time?
- What measures could be put in place to avoid adverse group effects such as groupthink or team conflict?

The task from this case study is to apply the consultancy cycle and write a report providing an analysis of the new project the organisation is proposing and recommendations for the set up and development of a new project team.

For details of the consultancy cycle, please refer to Chapter 2, which provides a comprehensive overview. Chapter 2 also provides details regarding the structure of a business report that you will find useful for this task.

13

Organisational structures, culture and change

Learning outcomes

After reading this chapter, you should be able to:

- understand the function of an organisation chart
- identify strengths and weaknesses of different types of organisational structures
- understand the importance and impact of organisational culture on the operation of an organisation
- critically evaluate theories of organisational change and factors that may cause resistance to change.

13.1 Introduction

David, the Chief Executive of Sammie Security Services, is undertaking a review of the organisation. The intention is to reduce the staffing costs, increase efficiency, and branch out into the fire industry, selling fire alarms, fire-retardant doors and water sprinklers. This will require a change in the structure of the organisation as branch managers will no longer be needed and regional managers will take on the staff management at branch level. The culture of the organisation needs consideration as the current organisation takes a traditional approach to sales by the use of word of mouth and recommendations rather than hard sell, which will be needed to ensure the survival of the organisation. The process of change will have to be considered to ensure it is a smooth process and should take into account its effect on customers, staff and the organisation as a whole.

Organisations are everywhere, with most of us being involved in organisations from birth. For example, most people are born in hospital, go to nursery, school, college, university and work. These all represent types of organisations. Organisations have an impact on all aspects of our life, from our education, our career, relationships with others, as well as our lifestyle (economic status). We humans also have an impact on organisations – for example, how we work with others, our leadership style and our values and beliefs. Therefore, much research has been carried out into how organisations are structured, the types of cultures within organisations, as well as how individuals and organisations as a whole respond to change. The present chapter will explore these factors.

13.2 Organisational structures

Organisational structure refers to the types of coordination to organise individuals and departments. Structure represents the way in which people and tasks are arranged in order to maximise performance and to reach organisational goals most effectively and efficiently. Within any organisation, an employee's role is typified by the tasks that they perform and who they report to. However, the development of a structure depends on the following building blocks: centralisation (discussed later in the chapter), formalisation, hierarchical level and departmentalisation, which all need consideration. Centralisation refers to the degree with which decision-making authority is concentrated, at the top levels of the organisation. If an organisation is decentralised, decision-making is delegated to lower levels of the organisation. Formalisation concerns the organisation's policies and procedures and the amount of authority a person has over decisions. Formalised structures control employees' behaviours through the use of written rules. Hierarchical levels represent the number of levels an organisation has in its hierarchy. For example, a tall structure has a high hierarchy and a flat structure has a short hierarchy. Departmentalisaton uses either functional or product structures (detailed later in this chapter). The type of structure an organisation adopts also depends on a number of factors including the size of the organisation, the type of work it carries out, and its finances.

Child (1988) suggested six major dimensions of an organisational structure:

1 allocation of individual tasks and responsibilities
2 formal reporting relationships, level of authority and span of control (discussed later in the chapter)
3 grouping together of units, sections and departments
4 systems for communication of information
5 delegation of authority
6 motivation of employees through systems for performance appraisal.

These types of structures are represented by organisation charts. An organisation chart depicts the structure of an organisation including job positions as well as the authority and reporting lines between them. Figure 13.1 (overleaf) provides an

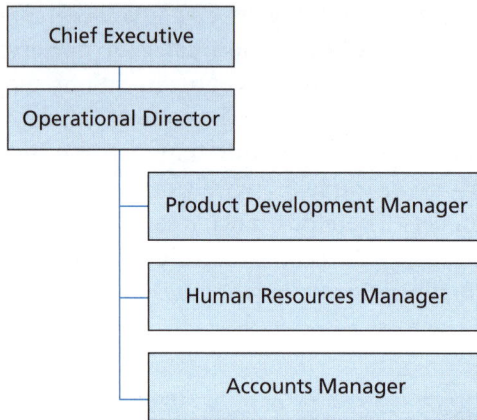

Figure 13.1 Functional organisation chart

example of an organisation chart depicting the management level of an organisation and the reporting lines. As can be seen from the chart, the three managers report to the operational director who reports directly to the chief executive.

The organisation chart in Figure 13.1 represents an organisation that is divided by function (product development, human resources and accounts). The advantage of splitting the organisation by function ensures that there is a coherent chain of command. For example, within a large organisation, the human resources department may be responsible for the arrangement of selection and assessment of staff, training of staff and performance appraisal. This ensures that staff recruitment and development are concentrated in one department, which allows for a seamless process. Another advantage is that as functions are housed within one area, the decision-making process should be speedier. If decisions were required by a selection and assessment manager, a training manager and a staff development manager (in separate departments), the decision-making process would be much slower than if the decisions were made within one functional area. A further advantage of a functional structure is that individuals develop their expertise in a specific area and this can become specialised. As individuals who have different skills are working in similar areas, they can help each other develop. For example, an individual working in career development can learn about relevant training programmes by working closely with an individual who assesses training needs of staff. (See Chapter 8 for a discussion of training needs.) The span of control is also represented in organisation charts that represent the number of people over which a manager has authority. For example, the product development manager may have 20 people working for them, therefore their span of control would be 20. The chief executive in Figure 13.1 would have responsibility for all members of the organisation, including direct and indirect reports, and thus would have a wide span of control.

Although the functional organisational structure has advantages, there are also a number of limitations. As functional structures are specialised, they may lose the perspective of the overall organisational objectives/goals and focus on their department only. Individuals also tend to have fixed ways of working and there is a lack of discussion with other departments/units. For example, Hollenbeck et al. (2002) found that organisations that adopt a functional structure perform poorly in unstable environments (such as changes in economic climates). This is because these unstable environments create change that overwhelms the simple subunits/ departments, whereas if they operated as a whole they might have the skills, knowledge and experience to react to the changes more efficiently.

A second type of organisational structure is the product organisation (see Figure 13.2). These organisations usually produce different product lines. For example, an electronics company may produce products that include televisions, audio equipment and computers. This sectioning of product streams creates divisions that are responsible for doing everything concerning that product (production, quality assurance, sales, etc). The advantage of this type of organisation is that the manager of the product can devote their resources to one product. There might also be a focus on the market segments for that particular product, which results in a good knowledge of the segment area, which aids in remaining competitive. However, as each area is devoted to its own product there is a duplication of resources. For example, in the example above, there would be a sales team for televisions, a sales team for audio equipment and a sales team for computers, rather than one sales team that covers the three products. This separation of products may cause coordination issues where different sales consultants may be trying to sell different products to the same customer. This would make the organisation look unprofessional in its sales approach and confuse the customer as to who their sales contact is.

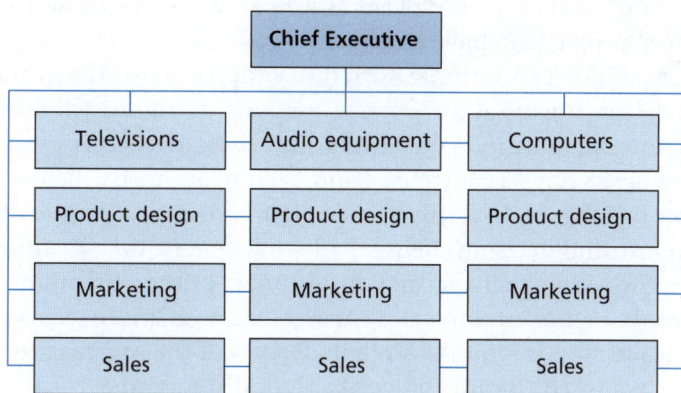

Figure 13.2 Product organisational structure

A more complicated organisational structure is the matrix organisation (see Figure 13.3, overleaf). Within these organisations each employee has two managers. One manager represents the functional manager (such as sales) and the second manager relates to the product or project (such as computers). In this type of structure there are three major roles. The first is the leader at the top of the structure (Chief Executive). This individual would have responsibility over both function and product managers. The second is the matrix bosses who are

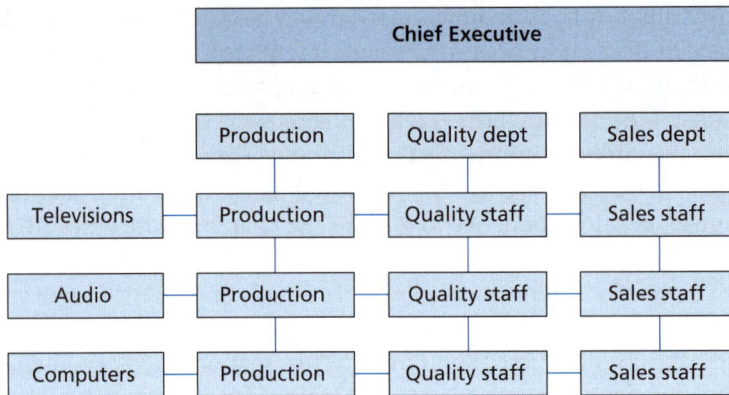

Figure 13.3 Matrix organisation chart

responsible for the functional departments or the product line. For this type of organisation to run effectively and efficiently, the functional managers and product managers need to communicate with each other and maintain a balance of authority between them. Finally, there are the two boss employees who must try to achieve their own individual targets while satisfying both managers. The benefits of this type of structure include a fluid workforce where individuals can be appointed to work on specific products or projects until completion and then be reassigned to another product or project once completed. However, disadvantages include conflicting loyalties to managers, which may cause anxiety and conflict of employees as well as slower decision-making due to the number of people who have to agree.

The type of organisational structure adopted depends on the environment in which the organisation operates as well as the distribution of authority within the organisation. Organisations where decisions are made by senior level managers have a centralised approach to authority. Benefits of centralised decision-making include the use of standardised procedures that employees understand, and decisions being made that benefit the organisation as a whole because the senior manager has an overview of the organisation. Where there are periods of uncertainty and change, such as in an economic downturn, strong leadership is required so that all parts of the organisation are aiming for the same goals. The disadvantage of a centralised approach is that it is very time-consuming as information has to be obtained from lower down the hierarchy so that the senior manager has a clear understanding of factors that may affect their decision. There is also less flexibility for the organisation to adapt to changes. This was exemplified by Hayward (1997), who commented on the British Army's first IT strategy. The strategy document contained over 800 pages and resulted in the managers feeling like prisoners over rigid methodologies and structures.

Organisations in which decisions are delegated throughout the organisation have a decentralised approach. The benefit of decentralised decision-making is that the workers who know the organisational processes best are involved in the decision-making. For example, a large supermarket chain would have decentralised decision-making as each store manager would have decision-making authority for their own store. Other benefits include senior managers having time to concentrate on the most important decisions as other decisions are taken by other people within the organisation. The delegation of decision-making also provides empowerment for individuals that increase motivation (see Chapter 10 – Motivation, job satisfaction, employee engagement and behavior modification). Weaknesses with this approach include the potential for a duplication of effort and resources. For example, three managers from different stores of a supermarket who have to decide on a recruitment process for cashiers would collect information about the job, advertising, shortlisting and selection process individually, whereas sharing the responsibility would reduce the amount of resources spent on the activity. There are also learning opportunities that may be missed due to not sharing ideas.

With the change in the way organisations operate, thought also needs to be given to the growing nature of virtual organisations. Virtual organisations have no physical presence. Two main types of virtual organisations exist. The first is where there is a structure where managers communicate with staff via electronic means such as email, telephone and video-conferencing. However, such organisations may be only partially virtual as they may meet face-to-face and have office space. Truly virtual organisations such as Amazon (the online provider of books and other goods) tend to be boundaryless and work with a small skeleton staff base, outsourcing a lot of work to other companies. For example, in the case of Amazon, customers place orders via the internet, orders are processed centrally and are mostly dispatched from the publisher's warehouse. Delivery of goods is handled by independent couriers. Disadvantages of virtual organisations include their high dependency on technology that is subject to limitations (network problems, internet access, etc.) as well as dependence on specific individuals (such as proprietor of the organisation).

Organisational structure theories

Two theories related to an organisation's structure are the classical and neoclassical theories. The classical theory assumes that there is a single, optimal way that organisations can be designed, where senior management have a tight control over their staff. This type of organisation has a tall hierarchy with lots of policies and procedures (centralised approach), where there is a narrow span of control (individuals only have a small number of people reporting to them). A structure that represents the classical theory is the functional structure. The neoclassical theory argues that the employee is important with employee satisfaction being key as well as the financial effectiveness of the organisation. These organisations tend to have flatter structures and there is less control from management over staff (decentralised approach). This type of organisation has fewer rules and procedures and staff are involved more in the decision-making process. Organisational structures are now moving towards a flatter, leaner structure that is representative of the neoclassical theory, as with organisations needing to change quickly due to technological advancements, economic changes as well as changes to political agendas, decisions need to be made speedily.

? Think about it

Think about the type of organisational structure that would be better suited to these two organisations.

1 The military, where there must be a tight control over the staff and there are lots of policies and procedures to follow.
2 An organisation that develops new computer software, where there is a need to respond to the marketplace quickly.

The type of structure an organisation has also influences the culture of the organisation. For example, where decision-making is decentralised, there is more room for creativity and thus the culture of the organisation must allow for an individual's expression of innovation.

13.3 Organisational culture

The culture of an organisation can be defined as 'the social glue that binds the organisation together' (Martins, 2000). Culture represents values, beliefs and attitudes that are common to its group members and represent the collective behaviour of people within that organisation. The culture of an organisation has several vital functions within organisations. First, it provides a sense of identity for members of the organisation (staff), as the more clearly the organisation and staff share values and beliefs, the more strongly a person can associate themselves with those values and beliefs. Secondly, it generates commitment and loyalty to the organisation as individuals feel a sense of belonging. Thirdly, it reinforces the standards of behaviour by making it clear how individuals should behave in certain situations such as whether to be creative in how to carry out a task. It is based on the beliefs and values of the organisation. Denison (1990) identified four distinct hypotheses for the function of culture within the organisation.

1 The consistency hypothesis, which views organisational culture as a common perspective with shared values and beliefs.
2 The mission hypothesis, where there is a shared sense of purpose, direction and strategy and individuals work towards the same goals.
3 The involvement–participation hypothesis, where the involvement from organisational members enhances commitment and loyalty to the organisation.
4 The adaptability hypothesis, where the norms and beliefs of an organisation allow it to receive, interpret and translate signals from the environment, which allows mental representations about the organisation to be formed.

Organisational culture manifests itself in various ways. Schein (1984) suggested that the three main indicators of organisational culture are artifacts/creations, values and basic assumptions. Artifact/creations represent both the physical and social environment and include stories about the organisation, the values of the organisation, the style of dress (e.g. police uniform), the use of technology, its customers and language (such as the jargon used within psychology) used by the organisation. The values (which determine the norms of that culture) guide work and determine the behaviour within the organisation. For example, bank managers wearing dark suits as a sign of respect to their customers and to portray knowledge. If they were to wear a bright green suit, then customers would not take them as seriously, especially to manage their money. The basic assumptions are based on factors that are taken for granted: beliefs, perceptions and thoughts that guide behaviour. For example, behaviour may be guided by the focus on customer satisfaction or its emphasis on providing quality products.

Organisational culture types

Theorists have attempted to characterise the variety of cultures found within organisations. Handy (1976) identified four cultures. The first is the power culture that represents a wheel (see Figure 13.4). The power is in the centre of the wheel and radiates out to other key people who then pass on information to other departments and staff. Decisions made in this type of organisation are centralised around one person. As decisions are made by one person, the organisation can react quickly to change. However, as staff are not involved in the decision-making process they may feel demotivated and undervalued.

The second type of culture is the role culture. This type of culture is common in most organisations today. The role culture is symbolised by a temple (see Figure 13.5, overleaf), where the decisions are made in the apex of the temple and the pillars represent the operational units. It is the employees in the operational units who implement the decisions. Individuals within this type of organisation have clear roles and responsibilities and strict reporting lines.

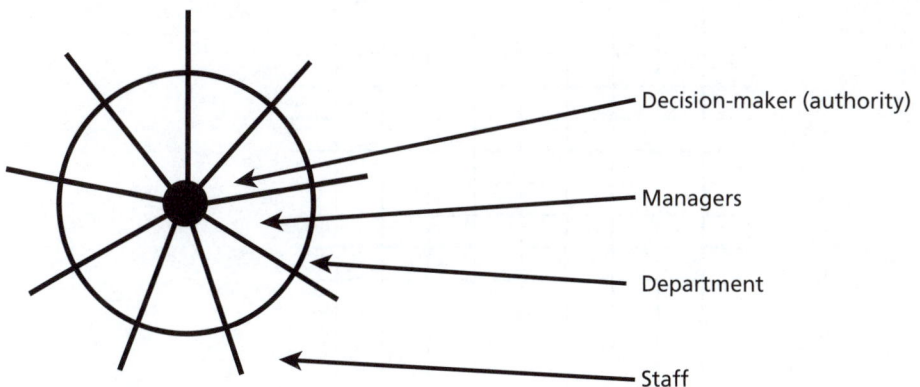

Figure 13.4 Handy's power culture

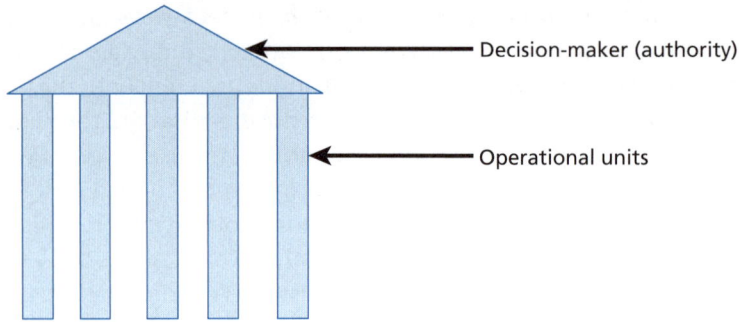

Figure 13.5 Handy's role culture

The third culture is the task culture and usually relates to organisations undertaking research and development activities. These organisations arrange their activities around teams. For example, a team would be set up to develop Product A. Once the product has been developed, the team would be disbanded and moved to develop another product. Due to the fluidity of the workforce, any change that is needed to be carried out quickly can be as there is an easy movement of staff from one project to another (as represented by Figure 13.6).

The fourth culture is the person culture, which is represented by a formalised structure. The structure, however, is developed for the purpose of its members. Within this type of culture, individuals are allowed to be creative and fully express themselves as there is no power base. Such organisations are typical of charities and barristers' chambers where individuals all operate at the same level. Decisions are made as a group rather than by an individual. (As can be seen in Figure 13.7, there is no central power base.)

It is difficult to provide a cultural typology that categorises companies taking into account all their activities. Whereas Handy's representation of culture considered the structure and reporting lines within organisations, e.g. role culture with decision-makers and operational units and person culture with no central power base, Cameron and Quinn's typology (1999) represented organisational culture as

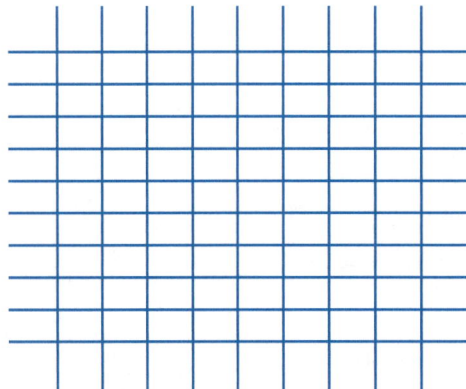

Figure 13.6 Handy's task culture

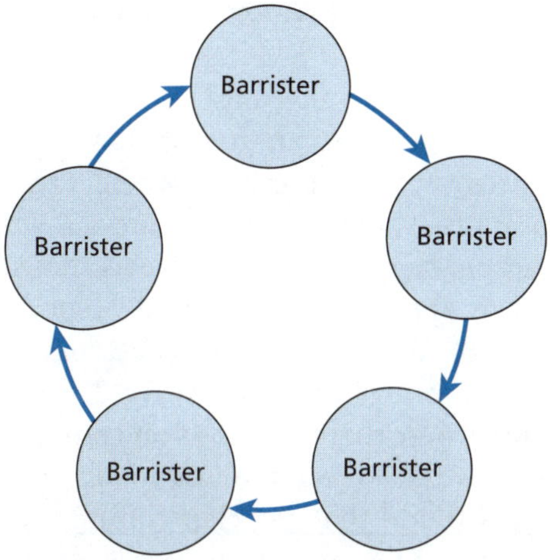

Figure 13.7 Person culture

a framework. The framework consists of two dimensions: 1) flexibility, discretion, stability and control; 2) external and internal organisation. These two dimensions form four quadrants (see Figure 13.8).

To determine the organisational culture, two questionnaires are completed by employees. The first asks the employee to consider the situation in the organisation as it has been for the last few years, and the second asks the employee to think of a perfect working environment. The results are then plotted onto the four quadrants. This allows senior managers to 'see' where the culture is currently and its ideal

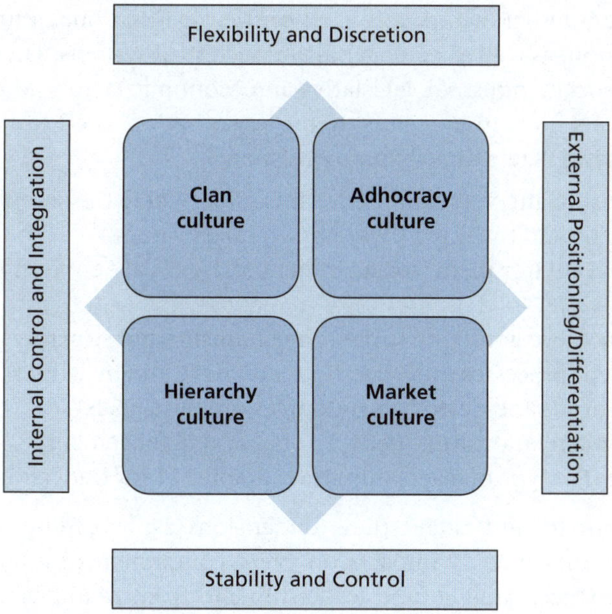

Figure 13.8 Quadrants of Cameron and Quinn's organisational culture

position. It also allows an assessment of whether employees are satisfied with the current culture by looking at how far away the present culture is from the ideal culture. It provides an insight into the most dominant culture within the organisation. Explanations of the quadrants are given below.

The clan culture has a friendly environment, where there is loyalty and commitment to the organisation. The hierarchy culture has strict policies, and procedures, and decisions are made at the top and passed down to lower levels for implementation (top-down approach). This culture type is similar to that of Handy's role culture. The third culture is the development culture where individuals are encouraged to be innovative and creative. The fourth culture type suggested is the market culture where there is a focus on getting the job done and the organisation is very competitive. Research by Cameron and Freeman (1991) investigating the culture types found that the clan culture increased employee morale, the market culture ensured resources were in place to meet the external market demands, the development culture was related to good performance, and the hierarchy culture was found to be too rigid and decreased the organisation's effectiveness. From this it could be suggested that for organisations to operate at their fullest potential they would need to have a clan, market and development culture. This may be possible as many organisations (especially large ones) do not have only one culture. Although there may be an overriding organisational culture (such as the market culture to get the job done), sub-cultures may also exist within the organisation (such as clan and development).

Although the culture impacts the internal makeup of the organisation (such as the vision of the organisation, its policies and procedures), the culture is also based on external factors. Martins (2000) developed a model of organisational culture based on both internal and external factors and the interaction between them. For example, the internal factors consisted of the organisational structure, values of the organisation, as well as managerial and technical systems. The external factors consisted of social, industrial, legislative and economic factors. Martin argued that the dimensions both in and outside the organisation need to be considered in decision-making. These dimensions consist of:

- mission, vision and values of the organisation (where the organisation is, where it wants to be and the way forward based on its values)
- the external environment (social, industrial, legislative environment, economic, etc.)
- means to achieve goals (the support mechanisms and structures)
- management processes (how decisions are made and by whom)
- employee needs and objectives (resources, pay and goals)
- interpersonal relationships (between staff and management)
- leadership (the type of leadership) (see Chapter 11 for leadership styles).

It is important to understand these dimensions as, according to Want (2003), 'corporate culture directly impacts on every component of a business organisation's performance, ranging from leadership effectiveness to business strategy and planned corporate mergers'. The culture impacts on the success of organisations,

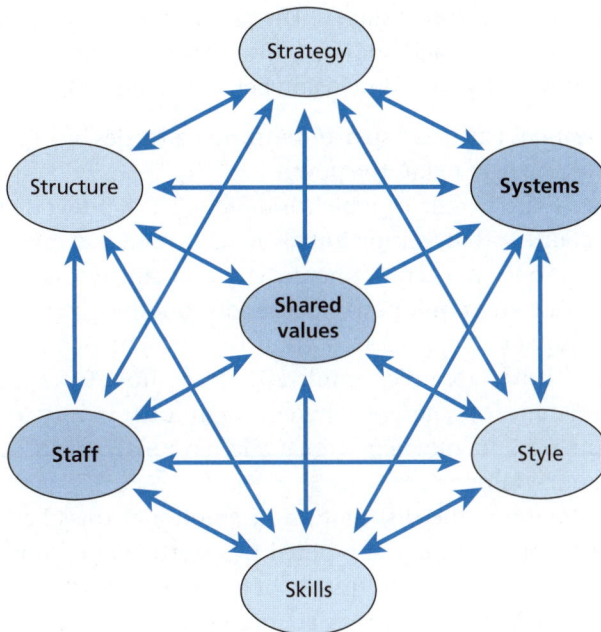

Figure 13.9 7-S framework (Peters & Waterman, 1982)

decision-making, customer services, policies, research and development approaches and organisational structures. A way to understand how a type of organisational culture develops is through the 7-S framework (the 7s represent the initials of the various aspects that make up culture as detailed in Figure 13.9 (Peters & Waterman, 1982).

The 7-S framework focuses on aspects of organising that are hard (at the top of the framework) and soft (at the bottom of the framework). The hard aspects consist of structures, systems and strategy whereas the soft aspects consist of style of management, staff skills and values. Peters and Waterman argued that, as the soft skills build up within the organisation, they become ingrained and represent the culture of the organisation. This then becomes the norm for the organisation and individuals' values and beliefs will be aligned with that culture, meaning that they are all aiming for the same goals. This increases both commitment and loyalty to the organisation.

Power distance represents the extent to which less powerful members of the organisation accept and expect power to be distributed unequally. A culture that has low power distance (such as Nordic countries) accepts power relationships that are more consultative where people relate to one another as equals. Those with high power distance are more autocratic and decisions tend to be made by one person. With the changes in the way organisations are now operating such as having worldwide clients/customers and offices of the same organisation being located in different countries, the issue of national culture needs consideration. The notion of national cultures was based on Geert Hofstede's work and more recent research by Bond and Minkov (Hofstede, Hofstede, & Minkov, 2010), which investigated differences across subsidiaries of IBM in 40 of the largest countries and then extended the research to 50 countries with over 117,000 matched employee samples completing an attitude survey. The primary analysis identified differences on four dimensions with Bond adding a fifth dimension based on results from an international study and a sixth dimension being added by Minkov.

1 *High power relations* (such as Asian and African countries) accept more autocratic power (where one person has the power).
2 *Individualism* is the extent to which individuals are integrated in groups. For example, a country that is individualistic (e.g. Britain, America or Germany), would focus on personal achievements where a country that is collectivist (e.g. South Korea, Taiwan or Indonesia) focuses on cohesive groups.
3 *Uncertainty avoidance* represents a country's tolerance for uncertainty. Low uncertainty cultures (Nordic countries) accept unstructured situations and are more tolerant of change whereas high uncertainty countries (Japan and Latin America) are more emotional and have plans, laws, rules and policies to deal with uncertainty.
4 *Masculinity* represents the distribution of emotional roles between males and females. Masculine cultures are typified by assertiveness, competitiveness and power. Feminine cultures value quality of life and relationships. Low masculine countries include Norway and Sweden; high masculine countries include Japan and the United Kingdom.
5 *Long-term v. short-term orientation*. Societies with a long-term orientation adapt traditions to changes in conditions. Short-term orientation exhibits great respect for traditions and the achievement of results quickly.
6 *Indulgence v. restraint*. Indulgence represents a society that allows for free ratification of human drives such as having fun, whereas restraint refers to a society that suppresses gratification and expects individuals to stick to social norms.

The differences between national cultures are important as they can be a cause of conflict as misunderstandings and misinterpretations can occur between organisations with offices and/or clients in different countries. To reduce conflict, it is important for individuals working across countries to be aware of differences such as etiquette and language, as well as different forms of management practices. However, although Hofstede provides us with issues to consider when working across countries, this does not enable us to compare organisations in the same country. This has led to research being conducted in 20 organisations in Sweden and Denmark (Hofstede, 1984), which identified six dimensions of practice.

1 *Process* (how things are done) *v. Results-oriented* (outcome)
2 Employee (employee satisfaction) *v. Job-oriented* (what work is required)
3 *Parochial* (identity from within the organisation) *v. Professional* (identity from outside the organisation)
4 *Open system* (easy to join) *v. Closed system* (difficult to join)
5 *Loose control* (casual) *v. Tight control* (serious, requires punctuality)
6 *Pragmatic* (market-driven) *v. Normative* (ideologically-driven).

Once there is an understanding of aspects that relate to the development of an organisational culture, processes can be employed to change the culture if required. Such a process was put forward by Eisenstat and Beer (1998) called the Organisational Fit Process (OFP). This process focuses on aligning the culture with the strategic direction of the organisation. For example, if a university had a strategy of providing face-to-face teaching only (adopting a traditional culture) but due to market demands changed its strategy to offer online learning including podcasts, video lectures and more interactive assessments, the organisation would have to change to a more dynamic culture that allowed it to move with technological advancements. The assessment of the organisation's culture relates to how the organisation needs to change to meet the demands of a changing business environment. Eisenstat and Beer argue that this is a circulatory process whereby the competitive environment has an influence on organisational strategy.

The process consists of a task force being set up to talk with employees and customers about the organisation's strengths and barriers to competing in the marketplace. A facilitator also interviews the senior management team about their perceptions of the organisation's effectiveness. Once the interviews have been completed, the task force get together to talk about the issues. This is then reported back to senior management as a group rather than from individual members of staff, which allows the feedback to be truthful without fear of retribution. Once this has been fed back to senior management, they can use the information to develop a vision and identify areas where change is required. When Eisenstat and Beer undertook the process within organisations, they found six main barriers that hinders an organisation from adapting to change:

1 an unclear strategy and/or conflicting priorities
2 an ineffective top management team
3 a leadership style that is too top-down (management dictate) or too laissez faire (not enough direction from management)
4 poor coordination across functions, business and geographic functions
5 inadequate leadership skills
6 poor verbal and/or written communication.

These six barriers stop management aligning their organisation with the changes in strategy in order to ensure survival of the organisation. The role of senior management is to overcome these barriers in order to achieve the strategic direction of the company. The achievement of the organisation's strategic direction may require organisational changes to be made that may include changes to working practices, structures, resources or direction of the business.

Stop and reflect

Going back to the introduction at the beginning of this chapter, what barriers do you think David, the Chief Executive, may face when making changes? How do you think these barriers can be overcome?

13.4 Organisational change

Organisational change can be defined as shifting from one state to another and is concerned with the breaking down of structures and creating new ones (Chonko, 2004). Such structures may include internal organisational structures, as discussed at the beginning of the chapter. Change may be small or large, but regardless of the scale is concerned with the variation or improvement of something. Change can be due to internal factors such as the growth of the organisation or external factors such as changes in the marketplace or legislative changes. Examples of change include changing the organisational structure (from tall to flat), changing technology (such as an automotive organisation changing from physical tests of vehicles to simulated tests), changing the physical setting (from centralised to decentralised – see explanation in the organisational structures section above), and changing people (creating a different culture or changing communication).

These different types of change can also be categorised into developmental, traditional and transformational (Ackerman, 1997).

- The developmental change can be planned or emergent, and corrects existing parts of the organisation. This type of change focuses on improvement.
- Transitional change aims to move from an existing state to a new one. It can be planned or radical.
- Transformational change requires a change in assumptions made by both the organisation and its members. This may be in terms of structure, culture or strategy.

Change can also be planned or emergent. Where change is deliberate it is planned. Emergent change, however, can be where external factors such as the economy, political change, legislative change or a change in competitive behaviour can influence the direction of the organisation. A further distinction can be made between continuous and episodic change. Continuous change is ongoing, and is characterised by individuals in the organisation constantly adapting ideas. Episodic change is infrequent, discontinuous and intentional (Weick & Quinn, 1999). Grundy (1993) explained change as consisting of three varieties.

- Smooth incremental change that evolves slowly is systematic and predictable.
- Bumpy incremental change has periods of peace and then an acceleration of change.
- Discontinuous change involves a rapid shift in strategy, the organisation's culture or structure.

Regardless of the type of change, before change is embarked on, there must be an evaluation of the likelihood that the change will be successful. This is important as research has shown that 70% of all change initiatives fail (Beer & Noira, 2000). Peltokorpi, Alho, Kujala, Aitamurto, & Parvinen (2008) argued that seven factors should be assessed before deciding on change. These are:

1 expected benefits such as cost-effectiveness and productivity
2 implementation challenges such as resistance to change and resource issues
3 the stakeholder's (staff, customers, trustees, etc.) influence such as their influence on decision-making of choices of change
4 motivation to participate, which is affected by potential costs and benefits of the change
5 capability to change taking into account individual skills
6 the complexity of the change that requires good project management
7 management's capability including the management of resources and ability to harness creativity.

It was argued by Peltokorpi et al. (2008) that, for change to be successful, six steps should be followed (see Figure 13.10).

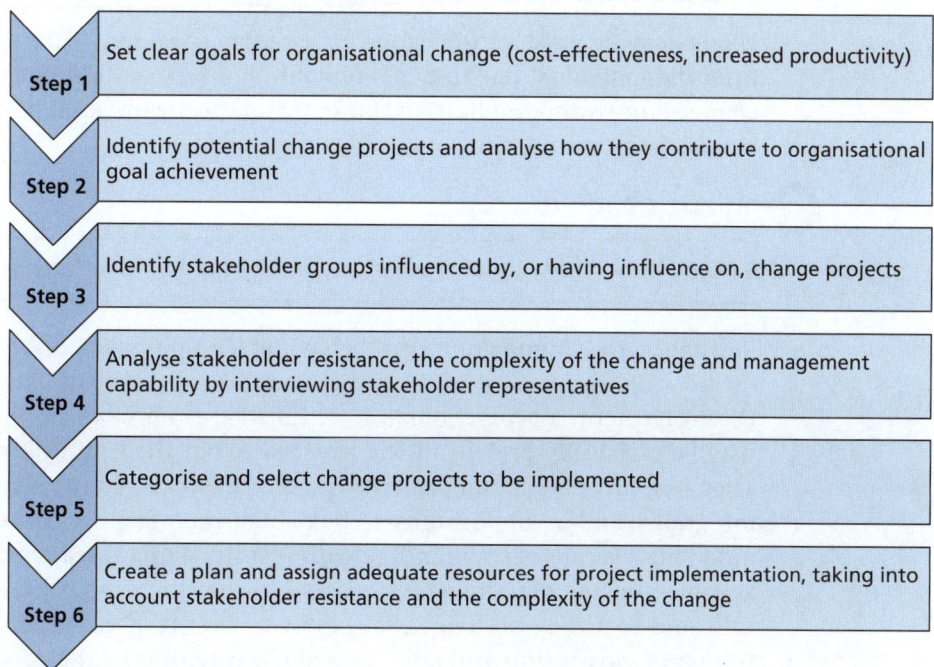

Step 1 Set clear goals for organisational change (cost-effectiveness, increased productivity)

Step 2 Identify potential change projects and analyse how they contribute to organisational goal achievement

Step 3 Identify stakeholder groups influenced by, or having influence on, change projects

Step 4 Analyse stakeholder resistance, the complexity of the change and management capability by interviewing stakeholder representatives

Step 5 Categorise and select change projects to be implemented

Step 6 Create a plan and assign adequate resources for project implementation, taking into account stakeholder resistance and the complexity of the change

Figure 13.10 Six steps to change

Although this is a pre-implementation change evaluation, this can also be used to evaluate whether the change has been successful once implemented by assessing whether goals were achieved, whether the plan was adhered to, and whether there were adequate resources to complete the project on time.

Responses to change

We have explored what is meant by organisational change, the different types of change and how to assess whether it is successful. Let us now consider individuals' responses/reactions to change.

During the change process, individuals within the organisation are likely to have one of two responses: readiness or resistance. Readiness refers to an individual's willingness to accept the change whereas resistance is an unwillingness to accept the change, which may be based on fear or the feeling of a loss of control. Rafferty and Simons (2006) believe that employee readiness to change is essential for the implementation of the change to be successful. If readiness is an important factor for successful change, an assessment of readiness is required. Palmer (2004) suggested a simple assessment method involving three steps.

1 The development of a list of all major activities in the organisation where there is competition for budget, staff, resources and management attention.
2 An estimate of the amount of effort required for the change to be implemented.
3 A calculation of the amount of load from steps 1 and 2 on the organisation is needed and its ability to take on the change.

People may be resistant to change for a variety of reasons. This may include fear from the individual due to a loss of control, a lack of full understanding of the change process and implications for staff and the organisation, lack of trust in the management and a feeling of job insecurity.

❓ Think about it

Can you think of any other reasons why employees may resist change?

Resistance to change comprises behavioural responses. Behavioural resistance includes disengagement, disidentification, disenchantment and disorientation. Disengagement is a psychological withdrawal from change. These individuals may be physically present in the workplace, but their mind is not on the job. They lack drive and commitment. These individuals require clarification of the intentions, and an opportunity to talk about their feelings. Disidentification of individuals is caused by an individual's identity being threatened by the change and their feeling of vulnerability. They feel that their job has changed dramatically and that they no longer have mastery over it. Resistance can be managed through empathising with the individual, listening to their fears and providing encouragement. Disenchantment is usually expressed through negativity towards the change process or anger. Destructive behaviours such as sabotage may be evidenced. Reasoning with these individuals can prove difficult, but their anger needs acknowledging rather than dismissing. Trying to discuss the change and the reasons behind it may alleviate the negative reactions. Disoriented employees may feel confused and unsure of their feelings. They may ask a lot of questions and may fail to be productive until their questions are answered. Individuals who feel this way need to be presented with a framework for the vision that explains the change and removes any ambiguity. Recognising these four reactions and applying the strategies discussed above may relieve some of the resistance to the change process. For successful change, a number of theories have been suggested.

Theories of organisational change

In this final section, the theories of organisational change will be outlined and evaluated.

? *Think about it*

When considering these theories, think of the effect they may have on both the structure of the organisation and its culture.

Systems theory of change

The systems theory of change, also known as systems thinking (Popper, 1972), focuses on the interrelatedness of the different parts of the organisation such as employees, functions, products or services. These systems are integrated in order to achieve the overall goals of the organisation. For example, the product development department of an organisation generates new products and ideas. The department consists of people, equipment, processes, policies and procedure – without them, the department would fail to function. Therefore, making a change to one part of the system requires consideration of the effects on the other parts of the organisation. When issues are identified that require change, a methodology for identification of change, analysis of options, implementation of choice and evaluation of outcome are needed. This involves a sequential step-based approach to change. Table 13.1 shows the steps to change and questions to be considered at each step.

Table 13.1 Hard systems step-based approach

Steps	Questions to ask
Definition of the problem	What changes are needed?
Analysis of the existing situation	Where are we now?
Identifying the ideal situation	Where do we want to be?
Identify ways to meet objectives	How do we get there?
Develop measurement methods	How do we know we have achieved?
Develop alternatives	What are our options?
Test alternatives	Are they feasible/cost-effective?
Choose the relevant option	What effects will it have on staff, policy?
Implementation	Are there any problems to be solved?

Organisational development

Organisational development is an episode of planned change. The process of successful change is dependent on agreement between individual and organisational goals. It is the agreement between these goals that ensure people are committed to the change. The organisational development change process is based on Lewin's (1951) model of change, which is based on three steps (see Figure 13.11, overleaf).

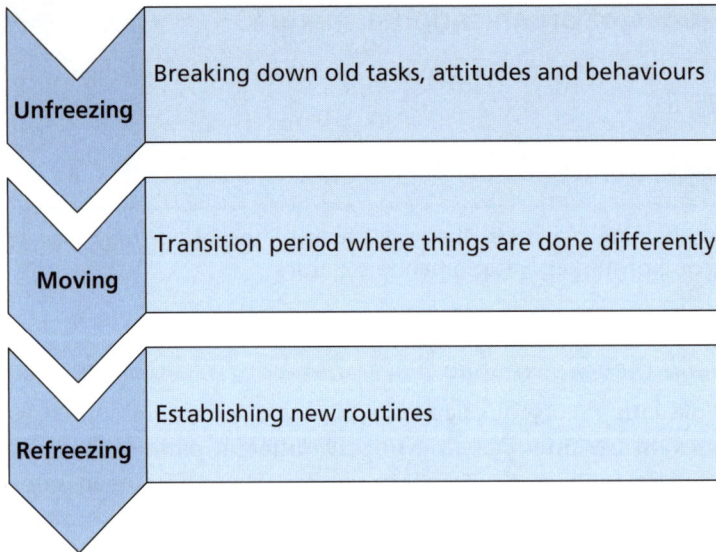

Figure 13.11 Lewin's model of change

The unfreezing stage involves the status quo being challenged. For individuals to accept this challenge, they need to be motivated by preparing them for change; asking them to participate in identifying problems and brainstorming solutions. The moving stage is to move the organisation and the individuals to a new level, different from the status quo. This involves convincing staff that the status quo is not beneficial to them; getting them to view the problem from a different perspective as well as providing clear communication between management and staff. The refreezing stage is integration of the new policies, procedures as values into the organisation and its staff.

Complexity theory

Complexity theory is the study of complex, nonlinear, dynamic systems. These complex systems are characterised by: 1) self-organisation and emergence; 2) learning and adaptive behaviour; 3) co-evolution.

1 Self-organisation and emergence is where the organisation can spontaneously self-organise itself into greater states of complexity without anyone being in charge. It is a result of agents/systems adapting to each other and are usually due to adaptations from changes in the external environment. For example, an organisation may adapt its strategy based on feedback from the marketplace/customers, changes in technology, legislation or political changes. These organisations will seek benefits from any situation. For example, a change in political behaviour would allow that organisation to change in order to embrace the new political agenda.

2 Learning and adaptive behaviour is where an organisation learns to adapt to cultural, social, economic and political systems. This may be an organisation moving to more global operations where this needs consideration.

3 Co-evolution is where there is a sharing of resources in a common environment (the organisation) and one system's (department/function) development would enhance another system's development. For example, the development of a new product would impact on the production department, the sales department, accounts department and quality control.

This theory views change as evolutionary rather than planned as it is based on changes in the environment. The process of change for this theory is not as clear as systems thinking or organisational development.

Social world theory

Social world theory suggests that change occurs as a result of negotiation and renegotiation between two or more social worlds. Strauss (1993) defines social worlds in terms of organisations as: 'Groups with shared commitments to certain activities, sharing resources of many kinds to achieve their goals, and building shared ideologies about how to go about their business'.

These groups are not structures or social units, but due to individual commitment allow for collective actions. For example, a social world could be a world of blog users in an organisation, a world of occupational psychologists or the world of an organisation. It is an interactive unit and a community. These social worlds inform what knowledge is important.

As with the complexity theory, the process of change for this theory is unclear. The status quo is challenged by an opposing view (such as two managers having opposing views as to the strategic direction of the organisation) and there is negotiation as to which process works best. Various issues are debated, negotiated, fought out and manipulated by its members. There is a historic course of events that can be traced back to individuals within the organisation. For example, if an organisation embarks on a new staff development process, the actions can be traced back in a time-related order.

Regardless of the theory adopted for change, the success of the change requires evaluation. Individuals can learn from things that went right in the change process as well as things that did not go to plan.

Evaluating organisational change

Once the change has been completed there needs to be an evaluation of how successful the change was. This allows for organisational learning where individuals can assess the parts that went well and those that did not, and learn from them for any future change.

Questions that need to be answered when evaluating include those shown in Figure 13.12 (overleaf).

Evaluation is time-consuming and expensive and thus if the change has been implemented and appears to be working, an evaluation of the process may not be undertaken. However, this does not allow for learning of good and extinguish of bad practices and this is paramount for future change projects.

Were the goals/objectives
of the
change project met?

Were the necessary
resources in place (staff,
materials, finances)?

What problems were
encountered in the
change process?

What aspects of the
change
project went well?

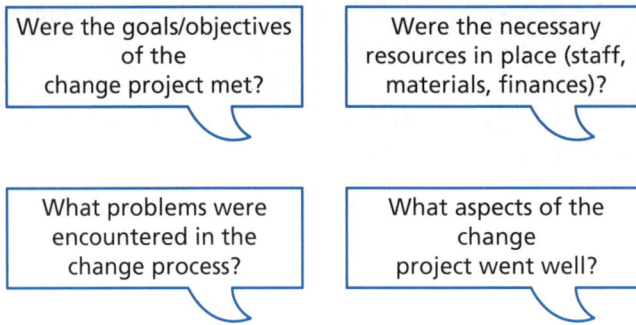

Figure 13.12 Examples of questions for evaluation of organisational change

Multi-level impact of organisational structures, culture and change

The impacts of organisational structures on the operation of an organisation, senior management, teams and staff are numerous. Having a tall organisational structure makes decision-making a lengthy process as individuals or teams need to make recommendations to managers who then need to take it to senior managers and so on. This trawling through the levels makes decision-making slow. The type of structure can also have an impact on teams, individuals and managers. For example, the matrix structure is difficult for managers as individuals are dual-managed, meaning that managers may come into conflict over workload and time constraints. It is also difficult for individuals as there may be a conflict between what is expected of them in terms of tasks and managing the expectations of two managers.

For organisational culture there is an impact on every aspect of the organisation and its staff. For the organisation, the culture guides its strategy for the future direction of the organisation, as the culture represents the values and beliefs of the organisation; for managers, teams and individuals, work has to be carried out based on those values and beliefs. Culture can also have an impact on staff (regardless of level) when their culture may be in conflict with the culture of the organisation. For example, a research and development department may have a very creative, innovative and no-blame culture whereas the overall culture of the organisation may be more dictatorial and traditional in its approach.

Organisational change has an impact on all aspects of an organisation and its staff. Depending on the type of change, it can influence the policies and procedures, the structure and the strategy of an organisation. These changes are then passed down and usually implemented by managers, teams and staff who have to work in conjunction with the changes being made. This can influence motivation, loyalty and job satisfaction, which can also have an effect on the productivity of the organisation (unhappy workers are unproductive workers).

In summary, the structure and culture of an organisation has an impact on the day-to-day operations of an organisation and also has an impact on the future direction of an organisation.

Legal context

For further details of legislative requirements for organisational development, please refer to the link below. Further details of legislative requirements are discussed in Chapter 3 – Legislation applied to the workplace.

Government Equalities Office (2010). *Equality Act 2010.* Available: *http://equalities. gov.uk/equality_bill.aspx*

Short-answer questions

1 Describe the different organisational structures and the benefits of an organisation chart.

2 Provide a definition of organisational culture and some of the core characteristics of an organisation's culture.

3 Critically evaluate Denison's (1990) four hypothesis of organisational culture and Handy's (1976) four types of organisational culture.

4 Describe Peters and Waterman's (1982) 7-S framework.

5 Discuss factors that may cause resistance to change and suggest ways to combat them.

CASE STUDY
Organisational change

The company

Sammie Printing Supplies is a small family-run business employing 15 people. It was established in 1995 by the current managing director who is the only individual who makes decisions within the organisation. The remaining 14 staff work in the printing room. There is no sales or marketing team. The company began by taking on any work that would come their way whether big or small. The majority of their work includes bulk printing of leaflets, business cards and other stationery for companies in and around Warwickshire.

The company was profitable and provided sufficient income for the owners and their staff. In 2009 this situation began to change as the UK began to go into a recession. This had a negative effect on local customers who cut back on ordering of stationery and business cards with orders declining dramatically. Secondly, the setting up of online print ordering providing cheaper services added to the decline in business. Thirdly, machinery is outdated and is slow in producing printing compared with more up-to-date machinery.

Sammie Printing Supplies' managing director recognises the need to change in order to survive through the recession. However, the staff believe in the traditional approach to providing print services.

The structure

The company is led by the managing director who makes all decisions regarding the operation of the business and the way the business should move forward. The managing director deals with all sales enquiries and face-to-face contact with customers and sees this as important to the image of the organisation. Print operators report directly to the managing director rather than through any line managers.

The culture

The organisational culture within Sammie Printing Supplies is very traditional. Print operators believe in traditional methods of printing and are resistant to changes in technology and operation. Staff have clear tasks to carry out with set procedures; there is no room for creativity or innovation. The managing director expects commitment and loyalty from staff and although there is no room for promotion, the managing director pays a £100 bonus every Christmas for each number of years served. For example, ten years' service would equate to a £1,000 bonus.

The problem

There has been a downturn in business since 2009. There is a need to change the way the organisation operates in order to survive. Staff are resistant to change and want to continue with traditional methods of printing.

Your task is to write a report to the Managing Director advising him about the issues related to the current operation of the business as well as issues concerning staff resistance. You should suggest interventions to overcome these problems. Ethical issues of implementing the interventions should also be considered.

Writing guidelines are provided in Chapter 2, section 2.3 – The consultancy cycle, which provides you with a structure to follow.

Further reading

Senior, B., & Swailes, S. (2010). *Organisational change* (4th ed.). Essex, UK: Prentice Hall.

14
Example consultancy reports

14.1 Introduction

Throughout this book, there has been a presentation of information related to the discipline of occupational psychology. From Chapter 4 through to Chapter 13 case studies have been provided at the end of each chapter so that you can start to think about how you would apply the knowledge gained from the chapter to practise within an organisation. The case studies allow you to practise analysing issues that may occur within organisations and gather information (theories and business information) to inform your decision-making of what interventions you may suggest. Although the style of the sample reports is academic in nature, it does provide a structure to enable you to consider pertinent issues and present them in a logical format. This will enhance your information-gathering and writing skills. The next section of this chapter provides you with two examples of academic consultancy reports that have been written in response to the cases presented in Chapter 4 – Personnel selection and assessment and Chapter 13 – Organisational structures, culture and change. These consultancy reports were written by students at Coventry University. As can be seen in each of these reports, an underlying area of occupational psychology is mentioned (e.g. personnel selection and assessment), but they are not discrete and other areas of the discipline need consideration (such as leadership). You must always consider issues within organisations in a multi-faceted manner and not by topic area. These reports follow the guidelines set out in Chapter 2.

Although this book is academic in nature and aims to develop you as you move into a practitioner role, it is important to note that differences do exist between academia and practice. The book has provided you with opportunities to consider how you would write a report based on business case studies, although real world examples may be very different and involve multiple issues that you may work on with other consultants. It is beyond the remit of this book to detail different approaches to writing business reports as this would represent a book in itself. Therefore, the chapter concludes with weblinks that lead to examples of consultancy reports that you may wish to use in developing your own style of writing. You will find that as you progress as a practitioner you will develop your own format, which represents what you deem the best way to present information to the client. One note of wisdom is to remain flexible in your approach so that you are continually developing your presentation of information to clients. Any report that is easy to follow is a good report and is valued by clients.

14.2 The case of Sammie Services: from Chapter 4 – Personnel selection and assessment

Case overview

The company

Sammie Services is a national supplier of CCTV and security equipment located in Birmingham city centre. The company provides products and services to both the domestic and commercial markets. It holds contracts with electrical suppliers and national house builders.

The company was established in 1999 as a family business and is managed jointly by the chief executive officer and the managing director. Both still maintain active involvement in the company and have ensured that it has prospered in times of economic downturn. The chief executive officer is an entrepreneur who has developed creative ways to secure business contracts. The managing director is a more 'hard nose' businessman who likes to maintain control of activities within the organisation and be involved in the recruitment and selection of individuals into vacant roles. At an interview for a local newspaper, on the success of the organisation, the managing director stated: 'the success is due to hard work, long hours, a tightly controlled workforce and financial acumen'.

Growth of the business

The company has grown from two senior managers, two engineers and two sales executives in 1999 to two senior managers, five middle managers, ten sales executives and 30 engineers. However, the company has gone through a 24-month period of losing sales executives to competitor companies. This is problematic as the sales executives are taking their network of customers to competitors, which is having a negative impact on sales within Sammie Services.

Sales executive role

The sales executive is responsible for securing sales in CCTV, security products and maintenance throughout the UK. This staffs is known within the organisation as 'baggers' as their aim is to bag business for the company. Of the ten staff, two cover the south of the UK, two the north of the UK, two the east of the UK, two the west of the UK and two in central UK. The baggers have a basic pay of £15,000 and a commission rate of 5% for the first £50,000 and 10% for sales over £50,000. For commission to be paid, a target of £20,000 sales per month has to be met.

Staff turnover has been excessive for sales executives within the last 24 months. Six of the ten sales executives have left for competitor companies. On an exit interview carried out by their direct line manager, reasons for leaving included unrealistic performance targets, a low basic salary, the job not being what they thought it would be, as well as confusion over their terms and conditions (such as the use of the company car for personal mileage).

Issues to be considered

The problems have prompted the chief executive officer to employ an occupational psychologist to evaluate the problems that exist in the recruitment and retention of staff and make recommendations to rectify those problems. Basic information provided by the chief executive officer includes the following.

- Six of the ten sales executives have left to work for competitor companies. Five of the six have gone to Stronghold Security Systems, which pays a good basic salary, although the commission basis is similar to Sammie Services.
- The highest earning 'bagger' has been with the company since 1999 and earns approximately £85,000 per year. For new sales executives, undertaking the company's six months on-the-road training has averaged about £1,000 commissions per month.
- The managing director selects all staff members by the use of an interview and a verbal reference from the candidate's previous employer. The chief executive officer has suggested using a situational judgement test to assess sales competencies but the managing director has made it clear that he does not believe in such 'rubbish' as he can identify a good salesperson as soon as they walk through the door.
- The company advertisement states that the salary is £15,000 per annum with an opportunity to earn unlimited commission. The advertisement also states that the company has other benefits such as a company car. Employment contracts state the rates of pay, but do not state the benefits that employees receive.

CASE CONSULTANCY REPORT
Written by Dela Lozanova

Executive summary

Sammie Services is a well-established CCTV and security equipment supplier, on a national level, in the UK. During the last two years, the company has been met with a large turnover of sales executives from Sammie Services to competitor companies. Some flaws in the personnel recruitment and selection process, deriving from the leadership styles used in the organisation, have been identified. Low levels of motivation and job satisfaction have been shown by the workers leaving the company.

This report will provide proposed solutions for the above issues, familiarising the organisation leaders with the most beneficial leadership style, the most effective personnel selection tools, and with various strategies to increasing staff motivation and job satisfaction.

Contextual theory

Leadership is a process in which a common goal is achieved through an individual's influence on the group. Since the early 1980s the idea of transformational leadership has been of great interest (Guest, 1996: 267). Tichy and Devanna (1986, cited in Shackleton, 1995:

124) described transformational leaders as being those who support and institutionalise changes in the organisation. Such leaders were also found to attract the commitment of staff through 'charisma', which refers to personal virtues that are perceived as worthy of a role model by the employees (Statt, 2004: 300). Transformational leaders have especially good communication with people and tend to keep being successful; therefore labelled 'arrivers' (Shackleton, 1995: 91). However, opposing the concept of 'arrivers' are the 'derailers'. This term refers to previously successful individuals who have met a downfall (Shackleton, 1995: 90). The 'derailers' have an autocratic leadership style and share the following traits: over-ambition, over-independence, being dictatorial and over-controlling, collapsing under the pressure of new situations, poor relationship and miscommunication with other managers (Shackleton, 1995: 91). It is crucial to understand that effective leadership is a key factor for the success of any organisation (Fiedler & Garcia, 1987: 1). Evidence has been found that transformational leadership style helps retain workers in the organisation (Lizzaro, 2010).

Personnel recruitment and selection appear to be of great importance for companies, as the cost of hiring the wrong person has been found to be larger than that of investing in a new recruitment scheme (Riggio, 2000: 81). The first thing an organisation must provide for its applicants is a realistic job preview (RJP). It has been found that people who apply for a job with a realistic view of the company are more willing to make a commitment to it and to stay loyal. If the organisation makes the effort to produce an RJP, it is viewed as more trustworthy and honest (Porteous, 1997: 128). A recent study has shown that one of the most practical ways of selection is through the use of psychometric testing (Carless, 2009). Since the beginning of the 20th century, psychometric tests have been proven to be highly reliable and valid. They can measure either personality and interests or aptitude and ability of the candidate, according to the needs of the company (Riggio, 2000: 89). Although interviewing is not a highly reliable method of screening and selection, it is very popular. Evidence has been found that interviews might be useful if they are carried out properly (Riggio, 2000: 108). However, very often those who do the interviews are not trained to do so, rendering the interview worthless. Two main types of interviews can be used – the situational interview, which asks the candidate questions about hypothetical situations that might appear at work, and the behavioural interview, which involves the interviewees answering questions about their experiences with difficult situations in their previous jobs (Riggio, 2000: 108). References, are found to be almost completely unreliable as their validity is low – about 0.14 (Porteous, 1997: 130).

Motivation is an internal state the intensity of which leads people either to engage, or not to engage in different behaviours. The higher the motivation is, the more likely the person is to show a particular behaviour (Spector, 2003: 188). Job satisfaction refers to an attitudinal variable that represents the extent to which people like their jobs (Spector 2003: 210). According to Locke's (1990) value theory, job satisfaction is an emotional state that could be reached if the job itself provides the workers with their values and desires (Porteous, 1997: 39). There are two types of values that lead to satisfaction (Porteous, 1997: 40): task-related (outcome of the job, goal achievement) and non-task-related (pay, promotion, recognition). Satisfied workers are likely to be more motivated and to perform better (Porteous, 1997: 37). According to Herzberg's two-factor theory (Spector, 2003: 192) there are two types of factors determining someone's attitude towards a job: hygiene factors and motivator factors. Hygiene factors refer to salary, co-workers and policies in the organisation. Motivator factors include recognition, achievement and the work itself. The employer makes the job itself satisfying through providing their employees with opportunities for personal growth (Smither, 1998: 208). A connection might be found with the reinforcement theory, which states that a reward should follow the occurrence of a desired behaviour as this might be viewed as a type of recognition (Porteous, 1997: 43). Expectancy theory also states that the more the employee wants the reward, the more motivated they are to work for it.

Supportive information

In order for Sammie Services to keep up with the constantly changing world of business, novel means of developing the business should be integrated into the company strategy.

Managers from Europe, USA, Canada, the Caribbean, Australia and Asia have already made use of various leadership training offered by LX Consulting (LX Consulting, 2011). The transformational leadership assessment and development programme uses the Transformational Leadership Questionnaire (TLQ) to identify areas and skills that need to be improved. The course includes a one-day workshop and one-to-one sessions. After two or three months, the TLQ is re-administered. Although this training runs over a lengthy period, it is beneficial for improving one's managing and leadership skills (LX Consulting, 2011).

Another important ability for an employer is conducting hiring interviews in a scientifically reliable way. Career Matters offer interview training for employers, which can be undertaken in small groups or individually. The course teaches not only how to select the best candidate objectively, but also how to leave a good impression on the interviewee.

Psychometric tests have proved to be a useful tool in the selection and recruitment process for many organisations. They aim to assess different aspects of human psychology such as how good people cope with stress, their teamwork skills and personality (Psychometric Success, 2011). Psychological research has found psychometric tests to be highly reliable and, as can be seen in Figure 14.1, 'over 80% of the Fortune 500 companies in the USA and over 75% of the Times Top 100 companies in the UK' use them extensively (Psychometric Success, 2011). Coventry University offers a Level A training in occupational testing; the cost is £500.

Finally, it could be of great importance for the organisation to be aware of the fact that the starting salary for a sales executive in the UK is £16,500–£35,000. Furthermore, salaries for people with three to five years' experience range from £22,500 to £45,000 (Prospects, 2011).

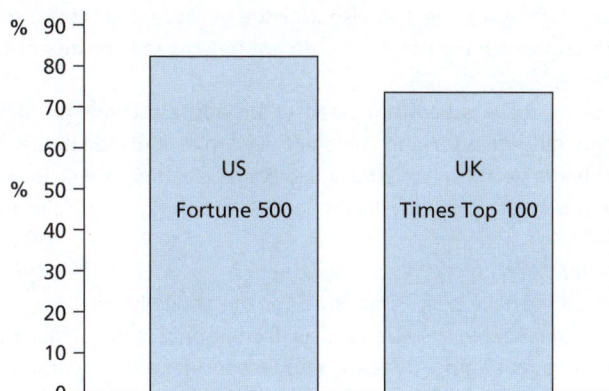

Figure 14.1 Percentage of companies using psychometric tests

Case analysis

There are a few issues arising in the Sammie Services case. First, the chief executive officer and the managing director display competing leadership styles. The chief executive is described as a person looking for more 'creative ways to secure contracts' and wants to use novel methods of personnel selection which makes him fit in the description of a transformational leader. The managing director appears to be a 'hard-nose businessman who likes to maintain control' and do the interviewing himself, which classifies him as a dictatorial leader. However, theory has shown that autocratic leaders are endangered by a 'derail' from the path of success. In critical situations, as in the Sammie Services case, a transformational approach towards the problem is more efficient.

The difference between the leadership styles leads to miscommunication and problems in the recruitment and selection process. The managing director denied the chief executive's proposal for integration of situational judgement tests in the recruitment process as he believes that he can 'identify a good salesperson as soon as they walk through the door'. However, theory has shown that, unlike interviews, psychometric tests are highly reliable. Psychometric tests are not only cheap, but also less time-consuming than hiring interviews. There is no evidence provided that the type of interviews the managing director conducts falls in the category of any of the scientifically reliable interviews – situational or behavioural. Furthermore, the managing director often appears to rely on verbal references, which have been proven to have extremely low validity. Another important issue seems to be the differences between the job advertisement and the work contract as the resigning employees were confused about their terms and conditions, being misled by the announcement for a company car in the advertisement. Such misunderstandings prevent the company from building the image of an honest and responsible organisation, which makes people lose their sense of loyalty and commitment, and therefore leave.

The employees who leave the organisation show signs of job dissatisfaction. They see their performance targets as unrealistic, their pay as low and the job as not meeting their expectations. Although pay is an issue, it does not seem to be the main one as the majority of the sales executives have moved to a company with a similar basic commission. This is a very important problem as the cost of sales executives leaving is extremely high, knowing that they take their business contacts, and thus their market, with them to the competitors. The unrealistically high expectations of the company and the low salary are affecting the motivation of the staff. Furthermore, almost no opportunities for promotion are available, so the expectancy of the employees is low, which leads to the job being seen as less satisfying. Viewing the staff as 'baggers' is also an issue because it creates a sense of a one-way profit relationship in which the employees do not get any reinforcement from the company they 'bag business for'.

In conclusion, the main issues that need to be addressed are the different leadership styles of the managing director and the chief executive contradicting each other, the outdated and unreliable recruitment strategies, the misleading advertisement, and the low motivation and job satisfaction due to the lack of promotion and reinforcements.

Proposed interventions

A number of solutions have been suggested for the above issues.

As the theoretical research shows that transformational leadership is the most beneficial for a company, the managing director should consider undergoing a transformational leadership assessment and development programme such as that offered by LX Consulting. A financial investment in improving managing skills will help Sammie Services benefit from better internal communication and more cohesive work between the managing director and the chief executive.

A new advertisement should be written for the vacant jobs so that there will be no confusion over the benefits the employees receive. Also, a realistic job preview should be prepared and presented to each applicant. This will raise the commitment towards the organisation and fewer people will leave due to unrealistic expectations for the job. Psychometric tests should be integrated in the personnel selection process as their reliability is much higher than that of interviews. They are also proven to be objective, standardised and non-discriminatory. Psychometric tests are not costly and they will save the managing director time by not having to interview each applicant. A training course in the use of psychometric tests, such as that offered by Coventry University, will cost only £500 per person. The managing director can still maintain his crucial role in the selection process by interviewing only those applicants who have successfully met the company's criteria at the psychometric tests. However, to do that he should undergo interview training for employers such as the one offered by Career Matters. In this way, Sammie Services can make use of the behavioural and situational interview techniques in order to get the best employees. Reliance on verbal or written recommendations is not recommended due to their low validity of 0.14.

There are several methods that Sammie Services could use to increase staff motivation and job satisfaction. Creating new positions in the company hierarchy should be considered as the opportunity for promotion increases expectancy and makes people work harder towards achieving their goal. The target sales of £20,000 per month should be lowered to £10,000 for new employees for the first six months as they still do not have their own market. Doing so, the company will eliminate the staff's dissatisfaction with unrealistic goals. Furthermore, the employees will be able to accept the goal and commit to it, which is a factor for effective improvement of their performance (Locke, 2000). The starting salary for the sales executive should be from £16,500 per year and in five years the minimum should be £22,500 as this is the expected standard base for the UK. These actions increase the number of hygiene and motivation factors being present. This leads to higher job satisfaction and better performance. Such actions also eliminate the risk of lowered performance due to extended underpayment resulting in lack of motivation and job satisfaction (Locke & Henne, 1986). Instead of viewing all workers as 'baggers', it is recommended to create 'Employee of the Month' and 'Employee of the Year' awards. A symbolic sum of money, such as £1,000 for the first and £500 for the second, can be awarded. Also, a picture of the winner should be hung in the common room or in the hall of the company building. This will enhance workers' motivation and will make them more productive.

If a transformational leadership style is used by both the managing director and the chief executive officer, Sammie Services can achive major improvements. The selection and recruitment process should involve both psychometric tests and professional interviewing techniques. To avoid misunderstandings all applicants should be provided with a clear view of the company through a realistic job preview. To retain personnel, the company should improve employees' job satisfaction and motivation to work by presenting them with promotion opportunities, achievable goals and public awards.

Recommendations

- The managing director should undergo transformational leadership assessment and development programme, e.g. LX Consulting.
- Development of a new job advertisement.

- Development of a realistic job preview to be presented to all applicants.
- Psychometric tests to be used for sifting applications.
- The managing director should undergo interview training for employers, e.g. Career Matters.
- The managing director to participate in the final selection interviews.
- References should not be used for decision-making as they are not reliable.
- Consider new positions in the hierarchy to enable promotion opportunities.
- Lower sales target to £10,000 for new employees for the first six months.
- Starting salary for the sales executive: minimum £16,500 per year; in five years minimum should be £22,500.
- 'Employee of the Month' award: first place £1,000 + picture of the winner in the hall/common room, second place £500 + picture of the winner in the hall/common room.

Summary

Taking into account the difficult situation Sammie Services is in, the managing director of the company needs to undergo transformational leadership training so that the organisation can go through some radical changes. The personnel selection process would benefit from a realistic job preview and the use of psychometrics. Interviewing should be conducted only by a trained individual and references should not be seen as valid. Higher basic salary, opportunities for promotion and monthly acknowledgements of the best salesperson would also help the company make the job it offers satisfactory, motivating and worth committing to.

14.3 The case of Sammie Printing Supplies: from Chapter 13 – Organisational structures, culture and change

Case overview

The company

Sammie Printing Supplies is a small family-run business employing 15 people. It was established in 1995 by the current managing director who is the only individual who makes decisions within the organisation. The remaining 14 staff work in the printing room. There is no sales or marketing team. The company began by taking on any work that would come their way whether big or small. The majority of their work includes bulk printing of leaflets, business cards and other stationery for companies in and around Warwickshire.

The company was profitable and provided sufficient income for the owners and their staff. In 2009 this situation began to change as the UK began to go into a recession. This had a negative effect on local customers who cut back on ordering of stationery and business cards with orders declining dramatically. Secondly, the setting up of online print ordering providing cheaper services added to the decline in business. Thirdly, machinery is outdated and is slow in producing printing compared with other more up-to-date machinery.

Sammie Printing Supplies' managing director recognises the need to change in order to survive through the recession. However, the staff believe in the traditional approach to providing print services.

The structure

The company is led by the managing director who makes all decisions regarding the operation of the business and the way the business should move forward. The managing director deals with all sales enquiries and face-to-face contact with customers and sees this as important to the image of the organisation. Print operators report directly to the managing director rather than through any line managers.

The culture

The organisational culture within Sammie Printing Supplies is very traditional. Print operators believe in traditional methods of printing and are resistant to changes in technology and operation. Staff have clear tasks to carry out with set procedures; there is no room for creativity or innovation. The managing director expects commitment and loyalty from staff and although there is no room for promotion, the managing director pays a £100 bonus every Christmas for each number of years served. For example, ten years' service would equate to a £1,000 bonus.

The problem

There has been a downturn in business since 2009. There is a need to change the way the organisation operates in order to survive. Staff are resistant to change and want to continue with traditional methods of printing.

CASE CONSULTANCY REPORT
Written by Sophie Ward

Executive summary

Sammie Printing Supplies is a small printing supplies business established in 1995, run by a family employing 15 people.

Until 2009 the business has been profitable, providing sufficient income for the owners and their staff. However, since 2009 when the UK went into recession custom has decreased leading to a loss in orders. Some issues have been identified within the organisation including leadership styles, employees' attitudes, performance management and motivation, all of which are impacting on the business and preventing it from change.

The following report suggests interventions to combat these problems, including leadership training, advice on organisational design and equipment, and motivation and job satisfaction strategies.

Contextual theory

Leadership is a process by which an inspirational figure attempts to 'unite and motivate their followers by offering shared visions and goals' to improve the future (Arnold et al.

2005: 487). Transformational leaders focus on motivating employees by communicating the organisation's 'values, beliefs and mission', along with encouraging loyalty to the business by setting goals to motivate subordinates and increase faith and commitment (Turner & Müller, 2005: 50). They empower employees to develop their own ideas, and focus attention on individuals who are in greater need of help and support (Jansen, 2011). They are successful leaders because they are good communicators, supporters and show increasing importance for social factors, which is linked to significantly more satisfied subordinates (Weed, Mitchell, & Moffitt, 1976). Successful leaders are known as 'arrivers' which links to the findings that 75% of 'arrivers' are said to have a 'special ability with people' (Shackleton, 1995: 90). This is in contrast to 25% of 'derailers' said to have the same ability. 'Derailers' are not as successful because of their autocratic leadership skills, including insensitivity, intimidation, arrogance, over managing and over-ambition (Shackleton, 1995: 90–91). It is essential that organisations benefit from successful leadership skills as they are needed to make a business thrive.

Motivation stems from an individual's motive for doing something, based on calculated risks, problem-solving and a need to succeed (Arnold et al. 2005: 316–317). The greater the motivation, the better the performance of the workforce will be (Cardone, 2006). Motivation contributes to a positive mood, often linked to the allocation of rewards seen to increase work satisfaction (Jansen, 2011), and **job satisfaction** (Llies & Judge, 2002). Herzberg's two factors theory suggests there are two main factors that contribute to job satisfaction and job dissatisfaction: the motivational factor and hygiene factor (Landy, 1985: 382–383; Chmiel, 2000: 317). Motivational factors are linked to the nature and challenge of the work (Landy, 1985: 382–383) and include 'achievement, recognition, responsibility and advancement' (Sharp, 2008) Hygiene factors relate to the psychological and physical aspect of the environment where the work takes place (Landy, 1985: 382–383) and include 'monetary rewards, competent supervision, policy and administration' (Sharp, 2008). If hygiene needs are met an individual is not dissatisfied but not satisfied either; however if motivation needs are met the individual is satisfied (Landy, 1985: 382–383), which emphasises the greater importance of motivational factors. In relation to this the expectancy theory suggests that a person will work hard if they believe successful performance will result in positive outcomes. This can depend on an individual's personality, values, and self-belief linked to self-efficacy and high intrinsic motivation (Chmiel, 2000: 311–324). Furthermore, the reinforcement theory suggests that rewarding positive behaviour will increase the chances of an individual repeating that behaviour (McKenna, 2000: 91). When a job provides the individual with the values that they hold and what is important to them personally, Locke's value theory suggests that job satisfaction will then occur, due to an emotional response to receiving these values (Landy, 1985: 389–390).

Organisational structure is the internal layout of positions within an organisation, the responsibility given to various roles and interrelationships between these positions (Jex & Britt, 2008: 429). First, managers must decide who will be making the decisions. Centralisation involves decisions being made only by the management, thus increasing uniformity but increasing employee job dissatisfaction. Decentralisation avoids this, as the decision-making power is passed down the hierarchy, allowing employees more opportunities, thus giving them a greater feeling of authority, responsibility and increasing job satisfaction (Theron et al., 2006: 92). The span of control enables managers to know how many subordinates are reporting to them, and the chain of command shows subordinates who they report to. A wide span of control has a flat hierarchy with very few managers exerting power over many subordinates. This is cost-effective, but can decrease the speed of work, cause stress and work overload for managers and result in a business that lacks a variety of ideas. A narrow span of control has a tall hierarchy with more managers and fewer employees reporting to each manager, meaning more efficient monitoring and support, and a quicker work process, which is effective in a changing environment and when there are competitors. However it is costly and can result in communication errors along the hierarchy (Theron et al., 2006: 92–93). The neoclassical design focuses on employee satisfaction and minimising managerial control, giving subordinates more power (Ghuman, 2010: 141). In contrast, the classical design in which organisations are a bureaucracy with set rules and a well-defined authority and many subordinates, productivity and orders increase; however, it is insensitive and unsuitable for a changing environment (Ghuman, 2010: 140–141). The contingency approach to organisational design suggests that stability of the environment should always be considered. An organic organisation responds quickly to a changing environment and requires less job specialisation but an expansive knowledge of many types of jobs. Emphasis is on self-control and coordination between peers, rather than authority from above (Theron et al., 2006: 92). Woodward also believed the structure of an organisation must adjust to match the technology as a mismatch will mean that productivity will suffer (Foo, 1997).

Supportive information

If Sammie Printing Supplies is to keep going with the constantly changing environment, it must adopt novel ways of developing the business through the use of company strategies.

Managers from many different companies such as Asda, Arcadia Group Limited, UCAS, British Transport Police and Bloomberg, have used transformational leadership training as a way of improving their leadership skills to help their organisations (Impact Factory, n. d). The training provides the opportunity to share your concerns about leadership and work together with other leaders to improve through the use of forums. It also focuses on you individually as a leader, identifying the type of leader you are and encouraging change through inspiration, motivation and passion. The course offered by Impact Factory is an intense five-day course that companies such as Arcadia have labelled as 'very insightful and motivating' (Impact Factory, n. d).

In addition to leadership-style training, managers have motivational management training courses available to them that have been used by many companies including Orange and DHL (Employee Engagement. n. d). These two-day training programmes enhance self-awareness in managers themselves and provide them with skills such as goal setting, commitment and communication to motivate their employees, increasing effectiveness, quality and productivity. Employee Engagement Training offers team workshops including the 'Blindfold tent team building activity', which aims to challenge employees directly, enhancing their team building skills and motivation.

Furthermore, Ipsos MORI has shown that businesses with high employee engagement are more positively rated by the public. From their work with a large number of organisations conducting employee research, ipsos developed a model of engagement (Figure 14.2, overleaf) with three main constructs: alignment, involvement and loyalty (Metropolitan Police Authority, 2011). The model is an excellent way to report staff engagement levels and identify areas for improvement.

The relationship between employees and their senior management, goals within the organisation, employee motivation, fulfilment within the current job, and the relationship to the organisation result in the amount of engagement employees have within the organisation (Metropolitan Police Authority, 2011). More employee engagement will result in an increase in job satisfaction and, in turn, improved productivity and performance.

Relationship to my company
- Feeling part of the organisation
- Individual perspectives
- Desire to stay

Employee experience

Loyalty

Involvement

Engagement

Alignment

Relationship to my job
- Satisfaction
- Fulfilment
- Best of you

Relationship to management
- Confidence
- Understand strategy
- Support change

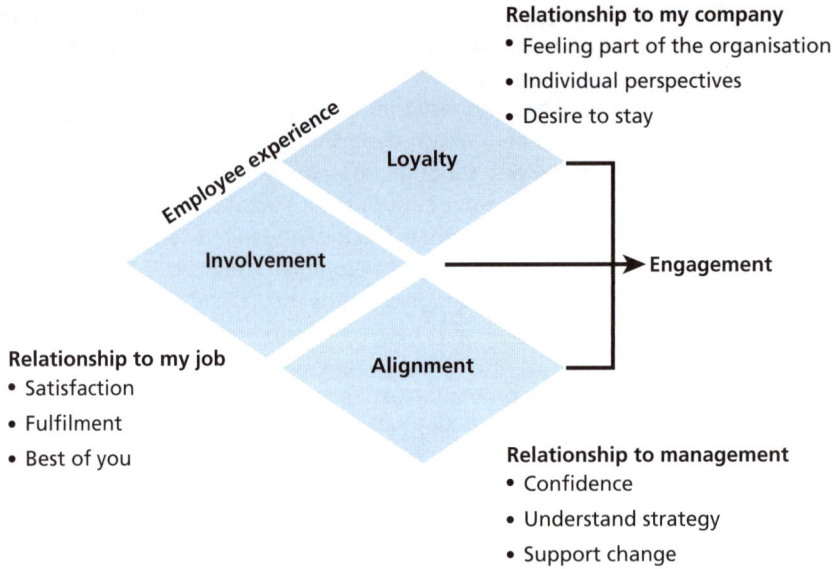

Figure 14.2 Ipsos engagement model (Metropolitan Police Authority, 2011)
Source: Ipsos MORI.

Case analysis

There are quite a few issues that have arisen in the Sammie Printing Supplies case. First, the managing director makes all the decisions in the business, suggesting a process of centralisation and a dictatorial leadership as all the power of decision-making is in his hands, leading to possible conflict between the manager and the employees. It can also cause great stress for the managing director to have sole responsibility for the company, and there is no one else to help manage this stress or manage the company if he is sick. This type of leadership has been found to be detrimental to business success, leading to a 'derail'. Instead, a more transformational leadership should be used as this has been proven to contribute to more successful leadership.

As the remaining staff work in the printing room and there is no sales and marketing team and no line managers, this also means there are fewer new ideas available to improve the business, which is characteristic of a flat hierarchy. The managing director 'recognises the need to change in order to survive' but doesn't know how to. This suggests there needs to be a line manager within the business to offer new ideas and help the managing director and the employees. In addition, a shortage of staff is causing problems such as no time planning, leading to customer disappointment because of the slow turn around, which is also linked to the out-of-date machinery suggesting a possible mismatch between technology and organisational structure. This is detrimental to the organisation during the recession, as competitors are more up to date and online. An organic organisation and slightly taller hierarchy would be more beneficial. Their order capacity is also too small and the business suffers from the narrow coverage area, therefore this requires expansion. They must first expand the workforce and improve the equipment.

It is essential that the current employees are happy and, due to the present management of the business, this seems very unlikely. The subordinates have 'no room for creativity or innovation'. They have set tasks and procedures typical of a classical design leading to a repetitive cycle. This repetition is likely to be leading to a decrease in job satisfaction and a resistance to change. The more dissatisfied the employees are, the greater the decrease in product quality, leading to loss of sales. All of these factors can contribute to personal illness and stress, which will result in an even smaller workforce.

The employees are also likely to be dissatisfied with their job as there is no learning curve and progress available to them. There is a lack of motivational factors as there are no promotional opportunities because there are no supervisory or managerial positions in the organisation. The only incentive to remain in the organisation is the bonus of money given for loyalty, which is linked to hygiene factors. However, loyalty is not the only thing needed within an organisation; performance and staff attitude should also be rewarded to increase job satisfaction. Those with a greater need for money will also be under more pressure to stay even if all the values they have are not being met and they are not progressing for themselves personally. This will lead to a lack of progress for the organisation as there is no turnover, resulting in a lack of new ideas.

In summary, the main issues that need to be addressed are the current manager's leadership skills and lack of higher management, the design of the organisation, including work technology, and also the lack of motivation and job satisfaction due to boredom, lack of rewards and no promotion opportunities.

Proposed interventions

There are a variety of solutions to help Sammie Printing Supplies.

As shown in the theoretical research, transformational leaders are successful leaders and are essential to making a business thrive. It would be wise for the managing director to undergo a training and development programme in transformational leadership skills such as the five-day training programme from the Impact Factory. This will improve internal communication between the managing director and employees, leading to a more positive and productive environment. The cost of the training will be outweighed by the benefits.

The managing director should also undertake motivational management training such as the two-day programmes offered by Employee Engagement. This will enhance the self-awareness of the managing director and allow him to develop skills to motivate the employees, such as by recognising achievement. As stated in the theoretical research, the more motivated a workforce is the better they will perform, and the greater the work and job satisfaction will be. Furthermore, to increase motivation, employees should be sent to team-building workshops to participate in a variety of activities similar to that of the 'Blindfold tent team-building activity'. This will not only train the managing director, but also train and develop employees, challenging them, enhancing their skills, motivation and cooperation within groups. This challenging environment will help employees to find new ideas and think outside the norm. This will encourage them to try out new ideas. Allowing the employees to explore new ideas and methods can widen their perspectives and help bring new ideas to the organisation. Employee ideas and input are essential to change within an organisation, which is greatly needed with the current recession.

Sammie Printing Supplies should take the form of an organic organisation in order to respond quickly to a changing environment and, rather than authority from above, employees should have more self-control and communicate with peers. Therefore, a neoclassical design is appropriate and decentralisation, which will allow employees more opportunities and give them a greater feeling of authority, responsibility and increased job satisfaction. New authority positions should be considered within the workforce, creating a taller hierarchy to reduce pressure on the managing director and increase more efficient monitoring, support, communication between managers and employees, and a quicker work process. Although this could result in some communication errors along the hierarchy and be costly, it is very effective in a changing environment such as the current recession and when there are competitors, and more authority positions will also allow for promotion opportunities.

Furthermore, it is important that the machinery and technology matches the organisation for it to be more productive. Sammie Printing Supplies should update machinery and start online services to improve efficiency and allow for a wider coverage area. This is possible with a taller hierarchy as an expanded workforce will mean an increase in productivity.

Sammie Printing Supplies will rapidly improve if the managing director uses a transformational leadership style and develops skills to motivate and support the workforce. The employees will also help the company by changing their attitudes, being creative and developing skills such as team-building skills. Moreover, the opportunity for promotions by adding new management positions, rewards such as employee of the month and expanding the workforce will increase employee motivation and product performance. Passing down power to employees will improve job satisfaction by giving them authority and responsibility.

Recommendations
- The managing director should be assessed and take a training and development programme to develop transformational leadership skills, e.g. Impact Factory.
- The managing director should undertake a motivational training programme.
- Employee motivation training and team-building workshops should be provided to improve employee attitude, motivation, communication skills, job satisfaction and performance.
- New authority positions should be considered within the hierarchy to allow opportunity for promotions.
- The workforce should be expanded so that more products can be produced and the coverage area can be expanded.
- Update machinery and introduce online services to improve efficiency.
- Rewards should be given to employees such as 'employee of the month award', consisting of a picture on the staff room wall and a bonus.

Summary
Overall, Sammie Printing Supplies must change certain aspects of the organisation in order to survive in a changing environment. The managing director should undergo transformational leadership training and motivational training to support the organisation through the dramatic changes it needs to undertake, by enhancing communication and encouragement within the workplace which can be done through the use of rewards. Furthermore, employees themselves should undergo motivation training and team-building workshops. New authority positions should be considered allowing for better communication and opportunity for promotions. The workforce should be expanded and machinery updated in order to increase the amount of products that can be produced, and therefore allowing for an expansion of the coverage area.

Useful websites

Example consultancy reports can be found at the following weblinks:

Economic and Social Research Council: *http://www.esrc.ac.uk/my-esrc/grants/RES-062-23-0904/outputs/read/372e419a-d3e6-4f45-abbc-d5615119f258*

Institute of Consulting: *http://www.iconsulting.org.uk/innovation*

London School of Economics and Political Science: *http://www2.lse.ac.uk/businessAndConsultancy/LSEConsulting/recentReports.aspx#ausaid*

15

The future of work

Learning outcomes

After reading this chapter, you should:

- have an insight into how the world of work may look in the future
- understand challenges that may be faced by workers and organisations
- consider how the changes to working practices may influence the work undertaken by occupational psychologists.

15.1 Introduction

The purpose of this final chapter is to identify some of the issues that you may be faced with, at work, in the future. This may be in terms of working for a company or advising clients on how to tackle some of the issues that arise as a result of changes in the workplace. The intention of this chapter is not to provide a complete overview of theory or answers to issues (as this would be a book in itself), but to raise potential issues for you to consider in your work.

The nature of work has changed dramatically over the past two decades. Such changes from an organisational perspective include the reduction in layers of workers resulting in changes to organisational structures; different ways of managing and different types of workers; organisational sustainability; globalisation; and technological changes. Changes from a team and individual perspective include cross-functional team working, location-independent working and youth unemployment.

There is also a change in the nature of the workforce where there is an increase in employment of the ageing population due to fewer financial incentives from occupational pension schemes. All these factors have an influence on how individuals and organisations operate. An overview of these issues will be discussed at an organisational and team/individual level.

15.2 Organisational changes

Flattening organisational structures

Many workplaces have had to downsize and remove layers of their organisational structure in order to survive an economic recession. Although this has meant that decisions are made faster, as they do not have to progress through as many tiers of decision-makers, it also affects the opportunities for advancement within the organisation. Fewer opportunities for promotion may result in talented staff leaving the organisation and looking for opportunities to fulfil their work ambitions elsewhere. According to Baruch (2006), modern careers are flexible and dynamic and mirror the impact of globalisation. Such changes have led to boundaryless/portfolio careers (discussed in Chapter 5 – Performance appraisal, career development, counselling and coaching) where individuals move between organisations rather than within organisations to pursue opportunities that lead to their career development. This leads to less loyalty and commitment to the organisation and loss of staff with important knowledge and skills. However, there are also drawbacks for individuals such as insecurity in securing work. This will lead to more location-independent working as individuals juggle many roles to fulfil their careers.

Challenges for the future: Career development opportunities for individuals will diminish, which may result in talented employees looking elsewhere for promotion opportunities.

For more details on organisational structures, please read Chapter 13 – Organisational structures, culture and change.

Management by objectives

Management by objectives (discussed in Chapter 11 – Management and leadership approaches) is becoming more and more paramount with the changing nature of work. For example, not being physically present in work (location-independent working, discussed later in this chapter) has an impact on how individual employees are managed. This is no longer managing by time (the time the employee is present in the workplace), but managing by setting goals and assessing if employees have attained those goals. This approach is participative in that the employee is involved in the goal-setting and chooses actions they should take to accomplish those goals. Goals should be linked to the overall organisation's goals as this allows individuals to understand how their own work contributes to the meeting of organisational goals. This can increase the motivation of employees (see Chapter 10 – Motivation, job satisfaction, employee engagement and behaviour modification). Drucker (1954) outlined a five-step process for managing by objectives, which can be seen in Figure 15.1 (overleaf).

The first step of this process is to define the strategic aims of the organisation so that all employees are aware of what these are and what the organisation is aiming towards. The second step is to set clear organisational goals and objectives that support the advancement towards meeting the strategic aim. These should then

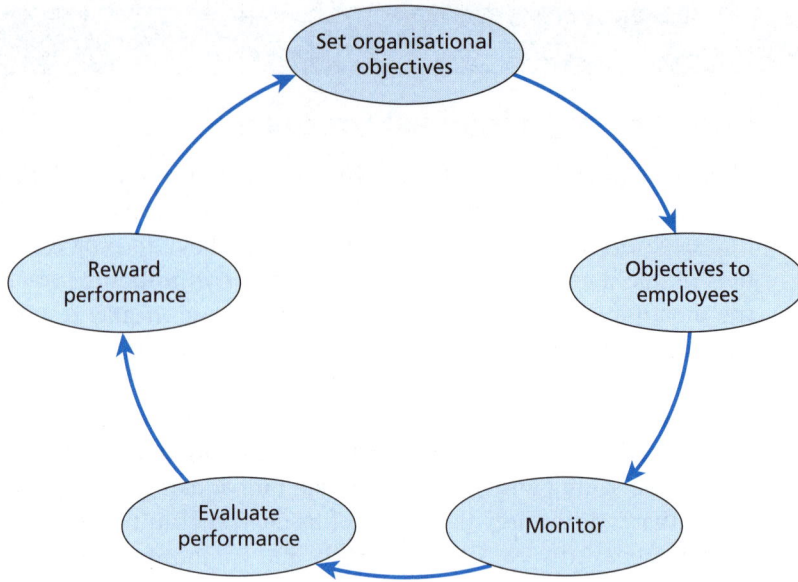

Figure 15.1 Drucker's five-step process for managing by objectives

be cascaded down the hierarchy so that they reach all employees. The third step is to engage employee participation in their own goal-setting, which aids in the achievement of the organisation's overall strategic aim. This provides employees with a framework of what they need to do and actions required to accomplish it. These should be SMART goals: specific, measurable, achievable, realistic and timely. Setting SMART goals ensures that the progress of individual employees on the achievement of these goals can be monitored. Issues that threaten goal achievement can be dealt with. Step four is to evaluate performance. This is a simple process as the SMART goals are measurable and evaluation is based on whether the employee achieved their goals. Feedback should be provided to employees on both their own performance and the organisation's. The final step of rewarding performance is along the lines of positive reinforcement, where employees are recognised for their achievements. Such management by objectives will also be applicable to the uprising of the knowledge economy.

Challenges for the future: These include setting realistic goals across cross-functional teams (discussed later in the chapter) and across working locations if operating globally.

Organisational sustainability

Sustainability refers to an organisation's ability to succeed and survive in a competitive marketplace. These organisations need to be able to adapt to changes quickly. Changes may include societal, political, technological, economic and environmental. Sustainability covers a number of issues including preserving the environment, health and safety, quality of products and services. As this chapter provides only a snapshot, an example of environmental sustainability is given. Worldwide environmental crisis has been discussed by a number of organisations including the Intergovernmental Panel on Climate Change (IPCC, 2007. The cause of the crisis has been attributed to human actions. Organisations are now becoming aware of this and are participating in green practices to address environmental concerns while still making a profit. A list produced by Global 100 of the top 100 clean organisations found Novo Nordisk in Norway rated at number 1; BG Group in the UK as number 6; and Toyota Motor Corporation in Japan coming at 21 for 2012 (Global 100, 2012).

Real case 15.1

BG Group – Environmental sustainability

To reduce freshwater consumption, a joint venture partnership with EXCO Resources Inc. (EXCO) in the USA implemented measures to re-use and recycle waste water. In Louisiana, EXCO signed an agreement with a local paper mill to re-use waste water discharged from paper pulp production. In 2010, 25 million barrels of water were used, of which 20–25% came from the paper mill, thereby directly reducing freshwater withdrawal by the same amount. EXCO has developed a pipeline network to transport water from the offtake point at the paper mill to the well sites, removing the need to transport the water by road. This has significantly reduced the impact on the local community.

Challenges for the future: These include creating products and services that distinguish the organisation from its competitors; and technological capabilities of delivering products and services worldwide.

Globalisation

The nature of work is also becoming more globalised. According to Blackmore (2000), globalisation is a trend towards a worldwide freeflow of goods, services, capital workforce and information.

Globalisation has, in part, been spurred by the internet in that services considered local can now be considered across countries and continents. An increase in these market links has also resulted in increased migration (OECD, 2006) with foreign workers becoming an important part of the workforce. The effect of such competitive marketplaces means that companies have to become more streamlined in their operations to ensure efficiency in order to reduce their costs. This also results in a reduction in wages. However, globalisation reduces financial risk by facilitating international diversification.

Challenges for the future: This may raise many challenges such as working across cultures and living in different cultures, managing across cultures, considering equitability in recruitment and selection. In Chapter 4 – Personnel selection and assessment, we considered the use of a variety of methods for selection of individuals into a job. Consideration needs to be given as to whether these translate across countries to ensure that there is no discrimination in the selection process.

Technological changes

Over the last 100 years, the world has witnessed an explosion in the advancement of technology (see Chapter 1 – Introduction to occupational psychology). From the industrial revolution, with an increase in machinery, to the present day with the use of wireless technology and portable computers and smart phones allowing individuals to work any time, anywhere. Robotics in manufacturing organisations has reduced the need to employ as many humans to carry out jobs. With so much information available, there is an increase in the need for knowledge workers to work in a knowledge economy.

The Work Foundation describes the knowledge economy as 'the interaction between technological change, workplace innovation and a highly skilled workforce'. This is due to the vast amount of information available to people through the increased development of information technology. According to Brinkley (2006), by 2014, 45% of UK workers will be knowledge workers. Knowledge workers are individuals who are valued for their knowledge and their ability to communicate and act on that knowledge within a particular discipline/knowledge area. They produce and distribute knowledge and ideas rather than products or services.

Challenges for the future: Knowledge workers need knowledge managers, who understand the 'work' they do. The focus of managing performance is developmental in nature as it is about the knowledge workers gaining more knowledge that feeds into their ideas. Having insufficient knowledge can cause problems and major disaster, as occurred in the Real case 15.2 (Feldman, 2004).

Real case 15.2

The wrong information

On 23 September 1999, NASA's Mars Climate Orbiter spacecraft disappeared. The spacecraft had flown flawlessly for nine-and-a-half months and 416 million miles. Scientists were stumped at first about what had gone wrong. They had checked and rechecked the calculations. It turned out that unbeknown to the metric-based NASA, its contractor had submitted acceleration data in pounds of force instead of the metric equivalent, Newtons. By not converting the pounds to the metric measurement, the spacecraft was lost.

15.3 Team/individual changes

Cross-functional work teams

The nature of team working will change in the new world of work. Although teams will work cross-functionally, there will be more working with groups of individuals who may be geographically distant and come together temporarily to work on a project and then disband when the project has been completed. This notion of 'work swarms' was coined by Gartner as 'a work style characterized by a flurry of collective activity by anyone and everyone conceivably available and able to add value . . . forming quickly, attacking a problem or opportunity and then quickly dissipating. Swarming is an agile response to an observed increase in ad hoc action requirements, as ad hoc activities continue to displace structured, bureaucratic situations' (Wailgum, 2010). This method of working is very problem-task/specific and once the task has been achieved the group is no longer required. As a result of such changes in working, the organisational structures will be flatter.

Challenges for the future: Work swarms limit the growth of individual skills as there is a focus on a particular specialism; other challenges include issues of reporting to more than one boss resulting in a confusing chain of command, being unable to express/evidence individual contributions to the task, working across cultures and constant changes in project team/department leading to stress.

Location-independent working

Location-independent work represents the ability to work remotely. This provides employees with flexibility as employees can work from any location – at home, on the move, at client sites or within the employing organisation. This can increase productivity as staff are able to conduct remote meetings (saving travelling costs), connect remotely to the office network at any time of the day or night, and it provides a better work–life balance by reducing travelling times and allowing employees to juggle work and family life more efficiently. From an organisational perspective there are also positive cost reductions as there can be savings on office space, heating and electricity costs. However, there are issues that occupational psychologists need to consider such as the impact of loss of face-to-face contact. This can result in a feeling of isolation for the remote worker and missing out on important information as well as feeling undervalued. This can result in a loss of identity where workers no longer feel part of the work team and/or the organisation. There are also issues with perceptions towards remote working, which may impact on its value. For example, the perception that remote working is an easy option can result in the remote worker feeling that they have to prove they are working hard, which leads to overwork and stress. Other issues concern the management of remote workers as there would be a move from presenteeism in the workplace to outcome-based assessments related to performance. This is known as management by objectives, discussed earlier.

Challenges for the future: Problems include employee withdrawal from social interaction, employees left out from the dissemination of information, issues surrounding working practices such as overworking leading to burnout, removal from the culture of the organisation leading to a loss of corporate identity and remote management control.

Youth unemployment

According to the Office for National Statistics (2012b), unemployment for April 2012 was at 8.3% of the economically active population with 2.65 million unemployed people in the UK. However, youth unemployment is at an all-time high. A study by the Office for National Statistics (2012c) reported that from January to December 2011, 26% of 16-year-olds leaving school with only GCSEs were unemployed, as were 18% of 18-year-olds who left school with A Levels and 25% of 21-year-olds who left university with a degree. Unemployment for 16- to 24-year-olds from October to December 2011 reached a staggering 1.04 million in the UK, the highest since 1986/87. However, the UK is not the only country with high youth unemployment. In Spain, 47% of its 15- to 24-year-olds were economically active from January to March 2011; Austria had the lowest figure, at 7%. Although some reasons for high levels of unemployment may be due to the global recession, other areas for consideration may be the mismatch between young people's skills and those required by the labour market. When work is found, it may be low-skilled jobs, jobs that lack career development opportunities, temporary contracts and low pay.

Challenges for the future: Challenges are to identify the gaps between skills that youths have and the skills the labour market needs, and provide training to bridge the skill gaps.

A comprehensive overview of youth unemployment and its challenges is provided by the International Labour Organization (2011). A link to the document can be found in the weblink section at the end of this chapter.

Ageing population

Individuals will be required to work past their normal retirement age, which will increase demand for work opportunities. The CIPD (2009) anticipates that by 2020, economically active (working) people below the age of 50 will drop from 75% to 69% and those above 50 will rise from 580,000 to 750,000. Many organisations, in response to new legislation on age, have removed their mandatory retirement ages (e.g. Asda). A survey conducted by the CIPD (2000) of 1,000 workers between the ages of 50 and 64 asked individuals what they planned to do when they reached the age of 65. Of those 1,000 workers, 38.2% wanted to continue working, with 67.8% of those stating it was due to financial reasons and 52.1% wanting to use existing skills and experience; 37.7% wanted continued social interactions. Organisations will need to consider the wants of individuals, in terms of benefits, for those over the age of 50 as these may be very different to those for people under the age of 50. For example, older workers may want to work fewer hours or take longer holidays, may have responsibility for older parents or may want to pursue hobbies. Aside from personal needs, there may also need to be consideration of the design of the working environment as certain medical issues may be more prominent in a population of older workers, for example, deterioration of eyesight.

As can be seen from the discussion in this chapter, the nature of work is changing and this will have an impact on individuals, teams, managers and the organisation as a whole, which is discussed below. This is where an occupational psychologist can aid in the transition from the old to the new by advising organisations of changes to make, based on both theory and empirical evidence.

Multi-level impact of the future of work

The impact on the changing nature of work has an impact at an individual, team, management and organisational level. For individuals, there will be a need to build networks so that individuals can develop their skills and look for alternative employment to meet their work ambitions. As the ageing population will want employment for longer, there will need to be a focus on ensuring equality in jobs. As work is becoming more globalised and businesses are operating in different time zones there will be a need for more flexible working and working across different countries, taking into account the culture of that country and their operating processes and procedures. From a team perspective, there will be 'pop up' teams who work on projects and then disband when projects are complete. From a management perspective there will be a need to change styles so there is management by objectives. From an organisational perspective, as layers of the organisational structure are removed, a challenge may be to keep talented staff as employees may look elsewhere to develop their career; organisations will have to consider how they promote their business and maintain their networks. For example, just over a decade ago there were no social networking sites such as Facebook and Twitter and just over two decades ago we did not have the World Wide Web. Organisations need to consider changes that may occur over the next 10–20 years and be ready to embrace them to remain competitive. In the future, location will not matter as organisations may employ contractors rather than employees, which reduces overhead costs. These contractors may be individuals from across the globe due to the increase in communications technology such as Skype and instant messaging.

Useful websites

International Labour Organization (2012). An introductory guide for employers' organisations: Tackling youth employment challenges – an overview of policy actions and policy considerations. Available: *https://docs.google.com/viewer?a=v&q=cache:nZNeIbGP72gJ:www.ilo.org/public/english/dialogue/actemp/downloads/projects/youth/tackling_ye_guide_en.pdf+youth+unemployment+challenges&hl=en&gl=uk&pid=bl&srcid=ADGEESiliI81oXGHzAcyGxSQoffD7iD3Osftpmok5PR1V9irXJ-MASJQY1oMBeBh0JSNqFOt1Xq_ito6mKfz5m1MtJyaBRkQ-gO5Xm9BWQioHe0LIF0dlT5X7umO20Lk_seVLU64NMMYS&sig=AHIEtbSHmz4x_-1_0gsoJ4gblcc5k6lFug*

The Work Foundation provides information on the future of work. Available: *http://www.theworkfoundation.com/default*

Glossary

Ability is the capacity to perform various tasks needed for a job.

Adverse impact is the potential unfairness in the treatment of a minority group.

Application form is a form completed by a job applicant that asks for background information.

Aptitude is an inherent ability to do or learn something.

Assessment centre is a standardised process that assesses a number of dimensions using many methods such as interviews, psychometric tests and work-based samples.

Behaviour modification represents the systematic reinforcement of positive work behaviour and non-reinforcement or punishment of negative work behaviour.

Beliefs represent ideas about something or someone and conclusions people make about them.

The **Big Five** factors of personality consist of five broad domains that define human personality and consist of Openness, Conscientiousness, Extroversion, Agreeableness and Neuroticism.

Biographical data represents factual information about life and careers.

A **boundaryless career** represents career paths that go beyond the boundaries of single employment.

Brainstorming is a group method where individuals meet to generate solutions to a problem.

The **British Psychological Society (BPS)** is a representative body for psychologists and psychology in the United Kingdom.

Bullying is an act of repeated aggressive behaviour (physical, verbal, emotional) to intentionally hurt another person.

Bureaucracy is an idealised form of an organisation whose characteristics have a clear division of labour, hierarchical control, written and inflexible rules, regulations and procedures and impersonal relationships.

Burnout is the feeling of physical and emotional exhaustion due to stress from working under difficult or demanding conditions.

Career development concerns the management of individual careers within an organisation

Career planning represents the steps an individual takes to achieve their goals.

Career management represents the process that organisations go through to select and develop employees.

Centralisation is the degree to which the authority to make decisions is restricted to higher levels of management.

Central tendency is where appraisers rate appraisees as average.

Coaching is a one-to-one relationship where the coach supports the coachee.

Cognitive ability represents our mental capacity to process information and solve problems.

Cohesiveness is the degree to which individuals are attracted to and want to remain part of a group.

Competency is a term that represents the task-related knowledge or skills possessed by an individual.

Conflict occurs when two or more people disagree.

Consultancy represents a professional practice that gives expert advice within a particular field or discipline.

Content theories of motivation identify the needs that energise individuals.

Contingency theories identify how situations can be understood and managed in ways that respond to their unique circumstances and characteristics.

Corporate culture represents a set of assumptions, practices, beliefs, attitudes and rules (both informal and formal) about how a company operates.

Counselling is a support process where the counsellor holds meetings with another to help them solve problems/issues.

Creativity represents the use of imaginative or original ideas in response to opportunities or problems.

Critical incidents is a technique for measuring job satisfaction that requires an employee to focus on a specific situation or event related to their work.

Decentralised is the degree to which decision-making authority is given to workers at lower levels within the organisation.

Decision–making is the process of identifying a problem or opportunity and choosing from alternative courses of action.

Departmentalisation is the segmentation of tasks/activities into discrete segments.

Discrimination is the unjust or prejudicial treatment of another person or different categories of people (such as age, gender and sexual orientation).

Emotional intelligence is a type of social intelligence that allows us to monitor and shape our emotions and those of others.

Employee is an individual who works for another in return for financial or other compensation.

Employee assistance programmes provide support to individuals, e.g. counselling them through problems such as alcohol abuse, financial issues and marital problems. The aim is to improve the employee's quality of life.

Employee turnover represents the rate at which an organisation gains and loses employees.

Empowerment is the process by which managers delegate power to subordinates.

Equity theory is based on an individual's perception of how fairly they are treated in comparison with others.

Empirical research refers to techniques for investigating phenomena, acquiring new language or correcting or integrating new information.

Employee engagement represents an individual's involvement with, satisfaction with and commitment to the work they are doing.

ERG theory categorises needs into existence, relatedness and growth needs.

Ergonomics is the study of designing equipment and devices that fit the human body, its movement and cognitive abilities.

Ethical issues refer to the way participants are treated in research and in the application of interventions within organisations.

Existence needs represent the desire for physiological and material well-being.

Expectancy theory argues that motivation is determined by individual beliefs about effort–performance and the desirability of certain work outcomes.

Experiment is a research design whereby subjects are randomly assigned to conditions created by the researcher.

Extrinsic rewards are positive work outcomes that an individual receives from some other person in their work setting.

Face validity is what a measure appears to assess.

Factor 'g' is a theory of intelligence by Spearman (1904) that suggests all individuals possess a general factor of intelligence.

Feedback is the process of communicating with someone how you feel about something they said or did.

Forming stage is the first stage of group development which is typified by initial entry of members into a group.

Globalisation is the movement towards financial, trade and communication integration.

Goal-setting is the process of establishing specific, measurable and time-targeted objectives.

Group is a collection of two or more people who interact with each other regularly to achieve common goals.

Group dynamics represent the interactions and relationships that take place between group members and the group as a whole.

Group norms are unwritten and unspoken informal rules that govern behaviour within a group.

Group polarisation is the tendency for a group to take more extreme positions than the mean of the individual positions.

Group think is the tendency for members of highly cohesive groups to lose their evaluative capabilities.

Growth needs represent the desire for personal growth and development.

Harassment represents behaviour that an individual finds offensive, even if it is not directed at them.

Hawthorne studies are the results of a study that is produced due to the participants' knowledge that they are participants in the study.

Health and Care Professions Council (HCPC) is a statutory regulator of health professionals in the UK (including psychologists).

A healthy workplace promotes and protects the health and safety of its people.

Heuristics are 'rules of thumb' or mental shortcuts that allow individuals to solve problems and make decisions quickly and efficiently.

Hierarchy of needs based on Maslow's (1954) theory that an individual's needs progress through a hierarchy based on physiological, safety, belongingness, esteem and self-actualisation.

Human relations movement refers to a critique of classical management and bureaucracy that suggests management styles should be more participatory and oriented to employee needs.

Human error is an inappropriate or undesirable human decision or behaviour resulting in the reduction, effectiveness and/or safety within the workplace or system performance.

Hygiene of factors represent dissatisfiers associated with aspects of an individual's work setting.

Individual differences represent the variations between one person and another on a number of different variables such as intelligence and personality.

Instincts consist of inherited patterns of behaviour that are often in response to certain stimuli.

Instructional design system aids in the design, development and delivery of training programmes.

Instrumentality is the probability that an individual assigns to a level of achieved task performance leading to a number of work outcomes.

Intelligence represents the capacity for learning, reasoning, understanding and similar forms of mental activity.

Internal consistency is a form of reliability where there is internal agreement between the ratings, or two or more raters on the same variable/subject.

Interview is a face-to-face meeting between two or more people for the purpose of exchanging information.

Intrinsic motivation is based on taking pleasure in an activity rather than working for an external reward.

Intrinsic rewards represent positively valued work outcomes that an individual receives as a result of task performance.

Job is one or more tasks that an individual performs as part of their occupation.

Job analysis is a process that produces systematic information about jobs.

Job characteristics model identifies five core characteristics (skill variety, task identity, task significance, autonomy and job feedback) as having importance in job design.

Job context refers to an individual's work setting.

Job description provides information about the main duties, responsibilities and working duties of a job.

Job design refers to the planning and specification of work tasks and the work environment in which they are to be accomplished.

Job rotation is a job design technique where individuals are moved between two or more jobs in a planned manner.

Job satisfaction is the degree to which an individual feels positively or negatively towards their job.

Job specialisation is a view of job design where jobs are specialised in accordance with principles of scientific management.

KSAs are the knowledge, skills and abilities required to perform a job.

Leaders are persons who influence others towards the achievement of an objective.

Leadership is the process whereby a person influences others to accomplish an objective and directs the organisation.

Learning styles are approaches or ways of learning.

Least Preferred Co-Worker (LPC) is a measure of a person's leadership style based on a description of the person with whom respondents have worked less well.

Location-independent working consists of working at a different place rather than an individual office.

A **Manager** is an individual who is responsible for certain groups, individuals, tasks or a certain subset (department) of an organisation).

Management represents the organisation and coordination of activities within an organisation.

Management by objectives is an organisational change technique that involves setting interrelated goals throughout an organisation.

Matrix structure is an organisational structure that represents a combination of functional and divisional patterns.

McDonaldisation involves rationalisation where tasks are broken down into smaller tasks in order to find the single most efficient way to carry out the task.

Motivation consists of internal and external factors that stimulate and energise people to be committed to job tasks/roles.

Need for achievement (NAch) is the desire for accomplishment, mastering skills and control or high standards.

Need for affiliation (NAff) represents the desire to establish and maintain friendly relations with others.

Need for Power (NPow) represents the desire to be responsible for others, to control others and influence the behaviour of others.

Negative reinforcement is the withdrawal of unpleasant consequences when a desired behaviour occurs.

The **Norming phase** refers to the third stage in group development that is characterised by close relationships and cohesiveness.

Occupational requirement represents discrimination in favour of particular protected characteristics for recruitment, training, promotion and transfers.

Operant conditioning is the process of controlling behaviour by manipulating its consequences.

An **Organisation** represents a social unit of individuals that is systematically structured and managed to meet collective goals.

Organisational behaviour is the study of human behaviour in organisations.

Organisation charts are diagrams that show the formal structure of the organisation and relationships and ranks between its parts and jobs.

Organisational change involves moving from a known state to an unknown or unfamiliar state.

Organisational commitment represents the strength of an individual's feeling of identification and responsibility to the organisation.

Organisational culture represents the values and beliefs that guide behaviour.

Organisational design represents a formal process for the integration of people, technology and information into an organisation.

Organisational development is a planned organisational effort to maximise an organisation's effectiveness and viability.

Organisational strategy represents the positioning of the organisation in a competitive marketplace and developing, implementing and evaluating actions in order to compete successfully.

Organisational structure represents the framework within an organisation that outlines its lines of authority and communications.

Path-goal theory is a theory of leadership where the main function of the leader is to assist the subordinate to attain his/her goals. The theory explains the relationship between leader and subordinate.

Participatory management is where employees are empowered to participate in organisational decision–making.

Performance is a measure of the quality and quantity of task/work contributions that is made by an individual/group or organisation.

Performance appraisal is a process where the performance of an employee is evaluated by superiors and others in order to maintain good practice and put right any weaknesses.

A **Person specification** provides detailed knowledge, skills and abilities required to perform a job.

Personnel represent people who are employed within an organisation.

Personality represents qualities and characteristics that form an individual's character.

Planned change represents change that is designed and implemented in an orderly and timely manner.

Planning is the process of setting goals/objectives and identifying actions needed to accomplish them.

Positive reinforcement is the administration of positive consequences that increase the likelihood of behaviour being repeated in the future.

Power is the ability to get someone to do something that you want done or to make things happen.

Predictive validity is where the predictor variable (score on test) is used to forecast a criterion that is assessed at a later time (performance on the job).

Process theories represent theories of motivation that aim to understand an individual's thought processes and how they motivate individual behaviour.

Productivity represents the quality and quantity of work.

Proficiency is the quality of having competence.

Protean career is a career shaped by the individual which may be redirected from time to time to meet the needs of that person.

Psychology is the scientific study of human and animal mental processes and behaviour.

Psychometric testing provides an assessment of an individual's key characteristics through controlled measures such as personality inventories or aptitude and ability tests.

Punishment represents the administration of negative consequences or the withdrawal of positive consequences in order to reduce the likelihood of the behaviour being repeated.

Refreezing is the final stage of the planned change process where changes are positively reinforced.

Recruitment represents the generation of an applicant pool for a job vacancy to provide a number of candidates for selection.

Reinforcement is the administration of a consequence (either positive or negative) as a result of behaviour.

Relatedness needs are the desire for satisfying interpersonal relationships.

Reliability refers to the consistency of a measure. Results would be consistent under similar circumstances.

Resistance to change is an attitude and/or behaviour that reflect a person's unwillingness to make or support a desired change.

Risk assessment is the evaluation of short and long-term risks associated with an activity.

Role is a set of expectations for the behaviour of a person holding a particular position.

Role ambiguity represents a lack of clarity about expected behaviour from a job.

Role conflict represents a conflict among roles due to having two or more statuses; for example, a mother and a manager.

Scientific management is a theory that focuses on efficiency and productivity in organisations with an emphasis on the interactions between the person and the job.

Selection represents a choice of candidates from an applicant pool through the employment of appropriate selection methods.

Self-actualisation is based on Maslow's (1954) hierarchy of needs theory and represents the most difficult to obtain stage which is characterised by self-fulfilment based on achievement (such as a challenging project).

Self-efficacy refers to a person's belief that they can perform adequately in a situation.

Servant leadership is a practice of leadership that gives priority and attention to the needs of colleagues and those they serve.

Situational Judgement Tests (SJT) are a type of psychological test which presents the test-taker with realistic, hypothetical scenarios and asks the individual for an appropriate response to the scenario.

Social loafing is the tendency for people not to work as hard when in groups as they would do if working individually.

Social support is the physical and emotional comfort provided to us by family and friends.

Span of control is the number of individuals reporting to a supervisor/manager.

Stereotypes is a belief about specific types of individuals, groups or ways of doing things; however, the belief may not represent reality.

Storming phase represents the second stage of group development and is characterised by high emotions and feelings of tension among group members. Conflict is more likely to occur at this stage as individuals are trying to determine what their roles are and where they fit into the group.

Stress represents the body's reaction to change that has a physical, mental or emotional response.

Stressors are things that cause stress such as conflict, work overload, etc.

Structured interview is an interview where questions are standardised across interviewees.

Swiss cheese model is a model of accident causation used for risk analysis and risk management of human systems.

Team are small groups/units of people who have complementary skills who work together to achieve a common purpose or goal.

Teambuilding refers to a range of activities that are designed for improving team performance.

Teamwork is when members of a team work together to achieve an overall goal.

Test taker refers to a person taking a psychological test.

Training is the teaching of a person or group of people in a particular skill or type of behaviour.

The **Training Cycle** is a cyclical process that identifies the training needs, designs the training, delivers the training and evaluates the training.

Trait is a distinguishing quality or characteristic that belongs to the person.

Transactional leadership is a style of leadership that is based on daily exchanges between leaders and followers to motivate and direct followers through a system of rewards and punishment.

Transformational leadership is a style of leadership where the leader identifies needed change, creates a vision and inspires employees to execute the change.

Unfreezing represents the first stage of the planned change process where a situation is prepared for change.

Unity of command represents the clear reporting relationship to only one supervisor/manager.

Unity of direction is where the group has the same objective.

Unplanned change is a change that occurs randomly or spontaneously.

Valence represents the value(s) that an individual assigns to work outcomes.

Validity is the degree to which an assessment, theory or construct measures what it is suppose to measure.

Values are beliefs that guide behaviours and judgements across situations.

Virtual organisations are those organisations that deliver goods and services but have no or few physical features of conventional organisations.

Well-being represents an individual's overall feeling (positive or negative).

Work–family conflict is a form of role conflict where work and family demands are in conflict.

Work–life balance represents the balancing of work hours with other responsibilities such as childcare, elder care or for individuals that want to take part in other activities such as sports.

Work-sample test is a standardised measure of an individual's ability to complete a task.

Work teams represent groups or units that include a manager and his or her subordinates.

References

Abraham, S. E., Karns, L. A., Shaw, K., & Mea, M. A. (2001). Managerial competencies and the managerial performance appraisal process. *Journal of Management Development, 20*(10), 842–852.

ACAS (2010). *Health, work and well-being*. London: ACAS.

Ackerman, L. (1997). Development, transition or transformation: The question of change in organisations. In D. Van Eynde, J. Hoy & D. C.Van Eynde (Eds.), *Organisation development classics*. San Francisco: Jossey Bass.

Adair, J. (1973). *Action-centred leadership*. New York: McGraw Hill.

Adams, J. S. (1965). Inequity in social exchange. *Advanced Experimental Social Psychology, 62*, 335–343.

Alban-Metcalfe, B., & Nicholson, N. (1984). *The career development of British managers*. British Institute of Management Foundation Management Foundation Report.

Albrecht, S. L. (2012). Handbook of employee engagement: Perspectives, issues, research and practice. Cheltenham, UK: Edward Elgar Publishing.

Alderfer, C. (1969). An empirical test of a new theory of human needs. *Organizational Behavior and Human Performance, 4,* 142–175.

Allport, G. W., & Odbert, H. S. (1936). Trait names: A psycho-lexical study. *Psychological Monographs, 47*(211).

Amason, A. C. (1996). Distinguishing the effects of functional and dysfunctional conflict on strategic decision making: Resolving a paradox for top management teams. *Academy of Management Journal, 39,* 123–148.

Anderson, N. R. (1992). Eight decades of employment interview research: A retrospective meta-review and prospective commentary. *European Journal of Work and Organisational Psychology, 2*(1), 1–32.

Argyris, C. (1957). *Personality and organisation*. New York: HarperCollins.

Arnold, J. (1997). *Managing careers into the 21st century*. London: Chapman.

Arnold, J., Silvester, J., Patterson, F., Robertson, I., Cooper, C., & Burnes, B. (2005). *Work psychology: Understanding human behaviour in the workplace*. Essex: Pearson Education.

Arthur, M. B., & Rousseau, D. M. (1996). *The boundaryless career*. Oxford: Oxford University Press.

Ashby-Cohen(2010) Requirment for degree does not constitute age discrimination for employee close to retirement [online]. Available: *http://legal-news ashbycohen. co.uk/discrimination/requirment-for-degree-does-not-constitute-age-discrimination-for-employee-close-to-retirement.*

Associated Press (2012). Developments in British phone-hacking scandal. Available: *http://news.yahoo.com/developments-british-phone-hacking-scandal-231658855.html*

Avery, R. D., Abraham, L. M., Bouchard, T. J., & Segal, N. L. (1989). Job satisfaction: Environmental and genetic components. *Journal of Applied Psychology,* 74 (2), 187–192.

Avolio, B. J., & Gardner, W. L. (2005). Authentic leadership development: Getting to the root of positive forms of leadership. *Leadership Quarterly, 16,* 315–338.

Avolio, B. J., Luthans, F., & Walumba, F.O. (2004). *Authentic leadership: Theory building for veritable sustained performance.* Working Paper. University of Nebraska, Lincoln: Gallup Leadership Institute.

Baker, B., & Warga, B. (2010). Building excitement for opening day: A case study on new employee engagement at Harrah's Entertainment. Available: http://www.aon.com/attachments/harrahs.pdf

Bandura, A. (1971). *Social learning theory.* New York: General Learning Press.

Bandura, A., & Locke, E. A. (2003). Negative self-efficacy and goal effects revisited. *Journal of Applied Psychology*, 88(1), 87–99.

Bar-On, R. (1997). *The Bar-On emotional quotient inventory (EQ-i): Technical manual.* Toronto, Canada: Multi-Health Systems.

Bar-On, R. (2006). The Bar-On model of emotional-social intelligence (ESI). Available: http://www.eiconsortium.org/measures/eqi.html

Barrick, M. R., & Mount, M. K. (1991). The Big Five personality dimensions and job performance: A meta-analysis. *Personnel Psychology,* 44(1), 1–26.

Barsade, S. (1998). *The ripple effect: Emotional contagion in groups.* New Haven, CT: Yale University School of Management.

Baruch, Y. (2003). Career systems in transition, a normative model for career practices. *Personnel Review, 32,* 231–251.

Baruch, Y. (2006). Career development in organisations and beyond: Balancing traditional and contemporary viewpoints. *Human Resources Management Review, 16,* 125–138.

Bass, B. M. (1985). *Leadership and performance beyond expectations.* New York: Free Press.

Bass, B. M., & Avolio, B. J. (1994). *Improving organisational effectiveness through transformational leadership.* Thousand Oaks, CA: Sage Publications.

BBC (2011). Blackberry problems spread to US. Available: http://www.bbc.co.uk/news/technology-15276481

Beal, D. J., Cohen, R. R., Burke, C. M., & McLendon, C. L. (2003). Cohesion and performance in groups: A meta-analytic clarification of construct relations. *Journal of Applied Psychology*, 88, 989–1004.

Becker, T. E. (2005). Development and validation of a situational judgment test of employee integrity. *International Journal of Selection and Assessment, 13*(3), 225–232; 225.

Beehr, T. A., & Bhagat, R. S. (1985). *Introduction to human stress and cognition in organizations.* In T. A. Beehr & R. S.Bhagat (Eds.), *Human stress and cognition in organizations: An integrated perspective* (pp. 3–19). New York: Wiley.

Beer, M., & Noira, N. (2000). Cracking the code of change. Harvard, May/June, 133–141.

Belanich, D., & Garven, S. (2008). Performance appraisal feedback: a foundation for effective self-development. Available: https://docs.google.com/viewer?a=v&q=cache:n4UqLyeyK-YJ:www.hqda.army.milari/pdf/TR_1233.pdf-+performance+appraisal+feedback&hl=en&gl=uk&pid=bl&srcid=ADGEESi6gjyVuArib0Hd_Lt10zb-56FITLw3wN0cpkhlmt09ndMXKN85EE3DH-mWDal6n6TsD-eqNM4bwtjMx_M4aRD_LdkxrdwXli90dDNzkkQpJQjpr-obAcUQBVRBpZRoTXVheQGK&sig=AHIEtbSwNuQtvJbkkKC5qkRjmkDDMMNCqA

Belbin, R. M. (1993). *Team roles at work.* Burlington, MA: Butterworth-Heinemann.

Bell, S., & Ford, J. K. (2007). Reactions to skill assessment: The forgotten factor in explaining motivation to learn. *Human Resource Development Quarterly, 18*, 33–62.

Bennis, W. (1998). *On becoming a leader.* Reading, MA: Perseus Books.

Bernardin, H. J., & Russell, J. E. A. (1993). *Human resource management – An experimental approach.* New York: McGraw Hill.

Bertua, C., Anderson, N., & Salgado, J. F. (2005). The predictive validity of cognitive ability tests: A UK meta-analysis. *Journal of Occupational and Organizational Psychology, 78*(3), 387–409.

Bevan, S. (2010). *The business case for employee health and wellbeing.* London: The Work Foundation.

Billings, A. G. and Moos, R. H. (1981). The role of coping responses and social resources in attenuating the stress of life events. *Journal of Behavioral Medicine, 4,* 139–157.

Blackmore, J. (2000). Globalization: A useful concept for feminists rethinking theory and strategies in education? In N. Burbles & C. Torres (Eds.), *Globalization and education: Critical perspectives* (pp. 133–156). New York: Routledge Press.

Blake, R., & Mouton, J. (1964). *The managerial grid: The key to leadership excellence.* Houston: Gulf Publishing.

Block, J. (2010). The five-factor framing of personality and beyond: Some ruminations. *Psychological Inquiry, 21*(1), 2–25.

Block, P. (2011). *Flawless consulting: A guide to getting your expertise used* (3rd ed.). San Francisco, CA: Pfeiffer.

Bobko, P., Rith, P. L., & Buster, M. A. (2005). Work sample selection tests and expected reduction in adverse impact: A cautionary note. *International Journal of Selection and Assessment, 13*(1), 1–10.

Bohlander, G., Snell, S., & Sherman, A. (2001). *Managing human resources.* Cincinnati, OH: South-Western College Publishing.

Boswell, W. R., & Boudreau, J. W. (2002). Separating the developmental and evaluative performance appraisal uses. *Journal of Business and Psychology, 16*(3), 391–412.

Bowling, N. A. (2007). Is the job satisfaction–job performance relationship spurious? A meta-analytic examination. *Journal of Vocational Behavior, 71,* 167–185.

Box, W. R., Odom, R. Y., & Dunn, M. G. (1991). Organizational values and value congruency and their impact on satisfaction. Commitment and cohesion: An empirical examination within the public sector. *Public Personnel Management, 20*(1), 195–205.

Boyatzis, R.E. (1982). *The competent manager: a model for effective performance.* New York: John Wiley.

BPS (2009). *Code of ethics and conduct.* Available: http://www.bps.org.uk/what-we-do/ethics-standards/ethics-standards

BPS (2012). *Qualification in occupational psychology stage 2: Candidate handbook.* Leicester: British Psychological Society.

Brannick, M. T., Levine, E. L., & Morgeson, F. P. (2007). *Work-oriented methods* (6th ed.). London: Sage Publications.

Branson, R. K., Rayner, G. T., Cox, J. L., Furman, J. P., King, F. J., & Hannum, W. H. (1975). *Interservice procedures for instructional systems development: Executive summary and model.* Tallahassee, FL: Centre for Educational Technology.

Brinkley, A. (2006). *Defining the knowledge economy: Knowledge Economy Programme Report.* London: The Work Foundation.

Briscoe, J. P., & Hall, D. T. (2006). The interplay of boundaryless and protean careers: Combinations and implications. *Journal of Vocational Behavior, 69,* 4–18.

Broucek, W.G., & Randell, G. (1996). An assessment of the construct validity of the Belbin self-perception inventory and observer's assessment from the perspective of the five-factor model. *Journal of Occupational and Organizational Psychology, 64,* 389–405.

Brutus, S. (2010). Words versus numbers: A theoretical explanation of giving and receiving narrative comments in performance appraisal. *Human Resource Management Review, 20*(2) 144–157.

Buch, K., & Bartley, S. (2002). Learning styles and training delivery mode preference. *Journal of Workplace Learning, 14*(1), 5–10.

Buckley, R., & Caple, J. (2007). *The theory & practice of training* (5th ed.). Bodmin, Cornwall: MPG Books.

Buhler, P. (2006). Engaging the workforce: A critical initiative for all organizations. *SuperVision, 67*(9), 18–20.

Bunderson, C. V., Inouye, D. K., & Olsen, J. B. (Eds.) (1989). *The four generations of computerized educational measurement.* Washington DC: American Council on Education.

Burke, J. M., & Day, R. R. (1986). A cumulative study of the effectiveness of managerial training. *Journal of Applied Psychology, 71,* 232–245.

Burns, J. M. (1978). *Leadership.* New York: Harper Row.

Bushnell, D. S. (1990). Input, process, output: A model for evaluating training. *Training and Development Journal, 44*(3), 41–43.

Cacioppe, R., & Albrecht, S. (2002). Using 360 degree feedback and the integral model to develop leadership and management skills. *Leadership and Organization Development Journal, 21*(8), 390–404.

Cadoret, R. J., Troughton, E., O'Gorman, T. W., & Heywood, E. (1995). An adoption study of genetic and environmental factors in drug abuse. *Archives of General Psychiatry, 43*(12), 1131–1136.

Callinan, M., & Robertson, I. (2000). Work sample testing. *International Journal of Selection and Assessment, 8,* 248–260.

Cameron, K. S., & Freeman, S. J. (1991). Cultural congruence, strength, and type: Relationships to effectiveness. *Research in Organizational Development, 5,* 23–58.

Cameron, K. S., & Quinn, R. E. (1999). *Diagnosing and changing organisational culture: Based on the competing values framework.* Reading, MA: Addison-Wesley.

Campbell Clark, S. (2001). Work cultures and work/family balance. *Journal of Vocational Behavior, 58,* 348–355.

Campbell, M. (2006). Demonstrating the value of learning, training and development. In: *Reflections on the 2006 learning and development survey.* London: CIPD.

Carbrera, D. D., Isla, R., & Vilela, L. (1997). An evaluation of safety climate in ground handling activities. In H. M. Soekkha (Ed.), *Aviation safety* (pp. 255–268). Proceedings of the IASC-97 International Aviation Safety Conference: Netherlands. 27–29 August.

Cardone, L. (2006). *Motivation at work: Transform your business in 6 extraordinary steps.* Virginia Beach: Profits with Purpose.

Carless, S. A. (2009). Psychological testing for selection purposes: A guide to evidence-based practice for human resource professionals. *International Journal of Human Resources Management 20*(12), 2517–2532.

Carlson, J. (1985). Recent assessment of the Myers-Briggs type indicator. *Journal of Personality Assessment, 49,* 356–365.

Carnevale, P. J., & Probst, T. M. (1998). Social values and social conflict in creative problem solving and categorization. *Journal of Personality and Social Psychology, 74*, 1300–1309.

Carron, A. V. (1982). Cohesiveness in sport groups: Interpretations and considerations. *Journal of Sport Psychology, 4,* 123–138.

Carson, J. (1993). Army Alpha, Army Brass and the search for army intelligence. *ISIS, 84,* 278–309.

Cascio, W. (2003). Managing human resources: Productivity, quality of work life and profits (6th ed.). Boston: McGraw Hill.

Casey-Campbell, M., & Martens, M. (2009). Sticking it all together: A critical assessment of the group cohesion–performance literature. *International Journal of Management Reviews, 11,* 223–246.

Cattell, R. B. (1943a). The description of personality: Basic traits resolved into clusters. *Journal of Abnormal and Social Psychology, 38*, 476–506.

Cattell, R. B. (1943b). Some theoretical issues in adult intelligence testing. *Psychological Bulletin, 38,* 592.

Cattell, R. B., Eber, W., & Tatsouka, M. (1970). *Handbook for the sixteen personality factor questionnaire (16PF).* Champaign, IL: Institute for Personality and Ability Testing.

Chan, D.C. (2005). Core competencies and performance management in Canadian public libraries. *Library Management, 27*(3), 144–153.

Chang, A., Bordia, P., & Duck, J. (2003). Punctuated equilibrium and linear progression: Toward a new understanding of group development. *Academy of Management Journal, 46,* 106–117.

Chang, A., Bordia, P., & Duck, J. (2006). Understanding the multidimensionality of group development. *Small Group Research, 37,* 327–350.

Chao, G. T., Walz, P. M., & Gardner, P. D. (1992). Formal and informal mentorships: A comparison on mentoring functions and contrast with nonmentored counterparts. *Personnel Psychology, 45,* 619–636.

Chiaburu, D. S., & Lindsay, D. R. (2008). Can do or will do? The importance of self-efficacy and instrumentality for training transfer. *Human Resource Development International, 11,* 199–206.

Child, J. (1988). *Organization: A guide to problems and practice* (2nd ed.). London: Paul Chapman.

Chiocchio, F. & Essiembre, H. (2009). A meta-analytic review of disparities between project teams, production teams, and service teams. *Small Group Research, 40,* 382–420.

Chmiel, N. (2000). *Introduction to work and organisational psychology: A European perspective.* Oxford: Blackwell Publishers Ltd.

Chonko, L. B. (2004). Organizational readiness for change, individual fear of change, and sales manager performance: An empirical investigation. *Journal of Personal Selling and Sales Management, 24*(1), 7–17.

CIPD (2000). *Recruitment Survey Report 14.* London: Chartered Institute of Personnel and Development.

CIPD (2005). *Annual Survey Report 2005: Training and Development.* London: Chartered Institute of Personnel and Development.

CIPD (2009). Managing an ageing workforce: The role of total reward. Available: http://www.cipd.co.uk/hr-resources/research/managing-ageing-workforce-total-reward-role.aspx

CIPD (2010). Recruitment: An overview. Available: http://www.cipd.co.uk/hr-resources/factsheets/recruitment-overviews.aspx

Clark, N. (2010). Women still missing out on top jobs at world's largest companies. Available: http://www.independent.co.uk/news/business/news/women-still-missing-out-on-top-jobs-at-worlds-largest-companies-1918433.html

Clements, R.V. (1958). *Managers: A study of their careers in industry.* London: George Allen and Unwin.

Cober, R. T., Brown, D. J., Levy, P. E., Cober, P. E., & Keeping, L. M. (2003). Organizational web sites: Web site content and style as determinants of organizational attraction. *International Journal of Selection and Assessment, 11,* 158–170.

Cockman, P., Evans, B., & Reynolds, P. (1999). *Consulting for real people: A client centred approach for change agents and leaders* (2nd ed.). Berkshire: McGraw Hill.

Coffman, C., & Gonzalez-Malina, G. (2002). *Follow this path. How the world's greatest organizations drive growth by unleashing human potential.* New York: Warner.

Collinson, D. L., & Hearn, J. (2003). Breaking the silence: On men, masculinities and managements. In R. Ely, E. Foldy & M. Scully (Eds.) *Reader in gender, work and organisation* (pp. 75–78). Oxford: Blackwell.

Conger, J., & Toegel, G. (2002). Action learning and multi-rater feedback as leadership development interventions: Time for re-examination? *Journal of Change Management, 3,* 332–348.

Cooper, M.D. (2000). Towards a model of safety culture. *Safety Science, 36,* 111–136.

Costa, P. T., & McCrae, R. R. (1985). *The NEO Personality Inventory manual.* Odessa, FL: Psychological Assessment Resources.

Costa, P. T., & McCrae, R. R. (1992). *Revised NEO Personality Inventory and NEO Five-Factor Inventory.* Odessa, FL: Psychological Assessment Resources.

Covey, S. R. (1991). *Principle-centered leadership.* New York: Simon & Schuster.

Cox, T., Leather, P., & Cox, S. (1990). Stress, health and organisations. *Occupational Health Review, 23,* 13–18.

Cranwell-Ward, J. , & Abbey, A. (2005). *Organizational stress.* Hampshire: Palgrave Macmillan.

Crozier, M. (2009). *The bureaucratic phenomenon.* London: Transaction Publishers.

Daft, R. L. (1999). *Leadership: Theory and practice.* Orlando, FL: Dryden Press.

Day, D. V. (2000). Leadership development: A review in context. *Leadership Quarterly, 11*(4), 581–613.

De Dreu, C.K., & Weingart, L.R. (2003). Task versus relationship conflict, team performance, and team member satisfaction: A meta-analysis. *Journal of Applied Psychology, 88,* 741–749.

Dean, M. A. (2004). An assessment of biodata predictive ability across multiple performance criteria. *Applied H.R.M. Research, 9*(1), 1–12.

Delarue, A., Van Hootegem, G., Procter, S., & Burridge, M. (2008). Teamworking and organizational performance: A review of survey-based research. *International Journal of Management Reviews, 10,* 127–148.

Denison, D. (1990). *Corporate culture and organizational effectiveness.* New York: John Wiley.

Depue, R. A., & Collins, P. (1999). Neurobiology of the structure of personality: Dopamine, facilitation of incentive motivation, and extraversion. *Behavioral and Brain Sciences, 22,* 491–569.

DeRue, D. S., & Hollenbeck, J. R. (2007). The search for internal and external fit in teams. In C. Ostroff & T. A. Judge (Eds.), *Perspectives on organizational fit* (pp. 259–285). New York: Erlbaum.

DeRue, D. S., & Morgeson, E. (2007). Stability and change in person-team and person-role fit over time: The effects of growth satisfaction, performance, and general self-efficacy. *Journal of Applied Psychology, 920,* 1242–1253.

Devito, A. (1985). A review of the Myers-Briggs type indicator. In J. Mitchell (Ed.), *Ninth Mental Measurements Yearbook.* Lincoln, NE: University of Nebraska Press.

Dignity at Work Bill (2001). Available: http://www.parliament.the-stationery-office.co.uk/pa/ld200102/ldbills/031/2002031.pdf

Direct Gov (2011). Employment. Available: http://www.direct.gov.uk/en/Employment/index.htm

Drucker, P. (1954). *The practice of management.* New York: Harper and Row.

Egan, G. (1990). *The skilled helper.* Pacific Grove, CA: Brooks/Cole.

Eisenstat, R. A., & Beer, M. (1998). *The organizational fitness profiling manual.* Waltham, MA: Center for Organizational Fitness.

Ellis, A. (1979). Toward a new theory of personality. In A. Ellis and J. M. Whiteley (Eds.), *Theoretical and empirical foundations of rational-emotive therapy.* Monterey, CA: Brooks/Cole.

Employee Engagement (n. d.). Training courses. Available: http://www.employeeengagementtraining.co.uk/index.php/training-courses

Employment Equality Directive 2000/43/EC. Available: http://www.diversiton.com/workplace/employment-equality/directive.asp

England, G. W., & Lee, R. (1974). The relationship between managerial values and managerial success in the United States, Japan, India and Australia. *Journal of Applied Psychology, 59*(4), 411–419.

Equality Act (2006) Available: http://www.legislation.gov.uk/ukpga/2006/3/contents

Equality Act (2010). Available: http://homeoffice.gov.uk/equalities/equality-act/

Equality and Human Rights Commission (2001). What forms does racial discrimination take? Available: http://www.equalityhumanrights.com/advice-and-guidance/your-rights/race/what-is-race-discrimination/what-forms-does-racial- discrimination-take/

Equality and Human Rights Commission (2011). Equality Act Codes of Practice. Available: http://www.equalityhumanrights.com/advice-and-guidance/information-for-advisers/codes-of-practice

European Commission (2010). *Report on equality between women and men.* Belgium: European Union.

Eysenck, H. (1987). The definition of personality disorders and the criteria appropriate for their description. *Journal of Personality Disorders, 1,* 211–219.

Falk, I. (2003). Designing effective leadership interventions: A case study of vocational education and training. *Leadership & Organisation Development Journal, 24*(4), 193–203.

Farkas, C.M., & Wetlaufer, S. (1998). The way chief executive officers lead. *Harvard Business Review on Leadership, 127.*

Fayol, H. (1949). General and industrial management. Available: http://www.hrmguide.co.uk/history/classical_organisation_theory_modified.htm

Feldman, S. (2004). The high cost of not finding information. Available: http://www.worldcat.org/title/high-cost-of-not-finding-information/oclc/63147044

Fennell, D. (1998). *Investigations into King's Cross underground fire.* Department of Transport. London: HMSO.

Festinger, L. (1950). Informal social communication. *Psychological Review, 57,* 271–282.

Fiedler, F.E. (1967). *A theory of leadership effectiveness.* New York: McGraw Hill.

Fiedler, F.E., & Garcia, J.E. (1987). *New approaches to effective leadership.* New York: Wiley & Sons.

Fine, S., & Wiley, W. W. (1971). *An introduction to functional job analysis.* Washington: Upjohn Institute for Employment Research.

Fisher, S.G., Hunter, T.A., & Macrosson, W.D.K. (2001). A validation study of Belbin's team roles. *European Journal of Work and Organisational Psychology, 10,* 121–144.

Fitts, P. M., & Jones, R. E. (1947). *Analysis of factors contributing to 460 'pilot error' experiences in operating aircraft controls.* Dayton, OH: Aero Medical Laboratory, Air Materiel Command, Wright Patterson Air Force Base.

Flanagan, J. C. (1954). The critical incident technique. *Psychological Bulletin, 51,* 327–358.

Fleming, N. (1995). VARK: A guide to learning styles. Available: http://www.vark-learn.com/english/index.asp

Fletcher, C. (2001). Performance appraisal and management: The developing research agenda. *Journal of Occupational and Organizational Psychology, 74,* 473–487.

Foo, C.T. (1997). Artificial firm: Technology, organisation and Woodward revisited. *Journal of High Technology Management Research, 8*(1), 37–61. Available: http://www.sciencedirect.com/science/article/pii/S1047831097900134

French, R. (2007). *Cross-cultural management in work organisations.* London: Chartered Institute of Personnel and Development.

Gallen, T. (2006). Managers and strategic decisions: Does the cognitive style really matter? *Journal of Management Development, 25*(2), 118–133.

Gallup Organisation (2004). Employee engagement: A leading indicator of financial performance. Available: http://www.gallup.com/consulting/52/employee-engagement.aspx/

Gallupe, R.B., Bastianutti, L.M., & Cooper, W.H. (1991). Unblocking brainstorms. *Journal of Applied Psychology, 76,* 137–142.

Gallupe, R.B., Bastianutti, L.M., & Cooper, W.H. (1994). Blocking electronic brainstorms. *Journal of Applied Psychology, 79,* 77–86.

Gardner, H. (1993). *Multiple intelligences: The theory in practice.* New York: Basic Books.

Gersick, C.J.G. (1988). Time and transition in work teams: Toward a new model of group development. *Academy of Management Journal, 31,* 9–41.

Ghaleb, T. (2008). Physicians suffer from higher levels of stress. Available: http://www.yobserver.com/sports-health-and-lifestyle/10014240.html

Ghuman, K. (2010). *Management: Concepts, practice and cases.* New Delhi: Tata McGraw Hill.

Giscombe, K. (2005). Best practices for women of color in corporate America. In R. J. Burke & M. C. Mattis (Eds.), *Supporting women's career advancement.* Cheltenham, UK: Edward Elgar Publishing.

Glanz, B. R. (2002). *Handle with care: Motivating and retaining employees* (p. 31). London: McGraw-Hill.

Global 100 (2012). 2012 Global 100 list. Available: http://www.global100.org/annual-lists/2012-global-100-list.html

Goldberg, L. R. (1990). An alternative 'description of personality': The Big Five factor structure. *Journal of Personality and Social Psychology, 59,* 1216–1229.

Golec, A., & Kahya, E. (2007). A fuzzy model for competency-based employee evaluation and selection. *Computers and Industrial Engineering, 52,* 143–161.

Goleman, D. (1998a). What makes a leader? *Harvard Business Review* (November/December), 93–102, 93.

Goleman, D. (1998b). *Working with emotional intelligence.* New York: Bantam.

Gornick, J. C. and Meyers, M. K. (2003). *Families that work: Policies for reconciling parenthood and employment.* New York: Russell Sage Foundation.

Government Equalities Office (2010). Equality Act 2010. Available from http://equalities.gov.uk/equality_bill.aspx

Grant, A. M. (2008). Does intrinsic motivation fuel the prosocial fire? Motivational synergy in predicting persistence, performance, and productivity. *Journal of Applied Psychology, 93*(1), 48–58.

Graves, L. M., & Powell, G. N. (1995). The effect of sex similarity on recruiters' evaluations of actual applicants: A test of the similarity attraction paradigm. *Personnel Psychology, 48,* 85–98.

Green, T. (2000). Three steps to motivating employees. *HR Magazine, 45*(11), 155–158.

Greenleaf, R. K. (1977). *Servant leadership: A journey into the nature of legitimate power and greatness.* New York: Paulist Press.

Gross, N., & Martin, W.E. (1952). On group cohesiveness. *American Journal of Sociology, 57,* 546–554.

Grove, C.N. (2005). Leadership style variations across cultures: Overview of GLOBE research findings. Available: http://www.grovewell.com/pub-GLOBE-leadership.html

Grundy, T. (1993). *Managing strategic change.* London: Kogan Page.

Guest, D. (1996). Leadership and management. In P. Warr (Ed.). *Psychology at work* (4th ed.) pp. 254–279. London: Penguin Books.

Hackman, J.R. (1976). Group influences on individuals. In M.D. Dunnette (Ed.), *Handbook of industrial and organizational psychology* (pp. 1455–1525). Chicago: Rand McNally.

Hackman, J. R., & Oldham, G. R., (1976). Motivation through the design of work: Test of a theory. *Organizational Behavior and Human Performance, 16,* 250–279.

Halfhill, T., Sundstrom, E., Lahner, J., Calderhone, W., & Nielsen, T.M. (2005). Group personality composition and group effectiveness: An integrative review of empirical research. *Small Group Research, 36,* 83–105.

Hall, D.T. (2004). The protean career: A quarter-century journey. *Journal of Vocational Behavior, 65*(1), 1–13.

Hallberg, U. E., & Schaufeli, W. B. (2006). 'Same same' but different? Can work engagement be discriminated from job involvement and organizational commitment? *European Psychologist, 11*(2), 119–127.

Handy, C. B. (Ed.) (1976). *Understanding organisations.* London: Penguin.

Hannah, S.T., & Chan, A. (2004). *Veritable authentic leadership: Emergence, functioning and impacts.* Paper presented at the Gallup Leadership Institute Summit, Omaha, Nebraska.

Hanson, M. A. (1994). *Development and construct validation of a situational judgment test of supervisory effectiveness for first-line supervisors in the US army.* Unpublished manuscript.

Hardy, G. E., Woods, D., & Walls, T. D. (2003). The impact of psychological distress on absence from work. *Journal of Applied Psychology*, 88–306.

Harter, J. K., Schmidt, F. L., & Hayes, T. L. (2002). Business-unit-level relationship between employee satisfaction, employee engagement and business outcomes: A meta-analysis. *Journal of Applied Psychology, 87*(2), 268–279.

Haslam, N. (2007). *Introduction to personality and intelligence.* London: Sage Publications.

Hassan, A., & Ahmed, F. (2011). Authentic leadership, trust and work engagement. *International Journal of Human and Social Sciences, 6*(3), 164–170.

Hattie, J.A. (1999). Influences on student learning. University of Auckland, New Zealand. Available: http://www.education.auckland.ac.nz/webdav/site/education/shared/hattie/docs/influences-on-student-learning.pdf

Hausknecht, J., Day, D. V., & Thomas, S. C. (2004). Applicant reactions to selection procedures: An updated model and meta-analysis. *Personnel Psychology, 57*, 639–683.

Hayward, D. (1997). Battlezone. *Computing, 36*–37.

Hazards (2011). Hazards News. Available: http://www.hazards.org/abouthazards/index.htm

Healey, A.N., Primus, C.P., & Koutantji, M. (2007). Quantifying distraction and interruption in urological surgery. *Quality & Safety in Health Care, 16,* 135–139.

Health and Safety at Work (2012). 'Thumbs up' system lets down press operator. Available: http://www.healthandsafetyatwork.com/hsw/SIG-manufacturing-puwer

Health and Safety Executive (1992a). The Workplace (Health, Safety and Welfare) Regulations 1992. Available: http://www.legislation.gov.uk/uksi/1992/3004/contents/made

Health and Safety Executive (1992b). The Manual Handling Operations Regulations 1992. Available: http://www.legislation.gov.uk/uksi/1992/2793/contents/made

Health and Safety Executive (1992c). The Health and Safety (Display Screen Equipment) Regulations 1992. Available: http://www.legislation.gov.uk/uksi/1992/2792/contents/made

Health and Safety Executive (1999). The Management of Health and Safety at Work Regulations 1999. Available: http://www.legislation.gov.uk/uksi/1999/3242/contents/made

Health and Safety Executive (2000). Work-related factors and ill health: The Whitehall II Study. CRR266.

Health and Safety Executive (2006). Health and Safety at Work etc. Act (1974). Available: http://www.legislation.gov.uk/ukpga/1974/37/contents

Health and Safety Executive (2007). Workplace stress costs Great Britain in excess of £530 million. Available: http://www.hse.gov.uk/press/2007/c07021.htm

Health and Safety Executive (2009). *Reducing error and influencing behaviours.* HSE Books: Sudbury.

Health and Safety Executive (2011a). *Risk assessment.* Available: http://www.hse.gov.uk/msd/risk.htm

Health and Safety Executive (2011b). *What are the management standards for work-related stress?* Available: http://www.hse.gov.uk/stress/standards/index.htm

Hersey, P., & Blanchard, K. H. (1977). *Management of organizational behavior: Utilizing human resources* (3rd ed.). Englewood Cliffs, NJ: Prentice Hall.

Hertel, G., Geister, S., & Konradt, U. (2005). Managing virtual teams: A review of current empirical research. *Human Resource Management, 15*(1), 9–95.

Herzberg, F. (1964). The motivation-hygiene concept and problems of manpower. *Personnel Administration,* Jan-Feb, 3–7.

Herzberg, F. (1974). Motivation-hygiene profiles: Pinpointing what ails the organization. *Organizational Dynamics, 3*(2), 18–29.

Higgins, E.T. (1998). Promotion and prevention: Regulatory focus as a motivational principle. In M. P. Zanna (Ed.), *Advances in experimental social psychology* (pp. 1–46). Academic Press: New York.

Hirsch, S., & Kummerow, J. (1989). *Life types.* New York: Warner.

Hofstede, G. (1984). Culture's consequences: International differences in work-related values (2nd ed.). Beverly Hills, CA: Sage Publications.

Hofstede, G., Hofstede G.J., & Minkov, M. (2010). *Cultures and organizations: Software of the mind* (3rd ed.). New York: McGraw Hill.

Hollenbeck, J. R., Moon, H., Ellis, A. P. J., West, B. J., Ilgen, D., Sheppard, L., Porter, C. O. L. H., & Wagner III, J. A. (2002). Structural contingency theory and individual differences: Examination of external and internal person-team fit. *Journal of Applied Psychology, 87*(3), 599–606.

Honey, P., & Mumford, A. (1982). *Manual of learning styles.* London: P. Honey.

Hooper, A., & Potter, J. (1997). *The business of leadership: Adding lasting value to your organisation.* Aldershot, UK: Ashgate.

Hooper, A., & Potter, J. (2000). *Intelligent leadership: Creating a passion for change.* London: Random House.

House of Lords (2009). SCA Packaging Limited *v.* Boyle. Available: http://www.publications. parliament.uk/pa/ld200809/ldjudgmt/jd090701/sca-1.htm

House, R. (1997). Path-goal theory of leadership: Lessons, legacy, and a reformulated theory. *Leadership Quarterly, 7*(3), 323–353.

Howard, A., & Choi, M. (2002). Do you assess a manager's decision-making abilities? The use of situational inventories. *International Journal of Selection and Assessment, 8*(2), 85–88.

HPC (2008). *Standards of conduct, performance and ethics.* Available: http://www.hpc-uk.org/assets/documents/10002367FINALcopyofSCPEJuly2008.pdf

HPC (2010). *Standards of proficiency: Practitioner psychologists.* Available: http://www.hpc-uk.org/publications/standards/index.asp?id=198

HPC (2012). *Standards of Continuing Professional Development.* Available: http://www.hpc-uk.org/aboutregistration/standards/cpd/

Hweidi, I. (2007). Jordanian patients' perception of stressor in critical care units: A questionnaire survey. *International Journal of Nursing Studies, 44,* 227–235.

Impact Factory (n. d.). Leaders with impact: A five day leadership experience. Available: http://www.impactfactory.com/p/leadership_programme/open_1311-7110-19769.html

IPCC (2007). Fourth Assessment Report. Working Group III contribution to the Intergovernmental Panel on Climate Change. Available: http://www.ipcc.ch/

Isenberg, D.J. (1986). Group polarisation: A critical review and meta-analysis. *Journal of Personality and Social Psychology, 50,* 1141–1151.

Jablonski, J. R. (1992). *Implementing TQM* (2nd ed.). Albuquerque, NM: Technical Management Consortium.

Jacobs, R. L. A. (1988). A proposed domain of human performance technology, implications for theory and practice. *Performance Improvement Quarterly, 1*(2), 2–12.

Janis, I.L. (1972). *Victims of groupthink: A psychological study of foreign-policy decisions and fiascoes.* Boston: Houghton Mifflin.

Jansen, E.P. (2011). The effect of leadership style on the information receivers' reaction to management accounting change. *Management Accounting Research, 22*(2), 105–124. Available: http://www.sciencedirect.com/science/article/pii/S1044500510000818

Jehn, K. (1997). Affective and cognitive conflict in work groups: Increasing performance through value-based intragroup conflict. In C. K. W. De Dreu & E. Van de Vliert (Eds.), *Using conflict in organizations* (pp. 87–100). London: Sage.

Jex, S. M. (2002). *Organizational psychology: A scientist–practitioner approach.* New York: John Wiley.

Jex, S.M., & Britt, T.W. (2008). *Organisational psychology: A scientist-practitioner approach.* Hoboken, NJ: John Wiley.

Jones, J. R., & George, G. M. (2004). *Contemporary management* (p. 405). Boston: Irwin/McGraw Hill.

Judge, T. A., & Bono, J. E. (2001). Relationship of core self-evaluations traits – self-esteem, generalized self-efficacy, locus of control, and emotional stability – with job satisfaction and job performance: A meta-analysis. *Journal of Applied Psychology, 86*(1), 80–92.

Judge, T. A., & Church, A. H. (2000). Job satisfaction: Research and practice. In C. I. Cooper & E. A. Locke (Eds.), *Industrial and organizational psychology: Linking theory and practice* (pp. 166–198). Oxford, UK: Blackwell.

Judge, T. A., Bono, J. E., Ilies, R., & Gerhardt, M. W. (2002). Personality and leadership: A qualitative and quantitative review. *Journal of Applied Psychology, 87,* 765–780.

Kahn, W. A. (1990). Psychological conditions of personal engagement and disengagement at work. *Academy of Management Journal, 33,* 692–724.

Kanouse, D. E., & Hanson, L. (1972). Negativity in evaluations. In E. E. Jones, D. E. Kanouse, H. H. Kelley, R. E. Nisbett, S. Valins & B. Weiner (Eds.), *Attribution: Perceiving the cause of behaviour* (pp. 47–63). Morristown, NJ: General Learning Press.

Karasek, N. (1979). Job demands, job decision latitude, and mental strain: Implications for job redesign. *Administrative Science Quarterly, 24,* 285–308.

Kelly, G. A. (1955). *The psychology of personal constructs.* New York: Norton.

Kikoski, J. F. (1999). Effective communication in the performance appraisal interview: face to face communication for public managers in the culturally diverse workplace. *Public Personnel Management, 23,* 301–323.

Kirkpatrick, D. L. (1959). Techniques for evaluating training programmes. *Journal of the American Society for Training & Development, 13,* 11–12.

Kirkpatrick, S. A., & Locke, E. A. (1991). Leadership: Do traits matter? *Academy of Management Executive, 5*(2), 48–60.

Kivimaki, M., Elovainio, M., & Vahtera, J. (2000). Workplace bullying and sickness absence in hospital staff. *Occupational and Environmental Medicine, 57*(10), 656–660.

Kolb, D. A. (1984). *Experiential learning.* Englewood Cliffs, NJ: Prentice Hall.

Kristof, A. (1996). Person–organization fit: An integrative review of its conceptualizations, measurement, and implications. *Personnel Psychology, 49,* 1–49.

Landy. F. J. (1985). *Psychology of work behaviour.* Homewood, IL: Dorsey Press.

LaRue, J. (1989). Assessing the assessment centre. Available: http://www.jlarue.com/assessment_center.html

Lau, D.C. & Murnighan, J.K. (2005). Interactions within groups and subgroups: The effects of demographic faultlines. *Academy of Management Journal, 48,* 645–659.

Lazarus, R. S. (1993). Coping theory and research: Past, present and future. *Psychosomatic Medicine, 55,* 234–247.

Lazarus, R.S., & Folkman, S. (1984). *Stress: Appraisal and coping.* New York: Springer.

Legislation.Gov.UK (2006). Work and Families Act (2006). Available: http://www.legislation.gov.uk/ukpga/2006/18/contents

Lessem, R. & Baruch, Y. (2000). Testing the SMT and Belbin inventories in top management teams. *Leadership & Organization Development Journal, 21,* 75–83.

Lewin, K. (1951). *Field theory in social science – selected theoretical papers.* New York: Harper and Row.

Lichtman, R. J., & Lane, I. M. (1983). Effects of group norms and goal setting on productivity. *Group & Organization Studies, 8,* 406–420.

Liedtka, J. M. (1998). Linking strategic thinking with strategic planning. *Strategy and Leadership* (Sept/Oct), 30–35.

Linder, J. R. (1998). Understanding employee motivation. *Journal of Extension, 36*(3), 1–7.

Lizzaro, K.E. (2010). The relationship between principal transformational leadership practices and teacher retention. *Dissertation abstracts. International Section A: Humanities and Social Sciences, 70*(7–A), 2322.

Llies, R., & Judge, T.A. (2002). Understanding the dynamic relationships among personality, mood, and job satisfaction: A field experience sampling study. *Organisational Behaviour and Human Decision Processes, 89*(2), 1119–1139. Available: http://www.sciencedirect.com/science/article/pii/S0749597802000183

Locke, E. A. (1976). The nature and causes of job satisfaction. In M. D. Dunnette (Ed.), *Handbook of industrial and organizational psychology* (pp. 1297–1349). Chicago: Rand McNally.

Locke, E.A., & Latham, G.P. (2006). New directions in goal-setting theory. *Current Directions in Psychological Science, 15*(5), 265–268.

Lord, R. G., De-Vader, L., & Alliger, G. M. (1986). A meta-analysis of the relation between personality traits and leadership perceptions: An application of validity generalization procedures. *Journal of Applied Psychology, 71,* 402–410.

Luthans, F., & Kreitner, R. (1985). *Organizational behaviour modification and beyond.* Glenville, IL: Scott Foresman.

Luthra, V. (2007). Business dictionary. Available: http://www.businessdictionary.com

LX Consulting (2011). Consulting services. Available: http://www.lxconsulting.com/business_management_systems_consulting_services_customized_to_your_needs_best_practices_benchmarking_leadership_risk_management_consultants_canada_usa_europe_ny.html

Macan, T. H., & Dipboye, R. L. (1990). The relationships of interviewers' preinterview impressions to selection and recruitment outcomes. *Personnel Psychology, 43,* 745–768.

Macdonald, K. B. (1998). Evolution, culture and the five factor model. *Journal of Cross-Cultural Psychology, 29,* 119–149.

Mannix, E., & Neale, M.A. (2005). What differences make a difference? The promise and reality of diverse teams in organisations. *Psychological Science in the Public Interest, 6,* 31–55.

Marchese, M. C., & Muchinksy, P. M. (2007). The validity of the employment interview: A meta-analysis. *International Journal of Selection and Assessment, 1*(1), 18–26.

Martin, G., & Pear, J. (2007). *Behavior modification: What it is and how to do it* (8th ed.). Upper Saddle River, NJ: Pearson: Prentice Hall.

Martins, E. C. (2000). *The influence of organisational culture on creativity and innovation in a university library.* MLnf dissertation, University of South Africa, Pretoria.

Martone, D. (2003). A guide to developing a competency-based performance-management system. *Employment Relations Today, 30*(3), 23–32.

Maslow, A. (1943). A theory of human motivation. *Psychological Review, 50,* 370–396.

Mauno, S., Kinnuen, U., & Pyykko, M. (2005). Does work-family conflict mediate the relationship between work-family culture and self-reported distress? Evidence from five Finnish organisations. *Journal of Occupational and Organisational Psychology, 78,* 509–530.

Mays, L., Graham, J., & Vinnicombe, S. (2005). Shell Oil Company US: The 2004 Catalyst Award Winner for Diversity Initiatives. In R. Burke & M. C. Mattis (Eds.), *Supporting women's career advancement.* Cheltenham: Edward Elgar.

McCarthy, J. M., Van Iddekinge, C. H., & Campion, M. A. (2010). Are highly structured job interviews resistant to demographic similarity effects? *Personnel Psychology, 63,* 325–359.

McClelland, D. C. (1978). Managing motivation to expand human freedom. *American Psychologist, 33*(3), 301–310.

McCormick, E. J., & Jeanneret, P. R. (1988). Position analysis questionnaire (PAQ). In S. Gael (Ed.), *The job analysis handbook for business, industry and government.* New York: John Wiley & Sons.

McCormick, E. J., Jeanneret, P. R., & Mecham, R. C. (1972). A study of job characteristics and job dimensions as based on the position analysis questionnaire (PAQ). *Journal of Applied Psychology, 56,* 347–368.

McDaniel, M. A., & Nguyen, N. T. (2001). Situational judgment tests: A review of practice and constructs assessed. *International Journal of Selection and Assessment, 9,* 103–113.

McDaniel, M. A., Morgeson, E. P., Finnegan, E. B., Campion, M. A., & Braverman, E. P. (2001). Use of situational judgment tests to predict job performance: A clarification of the literature. *Journal of Applied Psychology, 86,* 60–79.

McDonald, B. (2002). Designing better leadership development programs. Available: http://www.morassociates.com/better_ldr_dev_progrm.html

McDowall, A., & Kurz, R. (2008). How to get the best of 360 degree feedback in coaching. *The Coaching Psychologist, 4*(1), 7–19.

McGuire, W.J. (1985). Attitudes and attitude change. In G. Lindzey & E. Aronson (Eds.), *Handbook of social psychology* (pp. 233–346). Random House: New York.

McKenna, E.F. (2001). *Business psychology and organisational behaviour.* New York: Psychology Press.

McLelland, D., Atkinson, J. W., Clark, R. A., & Lowell, E. L. (1953). *The achievement motive.* Princeton, NJ: Van Nostrand.

McLeod, S. (2007). Psychodynamic approach. Available: http://www.simplypsychology.org/psychodynamic.html

Mead, A. D., & Drasgow, F. (1993). Equivalence of computerized and paper-and-pencil cognitive ability tests: A meta-analysis. *Psychological Bulletin, 114,* 449–458.

Meglino, B. M., and Ravlin, E. C. (1998). Individual values in organizations: Concepts, controversies and research. *Journal of Management, 24,* 351–389.

Melhuish, A. (1978) *Executive health.* London: Cornerstone.

Metropolitan Police Authority (2011). Metropolitan Police Service staff survey. Available: http://www.mpa.gov.uk/committees/cep/2011/0106/08/

Meyerson, D., and Fletcher, D. (2000). A modest manifesto for shattering the glass ceiling. *Harvard Business Review, 78*(1), 126–137.

Mills, T. (2004). The contrast effect in a competency based situational interview. Available: *https://dspace.lib.cranfield.ac.uk/bitstream/1826/3958/1/Contrast_effect-SWP2-04.pdf*

Morgan, H. (1996). *An analysis of Gardner's theory of multiple intelligences.* New York: Basic Books.

Motowidlo, S., Borman, W. C., & Schmit, M. (1997). A theory of individual differences in task and contextual performance. *Human Performance, 10,* 71–83.

Mullen, B., & Copper, C. (1994). The relation between group cohesiveness and performance: An integration. *Psychological Bulletin, 115,* 210–227.

Mumford, M. D., Marks, M. A., Connelly, M. S., Zaccaro, S. J., & Reiter-Palmon, A. (2000). Development of leadership skills: Experience and timing. *Leadership Quarterly, 11*(1), 87–114.

Munsterberg, H. (1913). *Psychology and industrial efficiency.* London: Constable.

Neuman, J. H. , & Baron, R. A. (1997). Aggression in the workplace. In R. A. Giacalone & J. Greenberg (Eds.), *Antisocial behavior in organisations* (pp. 37–67). Thousand Oaks, CA: Sage Publications.

Newell, S. (2002). *The healthy organisation: Well-being, diversity and ethics at work.* London: Thomson.

Nguyen, N. T., McDaniel, M. A., & Whetzel, D. L. (2005). *Subgroup differences in situational judgment test performance: A meta-analysis.* Paper presented at the 20th Annual Conference of the Society for Industrial and Organizational Psychology, Los Angeles.

NHS (2004). Choosing health. Available: http://webarchive.nationalarchives.gov.uk/+/www.dh.gov.uk/en/Publichealth/Choosinghealth/index.htm

NICE (2009). *Promoting mental wellbeing through productive and healthy work conditions: Guidance for employers.* London: National Institute for Health and Clinical Excellence.

Nijstad, B. A., & Stroebe, W. (2006). How the group affects the mind: A cognitive model of idea generation in groups. *Personality and Social Psychology Review, 10,* 186–213.

Northouse, P. G. (2007). *Leadership: Theory and practice* (4th ed.). Thousand Oaks, CA.: Sage Publications.

OECD (2006). *International migration outlook.* Paris: OECD.

Office for National Statistics (2012a). GDP and the Labour Market - 2011 Q4 - March GDP update. Available: http://www.ons.gov.uk/ons/rel/elmr/gdp-and-the-labour-market/2011-q4—march-gdp-update/gdp-and-labour-market-summary—gdp-march-update.html

Office for National Statistics (2012b). Labour Market Statistics 2012. Available: http://www.ons.gov.uk/ons/rel/lms/labour-market-statistics/april-2012/statistical-bulletin.html

Office for National Statistics (2012c). Better qualifications reduce chance of un-employment in your mid-20s. Available: http://www.ons.gov.uk/ons/rel/lms/labour-market-statistics/april-2012/statistical-bulletin.html

O'Moore, M., Seigne, M., McGuire, L., & Smith, M. (1998). Victims of bullying at work in Ireland. *Journal of Occupational Health and Safety – Australia and New Zealand, 14*(6), 569–574.

Orvis, K. A. (2008). Performance appraisal feedback: A foundation for effective self-development. Available: https://docs.google.com/viewer?a=v&q=cache:n4Uq LyeyK-YJ:www.hqda.army.mil/ari/pdf/TR_1233.pdf+peformance+appraisal+fe edback&hl=en&gl=uk&pid=bl&srcid=ADGEESi6gJyVuArib0Hd_Lt10zb-56FITL w3wN0cpkhLmt09ndMXKN85EE3DH-mWDal6n6TsDeqNM4bwtjMx_ M4aRd_LdkxrdwX1i90dDNzkkQpJQjpr-obAcUQBVRBpZsRoTXVheQGK&sig= AHIEtbSwNuQtvJbkkKC5qjRjmkDDMMNCqA

Owoyemi, O.A. (2011). Exploring workplace bullying in a paramilitary organisation (PMO) in the UK: A qualitative study. *International Business Research, 4*(2), 116–124.

Palladin Associates (2012). Available: http://www.paladinexec.com/resources/ strong_interest_inventory_general_occupational_themes/

Palmer, B. (2004). Overcoming resistance to change. *Quality Progress, 37*(4), 35–40.

Parrot, A. C. (1991). Performance tests in human psychopharmacology (2): Content validity, criterion validity, and face validity. *Human Psychopharmocology, 6*, 91–98.

Parsons, H. M. (1974). What happened at Hawthorne? *Science, 183*, 922–932.

Parsons, K. C. (2000). Environmental ergonomics: A review of principles, methods and models. *Applied Ergonomics, 31* (6), 581–594.

Paulus, P. B., & Yang, H. (2000). Idea generation in groups: A basis for creativity in organizations. *Organizational Behaviour and Human Decision Processes, 82*, 76–87.

Paulus, P. B., Larey, T. S., & Dzindolet, M. T. (2000). Creativity in groups and teams. In M. Turner (Ed.), *Groups at work: Advances in theory and research* (pp. 319–338). Hillsdale, NJ: Erlbaum.

Pavlov, I. P. (1927). Conditioned reflexes: An investigation of the physiological activity of the cerebral cortex. Available: http://psychclassics.yorku.ca/Pavlov/

Peabody, D., & Goldberg, L. R. (1989). Some determinants of factor structures from personality-trait descriptors. *Journal of Personality and Social Psychology, 56*, 586–595.

Pech, R. J., & Durden, G. (2003). Manoeuvre warfare: A new paradigm for business decision making. *Management Decision, 41*(2), 168–179.

Peel, M.(1992). Career development to realize potential. *Target Management Development Review, 5*(3), 13–16.

Peiro, J. M., Gonzalez-Roma, V., Tordera, N., & Manas, M. A. (2001). Does role stress predict burnout over time among health care professionals? *Psychology and Health, 16*(5), 511–525.

Peltokorpi, A., Alho, A., Kujala, J., Aitamurto, A., & Parvinen, P. (2008). Approach for evaluating organizational change projects. *International Journal of Health Care Qulity Assurance, 21*(5), 418–434.

Perrewe, P. L., & Nelson, D. L. (2004). Gender and career success: The facilitative role of political skill. *Organizational Dynamics, 4*, 366–378.

Peters, T. J., & Waterman, R. H. (1982). *In search of excellence: Lesson's from America's best run companies*. New York: Harper Row.

Pfeffer, J. (1998). Seven practices of successful organizations. *California Management Review, 40*(2), 96–124.

Pham, N. T. P., Segers, M. S. R., & Gisselaers, W. H. (2010). Understanding training transfer effects from a motivational perspective: A test of MBA programmes. *Business Leadership Review, VII*(III), 1–25.

Phillips, J. F. (1993). Predicting negotiation skills. *Journal of Business and Psychology, 7*, 403–411.

Phillips, J. J. (1991). *Handbook of training evaluation and measurement methods* (2nd ed.). Houston, TX: Gulf.

Pidgeon, N.F. (1991). Safety culture and risk management in organisations. *Journal of Cross-Cultural Psychology, 22*(1), 129–140.

Pidgeon, N.F., & O'Leary (2000). Manmade disasters: Why technology and organizations (sometimes) fail. *Safety Science, 34,* 15–30.

Pines, A. M. , & Aronson, E. (1988). *Career burnout: Causes and cures.* New York: Free Press.

Pitcher, G. (2008). Discrimination: Carer Sharon Coleman wins European case.Available: http://www.personneltoday.com/articles/2008/07/17/46759/discrimination-carer-sharon-coleman-wins-european-case.html

Polman, M. (2010). 7 powerful features of the 360 degree feedback system. Available: *http://ezinearticles.com/?7-Powerful-Features-of-the-360-Degree-Feedback-System&id=4822435*

Popper, K. (1972). *Objective knowledge*. Oxford: Oxford University Press.

Porteous, M. (1997). *Occupational psychology.* London: Prentice Hall.

Porter, L. W., & Lawler, E. E. (1968). *Managerial attitude and performance.* Homewood, IL: Irwin-Dorsey.

Primoff, E. S., & Eyde, L. D. (1988). Job element method. In S. Gael (Ed.), *The job analysis handbook for business, industry and government* (pp. 807–824). New York: John Wiley.

Prospects (2011). Sales executive: Salary and conditions. Available: http://ww2.prospects.ac.uk/p/types_of_job/sales_executive_salary.jsp

Psychological Testing Centre (2007). Psychological testing: A test taker's guide. Available: http://www.psychtesting.org.uk/download$.cfm?file_uuid=129C9234-1143-DFD0-7E7E-EF13CAD94319&siteName=ptc

Psychometric Success (2011). Introduction. Available: http://www.psychometric-success.com/psychometric-tests/psychometric-tests-introduction.htm

Pucel, D. J. (1989). *Performance based instructional design.* New York: McGraw Hill.

Pulakos, E. D., & Schmitt, N. (1995). Experience-based and situational interview questions: Studies of validity. *Personnel Psychology, 48,* 289–308.

Quine, L. (1999). Workplace bullying in NHS Community Trust: Staff questionnaire survey. *British Medical Journal, 318*(178), 228–232.

Quine, L. (2001). Workplace bullying in nurses. *Journal of Health Psychology, 6*(1), 73–84.

Racial Equality Directive (2000). Council Directive 2000/43/EC of 29 June 2000 implementing the principle of equal treatment between persons irrespective of racial or ethnic origin. Available: http://eur-lex.europa.eu/LexUriServ/LexUriServ.do?uri=CELEX:32000L0043:en:html

Rafferty, A. E., & Simons, R. H. (2006). An examination of the antecedents of readiness for fine-tuning and corporate transformation changes. *Journal of Business and Psychology, 20*(3), 325.

Randall, R., Davies, H., Patterson, F., & Farrell, K. (2006). Selecting doctors for postgraduate training in paediatrics using a competency based assessment centre. *Archive of Disease in Childhood, 91*, 444–448.

Rayner, C., & Keashley, L. (2005). Bullying at work: A perspective from Britain and North America. In S. Fox & P. E. Spector (Eds.), *Counterproductive work behavior. Investigations of actors and targets* (pp. 271–296). Washington DC: American Psychological Association.

Reason, J. T. (1990). *Human error.* Cambridge: Cambridge University Press.

Reason, J. T. (1992). The identification of latent organisational failure in complex systems. In J.A. Wise, V.D. Hopton & P. Stager (Eds.), *Verification and validation of complex systems: Human factors issues* (pp. 223–237). Berlin: Springer.

Reason, J. T. (2000). Human error: Models and management. *British Medical Journal, 320*(768), 770.

Reinhold, R. (2012). *Career choice and career development: Using the MBTI and personality type.* Available: http://www.personalitypathways.com/article/career-plan.html

Research Center for Group Dynamics. (2010). History. Available: http://www.rcgdisr.umich.edu/history

Revans, R. W. (1998). *ABC of action learning.* London: Lemos & Crane.

Riggio, R.E. (2000). *Introduction to industrial/organizational psychology* (3rd ed.). Upper Saddle River, NJ: Prentice Hall

Ritzer, G. (2008). *The McDonaldization of society.* Los Angeles: Pine Forge Press.

Robbins, S., Millett, B., & Waters-Marsh, T. (2004). *Organisational behaviour.* Sydney: Pearson Education.

Robertson, I. T., & Kandola, R. S. (1982). Work sample tests: Validity, adverse impact and applicant reaction. *Journal of Occupational Psychology, 55*, 171–183.

Robertson, I. T., & Smith, M. A. (2001). Personnel selection. *Journal of Occupational and Organizational Psychology, 74*, 441–472.

Robinson, D., Perryman, S., & Hayday, S. (2004). *The drivers of employment engagement.* Brighton: Institute for Employment Studies.

Roch, S.G., Sternburgh, A.M., & Caputo, P.M. (2007). Absolute vs relative performance rating formats: Implications for fairness and organizational justice. *International Journal of Selection and Assessment, 15*(3), 302–316.

Rodger, A. (1973). *The Seven Point Plan.* London: National Institute of Industrial Psychology.

Rushton, J. P., Bons, T. A., & Hur, Y. (2008). The genetics and evolution of the general factor of personality. *Journal of Research in Personality, 42*, 1173–1185.

Sainsbury Centre for Mental Health (2007). Mental Health at Work: Developing the Business Case (Policy Paper No 8). London: Sainsbury Centre for Mental Health.

Salas, E., & Cannon-Bowers, J. A. (2001). The science of training: A decade of progress. *Annual Review of Psychology, 52*, 471–499.

Salgado, J. F. (1997). The five factor model of personality and job performance in the European Community. *Journal of Applied Psychology, 82,* 30–43.

Salkey, K. (2005). *Employee engagement: Global survey.* Independent Melcrum Research Report, UK.

Salovey, P., & Mayer, J. D. (1990). Emotional intelligence. *Imagination, Cognition and Personality, 9*, 185–211.

Schein, E. H. (1984). Coming to a new awareness of organisational culture. *Sloan Management Review, 28*(2), 3–16.

Schmitt, N., & Gilliland, S. W. (1992). Beyond differential prediction: Fairness in selection. In D. M. Saunders (Ed.), *New approaches to employee management: Fairness in employee selection* (pp. 21–46). Greenwich: CT: JAI Press.

Schmitt, N., & Hunter, J. (1998). The validity and utility of selection methods in personnel psychology: Practical and theoretical implications of 85 years of research findings. *Psychological Bulletin, 124*, 262–274.

Schneider, B., & Schmitt, N. (1986). *Staffing organizations*. Glenview, IL: Scott Foresman.

Schwartz, S. H. (1992). Universals in the content and structure of values: Theory and empirical tests in 20 countries. In M. Zanna (Ed.), *Advances in experimental social psychology* (pp. 1–65). New York: Academic Press.

Scully, S. (2008). Transformational leadership during transformational change. Available: *http://theicor.org/art/present/art/AROB00050.pdf*

Seamster, T. L., Redding, R. E., & Kaempf, G. L. (1997). *Applied cognitive task analysis in aviation*. Brookfield, VT: Ashgate.

Seijts, G. H., & Crim, D. (2006). What engages employees the most or, The ten C's of employee engagement. *Ivey Business Journal,* March/April.

Selye, H. (1946). The general adaptation syndrome and the diseases of adaptation. *Clinical Endocrinology, 6,* 117–231.

Senior, B. (1997). Team roles and team performance: Is there 'really' a link? *Journal of Occupational & Organizational Psychology, 70,* 241–258.

Shackleton, V. (1995). *Business leadership*. London: Routledge.

Shamir, B., & Eilam, G. (2005). 'What's your story?' A life-stories approach to authentic leadership development. *Leadership Quarterly, 16*(3), 395.

Sharp, T.P. (2008). Job satisfaction among psychiatric registered nurses in new England. *Journal of Psychiatric and Mental Health Nursing, 15*(5), 374–378. Available: *http://onlinelibrary.wiley.com/doi/10.1111/j.1365-2850.2007.01239.x/full*

Sheehan, M., McCarthy, P., Barker, M., & Henderson, M. (Eds.) (2001). *The Standing Conference on Organisational Symbolism. A model for assessing the impacts and costs of workplace bullying*. Dublin.

Shin, Y., & Choi, J. N. (2010). What makes a group of good citizens? The role of perceived group-level fit and critical psychological states in organizational teams. *Journal of Occupational and Organisational Psychology, 83,* 531–552.

Shipper, F., & Dillard, J. E. J. (2000). A study of impeding derailment and recovery of middle managers across career stages. *Human Resource Management, 39,* 331–344.

Shore, L. M., Tetrick, L. E., Lynch, P., & Barksdale, K. (2006). Social and economic exchange: Construct development and validation. *Journal of Applied Social Psychology, 36*(4), 837–867.

Siegrist, J. (1996). Adverse health effects of high effort-low reward conditions at work. *Journal of Occupational Health Psychology, 1,* 27–43.

Simon, G. E., Revicki, D., & Heiligenstein, J. (2008). Recovery from depression, work productivity, and health care costs among primary care patients. *General Hospital Psychiatry, 22*(3), 153–162.

Skinner, B. F. (1953). *Science and human behavior*. New York: Free Press.

Smith, A., Johal, S., Wadsworth, E., Davey Smith, G., & Peters, T. (2000). *The scale of occupational stress: The Bristol Stress and Health at Work Study.* Sudbury: HSE Books.

Smith, J. H. (1998). The enduring legacy of Elton Mayo. *Human Relations, 51*(3), 221–249.

Smith, K. C., & McDaniel, M. A. (1998). In scoring situation judgment tests: Once you get the data, your troubles begin. *International Journal of Selection and Assessment, 14*(3), 223–235.

Smith, P. C., Kendall, L. M., & Hulin, C. L. (1969). *Measurement of satisfaction in work and retirement.* Chicago, IL: Rand McNally.

Smith, P.C., & Kendall, L.M. (1963). Retranslation of expectations: An approach to the construction of unambiguous anchors for rating scales. *Journal of Applied Psychology, 47,* 149–155.

Smither, R.D. (1998). *The psychology of work and human performance* (3rd ed.). New York: Longman.

Spearman, C. (1904). 'General intelligence' objectively determined and measured. *American Journal of Psychology, 15,* 201–293.

Spears, L. C. (2004). Practicing servant-leadership. Available: http://www.sullivanadvisorygroup.com/docs/articles/Practicing%20Servant%20Leadership.pdf

Spector, P. E. (2003). *Industrial and organizational psychology: Research and practice* (3rd ed.). New York: Wiley & Sons.

Stajkovic, A. D., Lee, D., & Nyberg, A. J. (2009). Collective efficacy, group potency, and group performance: Meta-analyses of their relationships, and test of a mediation model. *Journal of Applied Psychology, 94,* 814–828.

Stansfeld, S., & Candy, B. (2006). Psychosocial work environment and mental health – a meta analytic review. *Scandinavian Journal of Work, Environment and Health, 32,* 443–462.

Stark, E. M., Shaw, J. D., & Duffy, M. K. (2007). Preference for group work, winning orientation, and social loafing behaviour in groups. *Group & Organisation Management, 32,* 699–723.

Statt, D.A. (2004). *Psychology and the world of work* (2nd ed.). Hampshire: Palgrave Macmillan.

Steptoe-Warren, G. L. (2010). *The development of a situational judgment test to assess managers' strategic decision-making competencies.* Unpublished manuscript.

Sternberg, R. J. (1985). *Beyond IQ: A triarchic theory of intelligence.* Cambridge: Cambridge University Press.

Stogdill, R. M., & Coons, A. E. (1948). *Leader behaviour: Its description and measurement.* Columbus, OH: Bureau of Business Research, Ohio State University.

Stokes, G. S., & Cooper, L. A. (1994). Selection using biodata: Old notions revisited. In G. S. Stokes, M. D. Mumford & W. A. Owens (Eds.), *The biodata handbook: Theory research and applications.* Palo Alto, CA: Consulting Psychologsts Press.

Strauss, A. L. (1993). *Continual permutations of action.* New York: Aldine de Gruyter.

Straw, B. M., & Ross, J. (1985). Stability in the midst of change: A dispositional approach to job attitudes. *Journal of Applied Psychology, 70,* 469–480.

Stufflebeam, D. L., Foley, W. J., Gephart, W. J., Guba, E. G., Hammond, R., Merriman, H. O., & Provus, M. M. (1971). *Educational evaluation and decision making.* Itasca, IL: F.E. Peacock.

Sullivan, S.E., & Arthur, M.B. (2006). The evolution of the boundaryless career concept: Examining physical and psychological mobility. *Journal of Vocational Behavior, 69*(1), 19–29.

Supreme Court (2012). Homer v. Chief Constable of West Yorkshire Police. Available: http://www.supremecourt.gov.uk/decided-cases/docs/UKSC_2010_0102_Judgment.pdf

Tai, W. T. (2006). Effects of training framing, general self-efficacy and training motivation on trainees' training effectiveness. *Personnel Review, 35*, 51–65.

Tannenbaum, R., & Schmidt, W. (1958). How to choose a leadership pattern. *Harvard Business Review,* Mar/Apr.

Taylor, F. W. (1911). *The principles of scientific management.* Available: http://www.ibiblio.org/eldritch/fwt/ti.html

Taylor, R. (1990). Interpretation of the correlation coefficient: A basic review. *Journal of Diagnostic Medical Sonography, 6*, 35–39.

Telegraph (2011). Blackberry 'severely undermined' by outages. Available: http://www.telegraph.co.uk/technology/blackberry/8838854/BlackBerry-severely-undermined-by-outages.html

Tett, R. P., Jackson, D. N., & Rothstein, M. (1991). Personality measures as predictors of job performance: A meta-analytic review. *Personnel Psychology, 44*, 703–742.

Theron, R., Moerdryk, A., Schlechter, A., Nel, P., Crafford, A., & O'Neill, C. (2006). *Industrial psychology: Fresh perspectives.* Cape Town: Pearson Education South Africa.

Thompson, P., & McHugh, D. (2002). *Work organisations* (3rd ed.). Basingstoke: Palgrave Macmillan.

Thorndike, E. L. (1911). *Animal intelligence.* New York: Macmillan.

Thorndike, E. L. (1932). *The fundamentals of learning.* New York: Teachers College Press.

Thurstone, L. L. (1935). *The vectors of the mind: Multiple-factor analysis for the isolation of primary traits.* Chicago, IL: University of Chicago Press.

Tichy, N.M., & Devanna, M.A. (1986). *The transformational leader.* New York: Wiley & Sons. Cited in V. Shackelton (1995). *Business leadership.* London: Routledge.

Topf, M. (1989). Sensitivity to noise, personality hardiness, and noise-induced stress in critical care nurses. *Environment and Behavior, 15,* 19–28.

Towers Perrin (2007). Closing the engagement gap: A road map for driving superior business performance. *Global Workforce Study*, 1–21.

Tuckman, D.W. (1965). Developmental sequence in small groups. *Psychological Bulletin, 63,* 384–399.

Turner, J.C., Wetherell, M.S., & Hogg, M.A. (1989). Referent informational influence and group polarisation. *British Journal of Social Psychology, 28,* 135–147.

Turner, J.R., & Müller, R. (2005). The project manager's leadership style as a success factor on projects: a literature review. *Project Management Journal, 36*(1), 49–61. As cited in Jansen, E.P. (2011) The effect of leadership style on the information receivers' reaction to management accounting change. *Management Accounting Research, 22*(2), 105–124. Available: http://www.sciencedirect.com/science/article/pii/S1044500510000818

Turner, N., & Williams, L. (2005). The ageing workforce. Available: http://www.theworkfoundation.com/assets/docs/publications/144_theageingworkforce.pdf

Turner, R., Hudson, I., Butler, P., & Joyce, P. (2003). Brain function and personality in normal males: A SPECT study using statistical parametric mapping. *Neuroimage, 19*(3), 1145–1162.

Ulrich, R. S., Zimring, C., Joseph, A., Quan, X., & Choudhary, R. (2004). *The role of the physical environment in the hospital of the 21st century: A once-in-a-lifetime opportunity*. Princeton, NJ: Robert Wood Johnson Foundation.

Unison (2012). Stress at work: A guide for UNISON Safety Reps. Available: http://www.unison.org.uk/acrobat/18596.pdf

Van der Water, H., & Bukman, C. (2009). A balanced team-generating model for teams with less than nine persons. *Journal of Management Mathematics, 21*, 281–302.

Van Gundy, A. B. (1983). Brainwriting for new product ideas: An alternative to brainstorming. *Journal of Consumer Marketing, 1,* 67–74.

Van Gyes, G. (2006). Night work and shift work cause high stress levels. Available: http://www.eurofound.europa.eu/ewco/2006/09/BE0609019I.htm

Van Rooy, D. L., Alonson, A., & Fairchild, Z. (2003). In with the new, out with the old: Has the technological revolution eliminated the traditional job search process? *International Journal of Selection and Assessment, 11*, 170–174.

Visser, C., Altink, W., & Algera, J. (1997). From job analysis to work profiling: Do traditional procedures still apply? In Andersen & Herriot (Eds.), *Handbook of selection and assessment*. New York: John Wiley.

Vroom, V. H. (1964). *Work and motivation*. New York: Wiley.

Wailgum, T. (2010). The workplace in 2020: Gartner predictions. Available: http://www.smartconnectedcommunities.org/docs/DOC-1503

Walker, C. R., & Guest, R. H. (1952). *The man on the assembly line*. Cambridge: Harvard University Press.

Walker, H. J., Feild, H. S., Giles, W. F., & Bernerth, J. B. (2008). The interactive effects of job advertisement characteristics and applicant experience on reactions to recruitment messages. *Journal of Occupational and Organizational Psychology, 81*, 619–638.

Wallace, P. E., & Clariana, R. B. (2000). Achievement predictors for a computer-applications module delivered via the world-wide web. *Journal of Information Systems Education, 11*(1), 13–18.

Want, J. (2003). When worlds collide: Culture clash. *Journal of Business Strategy, 24*(4), 14–21.

Ward, P., Hodges, N. J., Williams, A. M., & Starkes, J. L. (2004). Deliberate practice and expert performance: Defining the path to excellence. In A. M. Williams & N. J. Hodges (Eds.), *Skill aquisition in sport: Research, theory and practice* (pp. 231–258). London: Routledge.

Watson, J. B., & Rayner, R. (1920). Conditioned emotional reactions. *Journal of Experimental Psychology, 3*(1), 1–14.

Weber, M. (1947). The theory of social and economic organization. Available: http://www.hrmguide.co.uk/history/classical_organization_theory.htm

Weed, S. E., Mitchell, T. R., & Moffitt, W. (1976). Leadership style, subordinate personality, and task type as predictors of performance and satisfaction with supervision. *Journal of Applied Psychology, 61*(1), 58–66.

Weekly, J. A., & Jones, C. (1997). Video-based situational testing. *Personnel Psychology, 50*, 25–49.

Weick, K. E., & Quinn, R. E. (1999). Organisational change and development. *Annual Review of Psychology, 50*, 361–386.

Welle, B. (2004). What's holding women back? Barriers to women's advancement as perceived by top executives. Paper presented at the 19th Annual Conference of the Society for Industrial and Organisational Psychology at Chicago, IL .

Wiegmann, D.A., Zhang, H., & von Thaden, T. (2001). *Defining and assessing safety culture in high reliability systems: An annotated bibliography.* University of Illinois Institute of Aviation Technical Report. Savoy, IL: Aviation Research Lab.

Williams, A. M., & Hodges, N. J. (2005). Practice, instruction and skill acquisition in soccer: Challenging tradition. *Journal of Sports Sciences, 23*(6), 637–650.

Yeandle, S. (2005). Older workers and work-life balance. Available: http://www.jrf .org.uk/sites/files/jrf/1859353444.pdf

Yerkes, R. M. (1921). Psychological examining in the United States army. *Memoirs of the National Academy of Sciences, 15*, 1–890.

Young, V., & Bhaumik, C. (2011). *Health and well-being at work: A survey of employees.* Sheffield: Department for Work and Pensions.

Zaccaro, S. J., Kemp, C., and Bader, P. (2004). Leader traits and attributes. In J. Antonakis, A. Cianciolo & R. J. Sternberg (Eds.). *The nature of leadership* (pp. 101–124). Thousand Oaks, CA: Sage.

Zapf, D. (Ed.) (2004). Negative social behaviour at work and workplace bullying. Paper presented at the Fourth International Conference on Bullying and Harassment in the Workplace. Norway: University of Bergen.

Zemke, R., & Kramlinger, T. (1982). *Figuring things out: A trainer's guide to needs and task analysis.* Reading, MA: Addison-Wesley.

Zohar, D. (1980). Safety climate in industrial organisations: Theoretical and applied implications. *Journal of Applied Psychology, 65,* 96–102.

Zohar, D. (2000). A group-level model of safety climate: Testing the effect of group climate on microaccidents in manufacturing jobs. *Journal of Applied Psychology, 85,* 587–596.

Zohar, D. (2002). The effects of leadership dimensions, safety climate and assigned priorities on minor injuries in work groups. *Journal of Organizational Behaviour, 23,* 75–92.

Index